Advance praise for *Illicit Flirtations*

"With insight, brio, and compelling empirical evidence, Rhacel Parreñas offers a novel interpretation of Filipino hostesses working in Japan. Boldly departing from standard accounts that treat all migrant hostesses as equal victims of sexual trafficking, *Illicit Flirtations* presents a nuanced portrayal of the women's multiple labor and sentimental experiences. Scholars and policy-makers should take note."

—Viviana A. Zelizer, Princeton University, author of
Purchase of Intimacy and Economic Lives: How Culture Shapes the Economy

"In this superb new study, Parreñas takes her rapt readers into the lives of scantily clad Filipina hostesses in Tokyo nightclubs and into the work of the professional flirter. Caught between money-gouging middlemen, club owners, and anti-trafficking laws, these women live in a labile moral world. They mix business, body, and heart in complex ways, each making peace with her own mix in her own way. A brilliant work, a must-read."

—Arlie Hochschild, author of
Commercialization of Intimate Life: Notes from Home and Work

"*Illicit Flirtations* brings together riveting ethnography, conceptual innovation, and significant policy implications. Parreñas breathes new life into gender and labor migration scholarship with an analytic focus on sexuality, morality, and money to challenge simplistic notions of trafficked victims. This book prompts us to rethink what we thought we knew about citizenship, intimacy, and work in transnational contexts."

—Pierrette Hondagneu-Sotelo, University of Southern California, author of
Doméstica: Immigrant Workers Cleaning and Caring in the Shadows of Affluence

"This book is a triumph from a leading scholar of migrant-female labor. In this work of daring ethnography and thinking, Rhacel Parreñas challenges conventional views about sex work and sex trafficking, revealing sex work as not solely prostitution but a continuum of practices, along which issues of volition, morality, and law collide and converge in complex dynamics."

—Mae Ngai, Columbia University, author of
Impossible Subjects: Illegal Aliens and the Making of Modern America

"*Illicit Flirtations* draws on ethnographic immersion to illuminate the little understood reality of Filipina hostesses in Japan. Rhacel Salazar Parreñas's courageous, nuanced ethnography and provocative analysis of 'indentured mobility' make vital contributions to our understanding of the social realities of migration and to the debate on the policies that regulate it."

—Robert C. Smith, Baruch College, CUNY, author of *Mexican New York: Transnational Worlds of New Immigrants*

"By now, Rhacel Parreñas's depth of knowledge about the migrations of Filipinas allows her to mark distinctions, unsettle commonplace understandings, and make legible that which is shrouded. Out of this depth also comes the possibility of genuine theorizing. This is an extraordinary book whose audience will go well beyond the specialists of the subject."

—Saskia Sassen, Columbia University, author of *A Sociology of Globalization*

"Avoiding broad-brushstroke mischaracterizations of sex-work, Rhacel Parreñas makes an important contribution to transnational feminist scholarship by productively reworking multiple binaries—motion and stasis, fixity and freedom, opportunity and risk—through her concept of 'indentured mobility.' She refuses to view her subjects as victims in need of rescue by Euro-American feminists, while simultaneously enabling a useful analysis of the vulnerability to human rights violations all these women experience."

—Susan Stryker, University of Arizona, editor of *The Transgender Studies Reader*

"*Illicit Flirtations* is a daring rethinking of the conditions of trafficking, the nature of sex work, the meaning of citizenship, and the moral classifications given by the workers themselves to intimate labor performed for pay. Bold and daring, this engaging ethnography breaks theoretical ground by advancing our understanding of the relationship between the economic and the sexual, focusing on global exchanges of people as well as cash."

—Eileen Boris, University of California, Santa Barbara, coeditor of *Intimate Labors: Cultures, Technologies, and the Politics of Care*

ILLICIT FLIRTATIONS

ILLICIT FLIRTATIONS

Labor, Migration, and Sex Trafficking in Tokyo

Rhacel Salazar Parreñas

Stanford University Press
Stanford, California

Stanford University Press

Stanford, California

Printed and bound by CPI Group (UK) Ltd, Croydon, CR0 4YY

Library of Congress Cataloging-in-Publication Data
Parreñas, Rhacel Salazar, author.
Illicit flirtations : labor, migration, and sex trafficking in Tokyo / Rhacel Salazar Parreñas.
pages cm
Includes bibliographical references and index.
ISBN 978-0-8047-7711-7 (cloth : alk. paper) — ISBN 978-0-8047-7712-4 (pbk. : alk. paper)
1. Women foreign workers—Japan—Tokyo. 2. Foreign workers, Philippine—Japan—Tokyo. 3. Hostess clubs—Japan—Tokyo. 4. Human trafficking—Japan—Tokyo. I. Title.
HD8728.5.F55P37 2011
331.4089'9921052135—dc23

2011018813

Typeset by Thompson Type in 10.5/15 Adobe Garamond Pro

CONTENTS

ILLICIT FLIRTATIONS

INTRODUCTION

THE INDENTURED MOBILITY OF MIGRANT HOSTESSES

Clad in a pink skin-tight polyester dress, I sat on a footstool across the table from a slobbering Japanese man, one too drunk not to slur his words as he asked me in English, "Can I touch your secret part?" Stunned by his request, I hid my urge to cringe with a smile, responding, "If we become friends, then maybe." I continued to smile and proceeded to pour him another drink, not knowing how long I was going to have to bear his harassments. He seemed to assume that the extra money he had paid the club, a mere ten dollars, to sit with me gave him free rein to manhandle and belittle me. He commented on my appearance, evaluating and voicing his approval of my face, skin, and body. I felt harassed and looked at him in disbelief, puzzled that he could not sense how irritated I was.

Sexual harassment is the norm in hostess work. I was not one of the more popular hostesses where I worked, but this particular customer seemed to take a liking to me. Hostesses can never overtly reject customers. If they ask us for a kiss, we must at least blow them a kiss. If they insist we eat, then we have to eat. When they hand us a microphone, we have no choice but to karaoke with them. Customers take the lead, and hostesses follow. The one who took a shine to me asked me to dance. I should not have been surprised that, as soon as we started dancing, he kept trying to rub himself against me. Attempting to minimize our contact, I danced with one foot forward and my behind protruding. Still, I felt a bulge rubbing against my leg as we moved on the dance floor. I recoiled in disgust, but at the same time I felt void of emotion and quite removed from the situation. Many of the hostesses I met told me that not long after working as a hostess one becomes immune to the customers' sexual overtures. A common saying shared in the Filipina hostess community is *"walang mawawala sa akin,"* meaning "nothing will be lost from me." After only a week of working as a hostess, I already knew exactly what they meant.

Though my stint working as a hostess was relatively short, it did not take long to learn how sex and romance work in that world. During my first week at the job, I was summoned to join the table of a group of frequent customers. Known members of the *yakuza*, this group included underlings with missing fingers and a higher-ranked boss I could tell they all listened to, obeyed, and protected. I cannot verify that they really were members of the *yakuza*, but all of the hostesses around me seemed to assume so, including my co-worker Aki, who had proudly told me that the "boss" is her boyfriend. As soon as the men came in, someone announced, "*Ito na ang mga putol*," meaning "Here are the ones with the cut-off fingers." In the community, *yakuza* is better known as *putol*, or "cut-off" in Filipino, a reference to the fingers that many of the *yakuza* lose when they make a mistake and are punished by their bosses.

When I was summoned to join the *yakuza* table that night, I saw it as a harmless invitation, as Aki had already been entertaining them for most of the evening. Not long after joining them, Aki's boyfriend grabbed my hand, examined my fingers and then in Japanese voiced his approval of my unpainted fingernails. He proceeded to tell me, in a combination of Japanese and Filipino, that he likes neither manicured nails nor thick makeup. Instead, he likes "*morena*," meaning dark-skinned women, with natural beauty. He ended his appraisal by telling me, "You are pretty." I thanked him, then grinned awkwardly at his girlfriend Aki. During my first night of working as a hostess, I had been told by one of the workers, Christine, that one should not steal a co-worker's customer. I took note of this, trying to keep my distance from him, deferring his offers of food and drinks to Aki. I did not want her to think I was stealing her boyfriend, let alone one who is *yakuza*. I also tried to keep our conversation platonic, playful but not sexually blatant. To make conversation, I innocently asked him, "What kind of work do you do?" To which he replied, "My work is dangerous." Teasing him, I prodded, "How dangerous?" Going along with our conversation, he said, "Very dangerous."

I had heard plenty of stories about the *yakuza*, knowing they are often blamed for the sexual trafficking of foreign hostesses, including Filipinos, to Japan. Yet the fear associated with the *yakuza* was not reflected in the attitude of most hostesses I met in Tokyo, many of whom seemed to have not only *yakuza* as customers but also *yakuza* as boyfriends, husbands, and fathers of their children. For them, the *yakuza* were not threatening criminals but potential sexual partners. They were also some of the most generous customers at hostess clubs. The welcoming attitude many Filipinas had toward the *yakuza* must have rubbed off on me, as I did not fear them at all during the entire time I worked in a hostess club in Japan.

While I was not afraid of the *yakuza*, I had no plans of ever becoming one of the many Filipinas in Japan romantically linked to one of them. Soon after my playful banter with the "boss," he asked me to join him on the dance floor. As I danced with him, I could not help but worry about Aki, wondering if she thought I was trying to steal her boyfriend. Sure enough, Aki had an anxious look on her face. Soon after we returned to the table, Aki told me in Filipino that her boyfriend never asks anyone to dance. Supposedly I was the only other hostess Aki had seen him dance with in the three clubs where he had visited her regularly in the many times she had returned to Japan as a contract worker. She then told me that she knew her boyfriend had other women and didn't mind, as long as she didn't lose him. I then realized that this had been Aki's way of giving me permission to sleep with her boyfriend. I wanted to tell her that she had nothing to worry about, that I had no intention of sleeping with this customer, or any customer for that matter, especially a member of the *yakuza*.

After working just one week in a hostess bar in Japan, I realized that I had entered an unfamiliar sexual world, one where people are more open about their sexuality, where both customers and hostesses seem to be open to extramarital affairs, and where men can sexually harass women with no punishment or admonishment. Yet this world has been dismissed not only for its debauchery and criminal elements but also for "crimes against humanity." Hostess clubs, specifically those that employ Filipinas, Eastern Europeans, Colombians, and Korean women, have been labeled by the U.S. Department of State as hotbeds of sexual trafficking. These are places where women are not just harassed endlessly but supposedly held against their will, forced into prostitution, and made victims of sexual violence by lecherous Japanese men. This book takes us inside the world of hostess clubs, where hostesses are indeed susceptible to exploitation, but where I also found more open attitudes and different moral standards when it comes to sex, marriage, and romance.

Despite the absence of an extensive study on the plight of migrant Filipina hostesses in Japan, we still hear unsubstantiated cries of their forced prostitution from both journalists and academics.[1] Such claims have led to their identification as sexually trafficked persons in the U.S. Department of State's *Trafficking in Persons Report* (TIP Report). According to the 2004 and 2005 TIP Reports, Filipina hostesses in Japan constituted the largest group of sex-trafficked persons in the world, making up more than 10 percent of the 800,000 estimated victims of human trafficking worldwide.[2] These migrant laborers were identified as trafficked victims under the assumption of their "sexual exploitation."[3] Though mostly speculative, we should not take such a claim lightly. Since their identification as trafficked persons, we have seen a near 90 percent decline in the number of Filipina hostesses who are employed as contract workers in Japan, from 82,741 in 2004 to 8,607 in 2006.[4] This decline might seem to suggest a victory in the global antitrafficking campaign, but I disagree with that interpretation.[5] Instead, I argue that it poses a setback to the emancipation of women. The drastic decline in the number of Filipina hostesses in Japan has stripped thousands of migrant women of their livelihood, forcing them to stay at home and helping to reverse the trend in Philippine gendered migration. In 2007, the number of men migrating from the Philippines surpassed that of women for the first time in twenty years.[6]

I challenge the identification of migrant Filipina hostesses as sex-trafficked persons because there are no hard statistics to support those claims. Instead, the numbers indicate that prostitutes are a small minority of all Filipinas in Japan, just 2.8 percent.[7] In fact, empirically grounded studies on Filipina hostesses in Japan consistently make no mention of prostitution, forced or otherwise. They actually repeatedly find that migrant Filipina hostesses sell drinks, not sex, in hostess clubs.[8] While Filipina hostesses in Japan are not prostitutes, they do perform sex work in the form of sexually titillating customers via commercial flirtation.[9] Rather than reducing "sex work" to "prostitution," I interpret it as encompassing a wide array of sexual provisions that include flirtation, stripping, escort service, and prostitution.[10] For hostesses, acts of commercial flirtation vary and include playful bantering via conversation, seductive dance and song performances on a stage, and, in rare instances, sexual acts such as groping and discreet masturbating of customers underneath the table.

When we take a closer look at the migration patterns of Filipina hostesses, we see that they generally migrate of their own volition. This calls into question their identification as trafficked persons.[11] For the most part, no one forced or coerced these women to seek work in Japan. They were not drugged, taken on a plane, and trapped in a hostess club. No one lied to them and explicitly told them that they would only be singing and dancing on stage.[12] With few exceptions, migrant hostesses go to Japan knowing that they will be doing the "illegal" work of talking to customers and interacting with them closely at a club.[13] Contact between a hostess and a customer is illegal for those with entertainer visas—that is, contract workers or "entertainers"—inside the club because it threatens the professional status of the migrant worker whose job is to do nothing but sing and dance on a stage.[14] While this is the case, most migrant entertainers come to Japan knowing that they would do more than just sing and dance. Most know they will engage in illicit flirtations with their customers.[15] Given this context, I argue that migrant entertainers are not trafficked persons, or individuals coerced to do hostess work, but instead labor migrants who face severe structural constraints.

Coerced labor is without doubt a problem that haunts millions of migrants around the world. The luring of young Mexican women and their entrapment in brothels in the United States by members of the Cadena-Sosa family;[16] the imprisonment of seventy-two Thai garment workers forced to work for $2 an hour in El Monte, California, in a compound behind razor wires and armed guards;[17] and the numerous convictions of individuals who forcibly enslave migrants as domestic workers or farmhands after luring them with false promises of well-paid jobs: All testify to the vulnerability of migrant workers to "modern-day slavery." Yet our view of the vulnerability of migrant workers to "human trafficking" suffers from a lack of systematic understanding of this grave problem. Individual cases become representative of everyone's experiences. The forced prostitution of one migrant Filipina hostess, for example, becomes proof of the sex trafficking of *all* of them. We also do not know the extent of the problem. The organization Free the Slaves gives the "conservative estimate" of 27 million domestically and internationally enslaved people worldwide;[18] the International Labor Organization estimates there are 12.3 million individuals in "forced labor, bonded labor, forced child labor and sexual servitude at any given time";[19] UNICEF speculates that 1.2 million children are trafficked every year;[20] and the International Organization for Migration as well as the U.S. Department of State provides the more conservative estimate of 800,000 individuals trafficked across national borders per annum.[21] The U.N. Office on Drugs and Crime admits that "it is very difficult to assess the real size of human trafficking because the crime takes place underground and is often not identified or misidentified." Still, they boldly claim that there are 2.5 million trafficking victims worldwide.[22] Solutions to trafficking also flatten the experiences of victims with the universal implementation, one advocated by the United States, of a one-size-fits-all template of the 3Rs (rescue, rehabilitation, and reintegration) and the 3Ps (prosecution, protection, and prevention).[23] Lastly, we see human trafficking on a case-by-case basis as if each is a random occurrence that could happen to anyone.

In the case of migrant Filipina hostesses, the limits of their migrant citizenship in Japan do indeed leave them susceptible to forced labor.[24] In a variety of ways, they face severe structural constraints: Contract workers cannot choose their club of employment but instead are bound to work for their sponsoring employer; criminalization leaves undocumented workers overly dependent on employers and other Filipinos who take advantage of their vulnerability by withholding their wages or overcharging their housing; and, lastly, the permanent residency of wives is contingent on five years of marriage to a Japanese spouse, an unequal relationship of dependency that leaves them susceptible to domestic violence. These constraints threaten the autonomy of migrant Filipina hostesses, in turn leaving them vulnerable to various human rights violations. Vulnerability, however, does not automatically make them trafficked persons. After all, we cannot reduce their experiences to the structures that shape them.

Yet migration arguably strips migrant hostesses of their freedom and autonomy. Hostesses who enter Japan with an "entertainer visa" are subject to middleman brokers who impose debt on them, which in turn discourages them from quitting their job prior to the end of their contract. Middleman brokers withhold their passports in both the countries of origin and their destination, retain their salary until the end of their three- or six-month contract, and penalize those who quit before their contract ends. These conditions do not automatically translate into forced labor. They do so, however, when the migrant wishes to quit because she is asked to do a task that she does not want to perform, be it cleaning the bathroom at the club or stripping in front of customers—but she cannot quit. Still, one who cleans the bathroom or strips of her own free will under the same conditions could not be so easily labeled a trafficked person.

How do we account for these severe structural constraints that hamper the autonomy of migrant hostesses, while also not disregarding their agency? The binary categories we currently have for thinking about the migration of Filipina hostesses—either free subject (migrant) or enslaved subject (trafficked person)—fail to capture the complex dynamics of coercion and choice that embody their labor migration experiences. We need to dismantle the binary framework that separates these two distinct migratory flows and construct a middle ground that recognizes the agency of migrants without dismissing the severe structural constraints that could hamper their freedom and autonomy. Filipina hostesses' labor migration inhabits a middle zone between human trafficking and labor migration, which I describe as a process of *indentured mobility*. This paradoxical position frames their labor migration as one of simultaneous progress and subjugation; the financial gains afforded by labor migration come at the expense of their freedom. This paradoxical position—obtaining financial mobility as unfree workers—is also one of coercion and choice; most migrant Filipina hostesses do not want to leave their situation, but if they did want to quit their jobs as entertainers, leave their marriages without the risk of deportation, or protect themselves from unscrupulous employers, they could not do so without facing criminalization as undocumented workers or without the burden of financial penalties. The framework of *indentured mobility* provides a nuanced picture of the Filipina hostesses' subjugation as labor migrants, one that acknowledges their susceptibility to human rights violations but simultaneously rejects the prevailing discourse on human trafficking that paints hostesses as helpless victims in need of "rescue."[25] So while *Illicit Flirtations* questions the labeling of Filipina hostesses as trafficked persons, at the same time it refuses to dismiss their vulnerability to forced labor.

GENDER AND MORALS

Given that even the U.S. Government Accountability Office says that most claims in the U.S. Department of State's annual TIP Report are based on scant information,[26] why have unsubstantiated assertions of human trafficking, including the supposed forced prostitution of Filipina entertainers in Japan, come to circulate as the truth?[27] In the case of migrant Filipina entertainers, the moralistic norm of antiprostitution undoubtedly shapes their experiences of migration, resulting in the mistaken basis of their identification as trafficked persons and, as a result, the near elimination of their migrant community. Yet unsubstantiated claims of the Filipina migrant entertainers' forced prostitution flatten our perspective on their experiences as well as diverting our attention from the need to closely examine the conditions of their labor and migration.

We need to recognize that unsubstantiated claims of forced prostitution are morally charged and spurred by abolitionist sentiments. In other words, what philosopher Philip Pettit calls "aspirational morality," meaning passionate zeal, and not practical reason undergirds spurious cries of antitraffickers.[28] According to Pettit, this zeal is dangerous because it refuses to recognize sex work as viable employment and therefore diverts our attention from solutions that target the regulation and protection of sex workers. Putting aside the assumption that Filipina migrant entertainers are forced into prostitution, this book, based on extensive interviews with Filipina migrant hostesses and my own experience working as one in Japan, provides a grounded and empirically rich discussion of their migration and labor conditions, which I show as involving both subjugation and mobility. Thus, to address the labor issues of migrant hostesses, we not only need to know the actual conditions of their labor but also need to disentangle our understanding of it from antiprostitution sentiments and free ourselves of the assumption of their forced prostitution.

Women and sexual minorities have long been subjected to moral regulation by states and communities.[29] Illustrating the legacy of women's moral regulation in migration, one maintained in the U.S.-led global antitrafficking campaign, prostitution for instance was the first category of migrant exclusion in the United States.[30] Today those "likely to be a public charge," meaning those who risk becoming welfare dependents, are excluded from entry to the United States.[31] Not immune from moral regulation, gays and lesbians were banned from entry in the United States until as recently as 1990.[32] Moralistic beliefs, particularly antiprostitution views, likewise motivate the feared global sex trafficking of women in the twenty-first century.[33] Looking at the situation of Filipina hostesses, this fear has resulted not just in unsubstantiated claims of their prostitution but also in false assertions of their forced prostitution.

Helping us make sense of the negative view of commercial sex are sociologist Viviana Zelizer, philosopher Martha Nussbaum, and anthropologist Gayle Rubin.[34] According to Zelizer, commercial sex is dismissed as immoral because such work defies the "hostile worlds view" on intimacy and economy.[35] By "hostile worlds view," Zelizer refers to the "rigid moral boundaries between market and intimate domains" that criminalize and make immoral acts of "sex for money."[36] The intersection of love and money, of intimate social relations and economic transaction, is said to result in moral contamination because intimacy and the private are shaped by sentiment and solidarity while economics and the public are motivated by calculation and efficiency. To put it simply, the "hostile worlds view" assumes that love and money are mutually exclusive. In this perspective, sex for money, including acts of sexual titillation for money, such as dancing on stage or serving drinks in Japanese clubs, would be morally wrong, while sex for love would be considered proper. The moral stronghold of the "hostile worlds view" over mainstream views on migrant hostesses, and the sentiment of antiprostitution that it espouses, eliminates the need for evidence in unsubstantiated claims of forced prostitution.

Feminist philosopher Martha Nussbaum would add that the "hostile worlds view" does not equally hinder the sexual activities of men and women. Nussbaum argues that the dismissal of sex work as immoral perpetuates and maintains a gender hierarchy that places men over women.[37] A gendered sex hierarchy defines our sexual activities with stigma limiting the tolerable sexual activities of women more so than those of men. This double standard, according to Nussbaum, emerges from "the view that women are essentially immoral and dangerous and will be kept in control by men only if men carefully engineer things so that they do not get out of bounds."[38] Speaking of sex as a vector of oppression, anthropologist Gayle Rubin further clarifies that it is not just women who are marginalized by the "hostile worlds view." According to Rubin, a "sexual hierarchy" dismisses certain sexual practices as immoral, including prostitution and sodomy, leading to the marginalization of particular sexual groups.[39]

The moralistic foundation of antiprostitution, the strength of which Zelizer, Nussbaum, and Rubin help us understand, is significant not only for helping us make sense of the unsubstantiated cries of forced prostitution of migrant Filipina entertainers, but it is also a key lens for understanding their very experience of migration.[40] The moralistic foundation of antiprostitution makes meaning of their labor, morally stigmatizing it and constructing it as morally transgressive. As such, hostesses' labor migration constitutes a "moral breakdown" from the moralistic norm of antiprostitution.[41] The process of negotiating the moral divergence of their labor migration and the means by which they negotiate their moral stance on prostitution underlies and defines their experience of labor migration.[42]

Illicit Flirtations documents how migrant Filipina entertainers negotiate, challenge, and reconfigure the moralistic view of antiprostitution that shapes their experiences of labor and migration. It does so to trace how gender and sexual inequalities determine their experiences. Following Nussbaum, moralistic foundations—often measured via sexual practices and hierarchies—limit the actions of women more so than those of men, and to this Rubin would add that they also limit the actions of sexual "deviants."[43] Hence, morality is a key lens for examining not just gender and sexuality but also gender and sexual inequalities. *Illicit Flirtations* thus uses morals to examine how gendered and sexualized hierarchies shape experiences of migration by looking at the negotiation of sexual morals as a process of subject formation for migrant Filipina entertainers: It traces how society attempts to morally control their actions not only via the law, as we see for instance in the current antitrafficking campaign to "rescue" them, but also through the stigmatization of their occupation; examines the impacts of the moralistic standard of antiprostitution; and finally analyzes the ways that they negotiate the moralistic control of their actions and, in doing so, attempt to reconstitute morality as a means of rejecting their moral disciplining.[44]

Helping us to some extent in making sense of this process is the philosopher Michel Foucault, who in *The Uses of Pleasure* asserts that morality supplies a set of norms and rules that govern everyday experiences.[45] These codes of morality do not overdetermine our actions, but they do impose moral standards that individuals negotiate.[46] While Filipina hostesses are guided and influenced by dominant moral norms and ideologies in society, they re-create alternative moralities.[47] The constitution of alternative moral norms and codes, which is a possibility not explicitly acknowledged by Foucault, emerges from the different social fields inhabited by migrant Filipina hostesses vis-à-vis dominant society.[48] The marginal locations of migrant Filipina hostesses, in the hostess club and the ethnic community, lead to the constitution of different moral codes and norms.[49] Yet, even in these social fields, a diversity of moral formations emerges.[50] In the world of migrant Filipina entertainers, there are multiple moralities, multiple moral codes, and multiple moral standards, differences that emerge from their multiple subject positions.

The recognition of the multiple moralities of migrant Filipina hostesses is key to understanding their labor experiences. It shows us that indentured servitude does not automatically result in forced labor.[51] Indentured workers could experience mobility despite the severe structural constraints that hamper their options. For a hostess unable to quit her job without financial penalty, the requirement of stripping, which she is sometimes expected to perform at work, would have different meanings for the worker. The experiences of those without any moral qualms over undressing could not be equated with the experiences of those who do. Thus, to fully understand the labor of hostesses, we must have a sense of their moral world and recognize that different hostesses have different codes and standards of romance, flirtation, and commercial sex.

CITIZENSHIP AND MIGRATION

Also flattening our perspective on human trafficking is its association with crime and illegality.[52] While criminals such as the Cadena-Sosa brothers from Mexico undoubtedly act on the vulnerability of migrants and enslave them in the process of migration, forced labor not only arises from the illicit activities of smugglers and traffickers but also emerges from the terms of migration enforced by nation-states. In the case of migrant Filipina hostesses, it is not so much the job of hostess work that automatically results in their forced labor but instead the circumstances of their migration that constrain their labor market flexibility; this in turn leaves them vulnerable to situations of coerced labor. On this basis, I argue that what has been identified as "human trafficking" is a labor migration issue, one that cannot be solved on a case-by-case basis via the prosecution of traffickers. Neither is it a problem of sexual victimization, one brought by sinister men who randomly kidnap naïve innocent women. Eradicating the threat of what we understand as human trafficking thus requires us to revisit migration policies worldwide with the goal of implementing policies that ensure migrant workers being granted greater control over their labor and migration.

Citizenship, broadly referring to one's terms of inclusion and membership in society, offers a lens for interrogating how migration regimes, the set of laws and policies that regulate the terms of membership of migrants, determine the susceptibility of migrants to forced labor.[53] In recent years, we have seen a spectacular growth in the field of citizenship studies, in which the category has been used as a trope for examining the struggles for political, cultural, and social recognition of groups marginalized by race, gender, religion, and sexuality.[54] Citizenship not only is a set of tangible rights and duties but also entails a social process by which individuals claim and stake their membership in the nation-state, including the articulation of their right to be different[55] and the negotiation of their contradictory position of racial exclusion and gender subordination.[56]

Influenced by the work of Michel Foucault, the anthropologist Aihwa Ong views citizenship as a process of subjectification, meaning a dual process of both subject-making and self-making.[57] Not discounting Ong's significant contribution to our understanding of migrant citizenship, I wish to point out, however, that subjectification is not a uniform process; instead, one's disciplining shifts according to one's particular subject position within what Foucault calls the biopolitics of the nation,[58] referring to the reproduction of the population, meaning the fostering of life and its care, by the state.[59] Indeed, the subjectification of an undocumented worker would be different from that of a documented worker. We could imagine that the former's citizenship would entail the negotiation of her or his criminalization, while the latter would be inculcated with the dominant values of the nation. Given this difference, we must distinguish the subject positions of migrants when examining the terms of their integration into the nation-state.

Emphasizing this point, sociologist Minjeong Kim uses the trope of "maternal citizenship" to examine the citizenship of foreign wives in rural areas of Korea.[60] For these wives, the inculcation of racial and gender ideologies, or in other words their subjectification, occurs via maternal expectations as imposed by the state, church, community, and family. By underscoring the subject-position of foreign brides in Korea as "wives," Kim's study reminds us that citizenship, or one's membership in the nation-state, is situated in and accordingly determined by one's particular sociostructural location and position in the biopolitics of the nation. Thus, I distinguish the subject-positions of hostesses when I discuss their integration into Japanese society. The terms and conditions of membership for migrant Filipina hostesses are not uniform but differ depending on their subject-position as long-term residents, temporary contract workers, or undocumented workers. Hostesses have different sets of vulnerabilities, different threats of human rights violations, and consequently different solutions to the problem of indentured mobility.

We could imagine that the integration of long-term residents, as their legal residency is conditional to their provision of sex as a wife or mother of a Japanese national, involves the inculcation and negotiation of traditional cultural mores of mothering or being a daughter-in-law.[61] For wives, permanent membership is contingent on five years of marriage to their sponsoring Japanese husband, which is a bounded relationship whose reward of legal status is contingent on the migrant's indenture to her spouse. In contrast to these sexual citizens are undocumented migrants, whose term of membership is defined by their criminalization and concomitant invisibility. Remaining in the shadows of the law engenders a different set of vulnerabilities in settlement. Forced invisibility places migrants in unequal relations of dependency with employers and coethnics. Perhaps not surprisingly, many undocumented hostesses I met in Tokyo had been denied their wages at least once by an employer. Lastly, migrant policies deny temporary contract workers the ability to migrate independently of middleman brokers. All of these constraints of membership limit the citizenship of migrant hostesses, threatening their autonomy by denying them full membership in the nation-state, subjecting them to indentured mobility, and finally leaving them susceptible to forced labor.

Notably, the conditions of indentured mobility are not uniform but instead distinguished by the terms of the migrants' citizenship. This diversity requires that we interrogate the susceptibility of migrants to forced labor with rich empirical research grounded in everyday experiences. Otherwise, our knowledge and understanding of the threat of forced labor suffers from generalizations that not only miss the nuances in people's experiences but also gloss over the specific vulnerabilities that people actually face.

BECOMING A HOSTESS

The supposed inaccessibility of trafficked victims justifies unsubstantiated claims of human trafficking; we imagine that victims are shackled and held against their will by traffickers. Yet, in 2005 and 2006, I managed to enter the community of what was considered at the time to be the largest group of trafficked people in the world. I spent nine months in Tokyo, where I worked as a hostess in a working-class club in one of many red-light districts,[62] a club frequented by members of the *yakuza*.[63] They not only controlled the area but were rumored also to finance the club.[64] Based on the reactions of my colleagues at the university sponsoring my visit to Japan, this type of club was often assumed to be a site of forced prostitution. This turned out to not be true, despite the club proprietor's questionable background and the seedy location.

Tapping into the world of migrant Filipina hostesses was not easy. During my first three months in Tokyo, I struggled to meet entertainers willing to participate in my study. My visits to clubs as a customer did not pan out any solid leads.[65] Church attendance among Filipinos, including many hostesses, did not gain the trust of those around me. Neither did visits to various ethnic establishments. Even hostesses whom I befriended would always decline my request for an interview. Seasoned journalists in Tokyo suggested I go to the Philippines. They told me hostesses would be more likely talk to me there because they would no longer be under the control of the *yakuza*. I was doubtful of the reporters' assumption; I had met many hostesses and knew that their unwillingness to participate in my study had not been for fear of the *yakuza*. Instead, many expressed the difficulty of talking about their experiences, which I could not help but assume meant that they experienced emotional distress from the stigma of their occupation. Having come to Japan with preconceived notions about hostess work, I had initially believed claims by other academics that "hostess work" was a euphemism for "prostitution."[66] Yet friends I made in the field soon corrected me.

Not quite understanding why hostesses were unwilling to participate in my research, I resorted to looking for employment as a way of circumventing my initial hurdle in the field. I did so with the reassurance that prostitution would not be in my job description. I actually had not sought to do fieldwork in a *yakuza*-operated establishment but ended up there only because it had been closest to where I was standing with a nun when I expressed my desire to work as an unpaid hostess. After I complained to her about the difficulty of locating hostesses to interview for my book and told her of my willingness to work alongside them, she literally walked me to the club closest to where we had been standing and introduced me to the management as a "journalist" wanting to investigate the lives of migrant hostesses.[67] They hired me on the spot and soon introduced me to my co-workers as a reporter writing a book on Filipina hostesses.[68]

Working as a hostess was just what I needed to gain access. After I began working as one, every person I approached to participate in an interview agreed to talk. By the end of my study, I managed to complete interviews with fifty-six Filipina migrant hostesses—forty-five females and eleven transgender.[69] We spoke about their migration, family, work, relations with customers, and plans for the future. I was struck by the complete shift in attitude of the hostesses toward me. Before I worked as a hostess, my offers of money could not lure one single person to an interview. Bribery did not get me very far. After I started working as one, my offers of money would be dismissed as insulting. I was repeatedly told that they could never accept payment from a "*kapwa* Filipino," meaning "fellow Filipino." Yet, interestingly, many did not hesitate to add that they would not think twice about taking my money if I were Japanese. To compensate research participants for their help, I spent around US$50 on each one of them, taking some out to eat in a local restaurant and bringing presents of chocolate, ramen, and occasionally the coveted delicacy of a bucket of Kentucky Fried Chicken.[70]

Although working in a club opened many doors to potential interviewees, my co-workers were not my main source of interviews. I interviewed only seven of my twenty-three co-workers. To diversify my sample, I solicited research participants in a wide range of areas in Tokyo, including the upscale Roppongi and the seedier Shinjiku, Kinshicho, and Akabane, as well as Nishi-Kawaguchi in the Saitama prefecture. I identified research participants at various places of gathering in the community including three churches, eight restaurants, one food store, and four clubs.[71] Prominent members of the community, including restaurant owners, old-timers, and religious clergy, also introduced me to potential interviewees.[72]

The difficulty of tapping into this community made sense to me only after I started working as a hostess. One mistake I had made was to initially seek them out in the middle of the day instead of the middle of the night, when they got off work at 2 o'clock or 4 o'clock in the morning. Another had been my insensitivity to the stigma of their occupation. Many individuals whose friends told me they were employed as hostesses even denied being one when I approached them about a possible interview. To them, I was a mere stranger, one they could only assume would morally judge them for doing a job dismissed as sexually immoral in mainstream society. Lastly, the misconceptions that circulate about their work as one of "prostitution" or "forced prostitution" dissuade many of them from taking to strangers about their experiences. Having to undo multiple misconceptions about their occupation made being interviewed a tedious and unwanted experience. Only after learning that I had been working as a hostess did people agree to participate in my study. It somehow reassured them that I would likely ask informed questions about the challenges of their work and not pose questions laden with misinformation. Contrary to my initial assumption that emotional trauma—from what I imagined had to be a result of their forced prostitution—dissuaded them from talking to me about their experiences, it was actually the fact that I would have such an assumption that put them off from speaking to me about their work.

While my study relies primarily on my interviews with hostesses and the data I gathered from conducting participant observation as a hostess, I also gathered supplementary data. I conducted participant observation as a customer and visited other clubs that solely employ Filipina hostesses. In all of these clubs, ranging from working to middle class, I would observe customer–hostess interactions and speak informally to hostesses about their labor and migration. Lastly, I spoke to club owners who employ Filipina hostesses and conducted supplementary interviews in both Japan and the Philippines with governmental and nongovernmental representatives who work on issues of labor and migration for hostesses in Japan as well as with middleman brokers.[73]

Altogether, I gathered a rich pool of information that allowed me to look at the lives of migrant Filipina hostesses from many angles and perspectives, gathering a set of interviews that represents their community. Among my interviewees were permanent residents, undocumented workers, and contract workers. They worked in high-end clubs as well as the lowest-end clubs. Perhaps most significantly, I had access to the group thought to be most inaccessible to outsiders because of their assumed status as trafficked persons: hostesses who worked for the *yakuza*. I did this by working alongside them in a hostess club, which inevitably would have exposed me to "forced prostitution" if it did ever occur. In contrast to unsubstantiated claims of their forced prostitution from those who have only looked at the hostesses' situation from a distance, I can speak with empirically grounded authority on the vulnerabilities and constraints that define the labor migration of Filipina hostesses in Japan.

THE HOSTESSES

The hostesses who participated in my study generally fell into two types of people: highly educated transgender women and economically disadvantaged females. Most entered with an entertainer visa—ten of eleven transgender and thirty-three of forty-five female interviewees—while most others entered with tourist visas they obtained through the sponsorship of a family member, usually an older sister who preceded their migration. Rarely did they enter illegally;[74] those who had done so did become susceptible to what we know as "human trafficking," or what I prefer to more accurately call "forced labor." Those who had entered illegally with a "fake" entertainer visa were usually saddled with a huge debt, while those who came illegally as tourists became vulnerable to forced labor. Regardless of whether they enter legally or illegally, what lures them to migrate to Japan? Considering that none of my interviewees had engaged in prostitution prior to migration, had they come to Japan open to this type of work? Or were they ignorant of the stories of prostitution and forced prostitution of migrant hostesses that circulate in the Philippines?

Female Hostesses

Most female hostesses sought employment in Japan to escape their lives of abject poverty in the Philippines as well as to pursue their passion for singing and dancing. Stories of prostitution and forced prostitution that have circulated in the media did not seem to deter their decision to come to Japan, as most knew prior to migration that such stories are generally untrue, while others had no problem with this kind of work. Because of lurid tales of the forced prostitution of hostesses, rarely did one venture to Japan without the urging of friends or relatives. Many followed older kin, neighbors, and friends, who provided them with some knowledge of the kind of work they would have to do in hostess clubs. While most came to Japan without the intention of engaging in prostitution, most migrated with a sense of risk and adventure for the work they knew would be sexualized, though many were not sure of the extent. Still they came, with some dreadfully open to the possibility of prostitution. This was the case even for those who came from conservative families that did not allow women to "go to the movies, let alone a club." Yet they sought work in Japan in hopes of escaping their life of poverty or to fulfill their desire to sing and dance on a stage.

With few exceptions, female migrants who entered with entertainer visas were members of the working poor.[75] All became their family's breadwinners after migration. When they first ventured to Japan, they ranged in age from fifteen to twenty-seven years old, with most no older than twenty. Rarely did I meet contract workers who had managed to renew their contracts more than three times. To stay in Japan, those who could not either secured a marriage visa or became undocumented workers. Prior to migration, those who worked usually held low-wage service jobs as store clerks or counter help, earning no more than US$3 a day in the Philippines.[76] For many, Japan had been their only option of going abroad due to its "fly now, pay later" system in which middleman brokers would cover the cost of training and travel for prospective migrant workers.[77] Among those entering with an entertainer visa, only two of thirty-three females had completed college.[78] Most others had not attained more than a high school diploma.[79] In contrast, female hostesses who entered with a tourist visa were usually highly educated. Six had completed a bachelor's degree prior to migration, one that was usually financed by an older sister who had been working as a hostess in Japan. Yet they opted not to secure professional jobs in the Philippines after graduation, choosing the higher income they could earn as hostesses in Japan over the salary they would earn as professionals in the Philippines.

While a much larger number of female migrants from the Philippines pursue domestic work abroad, not one of the hostesses who participated in my study had considered this job option. The placement fees that migrant brokers charge prospective migrant domestic workers would limit their employment option to the undesirable region of the Middle East, where stories of employer abuse of domestic workers abound in the Philippines. Such stories may have deterred them from pursuing foreign domestic work, but many claimed that it is a job they would never pursue regardless of destination. They generally considered domestic work as more dangerous than hostess work. As domestic workers, they would be more susceptible to being raped by employers, they told me, because they would be working in isolation in a private home. Seeing domestic work as a job that was beneath them, some even commented that they were too attractive to be domestic workers. They also saw domestic work as a low-skilled, low-wage occupation undesirable because of its greater physical demands. In contrast, they considered themselves to be skilled professionals with creative performance abilities requiring accreditation. The Japanese government requirement that foreigners with "entertainer visas" must be verifiably trained performance artists attested to their professional status. In other words, the hostesses I interviewed generally considered themselves professionals whose job was to entertain customers from a distance via performance on a stage or up close via conversation at a table.

Transgender Hostesses

Transgender hostesses constitute a visible minority of Filipinos in Japan.[80] Still, they remain absent in discourses of trafficking. Threats of prostitution, forced or otherwise, do not seem to apply to them; perhaps for this reason it was not a factor those I interviewed considered when deciding to secure entertainer visas to work in Japan. A highly educated group, transgender hostesses sought work in Japan to secure a professional status occupation that had eluded them in the Philippines, despite having degrees from some of the best universities in the country. Generally older than their female counterparts, transgender hostesses sometimes worked alongside females,[81] but they more often worked in transgender hostess establishments. Most transgender hostesses who participated in my study first sought work in Japan in their early and mid-twenties. Unlike their female counterparts, who generally are preferred to be in their mid-twenties at most, transgender hostesses can make a career out of hostess work and continuously secure contracts until their late thirties.

Of the transgender hostesses I interviewed, only three identified as transsexual.[82] Others had no plans of ever pursuing a sex change because they saw this process as inflicting a "wound" or committing a "sin."[83] In the Philippines, transgender women are referred to as *bakla*, which is a term that has been used loosely to include homosexuals, bisexuals, transsexuals, cross-dressers, and effeminate men. To distinguish them among those who fall in the general usage of the term *bakla*, I refer to my interviewees as transgender.[84] I do so because all were born male and presented a feminine persona in their everyday life.[85]

With the exception of the tourist visiting her mother in Japan, the transgender entertainers in my study all entered Japan with entertainer visas. At the time of my interviews, none of the transgender hostesses was a permanent resident or an undocumented worker. Five were still contract workers with three-month entertainer visas, one was a tourist with a three-month visa visiting her mother—a permanent resident—in Japan, and five were conditional residents, meaning they had one- to three-year *kekkon* (meaning marriage) visas that were renewable conditional to their continued marriage to the sponsoring Japanese citizen.[86]

While the female hostesses in my study generally came to Japan to escape their lives of abject poverty in the Philippines, the transgender hostesses migrated to pursue professional careers as entertainers. The transgender entertainers who participated in my research had attended some of the best universities in the Philippines, including Adamson University, Mapua Institute of Technology, University of the Philippines, University of San Carlos, and University of Santo Tomas. All five of these schools repeatedly rank in the top twenty universities in the Philippines. Among my interviewees, only one had not attained more than a high school diploma, while two had pursued vocational training in fashion design. Four completed college with bachelor's degrees in fine arts, mass communication, electronics communication engineering, and hotel management. Others dropped out because of financial difficulties or to pursue work as entertainers in Japan.

Transgender hostesses had not sought work in Japan to avoid their families. In fact, all of the transgender hostesses who participated in my study found tremendous support from their parents. Parents showed their acceptance of them as transgender by entertaining their lovers, supporting their passion for beauty contests, and introducing them to friends and co-workers as a "daughter."[87] These supportive parents include stereotypical patriarchs—police and military officers—whom one would assume would be likely to be homophobic. Once in Japan, many of the transgender hostesses provided financial support to their extended kin, but most, as they came from well-to-do families, provided only nominal assistance.

Like their female counterparts, transgender hostesses also pursued hostess work in Japan for the pleasure of entertaining men and performing on stage. Many identified as professional dancers. However, many also pursued careers as migrant hostesses to offset the discrimination that confronted them as transgender professionals in the Philippines.[88] Transgender professionals face dim labor market options in the Philippines. As the engineering graduate Peachy, a fourth-time contract worker in Japan, asked, "Who would hire a man who dresses like a woman and has boobs? No one." Peachy never bothered to seek employment as an engineer but instead started training to audition for a spot working as an entertainer in Japan soon after graduation from engineering school. Nikki, a student who had dropped out of the highest-ranked college in the country, University of the Philippines, explained why transgender individuals such as herself did not bother pursuing jobs in the domestic labor market:

> They expect you to be formal [in the labor market] and when you talk about formality . . . you are talking about abiding by gender roles. Formal for us means if you are a man, you have to dress like a man, and if you are a woman, you have to dress appropriately as a woman. . . . Now we have call centers. Many processors are gay, but they cannot accommodate the whole *bakla* population. It is a big help if we have the opportunity to go abroad.

Lastly, the transgender hostesses I met in Japan also repeatedly told me that Japan is a "*paraiso ng mga bakla*," meaning "paradise of the *bakla*." They pursued work in Japan for adventure and the promise of romance. Interviewees described Japan as a much better place for transgender women to seek sexual relations with men, and they could walk the streets free of harassment. This greater tolerance is perhaps a product of the normalization engendered by the mass media coverage in Japan of queer cultures in the 1990s as well as the campaign led by the Ministry of Education to celebrate individuality.[89]

Because of this tolerance, Peachy relished her life free of sexual harassment in Japan. As she described, "I am stable here. When I walk on the street, I am safe. No one will look at me, and no one will pay attention to me. Here they will just look at you to admire your beauty, unlike in the Philippines where they will call you names like faggot or *bakla*." Transgender hostesses appreciated the anonymity of their life in Japan; outside the club, they were not objects of spectacle. Hence, they felt that Japan provided them with the opportunity to be "normal," a far cry from the depiction of migrant hostesses as trafficked persons forced into prostitution.

OVERVIEW

Illicit Flirtations illustrates the indentured mobility of migrant hostesses by describing the processes of their labor, migration, and settlement. It begins with a description in Chapter One of the labor migration process for "entertainers" and explains why migrants who enter Japan with an "entertainer visa" are subject to relations of indentured servitude or peonage with middleman brokers, which are notably distinct from debt bondage.[90] The next four chapters move to a description of the labor process in hostess work. Chapter Two and Chapter Three describe the labor system in hostess clubs and the job requirements of hostesses. Chapter Two explains the organization and scientific management of flirtation and illustrates how club management disciplines the actions of hostesses by controlling their use of space and time while at work. Chapter Three then moves to a description of the job requirements of hostesses. Contrary to the common view that *hostess work* is but a euphemism for *prostitution*, I establish that the work of hostesses is not to provide sex but instead to bolster the masculinity of their customers. Chapter Four then elaborates on customer–hostess relations. My discussion of the labor conditions of hostess work ends in Chapter Five with an illustration of forced labor as situational and not universal. Forced sexual labor could occur when migrant Filipina hostesses face moral violations in the workplace, which I found not to be a frequent occurrence among them.

The last set of chapters describes the citizenship of migrant Filipina hostesses. It calls attention to the different set of vulnerabilities that plague them and shows how vulnerability to indentured servitude and forced labor differs according to their citizenship status. Migrant Filipina hostesses in Japan follow three patterns of settlement that accordingly determine their vulnerability to human rights violations. As I describe in Chapters Six through Eight, they are long-term residents (that is, wives), indefinite residents (that is, undocumented), or short-term residents (that is, contract workers). By distinguishing the citizenship patterns of migrant hostesses, I illustrate how each group faces a unique set of challenges that emerge from their particular terms of membership in Japan. Wives are vulnerable, among other challenges, to domestic violence; undocumented workers to employer and coethnic abuse; and contract workers to peonage. Notably, the flattening of their experiences to forced prostitution elides our recognition of the differences in their experiences and in turn prevents us from developing solutions that actually address their problems. The different challenges engendered by the terms of residency of hostesses attest to the variety of their needs, which in turn questions the applicability of uniform and top-down solutions to address their problems as migrants who are vulnerable to forced labor.

As a way of summing up, I address in the Conclusion the policy implications of my study. I underscore the need for us to shift from viewing forced labor, that is "human trafficking," as an individual problem that occurs randomly to seeing it as a structurally situated phenomenon that occurs in the context of labor migration regimes. Solutions to "trafficking" should not remain in the abstract, for instance with calls for the elimination of poverty or patriarchy. They should also not be universal. Instead, they need to address the particular needs of victims instead of glossing over them with one-size-fits-all fixes such as the templates of the 3Ps and 3Rs. Solutions need to be based on extensive grounded research. They must be empirically informed recommendations that work toward providing labor migrants with greater control over their labor and migration.[91]

The framework of *indentured mobility* blurs the distinction between human trafficking and labor migration by recognizing Filipina hostesses as labor migrants who face severe structural constraints. This framework does not dismiss their susceptibility to forced labor, but it rejects universal claims of their slavery as well as assumptions about the inevitability of forced labor for indentured workers. Blurring the lines between human trafficking and labor migration and recognizing trafficked persons as labor migrants would force us to rethink not only our understanding of the vulnerability of migrant workers to abuse, including enslavement, but also our solutions. The idea of *indentured mobility*, the recognition of "trafficked persons" as labor migrants, forces a realignment of our solutions from one of "rescue" to one of "harm reduction."[92] In other words, we would aim for job improvement and not job elimination, as our end goal would be not the "rescue" of supposedly helpless trafficked persons, as advocated by the U.S. Department of State, but instead their empowerment via continued mobility. Moreover, we would no longer tackle problems of forced labor on a case-by-case basis without an end in sight for its eradication. Instead, to eliminate forced labor, we would confront the severe structural constraints that hamper the autonomy of migrant workers, including exclusionary migration policies, the criminalization of migrants, the legalized servitude of contract workers, and the lack of sufficient regulation in the informal labor economies dominated by migrant workers. Such solutions would work toward increasing the control of "victims" over their labor and migration. We would focus our efforts on structurally ensuring the safe passage of migrant workers and not, as advocated by the United States in its global antitrafficking campaign, concentrate on individually prosecuting traffickers.[93]

CHAPTER ONE

THE MIGRATION OF ENTERTAINERS TO JAPAN

AMY TURNED EIGHTEEN YEARS OLD NOT long after I met her. At the age of seventeen, while many U.S. students are worrying over college applications or drivers' license tests, at an age where anyone is considered "severely trafficked" under U.S. policy guidelines,[1] she chose to leave her home to become a first-time contract worker in Japan. Amy fraudulently entered Japan with the use of another person's passport, but no one coerced her or forced her to do so. Instead, it was Amy who was quite determined to secure a contract as an entertainer and venture to Japan before she turned eighteen years old to help her parents financially.[2] Because all of her older siblings had gotten married quite early, Amy felt that this responsibility was left to her. She wanted to work in Japan for a few years to raise the funds that her parents would need to start a small business to support them in their old age.

Amy grew up as one of the working poor in Manila. Her fifty-six-year-old mother was a homemaker, and her father, whose age she did not know, hardly made ends meet with his daily earnings as a driver of a passenger jeepney.[3] Like Amy, many entertainers are among the poorest of the poor in the Philippines. Many had to drop out of school prior to migration. While some members of the middle class pursue hostess work in Japan because they have a passion for singing and dancing, most enter this line of work to escape their lives of dire poverty. Many of the entertainers I met grew up having to pick through garbage for food, sell cigarette sticks in bus terminals, and clean car windows in heavy traffic. Amy peddled pastries at the bus stop for a local bakery. She considered migrant hostess work her most viable means of financial mobility. Without financial resources, most other migrant employment opportunities had been closed to her. For instance, she could not afford the US$3,000 to US$5,000 fee that recruiters charge prospective migrant domestic workers in Hong Kong or Taiwan.[4] Yet, even if she could afford the fees imposed on domestic workers, Amy had no desire to become one, seeing their work as more difficult and dangerous than hostess work. For Amy, domestic work was made more perilous by the fact that it isolates the worker in a private home. Hostesses in Japan generally prefer their jobs over domestic work. Rikka, a veteran hostess, explained:

> Well, the salary is higher. In Hong Kong, it is only maids there. The contract workers who come back from Japan wear nice clothes, and the ones who come from Hong Kong have bags made of boxes. The women from Japan wear Louis Vuitton, and they have big earrings. The women from Japan, they have impressive necklaces, as big as dog chains. [We laugh.] The people from Hong Kong and Saudi Arabia, they are callused. The people from Japan, their hands are milky.

While migrant hostess work is considered desirable, it is not easily accessible.

Prospective migrant hostesses must undergo a highly selective audition in which they have to compete with around 200 other women for a handful of slots to go to Japan. At the audition, which is held at various promotion agencies in Manila, prospective hostesses are not judged on the merits of their talent but instead on their looks. Prospective migrants do not have to sing or dance at an audition but must instead look more attractive than the scores of other women around them. The local staff of the promotion agency, along with a Japanese promoter who has flown to the Philippines for the sole purpose of finding entertainers to place at various clubs in Japan, physically evaluate prospective migrants at an audition, where women parade in front of them as they would in a beauty contest. The women do not have to speak except perhaps to say their name, age, and how many times they have worked in Japan as an entertainer. Return migrants are sometimes tested briefly on their Japanese language skills, but their skills need not be more than rudimentary. For instance, they at most would have to demonstrate that they know how to throw a compliment to a customer in Japanese.

Amy had to undergo an audition at least three times before she was finally chosen to go to Japan. She described her slew of auditions as a disheartening process, one in which she had to undergo a series of rejections that she only managed to survive with the emotional support of the woman who had designated herself as her " talent manager." Amy's manager basically acted as her job coach, teaching her how to dress and apply makeup. In exchange for her services, she would receive at least 50 percent of Amy's salary, evidently not only for Amy's first labor contract but apparently for her next six. On signing a contract to be one of her manager's "talents," Amy agreed to complete six contracts for the next few years; yet securing six job contracts to work as a hostess in Japan is not easy. Unless Amy would be requested at the end of her contract to return to her club of employment, she would have to go through another round of auditions in various promotion agencies in Manila. Amy would have to do so because migrant entertainers cannot work continuously in Japan; instead they must return to the Philippines between contracts.

Refusing to complete six contracts in Japan would incur Amy a sizeable penalty of at least US$3,000. Amy could avoid this penalty without completing six contracts if she tried but fails to secure a contract at an audition, which is a risk that managers knowingly take when investing on the "training" of prospective migrant entertainers such as Amy. But Amy would probably have to go to at least twenty more auditions and do poorly, for instance not be selected as one of the top twenty candidates in any of them, before her manager would release her from future bookings. The point is that managers do not easily release entertainers such as Amy from their long-term contracts.

It would not only be Amy's manager in the Philippines who would be entitled to a portion of her salary. So would the promotion agency in the Philippines and the promoter in Japan. Between the two of them, they could legally obtain up to 40 percent of Amy's salary. For a number of reasons, a club in Japan technically cannot employ Amy; as I will later explain, the promotion agency in the Philippines and the promoter in Japan were her official employers. In most cases, a club would usually pay the promoter and promotion agency the salary of entertainers such as Amy prior to their arrival in Japan, but they in turn would withhold this salary from the entertainer until her very last day in that country. In fact, Amy had yet to be paid a dime of her earnings after having already worked in Japan for almost four months. Instead, she would not be paid the wages given by the club owner to her promoter until she completed her contract. It is common practice for the promoter to pay entertainers such as Amy at the airport when they are about to depart for the Philippines.

To survive, Amy lived off the tips she receives from customers, the commissions she received every ten days for her sales, and a daily food allowance of 500 yen, or US$5, that she received from the club owner. Some advocacy workers in Manila have said that the practice of withholding wages forces entertainers such as Amy into prostitution. Regardless, the fact that her wages were withheld not only violates Japan's labor laws but technically made her vulnerable to forced labor.[5] Also leaving Amy vulnerable to abusive work conditions was the fact that her promoter had confiscated her passport soon after she arrived in Japan. The promoter told Amy that he would return the passport to her at the airport on the completion of her six-month contract. Having her passport and wages withheld not only discouraged Amy from quitting but technically made her an unfree worker.

Although Amy had not yet been paid her salary, she already knew that she would receive only US$500 on her last day in Japan. The Japanese government stipulates a minimum monthly salary of 200,000 yen (approximately US$2,000) for foreign entertainers, but the middlemen who brokered Amy's migration are entitled to most of her salary.[6] Under the terms and conditions of her migration, Amy agreed to allocate US$1,000 of her monthly salary to the promotion agency and promoter who arranged her migration, while a US$500 monthly stipend was earmarked for her manager in the Philippines. These terms left Amy with a monthly salary of no more than US$500. Yet Amy knew that she was going to return home to the Philippines with a cumulative salary of only US$500 for six months of work in Japan, which is far less than the US$3,000 to which she should have been paid after the completion of her contract. This was the case because Amy had been paid US$500 of her salary prior to migration, and she additionally accrued US$1,000 in debt to her promotion agency, which compounded to US$2,000 due to the 100 percent interest rate the agency placed on it. Amy incurred this debt to cover various migration-related expenses such as the passport fee, medical exam fee, and so on.

Migrating to Japan is not free, as prospective migrants eventually learn they must pay the promotion agency for the dancing or singing lessons they must complete to qualify for an entertainer visa along with the cost of their passport, police clearance, medical examination, and other government requirements. Amy had borrowed money to pay for some of these costs. Most if not all entertainers accrue some debt before they go to Japan for the very first time, but most are not saddled with an interest by promotion agencies or managers, as Amy had been.

Disgruntled by her small salary, Amy admitted to selectively engaging in paid sex with customers. She knows that solely relying on her salary would not get her far. Amy did have certain boundaries. She had sex only with customers whom she found physically attractive. She also never received a direct payment for sex; instead, she received gifts. Amy told me that she engaged in compensated sex so as to guarantee that she would amass some financial gain from her time in Japan. However, still somewhat constrained by the moral stigma attached to prostitution, that is, the direct payment of money for sex, Amy wanted to clarify that she did not engage in prostitution. Interestingly, some of Amy's co-workers still ostracized her, as most of them would not engage in any form of commercial sex, suggesting that Amy's actions are the exception and not the norm among Filipina hostesses in Japan. The nineteen-year-old Reggie, for instance, was saddled with an even larger debt than her co-worker Amy but could not be tempted to accept the US$100 tip offered to her by a customer in exchange for a French kiss. The third-timer Kay, who also worked with Amy, also could not get herself to go to bed with her frequent customer, despite his threat that he would no longer give her gifts of jewelry from Tiffany's if she did not have sex with him after a month. The actions of Amy raise the question of whether she is a "severely trafficked person," not only because she was under age but also because her salary reductions pushed her into sex work in the first place. Some would say yes, but Amy herself would say no and insist that it had been her choice to engage in sex with some of her customers.

THE PROCESS OF MIGRATION

In the last twenty-five years, a steady stream of migrant women from the Philippines has entered Japan with entertainer visas.[7] These visas allow them to work as professional singers and dancers in Japan for a period of three months up to a maximum stay of six months. Because the government of Japan bans the labor migration of unskilled workers,[8] the visas of entertainers restrict their employment to singing and dancing on stage.[9] Their visas additionally bar them from interacting with customers because doing so would supposedly jeopardize the professional status of their jobs, as government officials fear that interacting with customers would mirror the activities of a waitress.[10] Still, most if not all entertainers closely interact with customers. Most enter Japan knowing that their work will require they do so.

While the government of Japan worries that close interactions between entertainers and customers would threaten the professional status of entertainers as performance artists, the U.S. government argues that such interactions suggest their prostitution. In the 2004 TIP Report, U.S Department of State identified migrant Filipina entertainers as sexually trafficked persons, asserting that the "Abuse of 'Artistic' or 'Entertainer' Visas" is a vehicle "used by traffickers to bring victims to Japan."[11] Disregarding the factor of consent, the U.S. Trafficking Victims Protection Act of 2000 (TVPA) defines sex trafficking as "the recruitment, harboring, transportation, provision, or obtaining of a person for the purpose of a commercial sex act."[12] This definition automatically renders any migrant sex worker a trafficked person, one who is assumed to be in need of "rescue, rehabilitation, and reintegration," regardless of their volition.[13]

Migrant Filipina entertainers are susceptible to forced labor. Their vulnerability arises primarily from their relation of servitude to middlemen, some of whom have been legally designated to broker the hostesses' migration. These include (1) the labor recruiter from Japan, otherwise known as the promoter, who places the entertainer at a club; (2) the local promotion agency in the Philippines, who makes sure that the terms of employment for hostesses abide by labor standards in the Philippines; and lastly (3) the talent manager, the self-designated job coach of prospective migrants whose responsibility is to increase the marketability and employability of prospective migrant entertainers.

Due to the presence of migrant brokers, going to Japan from the Philippines is not a simple process of moving from *A* to *B* for migrant entertainers. It begins with a prospective migrant signing on with a talent manager, who then takes the prospective migrant to an audition at a labor placement agency in the Philippines, otherwise known as a promotion agency, and the subsequent selection of the prospective migrant by what is called a Japanese promoter at

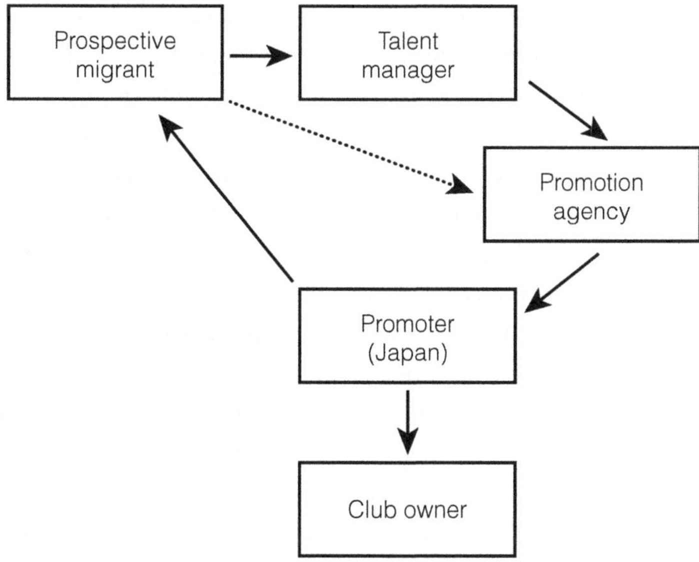

FIGURE 1.1 The migration process.

the audition. The Japanese promoter then places the prospective migrant in a club in Japan without much input from the club owner. Notably, the club in Japan is *not* the employer of the migrant entertainer, even though the migrant entertainer is technically working for the club owner. Instead, the Japanese promoter and Filipino promotion agency are the employers of the migrant entertainer. What explains this complex migration process? (See Figure 1.1.) Why the need for brokers such as the promoter or promotion agency? Can migrant entertainers ever circumvent this process and negotiate directly with the club, that is, their workplace, in Japan? In what sort of dependent position vis-à-vis brokers does the current migration process leave migrant entertainers? By addressing these questions, I unravel the relationship of entertainers and migrant brokers, specifically talent managers, promotion agencies, and promoters, and explicitly describe the legally sanctioned relations of servitude that these brokers maintain with entertainers.

By calling attention to the role of middlemen in the process of migration, I am acknowledging the susceptibility of migrant Filipina entertainers to forced labor. My discussion establishes that a culture of benevolent paternalism shapes the migration of women, resulting in the state's impulse to support their social and moral values with protectionist laws,[14] including minimum age requirements, a stringent professional accreditation system, standards of employment, and broker regulation. Protectionist laws in Japan and the Philippines—laws that emerge from the state's culture of benevolent paternalism—diminish women's capacity to migrate independently because they leave the women dependent on middleman brokers. The word *paternalism* in the most recent *Oxford English Dictionary* (*OED*) refers to "the policy or practice of restricting the freedoms and responsibilities of subordinates or dependants in what is considered or claimed to be their best interests."[15] In the case of migrant entertainers, "their best interests" would refer to the need to protect them not just from unscrupulous club owners but also from the immorality of close sexual interactions with customers, in other words, hostess work. Yet, rather than deter abuse, protectionist laws actually increase the likelihood of forced labor because they diminish women's ability to migrate independently. This tells us that it is the principle of wanting to protect women, including from human trafficking, that likely results in their exploitation.

The History of Government Accreditation

Protective measures engender relations of unequal dependency between brokers and entertainers. The first of these measures is the Japanese government's required professional qualifications for entertainers.[16] Requiring the professional certification of entertainers as singers or dancers supposedly deters the entrance of unskilled workers and reduces the likelihood that entertainers would engage in the unskilled labor of hostess work. For this reason, the Japanese government has imposed strict labor requirements that would ensure that each prospective migrant entertainer meets the highest level of professional skills for a performance artist.[17] As an officer of the Ministry of Justice told me, "Only those without real talent will do hostess work."[18]

Historically, Japan has given the Philippines the leeway to evaluate the professional qualifications of migrant entertainers. In 1981, Japan allowed the entry of Filipina entertainers without any work experience or training on the condition that the Philippine government would certify them to be bona fide performance artists. In contrast, prospective migrants from other countries were required to complete at least two years of training in the performance arts to qualify for an entertainer visa. With the discretion to determine the professional qualifications of their Japan-bound performance artists, Philippine government officials chose not to require them to fulfill two years of training. Instead, they required only that prospective migrants complete a much shorter skills training session at a government-accredited center. These training sessions could be as little as one month for singers and as long as six months for dancers. At the end of their training, prospective overseas performance artists must then be evaluated by a panel of judges and pass a skills-level examination to complete their certification; singers must perform two of five preselected songs in front of a panel of professional judges, and dancers must successfully complete a five-minute dance routine that shows their adeptness in a variety of dances including ballet, modern dance, and, sometimes, traditional folk dances of the Philippines. It is in the prospective migrants' vested interest to pass the accreditation exam. Those who do so qualify for an entertainer visa. Those who do not must resort to purchasing a visa under the table. Purchasing a visa would likely place an entertainer in debt to her broker, which would only diminish her control over her labor migration.

In the last twenty-five years, the Philippine government has consistently revisited and changed the requirements and process of certification for performance artists so as to deter the use of fraudulent credentials. For instance, the state has continiously revisited its age requirements, resulting in the last thirty years in an unpredictable flux of minimum age requirements from anywhere between eighteen and twenty-three years old.[19] The government has also evaluated its skills training requirements, for instance adding an academic course requirement for prospective migrants and forcing experienced entertainers to obtain recertification in certain years. While the requirements needed to qualify for a skills-level exam have changed through the years, what has stayed consistent is the evaluation exam. That is, singers and dancers must still perform in front of a panel of judges.

The labor migration of foreign entertainers to Japan preceded the institution of the Philippine Overseas Employment Administration (POEA) in 1982, which soon after in 1983 began to monitor the flow of entertainers to Japan with the issuance of the Philippine Entertainment Certification Center Card, otherwise known as the "blue card." Entertainers could obtain the blue card via the testing of their performance arts skills at an assessment center approved by POEA. Prospective migrants had to either sing or dance in front of a panel of judges, who often were members of the entertainment industry in the Philippines. Without much change in the requirements and standards of qualification to be a professional entertainer, the blue card was then replaced in 1989 with the yellow card or white card, which granted prospective migrant workers an Artist Accreditation Certificate.

In 1994, the Philippines instituted a major overhaul of its certification program for entertainers to make the categorization of their employment official under the category of "professional, technical, and related workers."[20] Under this new program, the Ministry of Foreign Affairs would no longer be in charge of assessing entertainers; instead, accreditation would fall under the responsibilities of the Ministry of Education. Consequently, centers for assessing prospective entertainers would now be accredited by the Technical Education and Skills Development Authority (TESDA) and instead of by POEA. Under this new system, the previous accreditation for overseas performance artists became null and void, and experienced migrant entertainers had to seek recertification. They now needed to secure an Artist Record Book (ARB), which would be their valid certificate of eligibility for employment as performance artists in Japan, one that they would have to renew every three years. To qualify for an ARB, prospective migrants would now also have to complete an "academic" skills training class. Administered by promotion agencies, academic training sessions would last between thirty and sixty days.[21]

After ten years of the ARB program, the Philippine government instituted another system for assessing overseas performance artists and replaced the ARB with the Artist Accreditation Certificate (AAC) in 2004. Not much difference exists between the two, but the AAC limits those who qualify for certification to prospective migrants with official bookings. This means that a Japanese promoter must have already selected and booked the prospective migrant worker for a contract in Japan prior to her eligibility for an AAC.[22] Only after her selection can the prospective migrant complete the required academic training to be an entertainer and secure certification as a performance artist by having her singing or dancing skills tested at an office of TESDA. An AAC also extends the eligibility of certified performance artists from three to ten years.

Only a year after the institution of the AAC, however, the Japanese government stopped recognizing the accreditation program of the Philippine government, making the shift from the ARB to AAC a moot effort. The Japanese government claims that the Philippine government does not accredit "real entertainers"[23] because they suspect that most deployed migrants from the Philippines still do hostess work. Since March 15, 2005, the government of Japan has required Filipino performance artists to complete two years of either training or work experience in the performance arts outside Japan to qualify for an entertainer visa. Disqualifying most experienced entertainers from reentry to Japan, this new policy does not count the experience of singing or dancing on stage in Japan toward a prospective migrant's qualification for an entertainer visa. What it does do is aggravate the dependence of migrant entertainers on middleman brokers, who now have to train them not for just six months but instead for two years to ensure they qualify for a visa to work in Japan.

Migrant Brokers: Promotion Agencies, Promoters, and Talent Managers

The dependence of migrant entertainers on brokers is not only because of Japanese government accreditation requirements. Philippine labor migration policies also diminish entertainer's ability to act as independent labor migrants, as they require overseas performance artists to work with middleman brokers to secure employment in Japan. Migrant entertainers must work with three groups of middleman brokers: the promotion agency, the promoter, and the talent manager. The Philippine government requires hostesses to work with various brokers to protect them from unscrupulous employers and to ensure that their work conditions in Japan meet labor standards in the Philippines.

The Philippine government displays their protective stance over entertainers by requiring them to sign a contract of employment within five days of their arrival in Japan, after which this contract is registered at the Philippine Embassy in Tokyo. Interestingly, the official employer designated in this contract is not the club owner but instead the Philippine-based promotion agency and its proxy of the Japanese job recruiter, otherwise known as the promoter. By registering the labor contracts of entertainers at the Philippine Embassy in Tokyo, the government makes official that the contract, which is made between two parties under the jurisdiction of the Philippine state, is subject to Philippine law. In actuality, foreign entertainers in Japan are not protected by Japanese labor laws as they are not considered workers but instead performers.[24] In this context, one could argue that establishing employment contracts within the jurisdiction of the Philippines, while providing some protection, only reinforces the lack of entertainers' rights in Japan. Notably, the employment contract could guarantee some protection for migrant entertainers by stipulating that a migrant entertainer could terminate her employment if subjected to "inhuman and/or unbearable treatment accorded to the Performing Artist by the Employer."[25] The glitch, however, is the fact that the "employer" is not the club owner but instead the promoter and promotion agency, who rarely if ever visit the club where the foreign entertainer might face "unbearable treatment" every night.

In recent years, POEA has accredited 322 promotion agencies to not only train and deploy but more importantly employ migrant entertainers in Japan.[26] Accreditation to become a promotion agency requires an initial capital of 2,000,000 pesos (approximately US$40,000),[27] the operation of a TESDA-certified training program, and lastly proof of a special power of attorney granted by a Japanese employer to hire on its behalf a minimum of fifty overseas performance artists from the Philippines per year.[28] In Japan, most clubs employ no more than twenty-five overseas performance artists, which consequently means most clubs *cannot* directly hire prospective migrants even through a promotion agency in Manila. To circumvent the minimum requirement of fifty hires per annum imposed by the Philippine government, hostess clubs in Japan have resourcefully turned to Japanese middlemen, that is, the promoters, who recruit the minimum number of prospective entertainers required of employers by the Philippine government and then assign them to different clubs in Japan, thus operating like the "body shops" that supply Indian information technology workers to businesses in the United States and Australia.

In his book *Global "Body Shopping,"* Biao Xiang describes "body shopping" as a system of subcontracting in high technology.[29] Body shops function as temporary placement agencies that assign migrant employees to companies on a short-term basis. Under this arrangement, the "body shop" remains the official employer of the worker and as such maintains responsibility for his or her temporary work visa, salary, and accommodations. A similar scenario of subcontracting occurs in the nightlife industry of Japan, where foreign entertainers are employed not by the clubs where they work but technically by the middlemen, that is, the promotion agency and promoter, who place them at a club in Japan. On behalf of the promotion agency in the Philippines, this promoter is responsible for finding an eligible place of employment for the entertainer, providing the entertainer with transportation to and from the airport at the beginning and end of her contract, and escorting her to the club officially listed as her workplace at the Office of Immigration in Japan.[30]

Promoters arguably function like "body shops." Similar to Japanese promoters that supply migrant entertainers to hostess clubs in Japan, "body shops" secure their business by placing workers in multiple job sites. "Body shops" would take a portion of the worker's monthly wages, charge workers a placement fee, and if possible transfer the costs of migration (such as airfare and visa fees) to the prospective migrant worker. Likewise, Japanese promoters receive the salaries of prospective migrant workers from club owners prior to their arrival to Japan. They have also been known to receive a commission from club owners and to incur a portion of the entertainer's salary and charge her for the cost of her travel. No one monitors the activities of promoters. As middleman brokers, they could double dip and charge both the migrant worker and her prospective employer the cost of her airfare. While the handful of club owners I spoke with claim to have prepaid the travel costs of migrant workers prior to their arrival in Japan, many hostesses likewise maintain that they incurred wage deductions from the cost of their airfare and travel documents.

Promoters in Japan as well as their counterpart of the promotion agency in the Philippines ironically emerge from the impulse of the state to protect overseas performance artists from harm. The Philippine government legally requires prospective Japanese employers to guarantee a large volume of placement, that is, fifty individuals per year, so as to protect prospective migrant entertainers from fly-by-night operations or small-scale establishments in Japan, where the Philippine government assumes migrant entertainers would be more vulnerable to unscrupulous labor practices. The state impulse to protect entertainers also results in their dependence on promotion agencies in the Philippines, which must oversee their labor protection and ensure that employment standards in hostess clubs abide by Philippine labor laws. The legal mandate for entertainers to work with middleman brokers unavoidably heightens the culture of benevolent paternalism that shapes their migration. Their presence institutionalizes this paternalistic culture, which in turn justifies the need for talent managers as a third group of brokers to oversee the protection of migrant entertainers.

Although the state does not sanction the brokering of talent managers, the salience of this group of brokers unquestionably emerges from the culture of benevolent paternalism around women's migration and more particularly the migration of entertainers. The cultural assumption of the need of migrant entertainers for protection results in the prominence of talent managers. The primary responsibility of talent managers is to assist prospective migrants through the predeployment process. Although promotion agencies are responsible for ensuring that contract workers meet all the requirements of POEA for prospective migrant entertainers, the talent manager often undertakes this responsibility. Frequently, managers are staff members of promotion agencies, who assist prospective migrants through the migration process by introducing them to representatives of local promotion agencies as well as promoters from Japan, walking them through the training process, and ensuring that they meet all of the predeployment requirements set forth by the government. These include the completion of a medical clearance, a one-day predeployment seminar, singing and dancing lessons (including ballet and modern dance), and finally securing a passport and the required government certification for performance artists.

Entertainers are not legally obligated to work with talent managers, but managers see themselves as necessary to the migration process. First, they claim to give entertainers the "opportunity" to work in Japan under the presumption that entertainers would otherwise have no access to such employment. For instance, an entertainer is unlikely to know about an audition without the help of a talent manager. Secondly, they perceive themselves to be the primary "protectors" of entertainers. For example, they supposedly ensure that promoters do not underpay entertainers. Lastly, they develop the marketability of the entertainer, increasing the likelihood of her selection in an audition by cultivating her artistry and looks. For this reason, talent managers are quite prominent during auditions.

Wage Reductions

Middlemen amass significant profits for brokering the labor and migration of entertainers. Brokering entitles them to a significant portion of the entertainer's salary. Under Philippine law, promoters and promotion agencies are obligated to pay overseas performance artists only 60 percent of their salary.[31] This means that Philippine law denies overseas performance artists the minimum wage stipulated by the government of Japan, which is 200,000 yen (approximately US$2,000) per month. Club owners usually pay middlemen the minimum wage stipulations of the government. If middlemen take no more than a 40 percent commission, then hostesses should earn at least 120,000 yen or US$1,200 per month. However, they do not. In fact, the standard employment contract that overseas performance artists sign at the Philippine Embassy limits their earnings to 100,000 yen per month. According to the standard employment contract, the minimum gross compensation of 200,000 yen per month could be reduced by a 30,000 yen food allowance, a 30,000 yen housing cost, and lastly 20 percent in income tax.

The frustration of seeing various forms of *legalized* deductions is the reason most of my interviewees refused to read the official labor contract that they signed and filed at the Philippine Embassy, claiming that it would only upset them to see their listed salary as more than what they actually receive. These employment contracts seem to be "just for show," many told me. They believed this was the case for many reasons. First, most knew they would receive far less than the stipulated amount of 100,000 yen as a monthly salary. They also knew that promoters do *not* provide entertainers with a food allowance and housing. Club owners provide both, and neither amounts to 30,000 yen. For instance, entertainers receive no more than 15,500 yen in food allowance per month.

In actuality, the earnings of entertainers fall far short of what is designated even in their contracts at the Philippine Embassy. They receive an average wage of only US$500 as first-time contract workers and not much more as experienced entertainers.[32] Second-time contract workers usually earn US$600 per month, while a third-time contract worker could negotiate a salary of US$700 per month. Among my interviewees, a few very experienced entertainers, for instance those who have completed eight or more labor contracts, earned close to US$2,000 per month, but these were rare cases, especially as clubs tend to hire only entertainers with minimal experience.

Most entertainers had only a vague understanding of the distribution of their income. While they knew that middlemen receive a portion of their salary, they usually could not explain why this was the case, for instance often responding to my request for an explanation of the logic behind their income distribution with the comment, "It is just the way it is." This was the case, for instance, with Elizabeth, a former contract worker who first migrated to Japan in the mid-1980s. Explaining her past income distribution, she stated:

It is just the way it is. See, our *papa* [club owner] cannot pay us directly. He really has to give our salary to our promoter. Then the promoter would give money to the promotion agency. So everyone gets our money. To be honest with you, we really did not know what happened to our salary. Our monthly salary before was $1500, but we know only $500 of that would go to us. We knew that $1000 would go to the promoter and promotion.

When I asked her what she thought of the financial distribution of her income, she gave an ambivalent response: "I think it is OK, because we probably would not be able to come here without them. But I think that they pay us too little. Work is hard." As the employer of entertainers, middleman brokers are entitled to a share of their earnings, a fact that does not always sit well with entertainers but one that entertainers have come to accept as the unquestionable norm and standard of employment for them.

One could conceivably argue that the situation of migrant entertainers does no more than follow the basic tenets of capitalism. After all, middleman brokers—as capitalists—own the labor of migrant entertainers and merely extract profits, or the surplus value, produced by this labor. As such, the relationship among promotion agencies, promoters, and migrant entertainers is sanctioned by the state. Yet the relationship between migrant entertainers and middlemen extends beyond a capitalist relationship and turns to abuse when middlemen fail to fulfill the responsibilities that entitle them to extract profit from the entertainer, which is to protect entertainers from labor violations.

Servitude

Middleman brokers ironically do not protect but instead violate the labor rights and freedom of migrant entertainers. They do this by subjecting them to peonage, that is, by binding them to servitude because of debt, and through indentured servitude, meaning work as "contractual but unfree" workers.[33] First, promoters withhold the salary of entertainers until their very last day in Japan, literally at the airport soon after they check in for their return flight to the Philippines. In other words, promoters do not pay entertainers during the entire time that they are contract workers in Japan.[34] Second, promoters deter entertainers from quitting by withholding their passports and restricting them to alien registration cards as their only proof of legal residency while in Japan. Third, entertainers must sign a legal document with the promotion agency in the Philippines prior to their departure, stipulating that they will incur the severe penalty of 150,000 to 200,000 pesos, approximately US$3,000 to US$4,000, if they quit their job prior to the end of their contract. Fourth, talent managers collect the passports of entertainers on their return to the Philippines and keep them until the entertainer goes back to Japan. None of the above conditions are sanctioned by the state.

Talent managers subject migrant entertainers to a longer period of servitude than other brokers. Prior to escorting an entertainer to her first audition, the talent manager usually binds the prospective migrant to an agreement that earmarks a sizable percentage of the entertainer's earnings to the manager, sometimes as much as 50 percent, in the next three to five years. Talent managers actually require entertainers to pursue and complete a set number of contracts, usually three to five, in the next few years. During this entire time, the manager would receive a percentage of the entertainer's salary. According to my interviewees, unscrupulous managers would demand a 50 percent commission, while "nice" managers would charge only a $200 monthly fee. The relation between talent managers and entertainers would be difficult to justify in court, but talent managers have been able to control the migration of entertainers by requiring them to sign blank checks prior to their departure or blank contracts, which they would later fill in with debt if they ever had a disagreement with the entertainer. As one interviewee told me, "You just sign the form." When I asked what form, she responded, "A blank piece of paper." Reneging on this arrangement with talent managers would usually cost entertainers a penalty of anywhere from US$3,000 to US$5,000.

One could argue that middleman brokers force entertainers to abdicate their freedom when they migrate to Japan. For some, servitude, regardless of context, would constitute unfreedom.[35] This is because servitude binds one to the will of another person.[36] However, servitude may accord material advantages that are otherwise closed to hostesses. Prospective migrant hostesses face two bad options of unfreedom: a life of servitude in Japan or one of abject poverty in the Philippines. Choosing between servitude and poverty, migrant entertainers evaluate their limited choices and make the "autonomous" decision to agree to a relation of servitude with middleman brokers.[37] We should recognize that they do so as thinking persons, who evaluate the risks of staying in the Philippines to those of going to Japan with "critical self-reflection."[38]

While one could argue that servitude indicates the trafficking of migrant entertainers, this assumption would risk the erasure of their will and desires; hence my insistence on viewing their migration as one of indentured mobility. In recognizing the limited choices of migrant Filipina entertainers, we should realize that freedom is more complicated than "the absence of restraints," as reasoned by the liberal thinker John Mill.[39] Freedom is not ontological but procedural. Significant in our conceptualization of freedom is the aim for what philosopher John Christman calls a "content neutral" conception, one that does not judge or dismiss migrant entertainers for making the illiberal choice of servitude.[40] When entertainers choose to be in a relation of servitude to middleman brokers, they take this risk conscious of their means of exit. For instance, many know of their option to escape their club and become undocumented workers. They also know that they can be free of their managers if they use another person's identity when returning to Japan. Amy was one of those who planned to do so. While unable to stake a claim on her current earnings (hence her reliance on the compensation provided by her customers), Amy knew that she could walk away from her middleman brokers free of penalty because the name they used in her contract was that of someone else, and the passport she used to migrate to Japan also belonged to another person. This means that the person whom her manager could sue for a "breach of contract" was fictive. Amy's situation, and her knowledge of the loophole in her labor agreement with middleman brokers, indicated that servitude had not completely subjected her to the domination of others. Yet her choice to become subjugated did not justify her subjugation. Migrant brokers could choose not to bind entertainers such as Amy to a relationship of servitude, but the fact is that they do.

To justify their actions, brokers claim that they, along with promoters, would incur a fee from the government of Japan for every entertainer who goes AWOL.[41] However, officials at the Ministry of Justice told me that their government does not penalize anyone if a migrant entertainer ever decides to leave a club before the end of her contract.[42] We could speculate that perhaps more than wanting to avoid government penalties, brokers do not want migrant entertainers to quit to avoid paying back to the club the advance payment that they had received for her labor before she arrived in Japan. They would have to do this, if she ever decided to quit before the end of her contract. Not all brokers charge migrant contract workers exorbitant fees to go to Japan, but most penalize entertainers for reneging on their contract.

While promotion agencies and promoters subject entertainers to servitude for six months, talent managers do so for at least three years. While still bound to talent managers, entertainers must continuously pursue contract work in Japan. Pregnancy, marriage, and other such life course events that could prevent a woman from returning to Japan would result in a penalty. Rowena, who first worked in Japan at the age of fifteen, paid her manager US$3,000 to be released from her "contract" to marry a customer who had proposed to her, a man nine years her senior. At that point, she still owed her manager the completion of four more labor contracts. Eleven years later, at the time of our interview, Rowena lived in Tokyo with her husband and two children. Living comfortably as a stay-at-home mother, she justified to herself the payment of US$3,000 she made to her manager by looking at it as a reward, otherwise known as a *balato* (shared winnings), to those who helped her meet her husband. Her logic was that without her manager she probably would never have had the opportunity to go to Japan and meet and marry a Japanese man, escaping her life of poverty in the Philippines.[43]

Middleman brokers reason that the "release fee" or penalty offsets their loss of future earnings. The former contract worker Irene explained the logic of the penalty, "There is an agreement that the woman will work in Japan for the next five years. But then, after two trips, you get married. Because you owe three more years, they make you pay them for those years for you to get your documents back from them." One manager further explained that the loss of earnings she would incur from someone failing to complete her contract was grounds for her to claim a "breach of contract." As she told me,

> Let's say you have a rich *papa* [customer]. You can get out of your three-year contract if the percentage of the salary that the manager was going to receive is paid for by the *papa*. This is on top of the debt. So it is illegal for the talents to turn their backs on their contract. That would be considered a breach of contract. You cannot get married until you are done with your [three-year] contract [with the manager]. You also cannot get pregnant because your travel has to be continuous.

To prevent hostesses from pursuing other options, including marriage, managers withhold the travel documents of hostesses in the Philippines and make their release conditional on the payment of a fee to offset their lost commission. Yet managers cannot force entertainers who wish to renege on their agreement to cover the penalty of their loss in future earnings. Some have rightfully contested "breach of contract" claims by their manager.[44]

The legality of the relationship between entertainers and managers is questionable, as it subjects the contract worker to indentured servitude or peonage. After an entertainer receives her earnings at the airport in Japan, her manager meets her at the airport in the Philippines and collects all the entertainer's travel documents. It seems managers do not have any legal grounds to hold the migrant worker accountable to this arrangement. By holding onto the entertainer's travel documents, the manager dissuades her from working with another manager or promotion agency, perhaps one who would take a smaller percentage of her earnings. It is common practice for middlemen to obtain the passports of contract workers whether in the Philippines or Japan. As Arissa, one undocumented worker, described, "When you are a *talent*, someone else holds your passport. You carry your passport yourself only when you are in the airport. When you are about to leave [the airport], they take your passport from you." In the Philippines, talent managers or promotion agencies hold onto the passports of migrant entertainers to deter them from working with other brokers, while in Japan promoters hold onto their travel documents to discourage them from running away from the club.

Once in the Philippines, an entertainer could potentially report her passport as stolen and then use new documents to seek work in Japan independent of her manager. However, some entertainers are convinced that not fulfilling their contractual obligation to their manager would land them in prison. For instance, Kay, a second-time contract worker, explained to me that she would be incarcerated if she reneged on her arrangement with her manager. She told me, "I signed a contract. And if I don't finish the contract, I will be put in prison. That is what it says in the paper. That I will be put in prison if I do not finish the contract."

Managers have the power to bully entertainers because the industry condones their presence. Managers could blacklist potential entertainers from various promotion agencies, as managers are often staff or owners of such agencies. Moreover, the government of the Philippines does not monitor the activities of middleman brokers, hence enabling them to abuse their power over entertainers. When I asked the labor attaché at the Philippine Embassy in Tokyo why managers have such a stronghold over the labor and migration of entertainers, she placed the blame on entertainers, explaining that they put themselves in that situation by signing a blank document.

It is a near universal occurrence for first-timers to be coerced into long-term contracts by managers. Most first-time entertainers are young women in their late teens, innocent and naïve, and hence easily bullied by middlemen. Those without managers are rare in this industry. The few able to secure contracts after a three- to five-year agreement with talent managers technically become what is called a "freelancer" in the community, which refers to their status of being free of the control of a manager. One such woman was my co-worker Teresa, a thirty-seven-year-old undocumented worker, who at some point had completed seven contracts to work in Japan. Teresa had to work with a manager only three times. Without a manager, Teresa—as a freelancer—could negotiate her salary directly with the promoter and the promotion agency. As a freelancer, however, she could not minimize the commissions of these two middlemen. Yet, according to Teresa, their commission had been of no concern to her because she cared only that her salary reached her own minimum wage requirement.

Irene, a former contract worker who was awaiting her *kekkon* [marriage] visa, also coped with her wage deductions by using the same strategy as Teresa. She set a minimum wage for herself and only cared that this wage was met regardless of the increases made to it by middleman brokers. As she explained, "You know how much your salary should be, and you ask for that salary. You tell your manager how much you want to take home, and you do not care how much they want to add to that amount." While this strategy allows hostesses such as Irene and Teresa to cope with their situation, it unfortunately invites conflict with club owners. The lesser salary received by the entertainer than the actual amount paid by the club owner to brokers could engender a conflict over the labor productivity of the entertainer, whose work expectations might be significantly lower than those of the club owner.

In general, hostesses suffer from the unfair distribution of their earnings with middleman brokers. Many complained to me that it was they, and not their managers or other staff members of the promotion agency, who were working hard in Japan. Most did accept the need to reward managers with a commission, but they also distinguished between what would be acceptable and non-acceptable commissions. According to most, a fair commission for managers would be no more than $200 per month. Because most migrant entertainers seem to know little about their rights, it is likely that many just tolerate their work even if they find it almost unbearable. Entertainers, for instance, can circumvent penalties if they can prove to the appropriate Philippine government agency, in this situation the Overseas Worker's Welfare Administration (OWWA), that they had been required by the club to perform illegal activities. However, rarely did the entertainers I met in Japan turn to the government for assistance. An entertainer who was disgruntled about her work would usually escape her club of employment and become an undocumented worker before she would formally complain to the Philippine Embassy.[45]

Talent managers justify the penalties they impose on entertainers as compensation for loss of investment. As one talent manager explained, "We have to feed them and shelter them. So we have to deduct that cost from their wages . . . *It is not possible for a manager not to get half of your salary. It is because she is the one that struggled and worked hard for you*" (my own emphasis). Surprisingly, brokers generally see their actions as falling within the purview of their legal responsibility to protect migrant workers and for the overall good of these workers. They consider their presence to be necessary to the well-being of entertainers. According to promoters, holding onto the passports of entertainers while they work in Japan assures them that these workers are unlikely to escape and place themselves at risk of becoming undocumented workers. Withholding wages for six months means migrant entertainers are more likely to take back their earnings to the Philippines instead of spending them on frivolous items in Japan, a reasoning that suggests the infantilization of these workers. Talent managers likewise claim that they hold onto passports once migrant entertainers are in the Philippines only to ensure their safekeeping. Replacing a passport stamped with the accreditation of the migrant entertainer supposedly entails an extended process that could delay the return migration of the entertainer. Not many would agree with the logic behind the arguments of middleman brokers. In contrast to their perspective, nongovernmental organizations in the Philippines consider migrant brokers neither as advocates nor as protectors of migrant entertainers. Instead, they consider them to be traffickers who shackle entertainers, perhaps not physically but without doubt mentally, and coerce them to do their job for the purpose of their economic exploitation.

OTHER VULNERABILITIES OF MIGRATION

Protective laws should be in place to ensure the rights of migrant workers. At the same time, the government should also monitor the administration of these protective laws. At the moment, they do not; instead they give migrant brokers free rein to do whatever they deem fit to protect migrant workers. As such, governments are not in a position to prevent migrant brokers from charging exorbitant fees to entertainers and obtaining a disproportionate share of their salaries. Currently, there is no system of checks and balances in the labor migration process of entertainers. Because the current system designates complete control to brokers, entertainers are left vulnerable to exploitation. In addition, brokers abuse their power over entertainers by also subjecting them to debt inflation and "flying bookings," meaning illegal club placements.

According to my interviewees, middlemen regularly inflate their debt. Prior to migration, middleman brokers will make entertainers sign a blank document, referred to as a *listahan* (list) that they will later fill with the expenses the entertainer has incurred. Thinking that this document is conditional to their migration, many entertainers sign it because "the only thing in your head is wanting to be able to leave." Those who abuse the power of having a signed blank piece of paper compound the debt of entertainers by charging them twice for travel documents, imposing large fees for minor services, and overcharging them for the food and housing expenses that they have incurred during their training period.

Most if not all entertainers incur a debt with middleman brokers because middlemen usually bear the cost of various premigration expenses, including the training required of overseas performance artists. Only the expenses of airfare and life insurance policy in Japan are covered by a middleman broker, in this case the promoter, because the Philippine government mandates it. However, promoters can still get away with passing this cost onto the entertainer with salary reductions as they are without government monitoring.

To cover the costs of migration, entertainers usually need to borrow funds from their promotion agency or talent manager because many are members of the working poor in the Philippines. The largest expense incurred by prospective migrants is the cost of training, which is an amount unknown to many of them, and the cost of their accommodation during this period. In interviews, promotion agency representatives and talent managers claim not to charge for food and lodging during the training period of prospective migrants, or, if they do, they claim to charge no more than 2,000 pesos a month (US$40). On the contrary, many entertainers whom I met in Tokyo claim to have paid significantly more for their food and lodging prior to migration. They accumulated debt while training because they were often required to live in the housing provided by either their talent manager or promotion agency. Due to the varied expenses that a woman incurs to secure her labor certification as a migrant entertainer, many do not earn an income during the first contract stint in Japan. As Irene, who has completed eight labor contracts in Japan, states, "The first time you ever travel is payment for your visa."

In addition to lodging, the prospective migrant must pay for the cost of a passport (1,000 pesos); POEA seminar (200 pesos); medical checkup for AIDS, tuberculosis, and other communicable diseases by a government-certified medical agency (800 to 1,000 pesos); TESDA exam (200 pesos); and lastly the certification fee (500 pesos). The largest debt among my interviewees reached 200,000 pesos (US$4,000), but most debts range anywhere from 10,000 to 50,000 pesos (US$200 to US$1,000).[46] According to a broker whom I interviewed in the Philippines, the average debt hostesses owe him is 20,000 pesos (US$400). Those requiring more than a year of training prior to certification amassed greater debt than others. While debts bind entertainers to talent managers and promotion agencies, rarely is the debt compounded with interest. The case of Amy, described earlier, was an exception.

It is not necessarily the accumulation of debt but the practice of debt inflation that bothers entertainers. One way middleman brokers inflate debt is by charging entertainers not once but twice for a service. This happened to many of the entertainers whom I met in Japan. They would pay twice for a passport, a medical exam, a certification exam, and other such expenses. During interviews, entertainers often laughed over this common practice. Rowena could only shake her head when she complained about having to pay twice for her passport. She recalled, "So you come home, and you are surprised that you have a debt. You paid for your passport before you left, and you pay for your passport again when you come home . . . They charged me 10,000 pesos for a passport." Rowena was not only overcharged US$200 for a passport that should have only cost her US$25, but she also had to pay for this expense twice. However, signing that blank piece of paper made her feel obligated to pay. She explained that, at the age of fifteen, she did not know any better.

Entertainers who migrated with "fake" identities provided by managers and promotion agencies are those most susceptible to debt inflation. Almost all of them incurred a fee of 60,000 pesos (US$1,200) upwards to 100,000 pesos (US$2,000) for the use of another person's identity. To subvert Japanese legal restrictions, for instance age requirements[47] or deportation restrictions,[48] hostesses commonly use others' identity to go to Japan. They use the passport of a relative they know is unlikely to venture abroad to avoid the penalty imposed by middleman brokers.[49] But while entertainers use others' identity to maximize their resources, so do middleman brokers. Many force their clients to use a "fake" identity that they have provided so they can impose fees on them. Promotion agencies would sometimes make it seem that the departure of the entertainer is conditional to her use of another's identity. This happened to Reggie, Amy's co-worker and, like Amy, a first-time contract worker in Japan. Reggie's use of another person's passport landed her a debt of 120,000 pesos (approximately US$2,400), which was slightly less than her projected six-month income of US$2,500. According to Reggie, her debts accumulated because she had used another person's identity. Reggie knew she was charged 60,000 pesos for her certification and 10,000 pesos for her passport, but she was unable to account for the remaining 50,000 pesos of her debt. She could only speculate that it had come from her housing cost; she had to live with the promotion agency for nearly four months while she auditioned in Manila. Reggie's story was complicated. She actually had been selected in two previous auditions, but those bookings got cancelled, holding up the use of her original travel documents.

Reggie desperately wanted to go to Japan and accepted the offer by her promotion agency to use "fake" travel documents when an opportunity to be deployed suddenly came while her other bookings were still pending and were holding up her original passport. Reggie did not mind the added cost of using another person's identity because she thought that her first labor contract would open the door to more contracts in the future. Reggie saw her first contract in Japan as part of a long-term investment. She agreed to the use of a false identity knowing she would earn only US$100 from her first contract stint but with the assumption that she would earn much more, at least US$3,600, from her second time around in Japan. Reggie's situation is a common one among entertainers as many accumulate debt nearly equal to if not more than the sum of their first six months of salary in Japan. They begin to earn from their work in Japan only during their second labor contract. In the past, promotion agencies would allow entertainers to spread the payment of their debt across two or even three work contracts. Reggie, for instance, hoped that her promotion agency would collect only US$1,000 of her debt after her first contract. However, promotion agencies are no longer agreeing to an extended installment plan to cover the debt of entertainers because they are unlikely to return due to the recent crackdown in Filipino migration to Japan. Plenty of first-time contract workers have consequently been returning to the Philippines without pay and without the guarantee that they will have another opportunity to work in Japan as an entertainer.[50]

Entertainers do not always know of their debt prior to migration. In some cases, they accumulate debt unknowingly. This happened to an undocumented worker, Marie, who was shocked to learn during her last day as a first-time contract worker in Japan that she was going to be paid only US$100 for six months of work in Tokyo by the promoter because of the debt she supposedly acquired prior to migration. Marie could not explain to me the source of her debt, but I assume that it must have originated from the cost of her training and housing as she resided at the promotion agency for over a year while preparing to go to Japan. Not wanting to return to the Philippines empty handed, Marie decided to escape her club during her last night of work. She had since been in Japan as a visa overstayer for nearly two decades.

Besides debt inflation, entertainers are also vulnerable to the practice of illegal club placements, which are otherwise known as "flying bookings." A "flying booking" is the practice of placing contract workers at a club other than the one where they had been registered to work at the Office of Immigration in Japan. Usually clubs where migrants are illegally booked are ineligible to hire foreign entertainers because they do not meet certain requirements, such as the provision at the premises of a stage measuring no less than thirteen square meters, the employment of at least five nonforeign employees, or the proprietor's lack of a criminal record.[51] Those not meeting government requirements would have to bribe promoters to place foreign entertainers at their clubs. Entertainers who do not perform adequately during their first three months are those likely to be placed as a "flying booking" at another club, as promoters—instead of sending them back to the Philippines as requested by the original club owner—would take advantage of the option to still earn a commission from them. "Flying booking" is a rampant problem for entertainers. An entertainer assigned to a "flying booking" is without legal rights to work in Japan, as she becomes an illegal worker who is subject to immediate deportation if caught by an immigration officer. If deported, she would then be banned from reentry to Japan for at least five years.

In their quest to protect migrant workers, the governments of both the Philippines and Japan have instituted protectionist laws that give middleman brokers control over the migration of entertainers. This in turn has diminished the capacity of entertainers to migrate independently. Bound to work with middleman brokers, they are unable to choose the club of their employment or directly negotiate the terms of their employment with clubs. Additionally, protectionist laws subject them to servitude. Some would argue that servitude would make all entertainers nothing but trafficked persons who are in need of rescue, while others would argue that it results in their susceptibility to forced labor and calls attention for their need to have greater control over their labor and migration.

THE U.S. ANTITRAFFICKING CAMPAIGN AND ITS UNIVERSAL SOLUTION TO TRAFFICKING

How has migrant Filipina entertainers' identification of as trafficked persons shaped their experience of migration? Has it improved the condition of their labor migration? Has it facilitated their greater control over their situation? At the turn of this century, the United States declared war on its two greatest perceived threats to democracy—terrorism and human trafficking. Unlike the war on terrorism, the war on trafficking gained momentum not overnight but slowly through a series of hearings with bipartisan sponsorship, calling attention to the forced labor, debt bondage, and coerced migration of 800,000 individuals, 80 percent of whom supposedly were women and children, throughout the world.[52] In these hearings, which culminated in the passage of the Trafficking Victims Protection Act (TVPA), much emphasis had been placed on the trafficking of individuals in the sex industry, which suggests that the "aspirational morality" of the antiprostitution movement and the quest to ensure the feminine respectability of migrant women had been strong motivations in the passage of this law.[53] As the legal scholar Jennifer Chacon notes, "Stories involving sexual exploitation were, by far, the most common stories invoked during consideration of the Act. Some members of Congress seemed convinced that they were enacting a sex trafficking bill."[54] As one of the bill's primary sponsors, Representative Christopher Smith, exclaimed, "It's time to declare war on sex traffickers."[55]

The U.S. antitrafficking campaign fits a historical continuum in which the migration of women has been subject to moral policing by the state. What is different is that, in the past, the United States monitored the migration of women only within its own borders.[56] Historically, the United States barred the entry of any woman suspected to be in danger of becoming a public charge, transgressing gender boundaries, and living immorally.[57] The protection of women's sexual morality also motivated the antiprostitution and antitrafficking hysteria in the late 1800s and early 1900s, which culminated in the passage of the U.S. White Slave Traffic Act of 1910, otherwise known as the Mann Act.[58] This law banned the interstate transport of females for immoral purposes with the intention of addressing prostitution and human trafficking. Interestingly, the intentions of lawmaker James Robert Mann are reflected a hundred years later in those of Congressman Christopher Hill. The only difference between them being is the global scope in Hill's antitrafficking campaign.

Reflecting the global scope of TVPA, this law requires the U.S. Department of State to submit to congress an annual report—the TIP Report—that describes the efforts of foreign governments to eliminate human trafficking. Foreign governments in turn are pressured to submit records and reports on their antitrafficking activities to the United States so it can accordingly monitor and evaluate their antitrafficking efforts. According to the U.S. Department of State,

> [The TIP Report] is intended to raise global awareness and spur foreign governments to take effective actions to counter all forms of trafficking in persons—a form of modern day slavery . . . A country that fails to take significant actions to bring itself into compliance with the minimum standards for the elimination of trafficking in persons receives a negative "Tier 3" assessment in this Report. Such an assessment could trigger the withholding of non-humanitarian, non-trade-related assistance from the United States to that country. In assessing foreign governments' efforts, the

TIP Report highlights the "three P's"—prosecution, protection, and prevention. But a victim-centered approach to trafficking requires us equally to address the "three R's"—rescue, rehabilitation, and reintegration.[59]

In its war on trafficking, the United States pressures other countries politically to implement policies and programs that follow its universal template of the Three *P*s and Three *R*s to avoid receiving a low mark in the annual TIP Report. According to TVPA, foreign countries must prohibit and punish severe forms of trafficking, punish so as to deter trafficking, and demonstrate sustained efforts to eliminate trafficking. To receive a Tier 3 ranking translates to social ostracism in the international community. In 2004, Japan was placed in the dreaded group of the Tier 2 Watch List, a deeply embarrassing position to be in as one of only two G-8 countries along with Russia to be placed in this low category. One primary factor for the demotion of Japan had been the migration flow of Filipina entertainers, which the United States highly suspected to be a back door to prostitution.[60] As the 2004 TIP Report notes, "It is reported that Japan issued 55,000 entertainer visas to women from the Philippines in 2003, many of whom are suspected of having become trafficking victims."[61] Explaining the low standing of Japan in the TIP Report is the fear of the U.S. Department of State that "women and children are primarily trafficked to Japan from Thailand, the Philippines, Russia, and Eastern Europe for sexual exploitation."[62] They supposedly come seeking "legal work but are deceived or coerced into debt bondage or sexual servitude."[63]

The TIP Report constructs supposed trafficked victims as dupes deceived or coerced into debt bondage. This assertion simplifies their situation and allows the United States to pose the easy solution of rescue. However, the situation of migrant Filipina entertainers, and perhaps also their counterparts from other countries, is much more complicated. First, middleman brokers, including those who have been legally sanctioned to protect Filipina entertainers in the process of migration, and not club owners are the ones who subject them to peonage and indentured servitude. Second, these women do not suddenly find themselves bound to servitude; instead, the legal system of their migration forces them to migrate under this condition. Faced with limited choices for mobility, they agree to servitude prior to migration, as their departure is almost always conditional to it. They see servitude abroad as a much better option than their other choice of immobility in the Philippines. Currently the solution to their human trafficking advocated by the United States, which is their rescue, not only fails to address their condition of servitude but also ignores their preference to be left with the option to work in Japan, albeit free of the control of middleman brokers, and instead forces them to return to their life of immobilized poverty in the Philippines.

Perhaps out of pressure or maybe in agreement with the U.S. government, the government of Japan designed a solution that abided by U.S. government recommendations. As of March 15, 2005, Japan imposed new visa requirements for migrant entertainers from the Philippines, in response to the recommendation by the U.S. Department of State for the Japanese government to impose the higher scrutiny of visa requirements and implement greater screening procedures "for repeat applicants and sponsors."[64] The most relevant change in policy concerning foreign entertainers involves the evaluation of artistic skills and the disqualification of the Philippine government to evaluate the artistic ability of entertainers they deploy to Japan. Notes the government of Japan:

> It has been recognized that not a few people who have entered Japan with the status of residence as entertainer, have become victims of trafficking in persons, in particular those who have entered Japan having fulfilled the criteria for landing permission by holding a certificate issued by the Government of the Philippines, which testifies that the holder is an artist, but as a matter of fact do not have capability as an artist. Given this situation, the paragraph below the description of the activities of entertainers—"The applicant who is qualified by a foreign national or local government agency or an equivalent public or private organization"—will be deleted from the [law]."[65]

This change in policy revoked the accreditation power of the Philippines and resulted in more stringent landing and resident examinations for foreign entertainers, with the most striking change being the extension of the training required of "overseas performance artists" to two years. Work experience in Japan does not qualify for training purposes. This means that an experienced migrant entertainer can become ineligible to renew her visa if she had received training to be an overseas performance artist for less than two years outside of Japan. As a reward for its efforts, Japan was taken out of the Tier 2 Watch List and placed back in the Tier 2 category in the 2005 TIP Report. Notably, the U.S. Department of State explicitly lauded Japan for its decision to curtail Filipino migration. As the 2005 TIP Report states: "During the reporting period, the government undertook major reforms to significantly tighten the issuance of entertainer visas to women from the Philippines, a process used by traffickers to enslave thousands of Philippine women in Japan each year."[66]

In its implementation of an antitrafficking platform, the government of Japan directly responded to the accusation that Filipina entertainers are prostitutes by implementing more stringent criteria for evaluating their professional skills as well as those of other foreign entertainers. Increased professionalism, according to Japanese officials, translates to a lower likelihood of prostitution. However, the longer training required of entertainers means not the validity of their professional status (or the combating of prostitution) but instead contributes to a longer duration of training under the control of middleman brokers. Longer training translates to the greater likelihood of larger debts for the few still able to enter Japan and thus peonage. This suggests that the solutions posed by Japan do not necessarily prevent trafficking but instead put prospective migrants at a higher risk of it.

If we look at the solutions implemented by Japan to protect migrant Filipina entertainers from human trafficking, we see that the enforcement of stricter visa regulations has not necessarily decreased migrant entertainers' desire to work in Japan. This means that prospective migrants are likely to seek illegal modes of entry. Nongovernmental organizations speculate that more have done so as a result of the greater scrutiny given to prospective migrant entertainers seeking entry to Japan.[67] Many, for instance, have resorted to buying fake marriage papers as a means of reentry.[68] According to representatives at the Philippine Embassy in Tokyo, migrant entertainers who enter illegally with false visas are those most susceptible to abuse by employers. They note that these workers are more likely to visit the Philippine Embassy to report cases of trafficking.[69] In his autobiographical account of his life as an undocumented worker in Japan *Underground in Japan*, Ray Ventura similarly observed that those who migrate via illegal brokers are more likely to end up in servitude.[70] Ironically, the new antitrafficking legislation encourages the illegal migration of workers, which in turn does not protect them from but instead leaves them even more susceptible to forced labor.

Across the globe, feminists have long fought for the greater protection of women from various forms of violence, including female genital mutilation, sex trafficking, and domestic violence. From transnational feminist efforts there have emerged particular norms regarding women's rights.[71] In the era that calls for "women's rights as human rights," few would argue against the claim that the need to protect migrant women from abusive work conditions is one such norm. A protectionist culture over the labor and migration of women has consequently emerged and affected the lives of migrant women, including entertainers in Japan. For instance, we see a cultural collusion between the Philippines and Japan over the need to protect migrant entertainers. But these protectionist laws have not necessarily protected entertainers; instead they have diminished these women's capacity to control their labor migration and accordingly have increased migrant brokers' power over them. Protectionist laws have made the entertainers vulnerable to coercion.

The solutions that have been implemented to combat the trafficking of entertainers have also done little to protect them. For instance, the "rescue" of migrant entertainers has simply curtailed their migration, while the increase in their training requirements has only heightened their susceptibility to peonage. Why do the current solutions used to combat trafficking fail to address the needs of migrant entertainers from the Philippines? Why do they perpetuate or even aggravate the susceptibility to forced labor of migrant entertainers? Current solutions are ineffective because they emerge not from practical design but instead from the passionate zeal of antiprostitution. Increased professionalism is supposed to lead to the less likelihood of sex work, but this comes at the cost of the entertainers' greater dependence on middleman brokers. This also tells us then that current solutions maintain the status quo because they uphold a culture of benevolent paternalism. In so doing, current solutions maintain the system that leaves migrant entertainers susceptible to forced labor. But instead of increasing their professionalism or barring their employment, hostesses such as Amy would like to be independent labor migrants. Only then could they remain gainfully employed, be free of migrant brokers, and be in control of their labor and migration.

CHAPTER TWO

THE LABOR SYSTEM IN HOSTESS CLUBS

ONE NIGHT AYA COMPLAINED TO ME THAT Sean had stolen one of her customers. The man was a first-time visitor to her club, Mr. Lady, and Aya had the good fortune of being asked to sit with him. As she was a first-time contract worker at Mr. Lady herself and without many customers, it was the unwritten rule that Aya would have first dibs on him and other new customers. But Sean supposedly broke protocol, exchanged phone numbers with the customer and called the man on the telephone behind Aya's back. The man then returned to the club a second time and requested not Aya's but instead Sean's company. As soon as Sean was requested, someone ran over to Aya and told her what had happened. I remember Peachy fuming next to me when she heard the story. Aya was seated at my table. She then told Aya that what Sean had done was wrong. Sean should not have called that man and invited him to go to Mr. Lady. It was supposedly only Aya who could do that to any newcomer. Then, if the man decides he does not like Aya, he can request another hostess but not before his third visit to the club.[1]

Elaborate rules organize the interactions of hostesses and customers in the club. Hostesses cannot freely flirt with customers but they instead must abide by the cultural protocols of flirtation that minimize competition between hostesses, maximize their camaraderie, and uphold sentiments of *tulungan* (helping out) among migrant workers. In clubs, I noticed that new hostesses and those without many visitors are assigned to sit with "fresh" customers as a means of boosting their business and sales, a practice that benefits not just the club but also the hostess in need of tips and commissions to survive in Japan. Unless one frequents clubs, one is not likely to learn that unwritten rules among hostesses abound in clubs, which I can only speculate informally develop not only for the purpose of increasing their sales but for mitigating the competition that would otherwise develop among the hostesses due to management demands at their workplace.

Filipina migrant hostesses refer to their workplace as an *omise*, meaning a shop. Technically, an *omise* could refer to any type of shop, but the socioeconomic reality of the limited labor market options for Filipinas in Japan has limited their opportunities, and thereby their linguistic use of this term, to the hostess establishment.[2] Among the Filipino community, the *omise* could indicate a variety of places—a club, a bar, or pub. In the clubs, entertainers perform a variety show on stage, otherwise referred to as *show time*, while in a bar or pub, entertainers work only as a hostesses, limiting their interactions with customers to the tables.[3]

Nongovernmental organizations that advocate for the welfare of Filipina migrant hostesses in the Philippines and Japan argue that entertainers' work as hostesses makes them trafficked persons.[4] The human rights advocate Fujimoto claims, "Another pattern [of trafficking] would be foreign women arriving with the legal status of entertainers as singers or dancers, but who are forced to work as 'hostesses,' an activity that falls outside of the scope permitted by their residence status, by nightclubs, where they are sent to work."[5] Aggravating matters is the supposed ignorance of prospective migrants about the nature of their jobs. But contrary to Fujimoto's stance, most Filipina entertainers whom I met knew prior to migration that they would be doing hostess work once they arrived in Japan.

It would actually be puzzling for prospective migrants not to know of their expected duties as hostesses. Not unlike other migrants elsewhere, networks direct their flow to Japan, mostly from the regions of Bulacan and Davao. Many follow neighbors, friends, and family, who openly share with the would-be migrants information about the work and life they could expect to experience once in Japan. In fact, most entertainers prefer hostess work to singing or dancing because they value the economic opportunities made possible by close interactions with customers. For instance, I met only two entertainers who would rather have restricted their work duties to performing on stage. Notably, these two were award-winning singers in the Philippines and hence as "real singers" distinguished themselves from the larger pool of passable singers who make up most of the Filipina contract workers in Japan.[6]

Another frequent but questionable claim that one hears concerning hostesses is that they are forced into prostitution. In Japan, customers are unlikely to patronize hostess clubs for the purpose of soliciting prostitution. We need to recognize that a variety of businesses exist in Japan's nightlife industry,[7] each marketing a distinct type of sexual labors and with its own defining features. Hostess clubs occupy a particular niche in the nightlife industry because men go there specifically to flirt. In contrast, men go to image clubs for sexual stimulation via role-play, pink salons for fellatio or masturbation, soap lands for a full-service bath with the option of sex, and lingerie clubs or no-panty bars for sexual excitement. The nightlife industry, referred to as *mizu shobai*, meaning water business, offers such an elaborate range of services for male consumers' sexual titillation that one could easily argue that commercial flirtation in a hostess club is the meekest of services one could receive in Japan's nightlife industry. Women in hostess clubs keep their panties on and provide no sexual services to customers. Still, the U.S. Department of State identifies only hostesses as trafficked persons in its annual TIP Report.

Examining the actual work of hostesses, this chapter takes us inside the *omise*. It describes the organization of the workplace and the labor system in Philippine hostess clubs. It shows that hostess work does *not* entail prostitution and in so doing questions claims in the annual TIP Report of the supposed "forced prostitution" of migrant hostesses in Japan. My discussion of the system of commercial flirtation begins with a general description of Philippine hostess clubs and the types of customers they entertain. Then, I turn to a description of the work system in clubs by describing the nightly routine of workers and the rules and regulations of clubs. My description of the labor system in hostess clubs reveals the bodily management of hostesses, meaning the minute control of their actions in the club. In so doing, my discussion establishes not just the institutionalization of commercial flirtation but also its scientific management.

PHILIPPINE HOSTESS CLUBS

Philippine hostess clubs are located throughout Tokyo from red-light districts in Shinjiku, Ikebukuro, and Kinshicho, to popular nightlife areas such as Shibuya and Roppongi, to working-class retail districts in the periphery of the city such as Jujo and Oyama. Regardless of where they are located in Tokyo, hostess clubs are usually ethnically segregated, with Japanese hostesses rarely working with foreigners, except perhaps when Koreans "pass" to be Japanese.[8] Clubs ethnically distinguish themselves in their marketing. Fluorescent signs would distinguish a club ethnically as featuring foreigners from particular countries with the Philippines, historically the largest source of foreign entertainers in Japan, being the most prominent.[9] In the red-light district of Kinshicho in the center of Tokyo, for instance, doormen of hostess clubs hound men walking on the streets. One can hear them distinguish their establishment to passersby as a Philippine, Russian, or Chinese venue. Rarely do Filipina hostesses work with anyone other than their coethnics; if they do, the doorman accordingly markets the establishment for its featured ethnic combination. One particular club I visited was a "Philippine-Russian" club.

Filipina hostesses prefer to work at establishments designated as a Philippine club. They wish not to work in an establishment that is generically advertised as a hostess club because potential customers would assume that such a place would feature Japanese women. They also wish not to work alongside other ethnic groups. They explain that cultural dissimilarities among them, such as native language differences, would make for a more difficult experience. For the most part, they prefer to work in Philippine clubs to avoid confrontation with xenophobic customers, some of whom, said the long-term resident Dianne, fear being touched by a Filipino "because they think you are contaminated as a foreigner." Julia, a hostess who migrated thirty years ago in 1981, added, "You will encounter a customer with anger toward Filipinos. They will pick a fight with you. They will ask you why you are working there—why don't you just return to your country?" Sometimes sadistic customers patronize Philippine clubs just to pick a fight with a hostess, but for the most part conflict arises only when customers unknowingly enter a Philippine club.

I did not visit hostess clubs of other ethnic groups for my research, but I did talk to a few customers about the ethnic distinctions of clubs. The ethnicity of hostesses supposedly makes for a different experience. Philippine clubs have a reputation for being lively. Indeed, Philippine hostesses describe themselves as *masayahin*, meaning happy and carefree, and *malambing*, meaning innocent and sweet. Being carefree and sweet do seem to embody the gendered persona of nearly all the hostesses I encountered in Philippine clubs, including the first one I visited where my arrival was greeted with much fanfare and excitement by hostesses who screamed out loudly in unison, "*Irasshaimase*," meaning welcome. At this club, hostesses would stomp their feet and clap their hands in unison, as they loudly shouted, "One, two, three, olé!" after each customer finished belting out a song—even if out of tune—in the karaoke machine. From the excitement of their applause, one would assume it was a rock star and not a regular Japanese man singing on stage.

Philippine hostess clubs vary in size. Some are snack bars that employ no more than a handful of hostesses and offer a limited food and drinks menu. Another type of hostess club is a pub, which usually employs ten to fifteen hostesses and provides not only a larger drink and food menu than a snack bar but also regularly features a variety show of singing and dancing. The first venue that I visited was neither a snack bar nor a pub but employed around thirty women. Much bigger in size, the place had a stage, which technically made it an actual club. In this type of establishment, hostesses must provide a variety show performance every night.

Regardless of type of establishment, Philippine hostess venues employ either a group of *talents* or entertainers, meaning contract workers with entertainer visas, or *arubaito* workers, meaning hourly wage part-time workers.[10] Unlike contract workers whose visa limits them to a six-month stay in Japan, *arubaito* include visa overstayers, that is, undocumented workers, and long-term legal residents, including wives and mothers of Japanese citizens. Snack bars usually employ only *arubaito* workers, while pubs and clubs employ a combination of the two, even though *talents* technically can work only in clubs, as there has to be a stage on the premises of their place of employment.

The work of a *talent* and an *arubaito* is quite similar; they often work alongside each other. The central difference perhaps is the greater likelihood that *talents* would be required to perform a variety show of singing and dancing on stage on a more regular basis. Another difference is the larger salary of *arubaito* workers. As independent workers, they are directly employed by the club and not by a middleman broker. Drastically distinguishing the two group of workers is their average age, with most *talents* being younger than twenty-five years old and *arubaito* workers being in their twenties and thirties, if not forties. Customers prefer the younger group of *talents* not only because of their youth but also because of the innocence that is assumed to come with it. For this reason, they generally prefer to visit hostess venues that employ *talents*. As the *arubaito* Marietta explained:

> *Talents* they think are less likely to be deceiving them. They think that *talents* are telling them the truth. *Talents* they think have virginal minds. In contrast, an *arubaito* they think has a child at home and is just fooling them. They worry that if they develop feelings for an *arubaito*, she will only leave them at the end. But even if they learn you are an *arubaito*, they cannot do anything about it if they are crazy about you.

Not surprisingly, clubs usually prefer to hire *talents*.[11] However, not all clubs qualify to employ *talents*, forcing some to rely on the much older pool of *arubaito* workers. Club owners prefer *talents* not only because of the marketability of their youth but also because they have greater control over their labor. Unlike *talents*, *arubaito* workers have the option of maintaining short work hours. Clubs solely employing *arubaito* workers usually close much earlier than the standard closing hour of four o'clock in the morning for clubs with *talents*. Many *arubaito* workers work only until midnight or at the latest two o'clock in the morning because they often have to attend to their families in the morning.

Regardless of whether one is a *talent* or *arubaito*, hostesses are expected to flirt with customers. Flirtation could occur up close at the table or from a distance via one's seductive performance of a song or dance on stage. In explaining their profession, hostesses—particularly those working at transgender clubs—view themselves as modern-day geisha. They often compare their work system and experience to those of geisha. For instance, Sean, explaining why *talents* at her workplace obey older and more experienced co-workers whether *talents* or *arubaito*, said, "In a gay club, we are adopting the geisha system.

There is seniority system like you need to respect; you need to have an elder system. So we are adopting the geisha system of seniority." Interestingly, Sean did not recognize the possibility that their seniority system also abides by the filial hierarchy that dictates relations among siblings in the Philippines.[12]

Filipina hostesses like to view themselves as similar to geisha, or courtesans, perhaps to upgrade the image of their work in Japan, which is often dismissed by outsiders as nothing but prostitution.[13] As the third-timer Nikki mentioned, "I am still in the process of learning the art of being a courtesan." Yet the hostesses whom I met, including Nikki, catered to a much lower income bracket of men than those who would typically engage with geisha, such as high-end corporate executives and business professionals.[14] For instance, a middle-range Philippine club in Tokyo charges no more than 5,000 yen per hour (approximately US$50), costing far less than the "lower-end" Japanese hostess clubs identified by the anthropologist Anne Allison nearly twenty years ago. According to Allison, in the late 1980s, "lower-ranked clubs" where hostesses "are more likely to be older, plumper, less educated, less sophisticated, less well dressed, less conventionally beautiful and certainly more brash" charged from US$80 to US$120 per hour.[15]

Regardless of the low status of most Philippine clubs, one could argue that some similarities do exist between Filipina hostesses of today, or hostesses in general, and geisha of the past, even if the likenesses are only slim. Like geisha, Filipina hostesses entertain customers. While they might not play a musical instrument such as a *shamisen* (Japanese stringed instrument), they do sing and dance.[16] Geisha refer to their male patrons (meaning frequent customers who subsidize their livelihood) as *danna*, meaning "father" in Japanese, and other customers as "Big Brother"; hostesses use similar terminology. Filipina hostesses, for instance, refer to their patrons as *papa* and their less frequent customers as *kuya*, meaning "older brother" in Filipino. More significantly, like geisha, most hostesses would not engage in the direct exchange of sex for money and tarnish their reputation by making themselves easily available to men on a nightly basis.[17]

Class

In her earlier study of hostess bars, Allison found a hierarchy in the nightlife industry of Japan in which levels of intimacy could be measured according to the class status of the venue. Allison asserted that the likelihood of sex between hostesses and customers increased in lower-ranked establishments. As she stated, "The more expensive and classy the club, the less the possibility of sex with one of the women; and, conversely, the sleazier and cheaper the club, the greater the chance."[18] In Philippine hostess clubs, the class of the venue does not determine the degree of sexual intimacy. The likelihood that flirtation would lead to sex is not greater in a lower-ranked establishment because, regardless of class, Filipina entertainers still remain mindful of the moral standards of social purity expected of them in Philippine society.[19]

In the community, hostesses distinguish Philippine clubs as either Class A, B, or C venues. Class distinctions are made according to the level of attractiveness of hostesses; the location of the club, with those in the center of the city usually of a higher class than those in the periphery; and the degree of professionalism of hostesses, as demonstrated in their language skills and creative performance. Corresponding with the class standing of the club is its price. High-class venues cost more to visit than lower-class ones. In one designated Philippine Class A club in Roppongi, for instance, an area known for its nightclubs and bars catering to both tourists and working professionals, a two-hour "set" would cost each customer 20,000 yen (US$200). During a "set," one has unlimited access to the house *shochu* or whisky, both of which the club serves with water or oolong tea, as well as one bowl of peanuts or Japanese snacks of crackers and soybeans. Class B bars generally cost significantly less, averaging 3,000 to 4,000 yen (US$30 to US$40) per hour for a "set" or 7,000 yen (US$70) for two hours, while most Class C establishments would charge no more than 2,000 to 3,000 yen (US$20 to US$30) for an hour of unlimited drinks, otherwise known as *nomehodai*. Transgender clubs, while providing similar services, cost significantly less than female hostess clubs. One infamous Class A transgender club for instance charges only 5,000 yen (US$50) per hour.

Despite the lure of the *nomehodai*, one should expect to incur a much greater expense than the minimum entrance fee whenever visiting a club. Once at the club, customers receive repeated invitations from hostesses to purchase food, lady's drinks, and songs in the karaoke machine.[20] As would be expected, food and drinks are pricier in higher-class establishments. A nonalcoholic lady's drink such as an eight-ounce glass of juice would usually cost anywhere between 500 to 1,500 yen (US$5 to US$15). An alcoholic beverage such as beer, which is considered a masculine beverage and hence not appropriate for hostesses to order, is usually between 2,000 to 3,000 yen (US$20 to US$30), while a sweetened mixed drink such as a screwdriver (a mix of orange juice and vodka), costs around 1,000 yen (US$10) to 2,000 yen (US$20).[21]

I mostly visited Class B establishments during the nine months I spent in Japan. After visiting a few hostess clubs, I learned to expect to spend at least 20,000 yen (US$200) per "set." Adding to the cost of my visits had been the fact that I sometimes had to be accompanied by a Japanese male into the club because hostess clubs generally restrict their clientele not only to men but more specifically to Japanese men. Sometimes I literally would have to pluck a random man from the street, luring him into the club by promising that I would pay for his entrance fee and treat him to at least two bottles of beer. Only through special arrangements with interviewees did I finally manage to visit hostess clubs unescorted. On my own, I did manage to visit transgender clubs, as women are allowed to enter these establishments without men. I did have to initially navigate through the restriction that requires visitors to be locals, meaning Japanese, and with the help of hostesses working there eventually convinced management to make an exception for my frequent visits.

As they do clubs, members of the community also group hostesses according to a particular "class." For instance, those who look like "fashion models" are considered Class A hostesses and accordingly have the option of working in a Class A establishment. These hostesses fit more conventional definitions of beauty than do others. They also tend to be more skilled, such as having a stronger command of the Japanese language and a keener ability to lighten the mood of customers, whether through song or dance or conversation. In contrast, members of the community would designate those who do not look like fashion models but are still conventionally beautiful as Class B workers. The class designation of a hostess is significant because it determines her salary. Among my interviewees, the highest-paid contract worker who fell under the category of Class A earned US$2,800 per month, but most took home no more than US$1,000 to 1,400 per month. Lower-paid Class A workers still earned significantly more than their Class B counterparts, as the average salary of a first-time Class B contract worker whom I interviewed was only US$500. Experienced Class B workers could also expect to earn no more than US$700 as a third-timer, meaning third-time contract worker.

What most Class B workers have going for them is their youth. Plenty of Class B workers are in their late teens and early twenties, as most clubs hire only first- to third-time contract workers. The higher "budget," meaning salary, of more experienced *talents* dissuades promoters from selecting them during auditions in the Philippines. Usually the exceptionally beautiful hostesses with adequate if not good language skills, that is, Class A workers, are those most likely to have the opportunity to return to Japan more than three times. Either they are requested by their clubs to return for another six months of contract work, or they repeatedly do well in auditions.

Not surprisingly, I did not meet anyone who described herself as a Class C worker. Members of the community claim Class C workers are "unattractive," but when asked to further explain what that meant, no one could qualify her statement with a more concrete description. In the Philippines, middleman brokers such as talent managers told me that Class C workers end up in the provinces and not in Tokyo, earn far less than hostesses in higher-ranked classes, and are likely to end up in small-scale operations such as a snack bar. Designated a lower budget than others by the promoter, Class C workers could expect to receive a starting salary as a first-timer, meaning first-time contract worker, of only US$350 per month. They are selected because some clubs cannot afford to hire a roster of all high-class workers and so as to lower their monthly expenses would mix their pool of hostesses to include a handful of Class C *talents*.[22]

Many Philippine clubs employ a mix of Class A and B workers. While they do, most hostess clubs still fall in the range of Class B, as most of the hostesses under their employ would fit this midrange ranking.[23] When working alongside each other, hostesses of various classes do not have different responsibilities in the club. However, clubs usually hold greater expectations of higher-ranked hostesses. Because they receive a higher salary, they have to have more customers than their lower-ranked counterparts. They also have higher sales quotas. To avoid conflict, hostesses usually do not talk about their salaries with others. However, hostesses often gauge the worth of their co-workers based on their appearance and talent.

Many clubs I visited usually employed at least one or two token Class A workers, who in addition to being more attractive could speak Japanese or sing better than others. The presence of a Class A singer usually gives an air of professionalism to the club, and management would often ask this "real singer" to sing whenever trying to impress a new group of customers. The "real singer's" repertoire would include classic Japanese ballads as well as popular American tunes. During the time of my research, Japanese customers frequently requested songs by Whitney Houston, Celine Dion, and Mariah Carey. The theme song to the movie *Titanic* was particularly popular.

For my field research, I worked in a lower-ranked Class B club, Manila,[24] one I personally labeled as a B-minus establishment because of the absence of extraordinarily beautiful hostesses among us and also because of our older age. My pool of co-workers in Manila was composed of mostly *arubaito* workers but initially included two *talents*, who left soon after I arrived there. My co-workers earned a base wage of anywhere between 1,000 and 1,400 yen (US$10 to US$14) per hour, which is around the average wage of Class B *arubaito* workers in Tokyo. In contrast, Class A *arubaito* workers could expect to earn around 2,400 yen (US$24) per hour. My youngest co-worker was twenty years old and the oldest thirty-seven years old. Most of us were in our late twenties to mid-thirties, making our pool of hostesses "over the hill" and undesirable. The women I worked with had limited labor market options in the nightlife industry. For instance, they were unlikely to find a job in the more expensive establishments in the center of Tokyo. Most of my co-workers were undocumented workers, in other words visa overstayers, who had escaped the last club where they had worked as a *talent*. Some had escaped their clubs as much as three years prior to working in Manila, while some had escaped only a few months prior to our meeting.

The median height of my co-workers was five feet and the average weight, excluding mine, was 100 pounds. My co-workers were lean as whippets while I, at 5′4″ and 145 pounds, loomed like an overpressurized dirigible. None of my co-workers believed that I would not be considered remarkably large in the United States. One customer, comparing me to my reedlike peers, disparagingly called me "Akebono's sister." Akebono was a former sumo wrestling champion of Japan.[25]

Also designating Manila's low status was its seedy location in a working-class area of Tokyo. Since the passage of the Sex-Oriented Business Management Law in 1984, businesses such as Manila can no longer operate near schools or residential zones.[26] Manila is located among other *fuzoku*, meaning "enterprises affecting public morals," in what could be described as a red-light district.[27] Neighboring Manila are pachinko parlors (gambling machine establishments), soap lands, pink salons, and numerous other hostess bars. Many of our customers were members of the *yakuza*, but we more often had to serve working-class men, for instance carpenters and painters, and low-level salaried men.[28] In the club, the women spoke a combination of Japanese, Filipino, and English with customers. Many of the customers had not yet visited the Philippines but had rudimentary knowledge of Filipino because they frequented Philippine hostess clubs—some as often as twice a week.

Conveniently located a block from the train station, Manila was nothing more than a dingy and darkly lit room on the ground floor of a four-story building in the periphery of Tokyo. A working-class bar, its limited décor included *feng shui*-inspired fountains with the running water representing the continued flow of money into the club as well as a statue of a cat and a small incense altar, both of which were supposed to stimulate business. On the walls of the bars were plastic flowers and pictures of random Japanese men on a fishing trip.[29] Disco balls adorned the ceiling along with neon-colored net coverings. Management often put up additional décor around the bar during the holidays. For instance, they managed to find and post a "Happy Halloween" streamer in October, and by November there were Christmas lights weaving in and out of wooden trellises leaning against the walls. A stale air of old cigarettes usually lingered in the windowless air-conditioned space. The only circulation of air came from the opening and closing of the sliding glass door. During the summer when I worked there, the cold blasting from the air conditioner left most of us hostesses shivering as we were—as might be expected—scantily clad. We often sought refuge from the cold in the bathroom, but its stench of what seemed to be a lethal dose of cockroach repellent was equally discomforting.

The furniture in Manila included no more than a long velvet cushioned bench against each wall, nine small tables, and green velvet footstools designed to seat hostesses, who would look quite small sitting across the table from their customers because of the low footstools. The bare furnishings at the bar left an open space in the middle that could function as a dance floor or a stage for variety show performances, which hostesses would sporadically be asked to perform on weekends. Like most other hostess clubs I visited, disco balls hung on the ceiling, a high-grade Bose sound system was prominently displayed with speakers installed in every corner of the room, and TV monitors strategically placed in the view of all the tables were connected to the karaoke machine. There was constant staff turnover at Manila. While I worked with twenty-three other women in the course of three months, I had only ten other co-workers at any given time.

My co-workers often complained that Manila charged too much. A one-hour "set" costs 3,000 yen (US$30), while comparable venues in the area offered a flat fee of 5,000 yen (US$50) for a one-hour set that would include all the lady's drinks. Two hours in Manila would usually cost a customer 15,000 yen (US$150): Added onto the cover charge would be the cost of each lady's drink (1,000 yen each or US$10); the cost for the request of an hour of the hostess's companionship, otherwise known as a *shimei* (1,000 yen or US$10); songs sung in the karaoke machine (200 yen each or US$2); and food, which was exorbitantly priced. For example, a ten-inch size pizza or a small plate of fried chicken would each cost 3,000 yen (US$30). The hostesses I worked with usually had no qualms handing a customer a 15,000 yen (US$150) bill, as the men seemed to have accepted this price as the standard cost for two hours of our company, but they would cringe in embarrassment whenever the customer's bill far exceeded this amount. As one of my co-workers once complained to me in Filipino while handing a 23,000 yen (US$230) bill to a customer, "We are not that pretty that two hours with us should cost that much."

Customers

Philippine hostess clubs attract a wide range of customers. They are mostly men but include a minority of transmen. Regardless of class level, customers visit Philippine hostess clubs for a variety of reasons. Some seek friendship, some romance, others companionship, others the thrill of flirtation; still others visit for the pursuit of sex. Yet not all patronize hostess clubs to pursue sex. Some truly want no more than the thrill of flirtation. Customers could be groups of co-workers or friends, lonely businessmen on an overnight trip in Tokyo, neighborhood regulars, widowers visiting their neighborhood bar, single or married men, and bored men without anything to do in the evening. They could also include someone who just wants to get a drink after work but would rather not drink alone and instead wants to go somewhere with the guaranteed company of a hostess—female or transgender. In the case of Philippine clubs, they could also include those who wish to practice their English. This had been the case even in Manila, where I was frequently assigned to customers who came specifically to speak English. Flirtation did also occur in this context, but to my relief it took place in the language with which I was actually familiar.

Among their customers, hostesses distinguish between passersby and regulars, with regulars being the greater focus of their energy and attention. This is because they are likely to garner more tips from a regular with whom they have established a meaningful social tie, whether as a friend or as a romantic partner. Hostesses do try to make every passerby into a regular customer but soon give up if they can see that their efforts are to no avail.

Stereotypes circulate as to the types of Japanese men who would seek romance and flirtations with Filipina hostesses, with the popular consensus being that they tend to be undesirable men, which as described by anthropologist Nobue Suzuki means they are "located in the bottom ranks of a masculine hierarchy and desirability."[30] As undesirable men, they are considered economically downtrodden, for instance farmers or blue-collar workers, and unattractive. Yet hostesses recognize a wider range of economies representing the sexual marketability of their customers. As Bambi, a married transgender hostess, described in a matter-of-fact tone, "There are ugly ones. There are good-looking ones. There are stinky ones. There are fat ones. There are some cross-eyed. There are toothless ones. All different kinds. There are crippled ones. There are ones with money. There are those without."

Explaining why customers visit hostess clubs, Allison perceptively described hostess clubs as a place of "male ritual."[31] Men patronize hostess clubs to bond with other men, and hostesses function merely as objects for strengthening this bond. Patriarchy being a relationship between men over women is fortified in the male bonding that takes place in the club.[32] According to Allison, hostess clubs are where men make business deals, build trust, and together enforce gender hierarchies. Whether customers visit clubs in a group or alone, displays of masculinity are part of the daily rituals in hostess clubs. For instance, male customers often brag about their material possessions. Once a customer took out his Cartier watch to prove to me its authenticity by showing me the insignia underneath its face. Another display of masculinity involves men bonding over their ability to objectify the physical appearance of hostesses with no admonishment. Customers often have no qualms commenting on a hostess's breasts, weight, hair, dress, and overall appearance. In the club Manila, customers usually made a comment about the appearance of the hostess assigned to their table immediately after being introduced to them, expressing either their approval or disapproval of the hostess and in some cases rejecting the hostess, telling the *mama-san* (female manager) of the club to replace her with a more attractive worker. Sometimes customers would make an explicit request for a hostess with a specific physical feature. A common one would be a request for a hostess with large breasts. Not exempt from the objectifying gaze of customers, I often heard customers describe me as *futote*, meaning fat, and *kuroi*, meaning dark. However, I could not reply with a sharp retort as customers patronize hostess clubs not only to avoid rejection but to experience male superiority. Because of this, hostesses can share only positive comments about customers and never any negative ones. Indeed, customers go to hostess clubs to "feel good." As one of my co-workers at Manila observed, many are "lonely. No one wants to listen to them. No one tells them they are good looking. No one admires them. That is why they go to the *omise*."

As well as wanting to participate in male rituals, customers, regardless of class, also visit hostess clubs for the thrill of romance. This includes customers who frequent transgender hostess clubs. While many customers go to such clubs for the cultural novelty of seeing male femininity, others go regularly in romantic pursuit of a hostess. Intended romances might be no more than a one-night stand or a casual fling but could also be a long-term relationship leading to the possibility of marriage. It is partially for this reason that customers wish not to engage in flirtation with married hostesses. Flirting with married women would diminish the romantic possibilities of the interaction. For this reason, most married hostesses hide their marital status and disclose it only selectively, for instance when wanting to sever a relationship with a customer.[33]

Some customers are open to the possibility of marriage with hostesses. Regular customers at the club Manila would sometimes gush over the culture of the Philippines and attribute their preference of marrying a Filipina to specific cultural traits, such as their assumed selflessness and devotion to family, loving nature, and fear of God. However, not all customers have such high regard for the Filipina hostesses who serve them. For instance, customers in Manila included those who viewed hostesses as nothing more than a possible sexual conquest. Once a customer told me that Filipina hostesses are "low society" women who would never amount to anything. As he told me, their purpose for being in the club is to be used by men. As soon as they "sag," they will have no worth in society. In short, the sexual desirability and accessibility of hostesses are the sole measure of their value.

Hostesses are quite aware of the low opinion that many customers have of them, which for some makes it all the more difficult to flirt with customers. Jeanne, a veteran hostess who had completed more than ten labor contracts in Japan, explained, "They say things like this, 'You Filipinas are so easy. Three *lapads*[34] (meaning 10,000 yen or US$100), and we can have you.' They really have a low opinion of Filipinas. That is why I tell the women here to realize that the Japanese do not see our faces when they look at us, but our vaginas. Of course there are nice ones, but most are not. Most have no respect for Filipinas."

Perhaps it is the low opinion of Filipinas that also make them undesirable sexual partners for some customers, who would want nothing more than the thrill of flirtation from visiting hostess clubs. Hostesses have sometimes complained about their failed attempts to seduce customers into bed. One experienced hostess, Ai, who had had her fair share of sexual partners after more than ten years in Japan, for instance, complained to me about how her favorite customer, the one who got her heart pumping as soon as he entered the club, continually rejected her sexual advances. The experience of Ai, and her feelings of rejection, tells us that not all customers visit hostess clubs to pursue sex.

While the perceived sexual accessibility of Filipina hostesses could be cause for rejection, it could also lead to harassment. Because many customers perceive Filipina hostesses as sexually accessible, a central part of the job of hostesses is to deflect invitations to go to hotels without rejecting customers, which is a skill not all easily acquired. Complained the first-timer Reggie, "It is so hard to get out of the situation when they are always asking you for sex . . . You do not know how to get out of the situation. You do not know what reason to give them to get out of the situation." Requests for sex place hostesses in a Catch-22 situation. Acceptance of propositions for sex results in the customer's lower opinion of them, for instance the view of them as easy, but the rejection of propositions likewise results in the loss of a customer, whose unsuccessful bid for a sexual encounter could result in his wanting to try his luck with another hostess at the same or a different club. Customers have the confidence to hound hostesses with repeated requests for sex because there is minimal risk of rejection, or at the very least minimal risk of face-to-face rejection. It is also for this reason that customers feel free to manhandle hostesses and speak crudely to them. For instance, once I told a customer I was thirsty, and he responded by telling me his cum in my mouth would take care of my thirst.[35]

Although customers repeatedly invite hostesses to engage in sex, many wish not to make their visits to hostess clubs public knowledge. Aware of this social constraint, hostesses know to pretend not to notice a customer outside the club unless the customer himself acknowledges them. Marie, a veteran hostess who had been an undocumented worker in Japan since 1991, described, "In Japan, when you are at an *omise*, and when a customer enters an *omise*, you interact; but outside the *omise*, you do not know each other. Even if you see them on the street, they will not greet you . . . You see them hiding from you. Then at the *omise*, you tease them for not paying attention to you on the street." Because hostess clubs are morally shunned places of leisure, customers might not want others to know of their patronage of these businesses. For instance, being recognized by a hostess in front of one's wife or friends could cause embarrassment for the customer. But despite the social stigma associated with visiting hostess clubs, customers still patronize these establishments.

THE NIGHTLY ROUTINE

Regardless of the romantic or sexual interests of customers, hostess clubs manage and organize the visits of customers to maximize profits. In that way, they are using a particular form of scientific management. Examining the distribution of labor on a factory shop floor in the late nineteenth century, Frederick Taylor proposed the need to synthesize work activities so as to maximize labor productivity, in other words to scientifically manage production.[36] Taylor called for a standard method for performing the job, minimal interruptions in the production process, wage incentives for worker output, and among others adherence to strict rules. The greatest legacy of Taylor is perhaps the minute breakdown of factory production into repetitive tasks along an assembly line,[37] which we now see also in place in the fast-food service industry.[38] In a different way, we see the principles of Taylorism reflected in the provision of flirtation in hostess clubs. Taylorism usually involves the breakdown of production to specific interrelated tasks that allow repetition and specialization for individual workers and the contingency of their labor on others. In the case of hostess work, the consumed product is an experience rather than a specific item built in piecemeal fashion by a number of connected workers. The experience, which in this case would be flirtation, is likewise regulated at a hostess club. It involves the minute control of the actions of hostesses to maximize not the production of goods but the number of customers to whom hostesses could sell flirtation and likewise the number of hostesses from whom customers have to buy flirtation.

Hostess clubs do not control the bodily movements of entertainers to the same extent that an assembly line subjugates the factory floor worker to the same repetitive motion, but they do so in other ways. The minute control of the body of hostesses emerges in the ways they are expected to evoke femininity in their actions. While at work, a hostess must constantly sit with her back straight, with her legs never wide open but instead one preferably placed in front of the other and with her head permanently tilted to one side. This pose is one that was constantly reinforced to me at the club Manila, where the cue for me to straighten my posture had been the floor manager screaming at me across the room "*babae ka*," meaning, "you are a woman." The scream always reminded me to evoke femininity in my posture. To abide by displays of femininity, one could also not yawn, rest an elbow on the table, chew gum, or turn one's back to a customer. As I had not been adept at the physical movements expected of hostesses, customers frequently reprimanded me for slouching but more often for yawning, which I could not help but do repeatedly after midnight.

In addition to monitoring the behavior of hostesses, clubs maximize the sales they generate by imposing a work pattern that controls the distribution of time and space. Time is managed by the enforcement of a table rotation system that limits the time customers can spend with a hostess and increases the number of customers with whom hostesses must interact in any given evening. In this system, entertainers rotate from one table to another in increments of twenty to thirty minutes.[39] A hostess who is not entertaining customers cannot freely circulate around the club but must wait in the space designated as the waiting area, where entertainers not in rotation are segregated from but are also left visible to the gaze of customers. Lastly, clubs frequently expect hostesses to perform a variety show performance to not only attract a steady flow of customers but to entice them to extend an invitation for a hostess to join them at the table.[40]

Moments of Waiting

Hostesses spend a great deal of time waiting for customers. They wait for customers not just anywhere inside the club but only in the designated waiting area, usually visible from the entrance to the club so that customers can see their selection of hostesses for the evening in one sweeping gaze. A hostess without a customer or between customers can be only at the waiting area. Not one hostess described being there as a welcome break from entertaining customers. For many, being in this area was almost a form of banishment, loudly announcing that they were without a customer. For example, at the transgender club that I frequented, I would always enter by walking past a row of entertainers. As I did so, I would be expected to point out the hostess whose company I would be requesting for at least one hour that evening.

Hostesses almost always express their delight on being selected because no one ever wants to be without a customer; time goes excruciatingly slowly without one. Additionally, management disciplines hostesses so as to make the experience of waiting for customers unbearable. Management does this by scrutinizing the physical movements of those in the waiting area more closely than those seated with customers. Notably, they do so to a much greater extent in female hostess clubs than in transgender clubs as the latter group of hostesses are expected to be lively and rowdy while waiting for customers. Generally, management requires hostesses in the waiting area to stay idle. By looking as though they are doing nothing more than wait, what is magnified for hostesses is the reality of the absence of their customers. Being idle consequently accentuates for them feelings of undesirability.

Clubs have different rules for hostesses in the waiting area, with some stricter than others. In some clubs, hostesses can talk to one another, even if rather inconspicuously, but in many they are required to wait for customers in silence. Other than wait for customers, perhaps the only acceptable activity for a hostess during moments of waiting is to send e-mail messages to customers using her cell phone.[41] However, a hostess can do so only discreetly. While waiting for a customer, a hostess should be doing nothing more than just that so as to underscore her availability to entertain the customers who are at the club. A hostess's availability means more than just her accessibility; it also connotes her unattached status. Just as it is considered to be unmannerly to speak of other romantic interests during a date, it is also considered to be in bad taste for a hostess to suggest she entertains more than one customer.

When business is slow, waiting for a customer can sometime take hours. During this time, hostesses must carefully monitor their bodily actions, which not only management but also customers scrutinize closely. Hostesses must sit or stand with their backs straight, maintain a positive and happy demeanor, and look as if they are excited about the opportunity of meeting a customer. Not surprisingly, some describe "being conscious of our movements the whole night" as one of the most difficult aspects of their job. Notably, the higher the class of the club, then the greater the level of professionalism expected of hostesses. In a lower-class establishment such as Manila, we could easily share and pass around a piece of bread, talk, make fun of the customers singing out of tune, or sneak in a slouch for a minute or two when in the waiting area. Still, we were not without reproach.

While most of the clubs that I visited were considerate enough to let hostesses sit at one corner of the room while waiting for customers, some forced hostesses to stand around awkwardly on stage or remain on the center of the dance floor. For example, the first-timer Amy complained that the management of her club tried to humiliate those without a customer by designating a space on the dance floor as the waiting area. With a grimace, Amy described the feeling of sitting in the middle of the room: "It is embarrassing to sit there—*alone*—with all these customers around you" (*emphasis my own*). Amy and her co-workers preferred the alternative waiting area given to them, which was right by the entrance of the club, where they were required to stand while waiting for customers. Amy much preferred to stand by the entrance of the club rather than sit at the center of the club without a customer because she considered the latter experience to be "humiliating."

The excruciating experience of waiting for a customer heightens feelings of camaraderie among hostesses. Notwithstanding the cliques and conflicts that inevitably form among co-workers, the waiting area is where hostesses give each other knowing, disgruntled looks over the constant barbs management directs at them; share their astonishment over the behavior of some customers; laugh together at customers for singing out of tune and dancing not quite in synch; and complain about their misfortune for being without a customer. Because they empathize with each other's struggles to secure a customer, hostesses usually find ways to help their friends get out of the waiting area. Seated hostesses would ask their regular customers to do them the favor of inviting their friends to join them at the table in hopes that their friends would do the same for them if ever they were ever without a customer.

Penalties

Clubs discipline the actions of hostesses not only via constant surveillance or via the strict regulation of their movements inside the club, what Michel Foucault describes as the "anatomo-politics" of the human body.[42] Clubs also impose a stringent penalty system as a means of ensuring that hostesses abide by their rules and regulations. Establishing a punitive culture at the club, penalties are generally imposed via wage deductions or verbal berating. The threat of penalties literally keeps hostesses on their toes. It is through penalties that management ensures that hostesses obey the rules of the club and abide by the work regime. The enforcement of penalties effectively instills fear and self-discipline among hostesses. Notably, female hostesses have to contend with more penalties than do transgender hostesses as the latter group is given more leeway to manage their own actions at work without much intervention from management. For instance, transgender contract workers rarely have a curfew.[43] In contrast, female contract workers always do. For missing their after-work curfew, which is usually 6:00 AM, hostesses' commissions are docked by 10,000 yen ($100).

With the exception of the curfew, penalties range from 1,000 yen to 5,000 yen (US$10 to US$50). Clubs often penalize the same digressive actions. For example, hostesses are frequently penalized for tardiness and for not following behavioral protocol in front of customers. At one club, hostesses "get a penalty for chewing gum, smoking cigarettes, falling asleep at work, crossing your legs." Providing other examples of digressive actions that would incur a penalty, my co-worker Melissa complained about the last club where she was a contract worker:

> We were supposed to wake up at the same time, at noon. If we did not, we received a penalty. That place was filled with penalty. By 4:00 PM, we had to be at the club. If you were late by one minute, then you would receive another penalty of 1,000 yen

(US$10). Then, at 4:00 PM, you practiced the dance performance. You had to practice ten dances. You had to know each dance. They have a *show time* there every day. If you made a mistake during *show time*, you were again imposed with a penalty. And if you made any kind of mistake, the *mama-san* would try to scare you and threaten to send you back to the Philippines.

This club was unusually strict, imposing penalties on hostesses who wore panties instead of thongs and also penalizing hostesses who made the most minute of missteps such as failing to return the microphone on its stand. While some clubs are stricter than others, they do all share a predilection toward the enforcement of penalties, using them to control hostesses' actions.

As Pierrette Hondagneu-Sotelo observed about domestic work, there is no standard of employment in hostess clubs.[44] Hostesses often described the nature of their job and the penalties they incurred at work as "*iba iba*," meaning different, and as distinguished by the system of the *omise*. Explaining the absence of a standard of employment in both of these migrant industries is their location in the shadow economy, with the former occurring in the informal sphere of the household and the latter occurring in the unregulated sphere of the nightlife industry. In Japan, the "liminal legality," meaning precarious legal status, of entertainers as temporary labor migrants also means they are outside the purview of local labor laws, consequently resulting in the absence of a labor standard in Philippine clubs that employ *talents*.[45] The same argument could be made of clubs that employ undocumented workers.

As a disciplining mechanism, the threat of penalties not only encroaches on the actions of hostesses inside the club but also leads to the conscious self-management of their bodies. This is particularly true for *talents* because management's corporal control extends to the monitoring of the hostesses' weight. Every month, management weighs contract workers and penalizes those who gain one or more kilos from their first weigh-in, which occurs during their first week at the club.[46] A gain of one kilo means a 5,000 yen (US$50) penalty, while two kilos would result in a penalty of 10,000 yen ($100). Experienced workers do become adept at circumventing penalties. Melissa, for instance, learned to put on extra weight before the initial weigh-in to avoid incurring penalties. She did this by placing coins in her pockets and inserting four ashtrays between her clothes, with one on each breast and buttock, altogether increasing her weight by four kilos.

Another punitive mechanism that management uses to discipline hostesses is the "meeting," which is consistently described by hostesses as an occasion for management to berate and infantilize them. During meetings, management tries to exert their greater power over hostesses. Whenever business is slow, management usually calls a general meeting during which time they scream and verbally abuse hostesses as a way of scaring them to find customers. At a club that I visited just outside of Tokyo, for instance, the hostesses complained to me that management singled out those with the worst sales and called them names in front of their co-workers. Management would use harsh Filipino words such as "*bobo*," meaning stupid, and "*buang*," meaning crazy, to describe them. These scare tactics sometimes backfire, as contract workers are more likely to escape abusive clubs and overstay their visas as undocumented workers. Still, hostesses wish to avoid penalties and for this reason closely monitor their behavior while waiting for customers at the club.

The Table Rotation System

Customers visit hostess clubs to spend time with hostesses. Yet their patronage comes not only with a fee but also a time limit. Clubs restrict the time that customers can spend with hostesses by enforcing a table rotation system. In this system, a hostess must continuously circulate from one table to the next, spending no more than twenty to thirty minutes at each table and then having to return to the waiting area if the customer does not extend a *shimei*, meaning request, for her company. Only with the extension of a *shimei* can a hostess be free from constant table circulation or banishment to the waiting area. A *shimei*, which guarantees a customer at least one hour with a hostess, costs a customer anywhere from 1,000 to 2,500 yen (US$10 to US$25) depending on the class status of the club. For instance, Manila charges only 1,000 yen (US$10) for a *shimei*, while many other clubs would charge 2,000 yen (US$20) for the same service.

Management explains that clubs have implemented the table rotation system so as to introduce customers to as many hostesses as possible during the one- or two-hour "set" that they have purchased on initially entering the club. However, hostesses see the table rotation system as a way for clubs to maximize their profit. Imposing a time limit on hostess and customer interactions may increase the number of hostesses catering to a customer per evening, but it also increases the expenses of the customer because the more hostesses that a customer meets in one evening, then the more lady's drinks he would feel compelled to purchase, especially as hostesses have been conditioned to request a drink from every customer. Explained the *arubaito* worker Charmaine, "You cannot just sit there and not offer the woman a drink. That is why the women are rotated constantly. You yourself will get embarrassed if you do not offer the woman a drink. That is the system there. You feel obligated to offer her a drink."

The table rotation system is geared toward every new customer who enters the club, every one of whom management intends will become a regular customer. Management assumes that customers would ever want to return to the club only to see a hostess who had somehow convinced him to see her again. Hence, a central job requirement for hostesses is to secure regular customers, who would request them to make her their "main," meaning primary hostess for the evening.[47] The attractiveness of the hostess need not be based solely on her sexual desirability; her allure could also be her skills as an entertainer, whether this is her comedic personality, talent as a singer, or flair as a conversationalist. What solidifies the status of a hostess as a main is the extension of a *shimei* by the customer for her company.[48] While a highly unlikely occurrence, the extension of a *shimei* to one hostess by multiple customers concurrently means she would have to alternate fifteen minutes of her time between various tables. Because a certain degree of possessiveness develops from the loyalty of the customer, hostesses usually defuse any potential conflict that may arise from the simultaneous arrival of customers by telling each one that the other is "just a customer," meaning someone who is not a boyfriend or love interest.

Securing the first *shimei* of every new customer is the goal of each hostess because the initial act of the first *shimei* would establish her hold over him.[49] This means that he would be expected to extend a *shimei* only to her in all of his future visits to the club. Undoubtedly a customer could sever his relationship with a hostess he had previously requested and choose another hostess at a club that he visits regularly. When this occurs, the new main would usually have to defuse the conflict likely to arise with the former main by establishing that the circumstances of the shift had not been her own doing, meaning that she had not actively lured the customer away from her co-worker. However, customers usually do not bounce around from one hostess to another and extend a *shimei* to a different hostess each time they visit a club. This would break the protocol of monogamy and loyalty that is practiced in hostess clubs. At most, a new customer could shop around for a main during his first three visits to a club, but soon after he would be expected not only to extend that initial *shimei* to a specific hostess but afterward also to maintain a certain degree of loyalty to her.

As a main, a hostess usually does not entertain her customer alone but is assisted by a "helper" at the table. The helper usually stays at the table for only thirty minutes as part of her table rotation duties. If not selected as a main, a hostess could potentially work as a helper throughout the evening. The helper does the dirty work of cleaning the table, including replacing ashtrays, wiping glasses dry, clearing the bowl of peanuts, and filling up the drinks of the customer. In contrast, the main is responsible for doing the intimate labor of entertaining the customer. She is expected to feed the customer, for instance peel a grape and feed it to him, as well as converse with him, sing along with him, and massage his shoulders or hands to make him feel comfortable. The task of making a customer feel good is relegated to the main.

The clear division of labor between the main and helper at the table relegates the helper to the periphery. She is there only to lend a helping hand and must not distract the customer's attention away from his main. Hence, a helper is considered disposable; she is replaced after thirty minutes and is there only as part of her continued table rotation duties. Sometimes a helper is actually requested to join the table by a customer; in this case she is requested as a *jonai* and not a *shimei*. By distinguishing requested helpers, the customer marks a boundary on the kind of service the hostess is requested to perform, which is to merely assist his main request—the one with the *shimei*—for the evening. A *jonai* costs a customer either 500 yen (US$5) or 1000 yen (US$10).

In most cases, helpers know to respect the division of labor at the table. They know not to flirt with the customer or attempt to steal him away from his main. Without doubt, helpers have often crossed the line—sometimes, as I have been told, resulting in actual fistfights among hostesses. In these cases, one hostess is usually fired or, if a contract worker, sent home to the Philippines prior to the end of her contract. Usually the hostess at fault would be the one who attempted to steal the customer. Stealing could occur in different ways. One could speak ill of the main, for instance telling the customer about her bad character, or she could outright just seduce the customer.

Stealing customers risks the end of friendships and the violation of hostess camaraderie. Yuki, a fourth-timer in Japan, explained the propriety surrounding customer ownership:

> Let us say that one person is the first one requested and that you are the helper. She has another customer [and leaves you with the customer]. You know that that person is the one who the customer likes, so you know not to flirt with the customer. You cannot flirt with a customer if there is already an owner. That would be wrong. You would get bad karma. If there was a woman requested before you and you were requested as a helper, you know to put yourself in the right place.

While hostesses expect their co-workers not to steal their customers, they do not take for granted the loyalty of customers but instead foster their allegiance. Hostesses expect customers to practice monogamy inside the club and not openly flirt with other hostesses in front of them. Extending regular phone calls to the customer outside the club and displaying acts of emotional affection inside the club are some of the ways hostesses foster loyalty. Once, with permission from my co-worker, I asked one of her customers if he would request me the next time he visited our club, to which he kindly replied, "No, it would hurt the feelings of Arissa." My interviewees explained to me that customers are not likely to replace their main for another hostess at the same club but are more likely to stop patronizing the club if they ever want to curtail a relationship with a particular hostess; or they would wait until she returned to the Philippines before soliciting the companionship of another hostess at the same club. Customers are not likely to replace their main for another hostess because, Yuki explained, "It would be insulting and disrespectful." Notably, this display of loyalty from the customer as well as his monogamous allegiance to a particular hostess is not a natural occurrence; they are sentiments cultivated by the hostess in the process of maximizing her labor at the club.

Show Time

Hostesses sometimes use the lure of what they call *show time* to keep the interest of customers. *Show time* refers to the variety show performance that *talents* must do while in Japan. With the exception of those with subpar artistic skills, the performance of *show time* comes as a welcome break from the routine of the table rotation system for most hostesses. Hostesses dedicate a great deal of effort and energy to the presentation of their shows, practicing in nonworking hours, either before or after their *omise* opens and closes, as many pride themselves on their talent as a singer or dancer. Many of the hostesses I met considered themselves to be "real performers." However, most did not delude themselves into thinking they were Class A performers. Still, they were confident about their ability to carry a tune and dance in step. Notably, those who feel they have subpar skills always qualified their migrant status as an entertainer to be "fake."

From circling hostess clubs around Tokyo and watching various *show time* performances, I found quite a wide range of skill levels in the delivery of these shows. This likely reflects the different class levels of the hostesses and the overall scarcity of Class A hostesses. In some cases, *show time* would be quite embarrassing to observe as hostesses on stage would neither complete the splits they attempted nor do in unison the Rockette-style kicks they tried to imitate. In other cases, *show time* could be better described as disappointing as the featured singer would not have the most commanding voice, or the featured dancers would attempt to perform only the simplest of dance steps. Attesting to the different styles and cultures of hostess clubs, some *show time* performances are more risqué than others, while others could be best described as "cute." In Manila, for instance, *show time* would fit the latter category, as my co-workers would only bounce around the middle of the dance floor and sway their hips without the elaborate foot movements one would see in dance performances at *hosto bars*, meaning the male version of hostess bars that Filipina hostesses frequent after work. Unlike in other clubs, most of my co-workers did not perform sensual dances or pseudo-stripteases during *show time*. They did not attempt to throw bedroom eyes at customers, engage in sexy hip rolls, or peel off layers of clothing. Despite the fact that they wore skimpy attire, they projected a more childlike image on the dance floor. In contrast, other Philippine clubs I visited sold the eroticism of their hostesses more blatantly. This was the case at the club Olympia, where the first dance routine in their *show time* showed bare legs, midriffs, and crotch grabs. In most *show time* performances I had the opportunity to see, the usual attire of hostesses would include bikinis, bare-midriff shirts, miniskirts, fishnet stockings, and "Daisy Dukes." This was also the case in Manila, a fact that made me grateful that the management there spared me from the requirement of doing this job even though they told me that they did not do so for my benefit but instead to spare customers from the ghastly sight of me in a bikini.

Show time performances usually last one hour. They include a combination of song and dance performances. Unless management expects the regular inclusion of a Japanese song in the ensemble, singers tend not to require too much preparation for *show time.* In contrast, dancers must spend at least two hours before or after work practicing their routine together for at least two weeks. Because of the additional and uncompensated labor of practicing for *show time,* hostesses prefer to minimize *show time* to an occasional rather than a regular feature of their daily routine. To abide by the government policy that requires *talents* to sing and dance on stage, many *omise* require a daily performance of *show time.* In such cases, hostesses usually alter their *show time* program every couple of weeks or monthly so as to keep the interest of customers.

Transgender Clubs

While the degree of professionalism in *show time* varies across clubs, the transgender hostesses are more professional than their female counterparts. There is no comparison between the sedate shows presented by female hostesses and the spectacular presentation of femininity one sees in *show time* performances at transgender clubs, where hostesses wear elaborate costumes and include slightly more complex maneuvers in their dance performances. Boasting to me about the higher caliber of the performances that she helped produce in transgender clubs, Ana, a strikingly beautiful transsexual woman with porcelain skin and a China doll face, remarked: "When you enter a *bakla* establishment, a show is a show. There are those who fly in the air during the show. Women do not have that in their show."[50] While transgender hostesses sell their performance, female hostesses sell nothing more than their female heterosexuality in *show time.* The most they as women have to do to entertain customers is look cute or sexy. In contrast, transgender hostesses must really perform. This is also true for transgender hostesses who work in a club that primarily employs female hostesses. There they usually are expected to do an extravagant solo performance or choreograph the entire *show time* production of the club.

In *show time,* transgender hostesses must do more than look cute or sexy. They must demonstrate a high level of artistic talent. Moreover, they have to act extremely feminine and look more attractive than women. Transgender hostesses generally refuse to appear "normal" at work but instead insist on always "look[ing] like they are Ms. Universe." In other words, a transgender hostess needs to be more of a woman than a woman is, which many explain they must accomplish because they are not women. Indeed, almost all of the transgender hostesses whom I met in Japan embody the unattainable and ideal femininity one associates with Hollywood. Many had won gay beauty pageants in the Philippines. Similarly, transgender prostitutes in Chiapas, Mexico, "better fit the current norms of beauty" than their female counterparts.[51] For not being women, transwomen occupy a space of liminality, which Victor Turner conceptualizes as the ambiguous location of being "no longer classified and not yet classified."[52] Helping us articulate the marginal location occupied by transgender gay hostesses, liminal beings refer to those who are "neither one thing or another; or maybe both."[53]

Pointing to the liminal space they occupy, Filipina transgender hostesses whom I met expressed their wish to be women and simultaneously not women. They did not aspire to be women because after all they have a distinct "embodied memory" that distinguishes their gendered subjectivity from women.[54] As feminist scholar Vera Mackie observes, "Gender identity is about the narration of shared experience. A person who is unable to share in the exchange of stories will not be interpellated as belonging to that group."[55] Transgender hostesses wish not to be women nor to occupy the same gendered category as women because they know that they do not have shared memories of becoming women. As they repeatedly told me, their experiences are distinct from those of women. Unlike women, for instance, the growing pains of becoming transgender as well as the experience of being one in the Philippines involve ridicule by classmates or people on the streets. Rafaela, for instance, complained, "In elementary and high school, you are always teased." Not unlike her transgender counterparts, teasing and harassment continue for her whenever she returns to the Philippines. As she continued, "In the Philippines, many harass you. You are just walking on the street and someone screams, '*bakla*.' You get annoyed. In the province when you go home, you cannot avoid that kind of behavior, that kind of negative attitude. You cannot move." The shared experience of harassment for those who occupy the liminal space of simultaneously being women and not being women distinguishes the gendered being of transgender hostesses from their female counterparts.

As the ultimate mimic and artisan of femininity, transgender hostesses claim not to be like women but instead assert that they are better than women. Indeed, their extreme personification of women makes them better than women.[56] By being better than women, they simultaneously remind us, however, that they are not women. In his classic book *Asian/American*, David Palumbo-Liu similarly describes the racialization of Asians in America as one of liminality in which Asians as the "model minority" are constructed as whiter than whites for the reason they are not whites. This outsider location looms over their membership in U.S. society and marks them as "perpetually foreign."[57] Following the argument of Palumbo-Liu, we must look at the liminal position of transgender hostesses as one of perpetual marginalization. Cross-dressing is not merely an act of resistance, as such a simple reading would ignore the marginal location of transwomen, who constitute a minority of the Filipino gay population. Yet, the marginalization of cross-dressers is one they wish not to end with their ultimate categorization as women but instead with the recognition of their feminine identity not-as-women. Hence, transgender hostesses perpetually aspire to be better than women, so as to find men who would fall in love with them for not being women. Many are in Japan, which they describe as the "*paraiso ng mga bakla*," meaning paradise for gay men, for the reason that in Japan, "men really fall in love with them" for not being women.

For transgender hostesses, the liminality of not being women results in their lesser material rewards and greater efforts than women. Because they are not women, transgender hostesses receive lesser pay for more work than their female counterparts. Among transgender hostesses, first-time contract workers on average receive only US$350 a month as compared to their female counterparts, who usually earn no less than US$500 per month. The greatest discrepancy between the two groups is seen in *show time* performances, which are often only an option for women but a daily requirement for transgender hostesses.

Because of the long hours of preparation required for *show time*, transgender hostesses must devote more hours at work. In the transgender club that I frequented, for example, the hostesses there had to do three *show time* performances every evening at 9:00 PM, midnight, and 2:00 AM. To maintain some variety in their performance, they redid the choreography of the program once a month. This required them to stay at work until 8:00 AM for at least two weeks in the month, in which time they would have mastered the program that they would then have to change again in a couple of weeks' time. Describing the long hours and rigor of their daily routine, Peachy, a third-timer, shared with me her schedule:

> Usual days, I wake up at 4:00 or 4:30 PM. I want to be the first to shower because I do not want to be the one to wait. [Note: there is only one shower per ten people in her housing unit.] Everyone is still asleep then. So, I can take my time and not rush and be done in five minutes. I cannot do that so I wake up early. I then get ready. Before work, I eat. By 6:30 PM, I am already downstairs at the club. This is because it takes me one hour to get ready, to put on my makeup, and to change into my outfit. By 7:30 is when we have to be at work. That is when we all have to be at the *waiting area*, waiting for customers. By 9:00 PM is our first show time, and that is about forty minutes. Then we go back to work after that show. Then the next show time is midnight. Then, the last show is at around 2:00 AM. We close at 3:00 AM, but we stay open until 4:00 AM on Fridays and Saturdays. We change our show every month, because customers do not want the same show all the time. So, we practice after work. We sometimes practice until 8:00 in the morning, but if we end early, we are done by 6:00 AM. Then we all go back home upstairs. We eat, we talk, and then we go to sleep. We repeat that cycle day after day.

The requirement of *show time* results in a more rigorous work pattern for transgender hostesses than for female hostesses. Explaining why they must do *show time* performances, they noted that the novelty of their male femininity is what they sell in Japan. The element of surprise is a huge part of the marketability and economy of transgender clubs. Customers go there to gawk at them for not only looking like women but for being better looking than women. Yet, the spectacle of what they are and are not comes not without emotional difficulty. Many transgender hostesses resent the attitude of customers who would sometimes even have the gall to ask them if they could touch their private parts. Nikki, who was close to departing for the Philippines when I first met her, described her stint in Japan as "six months of being like a clown." The exhaustion of performing extreme femininity does take its toll, and returning to the Philippines becomes a welcome break for many of them.

Although many customers initially patronize transgender clubs for the cultural novelty of the experience and the amusement of seeing men who are better looking than women, the intentions of their visit do sometimes transform and change toward the pursuit of greater intimacy, including sex and romance. Peachy described,

> It is like we have fans. They go to the club. They beg for your time. They pay yen to see you and talk to you and watch your show. It is like admiration. They are entertained. Customers are very different. I have customers who are just friends. There are other customers who are more. They think you are really cute. They look at you, and their problems disappear. There are some customers who want to make you a lover. That is when it gets hard.

Like female hostesses, transgender hostesses deflect the unwanted advances of customers. In their quest to be more womanly than women, transgender hostesses share the same struggles as women in hostess clubs with one aspect of the job they share being their need to constantly put off men's approaches. While the work experiences of female and transgender hostesses intersect a great deal, they differ dramatically when it comes to *show time*. The differences in their social location manifest in the greater demands placed on transgender hostesses, whose gender liminality results in the greater challenges they face at the workplace.

An intricate labor system exists in hostess clubs. In this system, the actions and behaviors of hostesses in the workplace are scrutinized and controlled, in other words managed, by the club. Management temporally and spatially controls the actions of hostesses by relegating those without customers to the waiting area and setting a time limit to customer visits. Clubs also manage the corporal bodies of hostess, resulting in the minute control of their actions, as we see with the enforcement of appropriate feminine postures in the club. To ensure that hostesses abide by the rules and regulations in the clubs, management then imposes a punitive culture with elaborate penalty systems. Lastly, the management of hostesses in Philippine clubs does not occur uniformly but is distinguished primarily by sexuality and not necessarily by class. For the most part, female and transgender hostesses have the same job requirements, but management scrutinizes the minute actions of transgender hostesses to a lesser degree. Yet transgender hostesses face greater labor market demands for lesser pay. Continuing with my discussion of the work of hostesses in the *omise*, the next chapter turns to the labor production in hostess work.

CHAPTER THREE

BUTTRESSING MASCULINITY

> When I first got here . . . my back would be hurting from thinking about whether I would be able to complete six months. I did not know if I could make it through six months or not. If I had no sales, I had at least pride. If I were sent home, I would use my own money to buy my ticket . . . Before I would go to sleep, I would have this knot at the back of my neck. It would hurt so much. I could not get rid of it. It would just hurt when you are lying in bed. You would think about your sales, and the knot at the back of your neck would hurt. Then, I got a cold. My runny nose would not disappear.
>
> *Janet, a ten-time contract worker, Tokyo*

IN RESPONSE TO MY QUESTION ON WHAT was the most difficult aspect of her job, Janet like many other *talents* described neither the constant monitoring of her actions by her employers nor the long hours required by *show time* of transgender hostesses. She did not even mention the sexual harassment of customers. Instead, she shared with me a vivid description of the physical ailments caused by the stress brought by her sales quota. Janet needed to generate at least 500,000 yen (US$5,000) in monthly sales at her club. Sales were made up of the cumulative expenses that her customers spent for food and drinks as well as for a *shimei*, meaning the request for the hostess's companionship inside the club, and a *dohan*, meaning a date with a hostess outside the club. Not meeting her monthly sales quota regularly would put her at risk of being sent back to the Philippines prior to the end of her contract. Not one of the highest-paid workers at her club, Janet actually had a low sales quota.[1] Still, she struggled to meet it. Janet told me that she worked on meeting her sales quota not only to maximize her earnings but also to avoid reprimand. According to her, those who failed to meet their sales quota were berated in a private meeting, ridiculed in public, and threatened with immediate deportation, if a *talent*, or firing, if an *arubaito*.[2]

Janet's dilemma raises the question of how she managed to meet her sales quota. How did she convince customers to spend an exorbitant amount of money on food and drinks inside the club? How did she convince them to extend a *shimei* and a *dohan* to her? Like Janet, most hostesses choose not to engage in prostitution to meet their sales quota. Influenced by conservative moral strictures of feminine respectability, most of them shun prostitution. Yet even if hostesses hold no moral qualms against prostitution, sex for money would not necessarily guarantee them more sales. This is because sex could repel as much as it could attract customers. Sex possibly deters future visits from a customer because giving in would eliminate the thrill of the chase. Yet surely customers are not altruistic and unlikely to visit hostesses without the guarantee of a return, raising the question of what their motivations would be if not for sex.

Hostesses need not rely on sex to attract customers because customers patronize hostess clubs not necessarily to obtain sex but to buttress their masculinity. By *masculinity*, I refer specifically to the customer's identity as a male provider and his feeling of being a sexually desirable male. With the wide range of sexual services available in the nightlife industry of Japan, customers could more easily obtain sex elsewhere, for instance a pink salon where fellatio is legally offered to them. In hostess clubs, customers bolster their masculinity not only via performances of what Anne Allison refers to as acts of "male ritual,"[3] such as objectifying hostesses or bonding with other men at the club. Because gender is always constructed relationally, they also rely on the cultivation of their masculinity via feminine acts by hostesses.[4] Hostesses perform femininity and bolster masculinity via the performance of bodily labor, aesthetic labor, emotional labor, storytelling, and acting.[5] These "immaterial labors"[6] are performed to cultivate particular forms of capital: bodily, emotional, and cultural. By *capital*, I refer to the hostesses' "accumulated labor."[7] *Bodily capital* refers to the physical attributes cultivated by hostesses, meaning their physical attractiveness; emotional capital underscores the emotional stronghold of hostesses over customers; and cultural capital has to do with their acquired knowledge of cultural norms in the club as well as their acquired cultural skills, such as command of the Japanese language.

Cultivating these forms of "capital"[8] fits what Michael Hardt and Antonio Negri call "immaterial labor," meaning the production of immaterial goods including affects.[9] Hostesses produce affects through the manipulation of the corporeal (via aesthetic and bodily labor), the generation of emotions (via emotional labor and storytelling), and the achievement of cultural familiarity. To engage in the production of affects, in other words to perform "affective labor," allows hostesses not just to increase their grip over customers but also to maximize their labor.[10] Notably, cultivating bodily, emotional, and cultural capital rewards not only the club owner with the surplus value produced by the hostess. While these forms of capital help hostesses meet their sales quotas, they also generate excess value for hostesses via the gifts that they induce from customers.[11] Gifts that hostesses obtain from customers, which could range from a US$10 tip to a house and lot in the Philippines, exclusively benefit hostesses as they occur outside the sphere of worker–employee relations.[12]

DOHAN

One of the most challenging job requirements for hostesses is the *dohan*. The *dohan*, which in Japanese parlance means "to go with, accompany, or a pairing," refers to the practice of a customer arranging a paid date with a hostess. Hostesses refer to the *dohan* as meaning no more than the practice of accompanying a customer into the club. Hence, one can literally go on a *dohan* by meeting the customer outside the door of the club and escorting him into the club. The *dohan* technically requires that a hostess spend some time with a customer outside the club, whether it is a few hours or no more than five seconds for those who literally do nothing for their *dohan* but escort the customer into the club. Regardless of how much time a hostess spends with the customer outside the club, the purchase of a *dohan* guarantees the customer at least one hour with the hostess inside the club.[13]

The *dohan* is a contentious issue for governmental and nongovernmental organizations, as they consider the *dohan* to be proof of "forced prostitution."[14] The U.S. State Department even cites the *dohan* as an indication of the sexual trafficking of Filipina hostesses in Japan.[15] On the contrary, most hostesses do not think that a *dohan* harms them. For instance, Nikki, a third-timer in Japan, argued that when sex does occur during a *dohan*, it happens by choice and not duress. Nikki explained, "If there is prostitution, then it is your choice. You can choose to allow them to take you to a hotel . . . Everything we do here is our own choice. There is nothing that we do that is forced." Most other hostesses agreed that coercive sexual relations were unlikely to occur during a *dohan*. As Mai commented: "A man cannot force a woman to go to a hotel." The claims made by Nikki and Mai could be construed as naïve, as hostesses without doubt are more vulnerable to sexual assault and harassment when outside the confines of the club and alone with the customer. For this reason clubs warn hostesses not to meet their customers in private venues such as a karaoke booth, residence, or hotel but instead encourage them to limit their *dohan* to a public place such as a restaurant, mall, or park.

According to Filipina hostesses, there are two kinds of *dohan*. Hostesses distinguish between an inside and outside *dohan*, with the former occurring only inside the club and the latter also taking place outside the club. Hostesses refer to the *dohan* that occurs inside the club as an *omise dohan* or *appointment dohan*, while the outside *dohan* is considered a "regular *dohan*," which suggests that the latter type of *dohan* is the more common practice in the community. Hostesses go on a "regular *dohan*" prior to the start of business hours, which would be eight o'clock in the evening, and they have to be escorted back to the club at least thirty minutes before it opens.[16]

In female hostess clubs, a *dohan* costs anywhere from 7,000 yen (US$70) to 15,000 yen (US$150), depending on the class of the establishment, plus the additional charge of a minimum purchase of 10,000 yen (US$100) of food inside the club, which is ironic because hostesses and customers usually go out to eat during a *dohan*. Transgender clubs charge less for a *dohan*, costing the customer 4,000 yen (US$40) and a minimum purchase of 5,000 yen (US$50) of food. The *dohan* is a huge source of revenue for clubs. For this reason, they provide incentives for hostesses to secure a *dohan* from regular customers, or they simply mandate them. Clubs usually do not require *arubaito* workers to secure a *dohan*, but they do *talents*. For instance, at the transgender club I frequented, contract workers such as Janet had to secure at least two every ten days. If not, they would incur a 4,000 yen (US$40) penalty from the club, which was deducted from their commission. Securing a *dohan* came not without incentive for hostesses. At the same club, hostesses secured 2,000 yen (US$20) for every *dohan* and an additional 300 yen (US$3) for every lady's drink. Notably, the *dohan* has not always been part of the work system in hostess clubs. According to old-timers in the community, the *dohan* started becoming more prevalent as the sales revenue of clubs declined beginning in the latter half of the 1990s.

While none of my interviewees had ever been violated during a *dohan*, many had experienced feeling at risk during one. For instance, the *talent* Jeanne, who complained earlier about her constant sexualization by customers, described how she once played "tug of war" with a customer trying to get her to go inside a "love hotel," meaning a short-stay hotel that operates primarily for the purpose of providing couples some privacy to engage in sexual intercourse. Once the undocumented worker Arissa had a screaming match with a customer who drove her to a hotel during a *dohan*. They had agreed to karaoke, but he insisted on singing karaoke in a hotel room.

Acknowledging the risk of going on a *dohan*, some clubs supply hostesses with mace for protection, require a minimum of two hostesses for every *dohan*, or limit the venues that a hostess and customer could visit during a *dohan* to those familiar to the hostess. Still, because most clubs have not taken any extra precautionary measures to protect hostesses during a *dohan*, hostesses have taken it on themselves to limit the risks of sexual assault in a *dohan* by never meeting a customer early in the afternoon, for instance meeting them only an hour before they must return to the club; never getting into a car with a customer; and insisting on going only to neighborhood venues familiar to them.

Despite the risks of the *dohan*, hostesses on a *dohan* are usually a source of envy and not pity, which would be the case if the *dohan* were an indication of forced prostitution. Hostesses look at the *dohan* as a lucrative and beneficial job requirement. For instance, most hostesses who are out on a *dohan* insist that customers take them to a Filipino restaurant. Filipino restaurants operate in various areas with a high concentration of Philippine hostess clubs and cater to the market of the afternoon and early evening *dohan*. Couples out on a *dohan* were a frequent sight in the Filipino food establishments I visited in the early evenings before hostess clubs open their doors at eight o'clock. Once I ran into a Filipino woman who looked no older than twenty years old eating with a young-looking Japanese man at a Filipino restaurant. Most likely out on a *dohan*, they were there to eat dinner. He ordered a beer while she took the liberty of ordering a few plates of Filipino cuisine including *linagang manok* (chicken soup), *ampalaya* (bitter melon), and grilled beef. She ate heartily while he seemed to be only picking at the grilled beef. As I observed them, I could not help but think about how this hostess must be relishing her meal, which she could not afford with her 500 yen (US$5) daily food allowance.

Clubs maintain different regulations concerning the *dohan*. While most require it of *talents*, clubs impose different reward and penalty systems. At one extreme, clubs have been known to ban hostesses who are without a *dohan* from leaving their apartment and to limit them to only a one-hour window to do their errands before they have to report to work. If with a *dohan*, they can leave their apartment as early as 1:00 PM. The penalty for leaving the apartment early is 10,000 yen (US$100). Technically, one could argue that hostesses are imprisoned under this policy. However, this is more the exception than the rule. Most clubs impose a less stringent penalty for the absence of a *dohan* and penalize hostesses who do not secure a sufficient number of *dohan* invitations by reducing their commissions.

Not all hostesses consider the *dohan* a risky venture, with a few even viewing it as harmless. After all, a *dohan* can take place only before a club opens and not after it closes.[17] To make their point that a *dohan* is not a backdoor to prostitution, two hostesses told me on separate occasions that a customer had even accompanied them to church during a *dohan*. I did frequently see hostesses with men who looked to be their customers at church on Wednesday afternoons. Attending mass is admittedly an extreme example and does not apply to most hostesses. For most other hostesses, the *dohan* is nothing more than providing companionship to an otherwise lonely customer. Many see it as a compensated date. Many know that customers likely hold romantic feelings for them when they willingly cover a *dohan*. A *dohan* allows customers "to have you solo," one hostess described, and gives them the opportunity to have more intimate conversations with the hostess. Yet hostesses also see a *dohan* as a favor from a customer willing to help them meet their sales quota.

Explaining why customers are willing to help hostesses meet their quota, my co-worker Melissa explained, "It is because they are really into the woman. They do not want the woman to get mad at them, to pout . . . They want you to be happy. A *dohan* makes you happy . . . You will tell them that you are not meeting your quota, and you will tell them that you are under pressure to meet your quota . . . That is when you really work hard to get them there." Contrary to the depiction of the *dohan* as an oppressive job requirement, Melissa considered the *dohan* a positive aspect of her work that "makes [her] happy" not only for increasing her sales and commission but also for making her feel desirable.

A *dohan* also suggests that relations between hostesses and customers cannot be reduced to a mere economic exchange. By constructing the *dohan* as an act of helping her out, Melissa assumed that the customer sympathized with her situation. This sympathy emerges in the context of a social tie that links customers and hostesses either as friends, lovers, or romantic partners. Emotional attachments, as we see in the desire of customers to help out hostesses, linger in the interactions between customers and hostesses, while hostesses such as Melissa also remind us that these ties are strongly gendered. Describing the *dohan* as an act of helping out underscores the role of the customer as a male provider and at the same time emphasizes the economic dependence of the hostess on his patronage of the club.

SALES QUOTAS

In addition to the *dohan*, management also expects hostesses to generate sales by consistently securing a *shimei*, meaning a customer's request for their company inside the club. The money spent by customers to pay for the two requirements of the *dohan* and the *shimei*, and the amount spent by a customer during them, would constitute the sales quota of a hostess.[18] Notably, the expenses of a customer seated with a hostess would not be part of a hostess's sales quota unless that customer had extended a *shimei* or a *dohan* to her. Clubs measure the sales of hostesses in two ways, either via the *oriage*, meaning sales, or via points. The *oriage* is a more straightforward system in which hostesses have to generate a minimum amount of consumption from customers. *Talents* who work in a club with an *oriage* system have to generate anywhere from 500,000 to 1,000,000 yen (US$5,000 to 10,000) in sales per month.[19] Most prefer the *oriage* system because one need not rely on the *dohan* to reach one's sales quota, which is the case with the points system. Hostesses dread the requirement of the *dohan* not necessarily because of the actual experience but more because of the difficulty of convincing a customer to spend for it. After all, a *dohan* is exorbitantly expensive.

Disregarding the preference of most hostesses, clubs tend to use the points system to measure the sales of hostesses. Under this system, a *dohan* is worth three points and a *shimei* worth one point. A *jonai*, which is a request for a helper, does not count toward the points system. A hostess must generate a set number of points every ten days, depending on her salary. A first-timer who earns only US$500 per month must generate anywhere from fifteen to seventeen points every ten days, while a second-timer who earns US$600 usually must generate eighteen to twenty points. Point requirements vary by club but usually fall within this parameter. To qualify these numbers, fifteen points could be earned, for instance, by securing five invitations to a *dohan* in ten days, or three invitations to a *dohan* and six extensions of a *shimei* from customers. The higher a hostess's salary and the greater her work experience, then the higher her quota. Hostesses receive a commission for their sales with one point usually equal to 1,000 yen (US$10). Thus, fifteen points would earn a hostess 15,000 yen ($150) every ten days. Not meeting one's quota results in penalty. Most clubs reduce the commission of hostesses who fail to meet their quota by 50 percent. This means that someone who generates only fourteen points out of a fifteen-point quota would earn only 7,000 yen (US$70) instead of 14,000 yen (US$140) in commission.

While most clubs penalize hostesses who do not meet their sales quotas, they do reward those who exceed it. For instance, in one hostess club, hostesses receive a bonus of 5,000 yen (US$50) if they secure seven *dohan* invitations in ten days. In some cases, a *dohan* would be worth four and not only three points if a customer spent 22,000 yen (US$220) for food inside the club instead of the minimum of 10,000 yen (US$100) required in a *dohan*. At another club, hostesses who generate thirty-five points in ten days would receive an additional 10,000 yen (US$100) in commission as a bonus. Although most hostesses barely make their sales quota, I did meet some exceptional hostesses who have benefited from their club's reward system. Considering that promoters withhold the salary of *talents* or entertainers during the entire duration of their six-month contract, hostesses have a great deal of incentive to generate as many points as possible. This is because, besides the 500 yen (US$5) daily food allowance, the commission generated by their sales is usually their only source of income while they are in Japan.[20] Making the commission all the more crucial for female hostesses is the fact that they depend on these funds to send money to their families in the Philippines.

As I mentioned briefly in Chapter One, the labor expectation of the club may far exceed what an entertainer perceives to be a fair workload because of the discrepancy between what a club pays the promoter and what this middleman broker pays the hostess. For example, one club imposed an exceedingly high sales quota on the former *talent* Lenlen during her eighth and last contract stint in Japan in 2003, demanding a sales quota of thirty points. Lenlen did not think that her salary of US$1000 per month warranted the requirement of securing an average of one *dohan* per night. Although she managed to meet this exceedingly high points requirement, Lenlen described her experience as abusive and a good example of why middlemen should charge only a nominal fee for their services and not collect 75 percent of the hostess's earnings.[21]

Club management measures the performance of hostesses not on the basis of how many customers they manage to lure into the club but on the basis of the amount of money customers spend inside the club. Wage rates of *arubaito* workers usually fluctuate according to sales, with higher sales leading to higher wage rates. In one club, for example, workers who generate fewer than sixty points in one month would earn 1,400 yen per hour, while those who generate at least 200 points in a month would receive 3,000 yen per hour. In the case of *talents*, sales determine whether they would be requested to return for another contract. Usually only the top earners of a club would be asked to return.

Generally, sales determine a hostess's treatment at the club. Management penalizes hostesses who fail to meet their sales quota. They do not hesitate to fire those with lackluster sales. Entertainers who are fired are not necessarily sent back to the Philippines by their promoters; they are likely to be placed at another club as a "flying booking," which leaves them in a precarious situation of illegality. As a disciplinary strategy, clubs also have no qualms about berating hostesses for their poor sales performance. Not surprisingly, along with having to be conscious of their bodily actions inside the club, hostesses describe meeting the sales quota as one of their most difficult job requirements. Noted the entertainer Jeanne: "This job is hard. You are thinking about many things. First, you worry about the customer. You strategize on how you can hold them. Second, you strategize about how you can get them to come here. How do you hold onto them without having them ask for sex?" Likewise, the first-timer Amy complained, "Me, I get tired thinking about the next day. I get tired of thinking about having to go to work the next day. I think that I am going to once again worry about which customer will come visit me. Who will *dohan* me? Will I meet my points?" Amy continued: "Then you stress out when your customers call and ask you, 'When are we going to have sex?' And if you do not give in, they will replace you. So, of course you worry. You have a hard time holding onto customers." Contrary to what many outsiders commonly think, hostesses do not always rely on sex to secure customers. This includes Amy, the once underage hostess who selectively engaged in compensated sex with some of her customers. More than turning to sex, hostesses try to generate sales by bolstering the masculinity of their customers.

BUTTRESSING MASCULINITY

Contrary to the assumption made by most outsiders that the stringent job requirements that clubs impose on hostesses would inevitably result in their participation in prostitution, hostesses demonstrate their agential behavior with the use of other forms of labor—bodily, aesthetic, emotional—to maintain the loyalty and continued patronage of customers. They do this work as part of the affective labor of bolstering masculinity. Without doubt, some hostesses provide sex as a strategy of cultivating customer loyalty, but it would be a mistake for us to think that they all do or that they rely primarily on sex to keep customers' interest. Instead of providing sex, hostesses bolster their customers' masculinity by performing various forms of labor, including bodily labor, aesthetic labor, emotional labor, storytelling, and acting. In this section, I describe how the performance of these forms of labor results in the accumulation of three forms of capital that organically define social relations between customers and hostesses: bodily capital, emotional capital, and cultural capital.[22] The cultivation of these forms of capital secures the loyalty of customers and in turn generates surplus value for clubs as well as excess value for hostesses.

The Bodily Capital of Hostesses

Bodily capital refers to the physical attributes of beauty and femininity among hostesses. These are the basic prerequisite of their employment and hence attributes they cultivate, manage, and maintain consciously in everyday life. Hostesses cultivate their bodily capital via the performance of "bodily labor," meaning their refurbishing and retooling of corporality, which in this case refers to the cultivation and maintenance of their physical appearance and features so as to remain sexually desirable and physically attractive to customers, as well as via "aesthetic labor," meaning the presentation of bodies to fit an organization's aesthetic image.[23] The companionship of a beautiful woman heightens the customer's masculinity by increasing his feelings of desirability. But what is desirable to customers is subjective and often depends on the type of club they visit. In some clubs, hostesses project a more demure physical appearance, while in others they cultivate a more risqué demeanor. Hostesses remain mindful of these different aesthetics, often changing their style of clothing to fit the aesthetics of a club from one contract to another, but what stays constant for them is the bodily labor of maintaining an optimal weight, skin tone, and physical appearance that fit ideal notions of beauty.

The conscious and unconscious monitoring of bodily capital shapes the behavior of hostesses to the point that it even shaped the dynamics of our interviews. Indeed, the pressure among hostesses to increase their bodily capital made an interview a cultural experience unto itself, as interview subjects would often not look at me but would instead gaze at their reflection in the mirror or the camera screen of their cellular phone while answering my questions. Offhandedly remarking on why she spent a lot of time looking at herself in the mirror, the fourth-timer Yuki commented, "It is very hard to control your vanity the longer you stay in this business."[24]

The efforts extended by hostesses to increase their bodily capital reflect those of prospective transnational brides from Latin America to the United States, as many alter their body to conform to the erotic desires of male tourists from the north.[25] In the case of hostesses and the transnational brides in feminist scholar Felicity Schaeffer-Grabiel's study, "bodily labor" refers not so much to the "physical labor of attending to the bodily appearance and pleasure of customers" as defined by sociologist Miliann Kang of "body labor" but instead refers to attending to one's own bodily appearance.[26] With the body being their primary source of income, hostesses see its management as not only an individual but also a community effort. As such, they openly monitor not only their physical appearance but also those of others in the community.

When spending time with hostesses, one soon notices that they frequently comment on one another's physical appearance and artistic talents, commending those whom they think belong in a Class A club and brutally reminding hostesses who are deluded about their ranking of their lower-class status. In the community, hostesses carry a keen awareness of their own class standing as well as the class standings of those around them, internalizing not only the objectification but also the standards of physical beauty imposed on them by clubs and customers. Hostesses comment on one another's physical appearance not just to deride others but also to assist one another with maintaining or elevating their beauty. Comments about the appearances of others extend to the sharing of beauty tips from improving one's wardrobe to learning how to pluck one's eyebrows into the correct shape. For instance, once a friend visiting me in my apartment reprimanded me for never using an eyelash curler. She told me that using one would make my eyelashes look longer, after which she insisted that we walk to the department store near my house so I could purchase one. The constant regulation of physical appearance in the community indicates its significance. Indeed, the marketability of hostesses depends on their beauty. How much they should receive in salary and the types of clubs they qualify to enter are all weighed according to the hostess's perceived class ranking, which is based primarily on her physical attributes. As such, hostesses do a tremendous amount of bodily labor. To heighten their marketability, hostesses in general manage their physical features by perpetually monitoring their weight, applying makeup and skin care products, and avoiding the sun not only to keep their skin tone light but to delay aging.[27]

In the transgender community, we see the performance of bodily labor as a community effort when hostesses advice one another on surgical processes, recommend doctors, and share tips on nonsurgical forms of bodily alterations. Illustrating the camaraderie among transgender hostesses, the gay beauty contest winner Sean, who had to "work very hard not to be a *batong bakla* . . . a masculine person with no touch of femininity," received advice from another transgender hostess on where to get hormone injections when she first arrived in Japan. Described Sean:

> When I arrived here I really looked like a man. I was very hard. Near where I worked was another *bakla*. She worked in another club, another branch of my club. She told me that we should take hormone shots. It is only 2,000 yen [US$20] per session. So I kept on getting injections. In one week, I would have two to three sessions for hormones. So that would be around 6,000 yen [US$60] per week. So I really saved my tips. I used to have tips that customers gave me in the other club. So I really saved my tips.

The marketability of transgender hostesses in the club is measured by the extent of their femininity, the achievement of which comes not without its risks, even for those who do not undergo surgery. Sean's body, for instance, eventually had an adverse reaction to her hormone injections resulting in acne as well as weight gain. She complained that she looked "like a pig" after three months of hormone injections, forcing her to stop. At the time of our interview, she took only a daily contraceptive to maintain her femininity.

Female hostesses tend not to invest in plastic surgery, which is unlike their transgender counterparts who would spend to not only look more feminine but also to achieve what they perceived to be Japanese features, such as slanted eyes and a more pointed nose. Club management regularly pressures transgender entertainers to turn to the bodily labor of surgery, especially those who still look like a "*batong bakla*." The first-timer Linda, for instance, had been told that her return as a second-timer would be contingent on her investment in plastic surgery. The club was telling her to "get a nose job, silicone implants, and waist reduction." Linda did not seem to mind these demands. As she told me, "I even see that myself. [My club manager] does not need to tell me that. I see that I am lacking." To attract customers, Linda agreed with club management that she needed surgery to look more feminine. Linda was beginning to save money for her planned surgeries.[28] The pressure to look feminine comes from the appearance of those around her. Many of her co-workers had in fact relied on plastic surgery to boost their marketability in the hostess industry.

Not all transgender entertainers turn to plastic surgery to achieve femininity. The third-time contract worker Nikki relied only on her weekly injection of hormones, which cost her 2,000 yen (US$20) per visit. Nikki had toyed with the idea of getting surgery, admiring her friends who had done so, but she feared going through the process herself. As she told me, "I am personally hesitant. Once you touch yourself, there is no turning back. Isn't that right? It hurts not only your body, but also your pockets."

Notably, the bodily labor of hostesses involves not only the management of their external corporality but extends the transformation as well to the upkeep of their most intimate body parts. This is the case for transgender entertainers who seek a sex change. Mama May, a club owner who worked in transgender clubs for nearly two decades prior to opening her own club, explained why her quest to be feminine extended to her sex. She stated,

> I had a sex change because us gays feel inclined to go there. If you have not yet had an operation, it feels incomplete. Your womanhood is not complete. That is what you feel. You have something to hide. You go to the beach. You have to hide it. You cannot wear a two-piece. Then, another matter is, when you are going to have sex, you have to hide it. They know usually, but you do not want them to lose interest. So you have to hide it.

Only a few of my interviewees opted to get a sex change. Most others actually feared the effects of this permanent change on their body, with some for instance calling this alteration a "wound."

Interestingly, the bodily labor of female hostesses also extends to their most intimate body parts. Available to the community are a host of products geared toward grooming and maintaining their intimate body parts, such as skin whitening creams for the thighs, vagina tightening lubricants, and douches. The availability of these products does not necessarily indicate that hostesses engage in sex-for-money, but they do suggest that some opt to pursue intimate sexual liaisons with customers. In some cases, they undeniably do so for money. As Amanda, a veteran hostess, described,

> You have sex with a grandfather if the price is right. If you really want something, you will do it. Like, if you say, I really want to buy a house, or my mother is sick. So even if the man smells like dirt and shit, you will accept him. Anyone will do it. You will just close your eyes because you need something.

In other cases, lust and not necessarily money motivates the pursuit of sex, though the two motivations are not mutually exclusive. As Amanda continued, "Filipinas, if there is a good-looking man that comes into the *omise*, and they have a crush, the Filipina will give sex for no money. No money, but the Filipina just wants to do that. But anybody will do that." Lastly, hostesses also have sex for love, even if "love" translates to only a small inkling of affection.

Magazines catering to hostesses such as *Pilipinos in Japan* regularly feature advertisements for products that improve intimate body parts including those that claim to "*tightening sa vagina, pangalis sa dumi sa loob at nakakaalis sa sakit ng puson,*" meaning "tighten the vagina, eliminate dirt inside, and remove stomach cramps." Other products are sold as "verginity soap" (*sic*) and "liquid vagina soap with aloe vera."[29] When among members of the community, I often overheard hostesses describe various intimate body creams and cleansers to one another, indicating how they help each other increase their marketability to customers. For instance, many swear by the effectiveness of "Magic Cream" for whitening intimate body parts. As one vendor once assured me, "*maganda yan sa pek-pek mo*," meaning "that is very nice for your vagina."

Emotional Capital

The term *emotional capital* refers to the emotions that hostesses strategically induce among their customers for the purpose of securing their loyalty and generating gifts. They accumulate and build particular emotions among customers via the manipulation of their own emotions, that is, through their performance of what Arlie Hochschild has called "emotional labor,"[30] as well as through storytelling. While the accumulation of emotional capital entails the performance of emotional labor, I distinguish the work of accumulating emotional capital from what we understand as emotional labor so as to underscore the productive value that workers could gain from the manipulation of their emotions.[31]

The accumulation of emotional capital, or the productive value of manipulating emotions, differs from emotional labor.[32] On one hand, *emotional labor* refers to the emotional regulation of a worker and the manipulation of feeling to generate a particular facial or bodily display. Emotional labor is "sold for a wage."[33] On the other hand, accumulating emotional capital refers to the excess value of emotions and affects generated in a particular social context that are to be used for personal gain. Hostesses accrue emotional capital through emotively and affectively charged storytelling and the use of acting as a consciously acquired skill. Such emotional capital includes love, benevolence, and sympathy, which potentially generate the excess value of a "*bahay, lupa, kotse,*" meaning "house, lot, car" for the most skilled of hostesses.

It would be a mistake to think that hostesses are merely doing affective labor.[34] Emotions are not just commodities for them. Although they participate in the "production of affects" in their labor, the values of the emotions induced in the accumulation of emotional capital differ in the context of particular social relations.[35] For hostesses, emotions are not just goods but are instead a form of capital. Thus, following Bourdieu's assertion that capital is a form of social relation, the emotions produced by hostesses among their customers only incur value in the context of the social relations of hostesses and customers.[36] Hence, to generate emotional capital involves "relational work" on the part of the hostesses.[37]

Hostesses flirt with customers to generate particular sentiments that would engender acts of gift giving among customers. For hostesses, the various feelings that encourage gift giving include, among others, love, compassion, sympathy, and benevolence. Hostesses induce certain feelings from customers so as to buttress the masculinity of a customer and in turn compel the customer to patronize their business.

One way that hostesses try to build their emotional capital is by continuously emoting love and affection, which they do via emotional labor as well as storytelling in the club or on the phone. In so doing, they are able to underscore the masculinity of customers by suggesting their sexual desirability. My co-worker Teresa, for instance, made a habit of calling her customers nearly every day to display what she personally described as acts of "sweetness":

> Here in Japan, even if you are married, I realize that if you have been together for a long time, they lose their sweetness. So, that is what I give them, sweetness. They become very, very happy that you worry about them and remember them. They are happy with a simple goodnight and sweet dreams.

By emoting affection, Teresa heightened her customers' sense of sexual desirability. Cultivating such sentiments, Teresa acquired emotional capital that could potentially be used to gain a *dohan*, *shimei*, tip, or gift.

Generating the feeling of pity is one other way hostesses induce acts of gift giving among customers, which they do via storytelling. Emotional ties between customers and hostesses emerge from their social situation. More specifically, they emerge from the context of not only their unequal relations of gender and class but also the marked differences in opportunities available to them from their politicoeconomic locations of being from either a downtrodden country such as the Philippines or an advanced capitalist nation such as Japan. Hostesses strategically underscore the disparity in their economic position by evoking the feeling of *awa*, or pity, from their customers, which is a feeling that elicits other emotions, including benevolence and magnanimity. Hostesses usually perform the emotional labor of projecting the emotions of sadness and despair to engender feelings of pity.

The strategy of evoking pity is one that men from richer nations seem to fetishize in their sexual desires for both men and women from poorer countries. Mark Padilla found that "performing poverty" reaped economic benefits for gay male sex workers in the Dominican Republic.[38] In her reading of gonzo pornography produced by white male sex tourists in Asia, feminist film critic Celine Parreñas Shimizu likewise identifies as central to their eroticism not only the poverty of sex workers but also their Third World status.[39] Scenes of the squalor of Third World countries serve as the frequent backdrop of sex tourism video productions. Like the Asian sex workers documented by tourists in gonzo pornography, hostesses utilize their poverty to generate feelings of chivalry and magnanimity among customers. In so doing, they can heighten the masculinity of customers without having to rely on sex.

To induce feelings of *awa*, or pity, among customers, hostesses frequently share stories of their hardships. A popular one is the story of how one's younger siblings in the Philippines would starve if not for the monthly remittance they receive from Japan. Another is the need to pay for a relative's medical bill. Hostesses also let customers know that they will face financial hardship once they return to the Philippines because of the lack of job opportunities in such a poor country. Likewise, they share with them the financial difficulties that they face in Japan, complaining to customers about the penalty management imposes on them or the ways management berate them for not meeting their sales quotas. To secure that *dohan*, hostesses will also not hesitate to cry on the shoulders of a customer, sharing with them stories about how difficult it is to survive on 500 yen (US$5) a day.

The work of projecting hardship through either storytelling or emotional displays of despair indicate that to be a main not only depends on the hostess's sexual desirability but relies as much if not more on her cultivation of emotional attachments. Notably, hostesses depend not only on love but also on sympathy to lure customers to the club. As I noted earlier, not every customer visits hostess clubs to pursue sex or romance. Some desire nothing more than friendship from hostesses. I found that feelings of sympathy, in other words feeling sorry for hostesses, are more often the reason shared by customers as to why they patronize hostess clubs and willingly shell out the money for a *dohan*. They go to clubs to help hostesses meet their sales quotas and avoid penalty primarily out of consideration for their plight as labor migrants from an impoverished country such as the Philippines. Clubs therefore gain surplus value from hostesses' emotional capital, and in this case, their accrual of sympathy, but the loyalty of customers engendered by emotional capital also produces excess value for hostesses. Customers often reward them with tips that are in excess of the profits made by club owners.

The flow of sympathy comes from the hostess's work of manufacturing and presenting her position of financial distress to customers so as to encourage their magnanimous acts. This tells us that the emotional capital of sympathy builds on the customers' heightened masculinity and their willing participation in traditional courtship exchanges between male providers and female dependents. Moreover, the emotional capital of sympathy emerges from the context of the unequal relationship between hostesses and customers, which we must locate in the geopolitical inequalities that shape uneven economic conditions in Japan and the Philippines. Customers visit hostess clubs for the sexual titillation of flirtation. Yet, besides the impulse to flirt, the desire to financially help out hostesses also keeps them coming back. By engendering sympathy, not only do hostesses use their sexuality to negotiate political and economic inequalities, but these very inequalities become a strategy used by hostesses to secure material gains.

Cultural Capital

The customers' want for a heightened masculinity pushes hostesses to cultivate a third form of capital, specifically the cultural capital of knowing how to maintain the customers' masculinity. Doing this of course requires language skills as well as familiarity with the norms that guide relations in the club. Yet the performance most saliently relies on the decommercialization of flirtation. Hostesses do this by never directly asking customers to spend money on them or by projecting the idea that their desire for the customer's company is always free of financial motivation.

One way hostesses make sure to decommercialize their flirtation is by never directly asking a customer to buy them a drink. Doing so could embarrass a customer with limited funds. Because the hostess's job entails stroking the customer's ego, putting him on the spot by requesting a drink that he possibly could not afford would go against the basic principle of hostess work while at the same time threatening the customer's masculinity. Skilled hostesses also develop ways of requesting a drink without having to ask for one directly, allowing customers the opportunity of taking the lead by initiating the offer of a beverage. Hostesses, instead of asking for a drink directly, make comments intended for the customer to hear such as "I don't have anything yet to drink," "I am so thirsty," or "My favorite drink here is the pineapple juice." Experienced customers usually know that such comments would be their cue to offer the hostess a beverage. Newcomers are taught the protocol that they should invite customers to spend money at the club only indirectly and not directly; acquiring strategies for inducing sales indirectly is something that hostesses develop only with experience.

The idea of decommercializing the hostess's interactions with customers suggests that she genuinely likes the company of the customer regardless of how much money he spends at the club. Acts of decommercialization ultimately stroke the egos of customers because they imply that commercial interests do not determine the hostesses' desire for their company. Providing us with solid examples, Yuki reinforced the idea of her genuine pleasure with the customer's company by suggesting to him that the time they spent together need not involve the exchange of money. In other words, she wished for customers to think that she sought their companionship not only for financial gain. To do this, she consciously told customers not to spend money on her, suggesting the possibility of noncommercial intimacy between them. Described Yuki:

> I put my heart in my work. I will say, "Oh you poor thing. No, let us not order that because it is too expensive." You say that if they offer to feed you. Sometimes you just refuse their offer even if you are so hungry. You tell them that you will just eat the peanuts on the table.

When interacting with customers, Yuki also consciously downplayed the material gains she came away with from their interaction. For instance, when coyly suggesting to a customer that he extend a *shimei* to her, Yuki would tell a customer that it was because she found his company (and not his wallet) pleasurable. As she described,

> You really have to develop tactics and techniques to amuse the customer, entertain him with song, and then coyly ask him for a *shimei*, telling him you don't want to

get moved [to another table] because you are having such a good time. You tell them that you want them to *shimei* you, so you can stay together. Then, they will agree.

After completing three terms as a contract laborer, Yuki had learned that articulating one's pure pleasure for the customer's company was likely to raise a customer's sense of specialness and consequently engender his sentiments of magnanimity and companionate desire toward her.

The decommercialization of hostess and customer relations also occurs outside the club. Like many other hostesses, the *arubaito* worker Alice threw in what she considered freebies of her time outside of work in hopes that they would result in a future *dohan*. Described Alice: "I am always there for them. I am always ready to meet them when they would like to see me . . . I don't count the hours when I am with them. Also, I don't limit it. For example, I don't meet them only in the day but also at night. If only in the day, then they might not feel satisfied." For hostesses, the devotion of unpaid time to customers, or the provision of noncommercial flirtatious encounters, increases the loyalty of customers. It also results in customers wanting to spend more money at the club.

The hostesses' success also depends on their ability to communicate in the Japanese language. This institutionalized form of cultural capital is one that hostesses cannot do without if they wish to reel in regular customers who would not only visit them at the club but also spend to help them meet their sales quota. My co-worker Dianne said it best: "No matter what, you need to learn how to speak Japanese so that you and the customer could understand each other." Some clubs provide a small language book for hostesses that does not provide an extensive and sophisticated range of topics but instead covers no more than the basic club lingo to describe various foods and customary introductions. In these books, Japanese words would be spelled out in the Roman alphabet. Hostesses are generally illiterate in Japanese and cannot follow complex characters in *kanji*, the Chinese characters that convey the most of the meaning in written Japanese. This is the case for even those who have lived in the country for more than twenty years, with the only exception being the Filipinas sent to Japanese language school by their spouse. While unable to follow *kanji*, many hostesses whom I met in Japan eventually learned to read *hiragana* and *katakana*, which are Japanese syllabaries typically used to spell out sounds for, respectively, Japanese and foreign words. This group includes new migrants; most if not all would diligently memorize *hiragana* and *katakana* characters so they could sing in Japanese with customers in the karaoke machine or send customers e-mails asking them to visit them at the club. For example, hostesses would spell out the lyrics of Japanese songs frequently sung by customers in the Roman alphabet and then memorize them so they could sing along with customers. Eventually, they would learn how to follow the Japanese characters without translation although usually without ever knowing the meanings to the songs.

For the most part, hostesses can get by with their limited reading skills. They can distinguish various foods, being able to figure out if the *onigiri*, meaning rice ball, at the convenience store has tuna, salmon, pickles, or pork inside it. Yet, when with a customer at a restaurant, they would usually leave it to him to read the menu, as the task of reading is, for them, mentally exhausting. Understandably, they never read the newspaper and cannot follow school memos handed to them by their children. They walk by businesses every day without always knowing what kind of businesses they are unless they have visited such an establishment in the past, have been told by someone else what it is, or have stopped to carefully make out the characters. For most, illiteracy becomes a way of life.

The difficulty of acquiring Japanese is the biggest struggle facing hostesses in their quest to secure customers. At the club where I worked, a number of regular customers, fortunately for me, had some knowledge of Filipino. Most had never been to the Philippines, but many had been frequenting Philippine *omise* for more than a decade, with some even visiting weekly. Many also spoke English, including for instance some members of the *yakuza* who frequented our establishment. Still, a rudimentary command of Japanese was necessary to do the job. Acquiring the Japanese language was a challenge not only for me but also for most of the hostesses whom I met in Japan. As they had a greater investment than I did on learning the language, unlike me, many of them had the habit of meticulously writing down the new words they would learn on a little notepad every night.

Most hostesses start to feel comfortable with holding a basic conservation in Japanese after about three months in Japan. One could imagine that they would eventually learn some Japanese as they are figuratively thrown into the lion's den soon after they arrive in Japan, spending nearly eight hours of every night with Japanese customers at a club with only two evenings off in a month. At the club, they would rotate from one table to the next, listening to men speak and sing in Japanese night after night. Although hearing Japanese continually might not guarantee they will speak with the correct grammar, it does give them the ability to communicate and forces them to acquire some of the language.

The first-timer Reggie, for instance, started feeling comfortable using her basic language skills with customers after two months in Japan. Describing her difficult transition, Reggie could only feel relief over the fact that she now understood the basic references to sex made by customers in Japanese. Stated Reggie:

> Before, I did not understand *iku* [orgasm], *hoteru* [hotel], and things like that. I would just say, '*hai, hai, hai*' [yes, yes, yes]. . . . I asked others what those words meant and they told me that I was stupid. They told me that those customers were asking me if I were hard up. He was going to take me to a hotel. So, I got all worried because I had said yes. I was told not to worry about it, because they know that I am a first-timer. Now, they can no longer do that to me . . . When someone says something like that to me, I now throw it back at them . . . No matter what, I know a little bit now. I can answer back now.

Hostesses face a tremendous amount of pressure to learn Japanese, because receiving tips, commissions, and presents from customers requires a rudimentary knowledge of the language. Some hostesses find it difficult to learn Japanese, although not for a lack of trying, and find themselves having the same conversation with different customers every night. The repertoire of the topics they could cover would never go beyond the weather, the elementary emotions of hunger and thirst, and recycled sex jokes. In some cases, customers even complained to them about their limited language abilities and described the experience of talking to them as "boring." Yet others undeniably find greater success in their language acquisition. For instance, the Class A hostesses whom I met could follow the news on the radio or television and more importantly could keep the interest of their customers with jokes, quick comebacks, and various topics of conversation, whether they were as basic as directing the customer's attention to her breasts, describing to him the dildo she owned, relating to him a sob story about her life of abject poverty in the

Philippines, or expressing to him how hungry she was after having only had a salmon *onigiri* for dinner that evening.

At Manila, the most successful hostess among my co-workers was Teresa, an older woman who relied on her language abilities to keep the interest of customers. Never without a customer, Teresa explained that her ability to balance the task of listening and talking increased her desirability. Described Teresa:

> You just tell them stories. You make them laugh. It is because they are stressed at work. I know that all the Japanese drink so that they can get rid of their stress. I think why they enjoy my company is because what is always in the back of my mind when I am with them is that they are here because of their stress. So they need to laugh. They need someone to talk to. That is always in my head. This is probably why it is easy for me to get a guest. They can feel that I am good to talk to. I have sense.

Indeed, Teresa seemed to know when to stop talking and when to start listening. As she said, "Sometimes they will share with you a sad story. And what you do is just listen. That is also a way for them to get rid of their stress."

Teresa learned Japanese after completing more than seven labor contracts in Tokyo. A former Class A hostess who had started working in Japan at the age of fifteen, Teresa had only recently returned to hostess work after nearly a decade's hiatus in the Philippines during which she started a family. Returning to hostess work only because her husband's shoe manufacturing business failed with the recent influx in the Philippines of cheaply made goods from China, Teresa was now working in Japan to raise the funds she needed for her children's private education in the Philippines. In her late thirties, Teresa was having to relearn Japanese, which is a task that I have noticed she did not take lightly, if the small notebook she carried with her around the club and her sly maneuvers to quickly write words and song lyrics on it were any indication.

When asked how she secured the flow of customers to our club nearly every night, Teresa ranked the importance of her language skills over her physical appearance and emotional stronghold over customers. Teresa however did not overlook these other assets of hers. For instance, she was mindful of her weight and constantly monitored her food intake, often complaining to me about the decrease in her metabolism in the last few years. Without doubt, her sex appeal greatly accounted for her success with customers. Teresa also utilized her sexual desirability, although only to the extent of kissing and petting inside or outside the club. Priding herself on her devotion to her husband, Teresa vowed that she had *never* had sex with a Japanese customer in all of her years in Japan. According to Teresa, a kiss is harmless and does not make her unfaithful, even though she herself admitted that she would probably never tell her husband in the Philippines that she had kissed some of her customers. Teresa's choice of engaging in a limited degree of sexual intimacy with certain customers was not required by our club but was one that she made herself.

Teresa's selective use of sex raises many questions about the sexual practices of hostesses. It suggests that they carry a different moral standard of monogamy from mainstream society in which they distinguish certain sexual intimacies as having no bearing on their faithfulness. It also indicates that sex does not occur only by force among them. Lastly, it establishes that, to varying degrees, hostesses do maintain sexual intimacies with customers. Teresa's behavior invites us to examine the unique configuration of sexual morality in their world, one that organically emerges from the institution of hostess clubs.

To secure customers, hostesses buttress their masculinity by accumulating various forms of capital—bodily, emotional, and cultural. Bodily capital enables them to heighten customer masculinity by giving them the pleasure of a beautiful companion when they visit a club. The accumulation of emotional capital bolsters the customers' masculinity by heightening their identity as a "good provider."[40] The emotions of love, affection, and pity, which hostesses consciously cultivate among their customers, are often performed via emphasizing the women's economic suffering. Lastly, the cultivation of cultural capital, which is centered on the practice of decommercialized flirtation, makes customers feel masculine, as such acts suggest the customer's sexual desirability as one who is wanted not for his money but for his looks and winning personality.

The work of buttressing masculinity via commercial flirtation suggests that hostess work is skilled labor, which is contrary to its dismissal as unskilled work that threatens the professional status of an "entertainer." As professionals, "entertainers" are supposed only to sing and dance on stage and not to engage customers in conversation.[41] Yet, the need to buttress masculinity, at the very least, tells us that hostess work requires acting skills. Utilizing these skills raises the material rewards of hostess work, generating gifts from customers that are in excess of the surplus value that the labor of hostesses generates for middleman brokers and club owners. Perhaps this is why hostesses consider the work of engaging customers at the table, work that supposedly makes them sex-trafficked persons, to be indicative not of their human trafficking but of their skilled employment. As one hostess whom I met at a popular trangender club told me,

> Working in an *omise* is like working in an office. After a few months, you better learn the ropes. If not, you will be embarrassed. Working in an *omise* is the same way. If you do not have customers, it is embarrassing to the others. It is a sign that you do not know how to do your job.

CHAPTER FOUR

THE RISKY BUSINESS OF LOVE

Cultivating bodily, emotional, and cultural capitals secures excess value for hostesses via their accumulation of gifts from customers.[1] These gifts could be as minimal as a US$10 tip, or they could be as extravagant as the US$700 in cash that a customer once handed Teresa as a goodbye present, one that she claims came "with no strings attached." They could also be as generous as the fifty-two-inch flat-screen TV that a customer gave Janet or the house and lot that my co-worker Arissa owned in the Philippines. To maximize the excess value of their labor, hostesses cultivate romance and participate in courtship rituals with customers. Hostesses pursue romance, or what we could call pseudo-romance or *gijiren'ai*,[2] not necessarily for the end goal of falling in love but for material gain.

The social field that hostesses occupy has a particular moral world when it comes to romance.[3] This moral world cultivates a unique set of principles in regard to sexual conduct, with the general rule being that the hostesses try continuously to secure gifts from customers whether inside or outside the club. To secure gifts, they often resort to the promise but not necessarily the provision of intimacy. For hostesses, obtaining gifts from men without conceding to sex proves their sexual desirability, erotic power, and skills as a hostess.[4] In contrast, conceding to sex without material gain would suggest that customers have the upper hand in the relationship. To win in the game of courtship, hostesses must accumulate emotional capital. They do this work with the dual and paradoxical goal of increasing the emotional attachments of customers toward them while simultaneously keeping their own feelings of emotional distance from these same customers. As one of my older co-workers once advised a newcomer at our club, "It is important that it is his heart that falls and not yours."

AMANDA: A WINNER IN THE GAME OF COURTSHIP

My entrance to the moral world of hostesses was my friend Amanda, whom I met fortuitously during my first month in Tokyo, in a place where someone would never expect to meet a Filipino. We met not in one of the Filipino grocery stores in the red-light district of Kinshicho in central Tokyo nor at church near the Yotsuya train station, where every Sunday afternoon a swarm of Filipinos crowds the sidewalk lined with food vendors. Instead, Amanda and I met in the ritzy neighborhood of Azabu Juban in central Tokyo. The neighborhood boasts many diplomatic offices and luxury apartments that cater to expatriate businessmen as well as a range of upscale restaurants and cafes that cater to the Western palate. On my way to Japanese language class, I took a quick detour to a nearby café to grab a cup of coffee. In the terrace near the entrance of the otherwise empty café sat two Filipino women. Both of them looked to be in their mid-thirties, significantly older than most hostesses, but because they were quite attractive I thought they might possibly be retired workers from the industry. Plainly dressed in T-shirts and jeans, the women wore no makeup.

Inside the café, I thought about whether I should introduce myself to these two women. During the previous week I had run into a young Filipina whom I had assumed from her appearance to be a *talent* from the Philippines. I had asked if I could interview her, but she practically ran away from me after

I handed her my business card. Her distrust and fear puzzled me. In other places where I have done research on Filipino migrants, for instance in Los Angeles, Madrid, and Rome, most members of the community welcomed me with open arms. In Tokyo, trepidation and distrust often greeted me. Though I hesitated, I still stopped on my way out—pleased to see the two Filipinos were still there—and introduced myself. To my relief, they did not ignore me. I became inseparable with one of them, Amanda, during the time of my fieldwork. Since I have returned to the United States, we have kept in touch often by e-mail and telephone.

Amanda is a short and plump woman with bangs and shoulder-length hair cropped along her cheeks to sharpen her round face. Amanda no longer works as a hostess, although she had done so for most of her adult life. She stopped working at night only five years before our meeting. Divorced, she lives with her three teenage children in a tiny three-room apartment in the outskirts of Tokyo, near one of the nightclubs where she once worked as a contract worker, three train rides from the neighborhood of Azabu Juban. An old-timer in the community, or a "veterana" as many such women call themselves, Amanda first came to Japan at the age of eighteen in 1986 to work as a *talent*. She subsequently married a Japanese man, bore three children, and divorced the man, which is not an unusual outcome for Filipino-Japanese marriages, as their divorce rate is higher than 40 percent.[5] Now a permanent resident of Japan, Amanda is a welfare mother who receives a monthly subsidy of 300,000 yen (US$3,000) from the state, one that is contingent on her twenty-hour-a-week day job selling *obento* (boxed lunches) in high-rise office buildings near where we met in Azabu Juban. A highly energetic woman, she often speaks with a dramatic flair, stressing her speech by always ending with a long drawl on an accented last word. Amanda is not my friend's real name, but it is the name she told me to use when telling her story. When I asked her why, she said it is because she thinks the name Amanda is sexy. Though I had no intention of ever using her real name, Amanda explicitly asked me not to after she heard me say that the title of my book might include the words *sex, love, money*. Her teenage children, she told me, would misconstrue the meaning of the words. She did not want them to assume she is a sexually "loose" woman, someone who freely has sex for money with various men.

Time spent with Amanda unavoidably exposed me to the moral world of hostesses. Every chance meeting with a man—whether or not he was a customer—was a financial opportunity for Amanda. One such opportunity came to Amanda during one of our late-night excursions to Roppongi, a place largely known to foreigners as "Party Central" with its late-night dance clubs that cater largely to the non-Japanese: Western businessmen, English language teachers, U.S. military men stationed near Tokyo, and tourists. Plenty of Japanese men and women also visit the area. Not many Filipinos do, except during the daytime, because the Philippine Embassy is located no more than two blocks from the strip of nightclubs that make up the area's main attraction.

One evening a group of Amanda's friends met at Roppongi. I was among the last of the group to arrive there. With Amanda were her co-workers and, to my surprise, a tiny South Asian man, perhaps no taller than 5'4", whom I had never seen before. I never caught the name of the stranger seated next to Amanda. I did not talk to him; if he did speak, I never heard his voice because he was quite soft spoken. In Filipino, I asked Amanda where he came from, and Amanda responded to me in English for everyone at the table to hear, "Our friend here saw me at the [dance] club next door earlier. He came up to me and whispered in my ear that he likes fat women. So, I said 'Really? Baby, c'mon then, let's spend the night together!'" Expressing his desire perhaps had been his downfall, as Amanda had refused to let him out of her sight afterward and insisted on keeping him by our side for the rest of the night. Amanda laughed as she shared this story. The man just grinned, seemingly made uncomfortable by the sudden focus of all our attention.

It was a warm summer night with crowds of mostly young white foreigners walking the streets of Roppongi and speaking loudly in English. Amanda, her friends, and I just sat there, enjoying a pitcher of beer and a large pizza. Amanda was her usual lively self, singing and bopping her head to the music and joining in the friendly chatter of the group. We were talking about mundane things, like the weather and clothes, but I noticed that as we chatted, Amanda never took her attention away from the South Asian man. While talking to the group, she kept her hand on his thigh. She sometimes without even glancing at him would hand-feed him a small piece of pizza. It made their intimacy seem all the more real. Amanda also made sure that his glass of beer was never empty. Once or twice she even blew him a kiss. If one did not know Amanda or this man, one would have easily assumed that they were a couple. But I knew that he is not her type, so I could not help but wonder why she brazenly flirted with him.

We asked for the bill a little more than an hour after I had arrived at the restaurant. The bill came and, on cue, I pulled out my wallet. I noticed neither Amanda nor the other women bothered to make an overture to contribute to the bill. Instead, Amanda looked at me, frowned, and almost barked in Filipino, "*Sensei*, hide your money." Then, she gazed at the South Asian man, looked at him with adoring eyes, tilted her head, smiled, and then said in English in a sweet and high pitched voice, "This is not too expensive. You can afford this, right?" I then realized that Amanda had been treating this man as a customer, who in exchange for her attention would eventually have to reciprocate by financially compensating her with food and drink. Since I met Amanda, she has not called me anything else but *sensei*, which means "teacher." Among Filipinos in Japan, a *sensei* carries stature because one of the few but central links of Filipinos to dominant society are their children's schoolteachers. Teachers broker Filipino women's inculcation to Japanese society. By referring to me with this title, Amanda also lets those around us know of my higher status than a hostess, which is something others would never assume due to my racial identity as Filipino.

As it was past midnight and the subway system was closed, we planned to stay in Roppongi until past 5 o'clock in the morning, after the subway operated once again. Otherwise, it would have cost each one of us at least 5,000 yen (US$50) to catch a taxi ride home. We all assumed that Amanda's "customer" would come along with us as well. Still, Amanda made sure he felt welcome. We wanted to go dancing, and Amanda extended a special invitation to him, uttering with that soft voice she hardly ever uses except when talking to men, "Boyfriend, you will come along with us, right? We will dance, boogie. Let's groove tonight."

Amanda is a singer; she often uses song titles and lyrics when expressing herself in English. This campy behavior is accentuated with frequent comedic bursts of song from her. She often relies on songs to express herself. Once she burst out singing "She Works Hard for the Money" after I asked her about her day selling *obento*. I often laugh when I am with Amanda, but then I think I am supposed to laugh because she intends to make me laugh. As she has told me repeatedly, the primary job of Filipinas in Japan is to entertain, and without doubt entertaining is what she does most of the time she interacts with those around her, including me. Amanda embodies the stereotypical image of a Filipina in Japan: funny, vivacious, and extroverted. She perfectly fits the usual hostess job ads that I saw posted in local Filipino community publications: "Wanted: Attractive Filipina with lively and outgoing personality."

Following the lead of Amanda, our group walked toward the main thoroughfare of Roppongi to look for a dance club. Amanda suddenly ran up to me, leaving her "customer" a few steps behind. She grabbed my arm, complaining, "Oh my god, *sensei*. He is so smelly." Immediately afterward, she turned around and waited for him, threw him a beaming smile, and put her arms around his. She walked along with him as if they were a couple out on their umpteenth date. I continued to walk behind them, not knowing what to think of the situation.

Based on appearance, one would never have guessed the exchange between Amanda and me had taken place. Once in the club, Amanda grabbed her escort and encouraged him to dance along with her. She jiggled her large breasts seductively in front of him, held his hands, and encouraged him to twirl her around the dance floor. I often had to look away because the exaggerated seduction performed by Amanda was so over the top. It was ridiculous. The two other women with us were livelier than usual, giggling throughout the night, and when I asked them why they were so happy, they replied that it was because the whole night had been a cost-free outing for them; they were gleeful about having Amanda's "customer" cover our expenses. Throughout the night they were teasing Amanda and this man, suggesting in their knowing glances and coy smiles that a mutual attraction did exist between them. As far as they were concerned, Amanda's seduction of this man was a collective effort on their part, one that obviously entailed more work from Amanda but one that they, as the self-appointed "helpers" of Amanda, also encouraged in their actions.

By four o'clock in the morning, I was exhausted. To pass time before the train station opened after 5 AM, we walked to the twenty-four-hour Filipino restaurant in the area, a small establishment no more than 100 square feet in size. This restaurant caters to the visitors at the Philippine Embassy during the day and the smaller stream of Filipino club goers at night. It seats no more than eight around a counter that practically fills up the space of the restaurant. The place was empty when we arrived there.

This restaurant is infamous for its *lugaw*, rice porridge, usually made with chicken and ginger, as well as *dinuguan*, blood pudding, a dish that I personally cannot stomach but one that seems to be the favorite of not only my mother but of many hostesses whom I met in Japan. In hostess clubs, including the place where I worked, entrepreneurial Filipinas make their rounds selling bags of *dinuguan* to hostesses. Because of the blood, it is easier for it to come out lumpy and rough than smooth and even. The dish is difficult to cook. The main ingredients of *dinuguan* are the blood and internal organs such as the liver and intestines of a pig. Whenever a vendor visited my club to sell a bowl of *dinuguan*, she usually told us, "I cook it clean," which made me wonder if the dish is usually cooked dirty.

Amanda and her friends all ordered *dinuguan*. Afterward, she announced in English, "I am going to eat pig's blood." As it was nearing the end of the night, I wondered if Amanda was strategically making herself less attractive to this man. Eating this dish could make one repulsive. *Dinuguan* is colored black, a charcoal black that leaves the internal organs in it indistinguishable. Thick with a spoiled milk kind of texture, it soils ones tongue and lips black. If kissing a person who has just eaten *dinuguan*, one cannot help but imagine the lingering taste of the dish due to the discoloration it etches on the tongue and lips. For someone repulsed at the thought of eating pig's blood, it would be disgusting to kiss someone who had just eaten it.

Instead of *dinuguan*, I ordered a bowl of *lugaw*, which I thoroughly enjoyed as I ate it slowly and in silence. I sat there quietly, savoring the sharp taste of ginger, and trying to imagine how the night would end. I wondered how Amanda would extricate herself from this man whom she had dragged along with us the whole night to cover most of our expenses that evening. My thoughts were suddenly interrupted by a scream from Amanda who suddenly exclaimed, "Oh my God! He just told me that he wants to have sex with me!" I looked over in surprise at Amanda who in dramatic fashion was acting aghast and offended. The man in turn looked embarrassed. If he had not been so dark, he probably would have been red in the face. Amanda reached for his groin and then pulled her hand away, dramatically flaring it in the air as she screamed, "Oh, he is very excited. He really wants to have sex with me."

I could not help but laugh, trying not to imagine the size of the bulge that Amanda had just felt with her hand. At the same time, I could not help but feel badly for him, as I could only imagine his discomfort and embarrassment. Assuming he was not one to visit hostess clubs, I could not deny that he must have thought that Amanda had been leading him on the entire night. Yet, I could also see how Amanda could construe her behavior not as an invitation to have sex but as merely the titillation of its possibility. After all, the job of a hostess is to titillate. As I mulled over the flirtation that had transpired between Amanda and her "customer," I suddenly heard Amanda laugh and tell the man that she was only joking. Her humor seemed to ease the tension in the room.

For many outsiders, Amanda's actions that entire evening could be construed as cruel and malicious, resulting in the duping of an otherwise lonely migrant worker from South Asia. Based on how he was dressed, I could only assume that he was a low-wage worker who had just spent most of his week's earnings on Amanda and her friends, including me, that night. Our expenses at the club and restaurant reached more than 20,000 yen (US$200). However, most hostesses would disagree with the interpretation of Amanda's actions as cruel. Instead, they would argue that this worker probably had the best time of his life during the few hours that he spent with Amanda and her friends. The least they could get for showing him a good time would be some pizza and beer.

For hostesses, acts of flirtation do not necessarily have any meaning outside the visceral pleasure they evoke at the moment. In their moral world, one should not assume that acts of flirtation invite or suggest sex. After all, they believe that men should not think anything of a woman putting her hand on their thigh or telling them they look good. They should expect no more than the good feeling that these acts evoke for them at that very moment. Experienced customers know these rules, but it seems that the South Asian man did not. Yet, his unfamiliarity with the cultural codes of flirtation among hostesses is not one that Amanda thinks that she abused, as she demanded little of him materially that evening.

Near the end of the evening, Amanda surprised me by suddenly saying, "Let me pay for the bill." However, this gesture by Amanda should not have surprised me, as it had most likely been a strategic gesture on her part. The act of covering the bill transformed the relationship between the man and Amanda. It ended his position as a customer whom she would entertain and shower with attention in exchange for the financial compensation of subsidized meals and drinks throughout the night. Sure enough, on our way to the train station, she no longer put her arm around his but instead stayed close by my side and completely ignored him. He struggled to keep up with us as we walked quickly to the train station. In Tokyo, the train and subway systems stop running around midnight until 5 AM, making it particularly crowded in the morning hours on the weekends when sleepy crowds of club-goers rush home. As soon as we arrived at the station, we hustled our way to the lines forming at the ticket booth, purchased our tickets, and continued to the gates. It was as if this man we had been with the whole night never existed. As we continued to walk, I asked Amanda what we should do about the man. She responded, "Nothing." Then, she turned around, met his gaze, smiled and waved goodbye. He looked surprised. We left him standing there in the crowd of half-asleep club goers as we proceeded to the subway that took all of us back home.

Amanda epitomizes the being of a hostess. She can turn the act of it on and off. The incident with the South Asian man had not been unusual. When I have been with Amanda, every situation with men could turn into an opportunity to hostess. Amanda provides those around her with care, entertainment, and sexual titillation; in exchange she receives some material compensation. In Amanda's lifetime, such material rewards have ranged from a free drink at a bar to more materially advantageous items such as luxury apparel, household appliances, and real estate in the Philippines. Quite skilled in her craft, Amanda has not had to give into unwanted sex to acquire any of these material rewards.

Amanda has a very straightforward and simple understanding of her craft: "We are here to comfort them . . . The job of a hostess is to mix drinks, sing, and flirt inside the *omise*. If you want to do monkey business, then it is your own desire. It is up to you. It is not required by the *omise* for you to have your body used by the customer. We did not enter a *casa*."[6] How does Amanda provide comfort, then, if not with sex? First, she provides comic relief by constantly sharing jokes. Most customers are "tired from work, stressed" and go to clubs to be "destressed," according to Amanda; she tries to destress them by helping them laugh. Second, she extends her friendship by demonstrating what would seem to be genuine concern for the customer. She listens to the customer complain about problems at home and work, which could include angst over a girlfriend, boredom with a marriage, financial difficulty in business, or conflict with a boss. Third, and perhaps most significant, she makes her customer "feel like a man."

She primarily does this by demonstrating *lambing*, meaning "affection," but more precisely a distinct way of displaying affection that one might call culturally Filipino. *Lambing* is to cajole for affection while acting impish, coy, amorous, and sweet. For instance, a hostess can just ask a customer for a drink or demonstrate *lambing* to obtain the drink. Doing the latter would involve asking for the drink in a coy and indirect manner, expressing one's thirst in an exaggerated manner, pouting and looking sad if the customer chooses not to buy a drink, and reacting ecstatically and dramatically displaying gratitude if given a drink. *Lambing* exaggerates the desire of the person for affection.

In addition to demonstrating *lambing*, Amanda makes her customer "feel like a man" by flirting and suggesting her attraction; persistently demonstrating servility; and finally constantly throwing him praise, perhaps by complimenting his looks, outfit, or hairstyle. Most importantly, Amanda would *never* reject a customer blatantly regardless of his physical appearance. At most, she would deflect their demands for intimacy. She treats them all the same, whether ugly or handsome, old or young, thin or fat, and hygienic or dirty. She does not reject even those who "disrespect" her with unwanted advances such as a grope on the breast or a stolen kiss on the lips.

After years in Japan, Amanda has mastered the craft of hostess work. In her everyday life, she transfers her workplace skills to her daily interactions. As she proudly told me, "I am very good at it." Indeed, she is. Since coming to Japan, Amanda has always had a prominent male provider in her life, someone who rewards her materially in exchange for her attention. One such man is her boyfriend Hiroshi, an older, comfortably middle-class man who works in hospital maintenance. Amanda met Hiroshi while working as a hostess in a Philippine pub five years ago. At that time, Amanda was divorced from her Japanese husband but living apart from their three children, who lived in the Philippines while she tried to get back on her feet without the help of her ex-husband.

Drawn to her outgoing personality, the quiet and soft-spoken Hiroshi soon became a regular customer of Amanda's. He visited her at the club at least twice a week. He often took her out on a *dohan,* helping Amanda meet her monthly *oriage* at the club. Hiroshi started liking Amanda not only because she is funny but also because she listens to him, because she shows concern for his woes regarding the distance between him and his teenage daughter who lives with his ex-wife, and finally because she flatters him endlessly. He also probably likes Amanda because she needs him. When they first met, Amanda used to frequently cry on his shoulder over her misery about being apart from her children in the Philippines, who could only wait while she tried to save enough money to cover their relocation expense. Amanda's strategic use of pity paid off. Soon after meeting her, Hiroshi felt magnanimous enough to offer Amanda the money she needed to send for her children from the Philippines. He not only paid for each of their plane tickets to return to Japan but also purchased all of the household appliances in her apartment to help in the children's transition back to the country.

I have spent a lot of time with Hiroshi and Amanda. Her displays of femininity so as to draw out his feelings of masculinity and magnanimity were continuous to the point that they became natural. Whenever we ate out, I would notice Amanda always filled Hiroshi's plate. He would otherwise not touch any of the dishes on the table. Sometimes, Amanda would emphasize her servility by feeding Hiroshi, who would always giggle in excitement over this overt display of affection. Her servility and his paternalism are the norm in their relationship. In other words, she serves, and he pays. Her service also includes the work of magnifying his paternalism. For example, during dinner at a restaurant, she would often throw out the comment, "Oh, this is so expensive," to make him feel even more masculine and magnanimous. The consistency of her servility is sometimes exhausting to watch. At one point, I could not help but comment on how tiring it is for me to observe the unrelenting effort that she exudes when it comes to serving Hiroshi. To my surprise, she responded by telling me that she performed an even more extreme version of servility in the beginning of their relationship. As she said, "I was better before. For example, I used to give him a massage always. But now that I have him, I do not do so much. He complains. He asks why I don't serve him as much as I did before."

Interestingly, the lesser attention extended by Amanda has not translated to her lesser material rewards. Hiroshi still pays for most of the bills when we eat out, and he still lavishes Amanda with presents when she asks for them, including her new Sony Cyber-Shot digital camera and her even newer video iPod that she admits to me she does not know how to use. I even benefited from their relationship, for instance receiving two sweaters from Hiroshi under pressure from Amanda after I had dragged them both to one of my favorite clothing stores in Tokyo for one last look during my very last night in Japan. Amanda sees one of her central missions in life is to make her partner—whoever he is—"feel like a man." Indeed, spending money on Amanda and her friends makes Hiroshi feel like one.

Hiroshi is only one of many men who have had the pleasure of receiving Amanda's affections. Prior to Hiroshi, there was Tomo, who also met Amanda at a hostess club in Tokyo. Except for the last few years, Amanda has worked consistently as a hostess in Japan, initially as a *talent* in the late 1980s and then as an *arubaito* in the 1990s. In the early 1990s, Amanda worked as a hostess not far from the apartment she shared with her husband. She also kept a day job as a cashier in a vegetable store but opted to continue to work at night to earn extra money that she could send to her family in the Philippines. Back then, Amanda earned 1,800 yen an hour as a hostess, which had been more than double her minimum wage salary as a cashier.

Tomo had been a customer of Amanda's at the bar. Attracted to him not for his looks but for his generosity, Amanda soon turned him into a "boyfriend" and not just a regular customer. Amanda had a full-fledged affair with Tomo, who she claims was a much better father to her children than her husband was. Tomo, unlike her husband, helped her children with their homework every afternoon. Within one year of their relationship, he managed to convince Amanda to leave her husband and return to the Philippines with her children. He promised that he would financially support Amanda while she awaited her divorce in the Philippines, after which he would marry her and bring her back to Japan with her children. Amanda's marriage had been failing for some time before she met Tomo, so she was only too happy to accept his offer. For almost six years, Amanda and her children lived in the Philippines with the US$5,000 monthly allowance provided by Tomo, who could afford such a large remittance because of his work as an established film director in the pornography industry. With this money, Amanda purchased a house in the Philippines. She could not save much, because she sent all of her children to private schools and hired full-time nannies for each of them. She also had not set up a self-sustaining business because, as she said, "I was stupid. Easy money, easy gone." Tomo visited Amanda in the Philippines regularly, at least four times a year. However, their romance ended after six years, which forced Amanda to sell her house, go back to Japan, and set out on her own without her children. As she said, "I think Tomo got sick of sending me money, so it stopped. Before I knew it, I started accumulating debt to keep up with the expenses. So I decided to come back to Japan."

In addition to her two "real boyfriends," Hiroshi and Tomo, Amanda held onto many other "boyfriends" from the *omise* but, as she clarified to me, "only in the *omise*" and with no "private relationship" outside the club. Amanda did not maintain a sexual relationship with any of her "*omise* boyfriends" but treated them with affection as she did the South Asian man we met at Roppongi. Amanda admits that many thought or hoped that they would eventually have a sexual relationship. So she usually received more than just a free meal from these men. Two even sent her close to US$1,000 a month for some time during her hiatus in the Philippines. But those "gifts" did not last as long as those from her "real boyfriend" Tomo.

Perhaps Amanda tries to maximize her material gains from men because of her tremendous financial responsibilities in both Japan and the Philippines. Since her divorce, Amanda has not received any financial support from her ex-husband. She is also saddled with the responsibility of financially supporting her mother in the Philippines. To supplement her subsidy from the state, she sometimes works in a small *izakaya* (after-work restaurant for shared dishes and drinks) for ten hours a week. She sends all of her earnings from the *izakaya* to her mother. Still, the money that she makes is not enough. Amanda tells me, "It hurts to send money to my family in the Philippines. I do not work at night in an *omise* anymore. You have children yourself, and you cannot help but think that you wish you were just putting the money to pay for the insurance of your children or in an educational plan."

Despite her ambivalence, a deep-seated obligation prevents Amanda from turning her back on her family in the Philippines. As far as Amanda is concerned, ignoring those who need her would translate to bad karma. As she explained,

> But you are thinking you are a mother, too. And you want your own children to do that same thing to you in case you need it when you are older. You do not know what is going to happen to you when you are older. Someone like me, I have no savings. So, I am just thinking that if I do good to other people, it will return. So, I am good to my mother and do good things for my mother, because I know my children will not abandon me later . . . If you do bad, that will come back to you.

Amanda knows that the limited financial resources of her extended family in the Philippines make her a valuable resource. None of her other siblings work abroad. Although all of them graduated from college, each one of them only earns enough to support his or her immediate family. Not without difficulty, Amanda sends US$400 to her mother every month. Sometimes resentful of her obligation, Amanda recently shared with me her annoyance over her mother's parting comments on the telephone, "Please take care of yourself. What will happen to us if we lose you?" These comments made Amanda feel like a money machine.

Ironically, Amanda complains about being for her family what she makes the men in her life be to her. Yet, without these men in her life, Amanda could probably not afford to be there for her family. Because of her many "boyfriends," it is rare for Amanda to ever pay for her own expenses. From her pantyhose to her facial cream, she has continuously managed to find a customer willing to buy these items. Not all hostesses have been as successful as Amanda. Her dynamic personality, confidence, and skills make her exceptionally talented as a hostess. It is ironic that Amanda and I became friends because, in sharp contrast to Amanda, I have never had a male provider take care of me in my adult life. For this reason, Amanda feels sorry for me.

Amanda is troubled that I am without a husband or children. She also pities me for never having had a man buy me an iPod or a digital camera. To help me out, she has taken it upon herself to consciously demonstrate to me the skills that I would need to acquire a male provider. One such opportunity for a lesson came when an old customer from the last bar where she had worked as a hostess five years ago called and invited her to dinner. Amanda insisted I come along to not only get "a free meal," but to "practice your femininity." Unlike my *mama-san* at the bar, Amanda does not care whether my posture exudes femininity. Amanda instead wants me to acquire feminine mannerisms like those she displayed to the South Asian man. Among other feminine virtues that she believes that men want of their prospective wives, she wants me to practice deference and servility.

The old customer turned out to be a salaried man in his early forties who wore a crisp short-sleeved white shirt neatly tucked in black slacks. He met us after work, closer to nine o'clock in the evening. He looked tired, as he stood there waiting for us near the train station, but his eyes lit up and he smiled from ear to ear as soon as he saw Amanda. The customer was not very attractive. Yet, Amanda still told him in Japanese, "You are looking very handsome. Nice hairstyle." In the way that Amanda had become immune to the unwanted sexual overtures of her customers, I had become indifferent to the empty compliments that she consistently threw at men. Amanda gives men these compliments not only for their benefit but also for my own. She does it to fulfill the job she gave herself of training me to acquire femininity. Amanda introduced us, and afterwards we proceeded to the ramen shop around the corner. While we ate, Amanda continuously gave compliments to the Japanese man, asking him questions to show interest in his life and repeatedly asking him if he wanted something else to eat or drink. When he got up to go to the restroom, she turned to me and asked if I noticed how she acted and to remember to do the same whenever out on a date. When alone with Amanda, I usually received unsolicited suggestions on how to act like a woman, from the proper application of makeup to the comments I should make to men. For instance, she once advised me to tell my dates, "Oh, honey, are you tired? Let me massage your shoulders." I took note of her advice but cringed at the thought of displaying servility to men.

Near the meal's end, our bill arrived. To our surprise, the customer then asked Amanda, "Should we split it?" Knowing that Amanda had been short of money, I volunteered to pay for our share of the bill, which did not even amount to 2,000 yen (US$20). Amanda then tried to part ways with the customer, telling him, "My friend has to buy all these things at Don Quixote [the 24-hour discount mall]. So we have to go." The man should have gotten the hint, but instead he protested and complained that he thought we were going to a karaoke bar. Trained to never reject a customer directly, Amanda relented but told him that we first had to go to the mall. But the man should have known better, because Amanda completely ignored him as we walked for more than ten blocks to the mall.

Relieved that the customer had volunteered to ride my bicycle so she and I could talk, Amanda was fuming. In exchange for her flattery, Amanda expected a free meal. Customers are always supposed to pay for a bill unless the hostess insists otherwise. While glaring at the back of the customer, who leisurely peddled my bicycle, Amanda complained, "I cannot stand cheap men." Amanda could not believe that he made us pay for the ramen. As she explained to me, we would not have spent any time with him if not for a free meal. Otherwise, his company would not have been worth it. We did not need him to have a good time, but he needed us to have a good time. We can entertain each other. We often do without men. He, like most men, did not entertain us. We entertain them. We entertained him. We exerted energy for him. We gave him attention. And for our work, we had gotten nothing. Explaining this to me further irritated Amanda.

When I asked how we were going to get rid of this man, she replied, "Do not worry, *sensei*. I am a master at this, getting rid of men whom I do not want." I was ready for anything but fearful that a confrontation would erupt, as I am not adept at handling customers outside the club—or, for that matter, inside the club. In amazement, I wondered how this customer could not sense the irritation of Amanda. How could he be so clueless? A beginner in the world of hostesses, I myself knew that he had stepped outside the script.

I did not know how Amanda planned to retaliate, but I assumed that she was concocting a plan. Once we arrived at the mall, I retrieved my bicycle and parked it along the row of other bicycles. She told the customer to wait for us inside the mall in the lobby by the front entrance while we shopped for gifts I would later give other hostesses helping me out in my study: boxes of ramen and bags of chocolates. We shopped for about an hour, during which time he would regularly call Amanda who would then tell him to hang in there. But Amanda never planned to meet him again. She told me that we would keep him waiting there. I suddenly became concerned, asking Amanda what would happen to him if he no longer had a train ride home as it was near midnight. She told me she did not care. Both Amanda and I lived in the neighborhood, while he lived across town in a neighboring city. A cab ride home would cost him more than 10,000 yen (US$100). I worried that he would see us. I started panicking, fearing the customer would find us and stop us in our tracks. Amanda calmly told me not to worry, to go home, and that she would talk to me in the morning. She was so nonchalant that it seemed like she had frequently left men waiting for her; indeed, she assured me that she had as we walked outside the mall, picked up my bicycle, and proceeded to hail a taxi for Amanda.

Although my lessons in femininity did not quite pan out that evening, I did learn from Amanda about the moral compass that guides her interactions with customers. Amanda knows the value of her time and company. She thinks that those around her should do so as well. Unfortunately, the customer whom we met for ramen did not. According to Amanda, neither did the South Asian man. As far as she was concerned, the acts of affection she displayed had not intentionally suggested the possibility of sex between them. She was quite insulted that he had thought so. As she explained, "That man was so offensive. He expected me to have sex with him after letting me eat pizza and drink beer. Oh my God! How cheap does he think I am? You cannot pay me even US$500. If you are not my type, I cannot go for you." If Amanda had not at all been attracted to the South Asian man, then why did she flirt with him? Why did she hold his thigh? For Amanda, the answer to these questions is simple. She did it out of recognition for what he gave her. As she told me, "It's because he was buying food for me." Amanda held his thigh to express her gratitude and not to suggest sex. By holding his thigh, Amanda reciprocated for his material generosity with the gift of ensuring his emotional satisfaction at the temporally bound moment of its occurrence.[7]

Amanda explained, "That man enjoyed the moment. At that moment, he felt we were a couple . . . He wanted to come with us, so I let him come along with us." Giving him the pleasure of feeling like her boyfriend at the moment enabled Amanda to accept his offering of beer and pizza with no guilt, no qualms, and no feeling that she had taken advantage of him. Reciprocating allowed her to walk away from the moment with no sense of further accountability for the free food and alcohol. The payment of emotional gratification during that moment was a fair exchange, in Amanda's mind. After all, in the moral world of hostesses, visceral pleasures that one grants men do not necessarily mean anything more. In other words, we could assume them to be temporarily bound or, in the words of sociologist Elizabeth Bernstein, see them as moments of "bounded authenticity."[8] Yet, differentiating the situation of hostesses from the sex workers studied by Bernstein, the acts of affection displayed by hostesses could also mean more. They could transform to a more durable romantic relationship. Knowing of this possibility, some customers take the risk of extending gifts to hostesses for the purpose of winning them over romantically or sexually. The South Asian man clearly took such a risk, but he unfortunately lost.

Notably, Amanda does not solely inhabit the moral world of hostesses. Different moral codes concerning love, sex, and money apply to Amanda when it comes to the social relations that she maintains with friends and family. Solely out of sympathy for a fellow migrant, for example, Amanda is currently debating whether she should marry a Kurdish refugee whose visa is soon to expire. Amanda expects no financial reward for this act. My relationship with Amanda also occupies a different moral world, which is something I cannot say about all the hostesses whom I met in Japan. Some hostesses I met formulaically turned me into a customer, constantly extending to me acts of affection in the apparent hope that I would reciprocate with visits to their club. Peachy for instance constantly sent me e-mails telling me to "take care" and asking me to visit her at the club because she supposedly missed me. In contrast, most hostesses did not consider me a customer. Peachy's co-worker Sean, for instance, always insisted on paying for our meals outside the club so as to reciprocate for the money I spent inside their club. Amanda likewise did not want our "friendship" to fall within the parameters of a hostess-and-customer relationship. For instance, Amanda visited me at home when I was bedridden with the flu, cooking me a pot full of *lugaw* spiced with ginger. After I sprained my ankle from falling down a flight of stairs at the subway station, Amanda picked up an ice patch for me at the pharmacy. When I asked for the cost of the patch, she responded, "Priceless, because it comes from my love."

THE RULES OF ROMANCE

In the moral world of hostesses, certain rules shape the play of sexual titillation for money. First, romance is conditional on the provision of material goods by customers. Similar to the sex workers observed by anthropologist Patty Kelly in Chiapas, hostesses usually measure the worth of a relationship with a customer based on its material benefits.[9] Most hostesses would not entertain romantic relations with customers who are unable or unwilling to provide them with material goods. Second, in their moral world, signs of affection and demonstrations of sexual attraction—a caress on the cheek, a hand on the thigh, whispers of affection, or the holding of hands—cannot be assumed to mean something beyond the visceral pleasure they evoke at that very moment. In the mainstream local culture of Japan or the Philippines, signs of affection usually insinuate a desire for companionate romance. In the world of hostesses, they do not. Similar to the sex workers studied by Bernstein, hostesses manufacture love so as to induce a temporally bound emotional thrill among their customers.[10] While this is the case, porous boundaries also define the emotions of customers and hostesses, enabling the possibility of a more durable relationship, such as marriage, to form between them.[11] However, this is a risky assumption for either customers or hostesses to make because it is highly likely that each is just feigning love. As the undocumented worker Marie once said of customer–hostess relationships, "Many are fooled, and many place themselves in a situation of getting fooled." This leads to the third rule of romance in the moral world of hostesses: Performances of love often do not reflect the feelings of hostesses. In other words, they are not necessarily in love when performing the "emotional labor" of acting in love.[12]

In explaining emotional labor, Hochschild draws from the work of Konstantin Stanislavski to distinguish between "surface acting" and "deep acting." In "surface acting," one merely pretends to be the character.[13] For instance, a hostess acting in love is not really in love. In contrast, in "deep acting," one embodies the traits and emotions of their character, becoming the actual character. In this scenario, a hostess genuinely feels love for the customer. I found that Filipina hostesses more frequently engage in "surface acting" and not "deep acting" when projecting emotions of love toward their customers.[14] Although some hostesses fall in love with customers, most are dissuaded by the likelihood of various emotional risks, including unrequited love, unacknowledged pregnancies, and forsaken promises of love and money. These risks encourage hostesses to impose stopgaps against the development of their feelings for customers.

THE QUESTION OF DECEPTION

Romantic affairs between hostesses and customers are highly risky ones. Each party frequently throws empty promises of love to the other to maintain the façade of romance. Because of the high likelihood of deception, hostesses minimize the risk of getting hurt by seeking inexperienced customers. The lesser the experience of the customer, then the more likely that he will buy into her professions of love and reciprocate by spending liberally on her. The greater their experience, then the less likely he would do so. As one experienced *talent*, Angie, explained,

> We target the people who do not know any better. We go for those who have never been to the Philippines. That is why they think that we have feelings for them, that we are boyfriend-girlfriend. When you go back to the Philippines, they support you. When you come back from the Philippines, you are still talking. But then it is impossible to avoid them from asking, for looking for something in return. What we

tell them is to wait. A veteran customer will request you for three weeks, and if they look for something, then you come up with an alibi. Any alibi. You tell them to wait. Others disappear right away, the veterans. That is why we prefer to get those who are not veterans. . . . If you are with a veteran customer, it is hard, because the customer already knows your ways. They become a veteran because they were once broken-hearted. When they court someone else, they immediately look for sex.

Veterans are those who are likely to know how to speak Filipino, have visited a hostess in the Philippines already, and have maintained long-term relationships with other Filipina hostesses. They are also those likely to be familiar with the styles used by hostesses to display affection. Due to their familiarity with the culture of romance in Philippine clubs, they are likely to brush aside and ridicule the recycled ways that Filipina hostesses express love and affection. Charmaine, for example, told one of her customers who invited her to accompany him in an out-of-town weekend excursion, "I like you, but you have to wait for me if you really love me." Charmaine, who had recently returned to hostess work after a ten-year hiatus in the Philippines, was surprised when her customer scoffed at her response. A veteran customer of Philippine clubs, he explained to Charmaine, "In this day and age, that style no longer works. That is no longer effective." Charmaine learned that her style is "old school." She further explained: "He told me that my style was from three years ago. That style no longer exists. He told me courtships only last for one month these days. If you do not give [into sex] after one month, they will move to another woman. They will request another woman."[15] Experience makes veterans much wiser than other customers. They are the customers who know that signs of affection from hostesses do not necessarily bear any meaning outside the act.

In the distinct moral world of hostesses, perils would await inexperienced customers, as patrons would need specialized knowledge of the codes of conduct of hostesses to understand their gestures of affection. Experienced customers usually know better than to read into displays of love demonstrated by hostesses. At the same time, they know that they must also lavishly spend on hostesses to open the possibility of love and sex. However, lavish expenditure does not necessarily guarantee a customer sex with a hostess. After all, the goal of hostesses is to facilitate the liberal spending of customers and the provision of sex could lead to its abrupt end.[16]

Seasoned customers are not always so easily duped. Their skillful manipulations could actually result in hostesses chasing them rather than the other way around. Adept means of promising money and marriage could also lead to the deception of hostesses. For instance, some hostesses shared with me stories of being defrauded by customers who disappeared after borrowing their money or offering to have their jewelry professionally cleaned. Even worse, some told me that the men who impregnated them refused to recognize the paternity of their children. These examples suggest that as much as hostesses can deceive customers, they can also fall prey to deceitful customers. To minimize these risks, hostesses not surprisingly enter romantic affairs with extreme caution.

Regardless, romantic affairs are quite risky for customers as well. Without doubt, many customers become victim to the seduction of hostesses. Many—although not all—cannot help but feel that there must be more to the acts of affection extended to them by hostesses. Likewise, many refuse to believe that these acts mean nothing more than calculated suggestions of love. As one customer, Mr. Takahashi, astutely put it, "Going to a hostess club is like going to a casino. You know the odds of winning are against you, but a good hostess fools you every time."[17]

Perhaps because many hostesses cater to a working-class clientele or perhaps because most hostesses do not have sex with customers, I found that they usually receive nothing more than token presents from customers, such as an occasional gift of perfume, a handbag, and/or expensive jewelry. Courtships could also best be described as a practical means of survival for hostesses. As part of their courtship ritual, it is not unknown to hear of customers providing a hostess with a weekly supply of groceries or a case of ramen. These examples suggest that courtships are not so much glamorous as merely a practical means of livelihood for hostesses.

We do hear of hostesses receiving substantial material rewards from customers. Stories of hostesses winning the jackpot of a *bahay, lupa, kotse,* meaning "house, lot, car" from customers abound in the community. *Suwerte,* meaning "lucky," and "wise" are the words used to describe these winners. While members of the community look up to the winners of a *bahay, lupa, kotse,* they interestingly also condemn those who win these gifts deceptively. Members of the community frown upon those who secure these presents with false professions of love or stories of a sick mother in need of expensive medical care in the Philippines.

A few hostesses did admit to deceiving customers. Stories of scamming customers for thousands of dollars circulate among hostesses in Japan with some of my interviewees still reeling with guilt over their own deception of previous customers. One admits to taking US$10,000 from a customer to cover their supposed wedding in the Philippines only to leave him waiting for her at the airport in Manila. Another had one customer purchase a house and lot in her name in the Philippines only to break up with him as soon she had the title in her hands. She also never told him that she already had a family in the Philippines. However, the actions of these few hostesses had been more the exception than the rule.

"WHAT IS INSIDE THE HEAD IS DIFFERENT FROM WHAT IS IN THE HEART": SURFACE ACTING AND THE DISPLAY OF LOVE

Performing the emotional labor of love, which is one of the central ways that hostesses try to accumulate emotional capital, eventually becomes routine for them. They continuously evoke emotional displays of affection, whether inside or outside the club. For instance, one regularly sees a hostess gaze lovingly at the most unattractive customer and hears her passionately utter such comments as, "You are looking handsome tonight." Sometimes a hostess would intersperse these displays of affection with demonstrations of jealously, which in effect naturalizes her emotional performances. Angie, for instance, described, "Let us say that he looks at another woman and he makes a comment that she is sexy. I pretend that I am jealous. Then, I respond, 'well, go *shimei* her then.' Then their feeling is that you really like them." Her co-worker Jeanne added, "Sometimes they do it just to challenge you. They do it to find out if you have feelings for them. Of course, that is work, so you let the customer think that you are jealous. What is inside the head is different from what is in the heart."

The use of calculated displays of emotions suggests that hostesses resort to surface acting when attempting to forge an ongoing relationship with customers. It has been said that surface acting, or the feigning of emotions, comes at the risk of "emotive dissonance."[18] However, recent studies on emotional labor have found that experiences of emotional discrepancies at work, meaning having to display what one does not feel, do not necessarily lead to feelings of alienation; instead, alienation emerges from one's lack of autonomy over one's display of emotions.[19] Moreover, the provision of good service that arises out of emotional labor, even in situations of "emotive dissonance," could lead to worker satisfaction.[20] This happens when hostesses find satisfaction in the emotional thrills that their actions generate for customers. In other words, they relish showing their customers a good time.

Distance more than dissonance defines the experience of emotional labor for hostesses. Hostesses can keep their distance because they have redefined their displays of love to mean little outside the actual act.[21] By redefining the moral signification of their displays of love, hostesses avoid feelings of estrangement. However, the porous boundaries between "surface acting" and "deep acting" could turn a customer into a romantic interest and potentially could leave hostesses at risk of emotional vulnerability. Such a risk discourages hostesses from plunging into sexual liaisons with customers at the same time that it encourages them to develop sentiments of emotional distance.

Hostesses use particular strategies to keep their emotional distance from customers. These include the creation of a public, that is, club, identity distinct from their private identity. Sociologist Wendy Chapkis likewise found that sex workers construct multiple identities as a strategy of managing their emotions at the job.[22] Switching identities allows them to control their emotions at will. Hostesses distinguish their identities inside and outside the club by using a different name at work, rarely ever using their given name at a club. Some hostesses use a different name for every six-month stint they do in Japan. Others use the same name throughout their careers. At one club I visited, the names of hostesses who served me one evening included Prada, Fendi, and Smile. Despite the popularity of kitschy names in the Philippines, where it would not be unusual to meet women named Apple, Baby, Honey, and Melody, I could only assume that these particular monikers were pseudonyms.

A hostess also uses a different name at work to more easily hide her personal information from customers. Hostesses can lie more easily about their marital status or relations with other customers when using a different name. Interestingly, many morally conservative hostesses think of their job as sinful not because it requires sexual flirtation but because it requires them to lie to customers. As Serela, a hostess who is now a born-again Christian, complained, "If you work at night, you have to deal with customers. They will ask you if you are married, and you cannot tell them the truth. There are times like that. So it is not good."

For a hostess, the use of a different name at the club distinguishes her club persona from her "real" persona. Many told me that who they are inside the club is quite different from who they are outside the club. Yuki, for instance, clarifies that her persona in Japan is very different from what it is in the Philippines. She described:

> If you are in the Philippines, and there is someone you like, you are shy, you do not look like a flirt. Here, you look like a flirt. Because you have to tell them, "I love you. You are my boyfriend. Marry me." Could you do that in the Philippines? No, right? If he is not my boyfriend, I will not call him "honey." I will not call him "my husband." But here you are able to do that. You are like an actress. Whatever opportunity there is, you grab it. You ride every opportunity. You go with the flow. That is the way it is here. Who would do that in the Philippines?

For Yuki, different moral standards control her behavior with the opposite sex in the Philippines and in Japan. Her actions accordingly change from one place to another, subverting the notion that one ever holds real and authentic feelings. In the Philippines, romantic overtures carry plenty of underlying connotations, most significantly the suggestion of one's genuine feelings of love, while in Japan they do not. In the club, romantic overtures and references to customers as "my husband" or "honey" often mean nothing beyond the erotic thrills they engender at that particular moment.

Because they feel that their actions inside the club do not reflect their "real" persona, hostesses can be more forward with customers. To passionately pursue men is not a reflection of being easy and loose women, as would be the case in the Philippines. For example, hostesses often rely on the infamous "missed call" to lure customers into the club. In the community, to do a "missed call" means to call another cellular phone with the intention of hanging up the line before the person answers the phone. Knowing that their cellular phone number would appear on the phone of their customer after a "missed call," hostesses wish for customers to return their "missed call." "Missed calls" enable hostesses to avoid charges on their cellular phone. Unlike in the United States, cell phone companies in Japan do not charge receivers but only callers for their usage. If customers choose to return their "missed calls," hostesses immediately try to entice them back to the club. If customers ignore their "missed calls," hostesses usually know not to take their rejection personally. Yet they can only do so if they manage to keep a certain degree of emotional distance from customers.

In addition to relying on "missed calls," hostesses also bait customers with flirtations. Some do with humor. Charmaine, who had more than a decade of experience in Japanese hostess clubs, would joke around with the customer, for instance, telling him over the telephone: "I am hungry. I have not eaten yet. Why don't you come over? Maybe you would like to feed me." Others would boldly project feelings of emotional attachment to the customer. This includes Yuki, who described her strategy as "*walang hiya*," meaning "shameless." She stated, "I would 'missed call' them. Then, they call me back. I do not force them to come. If they call back, I do not tell them, 'Come here. When are you going to come here?' I will just tell them, 'Are you busy? That is too bad because I am missing you.'" Yuki explained that she could only be so forward with customers because she knew not to take their rejection personally. Her emotional declarations of missing them did not reflect her genuine feelings of ambivalence.

To keep customers on their toes, hostesses must design creative styles of emotional titillation and develop a wide range of strategies for demonstrating feelings of love and devotion to customers. For example, Yuki claimed to have multiple scripts that she selectively used with customers. Sharing many of them during our interview, the following is one scenario that she used to avoid sex while keeping its possibility still open:

> Customers ask for sex. . . . They always say that if I really loved them, then that I need to have sex with them. Of course, you tell them that you love them even if you do not love them. . . . I will tell them, "I realized that I like you. You are in my heart, but I am controlling it because I am only going to be here for six months. We are not going to be together for a long time. So it is probably fate that nothing more will happen between us." Those are the kinds of things that I tell customers.

Yuki did not need to tell us that her job as a hostess required the talent of an actor. It clearly did. As she put it,

> The work here, *ate* [older sister], is like being an actor. You actually are better than the actors in the Philippines. In the Philippines, they have a script. They have the opportunity to redo the scene. The director can say, "Cut." You can ask the director for

guidance on what you need to say. You get the assistance with your makeup. It is very upscale. Here we do not have a script. We come up with whatever we tell customers. We do different dramas. We give different reasons. We give different stories . . . I have learned many skills. It is funny.

Yuki was not alone in channeling her acting abilities while at work. All the other hostesses do, particularly in their declarations of love and affection for customers.

There is no formula to the romance that transpires between hostesses and customers. In response to my question of how long they are able to keep the interest of a customer, hostesses gave quite a wide range of time periods. I heard that most customers stay around for no more than a month, as they usually know that hostesses are unlikely ever to give into sex if they have not already done so by then. In the case of contract workers, hostesses complained that customers with sexual interests began to disappear a month prior to the end of their contract, as these customers suspected that they would end up losers in the courtship exchange. Yet hostesses have learned that the provision of sex does not necessarily prolong courtships, teaching some to refrain from sex and others to demand a material reward prior to every sexual encounter.

MAINTAINING EMOTIONAL DISTANCE WHEN CUSTOMERS BECOME BOYFRIENDS

Without doubt, the presentation of gifts, promises of marriage, and pronouncements of love by customers nurture romantic sentiments among hostesses and encourage the possibility of sexual intimacy. As Lenlen told me in passing one day, "[Customers] visit you a lot. They give you presents. They are sweet to you. It is just natural that you develop feelings for them." Hostesses sometimes cannot help but engage in deep acting when flirting with customers. Deep acting occurs when the display of emotions by hostesses coincides with their inner feelings. Moments of deep acting are likely to result in greater physical intimacy between hostesses and customers because hostesses determine the extent of intimacy they maintain with customers based not only on their material benefits but also on their feelings of affection and sexual desires. In other words, greater physical intimacy is more likely to take place when hostesses feel love or lust for their customers.[23]

While a customer could stay "nothing-but" a customer, he could also become a friend, lover, or partner.[24] To distinguish their social ties with each customer, hostesses engage in "relational work" and distinguish their rules of behavior and meanings of monetary exchange with customers according to the type of relationship that ties them.[25] In other words, the rules and meanings of the monetary exchange between hostesses and their customers would change depending on whether the customer was a boyfriend, just a friend, or a mere customer. Displays of affection from hostesses, initially representing nothing more than the actual act, could transform to connote affection, love, and other emotions, whether fleeting or durable, with the meanings of these acts changing according to the relationship between the hostess and her customer.[26]

In their performance of relational work, hostesses often use different strategies to protect and shield themselves from emotional vulnerability. To maintain their emotional distance from customers, hostesses carefully and selectively earmark the type of relations they will pursue and maintain with each one of them. Notwithstanding those who choose to engage in commercial sex freely, in most cases a hostess engages in physical intimacy only with a customer who has become a "boyfriend," meaning not just a regular customer but someone with whom she actually maintains a relationship outside the club. In many cases, those who shower hostesses with presents such as jewelry, electronics such as a TV or DVD player, designer handbags, and other luxury items are those likely to be chosen as "boyfriends," telling us that money talks when it comes to romance. However, not all those who lavish hostesses with presents become "boyfriends." Additionally, not all "boyfriends" can expect sex. It seems that material generosity alone is rarely reason enough for sex. Hostesses are selective, choosing to become lovers only with those for whom they develop some level of physical attraction. They tell me this is true even if only "5 percent."

Sometimes, insatiable lust and not money accounts for their want of a "boyfriend." It is in these cases that customers are likely to reject the sexual advances of hostesses. Those who do not lavish hostesses with gifts, meaning those who do not participate in the courtship ritual of clubs, are more likely than those who do to want no more than just platonic flirtations with hostesses. Some interviewees shared with me stories of their rejection by such customers. One of them was the eighteen-year-old Amy, who complained to me about how her "crush" rejected her proposition for them to have sex. As she said, "He is my crush. If he invited me to go to a love hotel, I would go. But he does not want to make me his girlfriend because he said I am too young . . . He is forty-three years old. But he really is my crush . . . I am the one who kisses him. But the only thing he wants is friendship." Rejections by customers are as surprising as they are rare. Hostesses usually have to deflect the sexual advances of customers.

In addition to earmarking their relations with customers, hostesses also attach moral values to various forms of intimacies, distinguishing certain sexual practices, particularly those involving genital penetration, as more sacrosanct, reserved for the most special of customers.[27] These would include those who have lavished them with the most gifts, those they find attractive, or those whom they love. Hostesses frequently abide by the moral compass of "*walang mawawala sa akin*," meaning "nothing will be lost from me," when determining the level of physical intimacy they allow customers. As such, the physical intimacies that hostesses maintain with "boyfriends" need not involve genital penetration but can involve merely what they consider pragmatic acts of heavy petting, kissing, and oral sex. Hostesses maintain this moral compass to somewhat abide by the script of moral purity that Philippine society upholds for Filipinas. They also do it to protect themselves from disease and unexpected pregnancies and lastly for their emotional protection. Denying genital penetration, they reason, enables them to keep some emotional distance from their customers. For instance, one of my co-workers, Erika, maintained an ongoing relationship with a married customer who gave her a 30,000 yen (US$300) monthly allowance. When I asked Erika what her "boyfriend" received in exchange for her allowance, she told me a "*chupa*," meaning fellatio, but "never sex." Although many hostesses claim to limit the extent of intimacy that they maintain with their "boyfriends," the estimated 150,000 Japanese–Filipino children in the Philippines, unrecognized by their Japanese fathers, do remind us that many hostesses do choose to engage in sexual intercourse with customers.[28]

Hostesses also protect themselves from emotional vulnerability by delaying sexual encounters with "boyfriends," assuming that the longer they fend off and string along a customer, the greater the likelihood that he would give her presents. Regardless of the inner feelings of hostesses, they prefer customers who wish to pursue durable and not only fleeting romances. The risk of choosing the wrong "boyfriend," however, is perhaps the reason why most of the hostesses whom I met in Tokyo did not have a boyfriend outside the club. Hostesses admit that they have lost in courtship exchanges by choosing a "boyfriend" who, soon after sex, rejected them, reneged on his promise for a visa or material support, disappeared after impregnating them, and ignored their repeated "missed calls." Stories of these types of heartbreaks circulate among hostesses. Knowing and hearing of such experiences make hostesses all the more cautious. Consequently, they hold out on sex as long as possible and give in only if such an experience would also give them physical pleasure or the guarantee of material reward. In this way, they can avoid a catastrophic loss in their pursuit of romance.[29] To avoid getting hurt, hostesses also retain multiple "boyfriends" inside and outside the club. Maintaining relations with multiple partners—not necessarily in equal degrees of intimacy—eases the pain of rejection, many told me. When maintaining multiple boyfriends, hostesses usually designate one as their "favorite" boyfriend.

Lastly, to protect themselves from getting stiffed and consequently hurt, hostesses also participate in a straightforward exchange of sex for goods, meaning that they would not engage in sex with boyfriends unless they were somehow compensated materially beforehand. In some cases, the hostess would demand to be taken shopping prior to visiting a hotel. One hostess who uses this strategy is Nikki, who secured material rewards prior to every sexual encounter as a way of protecting herself from losing in the courtship exchange. Nikki said, "Whenever I need money, he gives me. We meet and every time we do, he already expects us to be sweet and loving. But before we become sweet, he takes me to a shopping center, and I point to him the thing that I would like." When I asked her what kinds of presents he purchased for her before they "become sweet," she enumerated:

> Different things like a stereo, DVD player. Usually things that many people can use in the Philippines. My personal things are not very nice, they are not brand-name materials, but when you enter my house, it is very nice. What I want is to go home to a nice place that is comfortable. Luxurious a bit. I live in the province, so there is no point in owning Rolex or Bulgari. There are people who give presents like that. But me, if someone is going to give me something that expensive, I would rather they just give it to me in cash. In that way, I can invest the money in business.

Nikki is not the only hostess who received material compensation for sex. Many, but not all, did. As Amanda once explained to me, the provision of a gift guarantees that they get something out of the sexual encounter with the customer. If rewarded with a gift, then a hostess would not mind having a disappointing sexual experience. Moreover, if the boyfriend opted never to see her again after the sexual encounter, then at the very least she had received some compensation for her provision of sex. In other words, hostesses seek material presents before a sex act so as to guarantee they do not lose in the game of courtship. In the community, hostesses who are able to secure material compensations prior to sex are described as "wise."

Interestingly, hostesses were keen on explaining to me that their performance of sex in exchange for money and goods does not entail prostitution. Perhaps the moral stigma of prostitution makes them shun any association with the act despite the fact that what they do fits the definition of the term, that is, performing sexual acts in exchange for money. According to Nikki, prostitution would mean the absence of selectivity, meaning that would imply that it had not been her personal desire regardless of money to engage in sex with that particular person. She explained that she could get a present from that boyfriend, as she could from many other customers, even without sex, but instead she chose to engage in sex with that particular person.

Dismissing the common assumption that Filipina hostesses in Japan are prostitutes, Nikki explained,

> I think they pick on Japan, because they see we do well when we go home. We dress in glamour. We wear brand name clothes when we go home. That is why they think that we are all prostitutes. People do not imagine that we are appreciated here, that people give us expensive things because that is the way Japanese people are. When they appreciate people, they do not say "I love you"; instead they show it by giving material things or money. But people, when they see us, they think, "Oh, this person probably [had sex with] that person, that is why they get something in return." But you could easily fool someone here, and the next day you have a present. That is probably why they think prostitution happens here: because we get so many material things. They think that it is brought by prostitution. Me, I do not think of myself as a prostitute, because I do not do that.

Although Nikki rejected the idea that she engaged in prostitution, she nonetheless would still insist on receiving material compensation prior to sex.[30]

If not prostitutes, what are they then if they expect the provision of goods for sex? In the viewpoint of hostesses, the logic of prostitution assumes a "nothing-but" perspective in the exchange of sex for money, meaning the performance of sex by the prostitute is solely for the purpose of obtaining money.[31] In their world, sex with "boyfriends" involves more than the simple acquisition of material compensation. Hence, they insist that it cannot be reduced to prostitution. For them, sex sometimes involves a degree of emotional commitment on their part.[32] Moreover, sex is not always just a one-time occurrence. Lastly, the experiences of sex with customers are as diverse as the multiple social ties maintained by hostesses with customers, pushing us to acknowledge the different social meanings underlying declarations of love, acts of sex, and more generally displays of affection that hostesses project at work.

An emotional paradox of distance and entanglement underlies the labor of hostesses. While they keep their emotional distance from customers, they struggle to bolster the emotional attachments of customers toward them. This paradox potentially engenders feelings of emotive dissonance among hostesses. Yet, such an estrangement would occur only if hostesses have a unitary identity. I find that they do not, as evidenced by the fact that hostesses maintain multiple moral standards. For instance, their rules of behavior in the Philippines are quite different from the rules they follow in Japan. In the Philippines, they act demure and shy when around men; in Japan, they shamelessly flirt with them. The moral standards of hostesses also shift according to their social relation with customers. Hostesses demonstrate not only the multiplicity of their identities but also the multiplicity of their emotions when they gauge their actions according to multiple moral standards. We should thus recognize that the conscious and unconscious manipulation of emotions by hostesses is a labor strategy they use for financial gain.

CHAPTER FIVE

CULTURES OF FLIRTATION

The opinion of hostesses is so low. But the reality of hostessing is that you are the one who does your job. You are the one who sets your boundaries between you and your customers.

Marie, former talent, *visa overstayer since 1991*

HOSTESSES OFTEN FROWN ON THE DISmissal of their work as prostitution. *Prostitution* has been defined as the "act or practice of engaging in promiscuous sexual relations especially for money."[1] Following this definition, one could argue that to flirt is in itself a promiscuous activity, and hence the act of flirting for money would constitute prostitution. Yet most hostesses I met in Japan would disagree with this assertion; they make a marked distinction between flirting for money and having sex for money, with the latter constituting prostitution in their perspective. At the same time, they would also qualify that to have sex for money is not automatically prostitution. The context and dynamic of the exchange would distinguish its meaning, with those who receive money from their boyfriends considered not to be prostitutes and those who do from strangers for one-time encounters perceived to be so.[2] Hostesses may disassociate their work from prostitution because of the stigma of the occupation; yet they also tend to have an unsophisticated view of prostitution, dismissing it as nothing but a casual sexual encounter that does not require the skills of flirtation that they as hostesses must cultivate to secure customers.[3]

Regardless of these distinctions, most hostesses do not engage in sex with their customers. Most offer customers nothing more than the lure of sex or the promise of sex, a promise that oftentimes remains unfulfilled. Some clubs, including transgender clubs, are even known to ban sexual relations between hostesses and customers. After all, people know they can patronize establishments other than hostess clubs to buy sex in Japan. Clubs frequently advise hostesses to avoid sexual relations with customers to protect their business reputation as legitimate venues for professional entertainment. While most clubs do not promote the formation of sexual relations between hostesses and customers, they do usually turn a blind eye to such activities when they occur outside the club.

Although the provision of sex is not necessarily part of the hostesses' jobs, the public in Japan, the Philippines, and the United States still view all hostesses as victims in need of rescue from forced prostitution. Fueling this myth is their representation as victims of forced prostitution in sensationalist media reports.[4] This one-dimensional image clouds our view of foreign hostesses in Japan. Not accounted for in this characterization is the fact that hostesses maintain varying degrees of sexual intimacy with customers. Aware of this, most hostesses who participated in my study could not give me a uniform description of their sexual activities at the club. When asked to describe the nature of sexual relations between customers and hostesses, most said, "*Nasa kanya*," meaning, "It is up to the person." Interestingly, hostesses did not say, "It depends on the relationship," which is an answer one could expect, considering that hostesses are more likely to engage in sexual relations with a boyfriend than someone who is just a customer.

By saying "*nasa kanya*," hostesses suggest that they believe—perhaps naïvely—that they and not customers and club management centrally determine the degree of sexual intimacy that they maintain with customers. From spending time with hostesses inside and outside clubs, I did learn that many of them do not have sex with customers but also that some do. From circling Philippine clubs in Tokyo, I also noticed that customer-hostess interactions could sometimes remain platonic throughout the evening but at other times could become sexually charged immediately. In some clubs, I observed customers freely touch the bodies of hostesses; in many others I noticed that hostesses and customers barely made any physical contact. These different gradations of sexual intimacy are not at all addressed in media depictions of hostesses but suggest a more complex picture of their work. To correct misconceptions not only on the forced prostitution of hostesses but also more generally on the sexual activities tied to hostess work, this chapter describes the extent of sexual intimacy between hostesses and customers, illustrates the contexts in which sex is likely to occur between them, and lastly describes the circumstances in which hostesses find themselves vulnerable to coerced sexual labor.

Contrary to hostesses' one-dimensional portrayal as victims of forced prostitution, I found that they carry a semblance of control over their interactions with customers and accordingly maintain different levels of sexual intimacy with them. Migrant hostesses play with their gender and sexuality at work, where customers pay per hour to receive care, accolades, sexual titillation, entertainment, and servility. Hostesses accordingly feed, praise, touch, perform by singing or dancing, and playfully flirt with customers. Yet they do so not uniformly but instead according to their morality. The extent of sexual intimacy between hostesses and customers usually coincides with the moral boundaries of both the hostess and the customer as well as the moral regime of the club. I found that the moral views of migrant Filipina hostesses could be placed in three groupings: *moral conservatives* (those who view paid sex as immoral), *moral rationalists* or *amoralists* (those who have no moral qualms with paid sex), and *moral in-betweeners* (those who morally reject the direct purchase of sex but accept its indirect purchase). While I place hostesses in these moral categories, I recognize that their moral views are not static but instead shift according to ideology and experience.

While the moral boundaries of hostesses establish their sexual limits, the club's moral regime ascertains the customers' and management's sexual expectations. By *moral regime*, I refer to the moral standards and prevailing notions of proper and improper uses of sexual intimacy in hostess clubs. We could imagine problems potentially arising when the moral views of a hostess clash with the moral regime of her workplace. Without question, moral clashes between hostesses and clubs could leave hostesses vulnerable to forced labor. For instance, a morally conservative hostess placed in a club that promotes sexual liaisons between hostesses and customers could be pressured to engage in sexual acts. Still, we should not assume that her situation would inevitably result in forced labor. After all, she could escape. She could also expand her moral views and come to see paid sex as an acceptable activity. However, she could as easily stay morally adverse to paid sex and find herself stuck at her club because of her unpaid debt to middleman brokers. It is in this latter circumstance that she could find herself coerced to perform sexual labor. The possibility of sexual coercion, in other words "human trafficking," raises the question of whether the vulnerability of a few hostesses warrants the rescue of all of them as advocated by the U.S. Department of State and its supporters. In this chapter, I argue that it does not.

HOSTESS WORK

Comfort. It is called comfort work. We are to comfort them. We are there for someone to lean on, so they have a friend. Here in Japan, everyone is working and staying alone. They are not with their mothers. So, if they go to the *omise* of the Filipino, they think that they have their friends there, their family. In the Philippines, it is different. If the men go to the club, they get sex. But that is not the case in Japan. It is different. It is not a brothel. (Amanda, former *talent* and *arubaito*, now an elderly caregiver, long-term resident of Japan)[5]

The culture of Japan is that, after work, they need to relax and unwind. What we do for them is we are there to make them laugh. We are there to amuse them. How does that make us bad? It is not like we go out to . . . do you know what I am talking about? Our work is not like that. That is why I can say that I never saw anything bad that I can say is bad. (Irene, former *talent* and *arubaito* hostess, now a housewife with a pending long-term resident visa)

What is hostess work? To be a hostess does require one to wear scanty attire; but, as the former hostesses Amanda and Irene claim, it does not require sex. While flirtation is the basic premise of the job, hostesses flirt to provide what I have identified as care work, sexual titillation, entertainment, and boundary work.

"Care work" involves paying attention to all of the customer's needs: serving his drinks, lighting his cigarettes, feeding him, and constantly singing his praises "to make him feel special" or "to make him feel like a man." At hostess clubs, care work is as personalized as it is routinized.[6] The demonstration of care, for instance, begins when hostesses welcome customers into the club by screaming in unison, "*Irasshaimase*," meaning "welcome." At some establishments, management even requires hostesses who are not seated with customers to stand up and scream "*Irasshaimase*" when a customer enters the club. At Manila, the club where I worked, the hostess assigned to the table would have to kneel and bow her head before proceeding to wipe the customer's hands clean with a moist *oshiburi* (washcloth). Then, she had to prepare the customer's drink, asking whether he wished to mix his alcohol with water or tea. After mixing the drink to his liking, she then offered him the beverage with her head bowed down. As the *mama-san* repeatedly demonstrated to us, we had to take care of the needs of the customer while establishing a feminine and submissive demeanor. For instance, I had to mix drinks with my head slightly tilted to one side, my face set in an idiot grin, and my legs slightly crossed with one leg placed in front of the other. Then, if the customer offered me a beverage, I would have to wait for him to drink his before drinking mine. Before taking a sip of my drink, I would also have to remember to thank the customer for his generosity and demonstrate my subservience by sharing a toast, not only with my head bowed down but also with my glass lower than his. As one coworker once said to me, "You are below a customer. So your glass must always be below his."

Servility manifests not only in these displays of subservience but also in hostesses having to stay attuned to the needs of the customer. The *arubaito* Jane explained:

> Our master [meaning boss or club owner] tells us to improve our work. [pauses] What our master likes is the ashtray is replaced right away when it is full; and when a customer smokes, it is lit right away. When the glass is empty, you refill it right away. When they want to sing, you immediately get the [song] book, or you program the song in the karaoke machine. The master is happy when he sees you are attentive to the needs of the customer. That is it.

Demonstrations of extreme subservience heighten the masculinity of customers. Because the construction of masculinity always occurs in relation to femininity and vice versa,[7] the demonstration of *feminine* subservience in the performance of care work by hostesses such as Jane ensures that customers feel masculine or "like a king," as many of my informants expressed to me.

In having to always demonstrate their subservience, hostesses with rare exception are never in a position to blatantly or directly reject customers. For this reason, they cannot refuse any request made by a customer. For instance, I learned that if a customer asked me to sing, I must sing. If he asked me to dance, I must dance. If he asked for a kiss, I must blow a kiss, as I never wanted to give him an actual kiss. And when he offered me food, such as the fried sausages customers ordered for 1,000 yen (US$10), I had to hide my urge to cringe and must actually take a bite of it if I could not come up with a clever excuse not to eat it. Care work, I learned, entails the practice of selflessness, completely ignoring one's needs and desires for those of the customer.

In addition to providing care work, hostesses must also entertain customers at the club. Hostesses entertain customers not only by singing and dancing on stage but by also providing lively conversation in the hybrid language of English-Tagalog-Japanese.[8] Giving us an example of how she entertained customers at the table was the *arubaito* Maki, who described, "I just amuse them. I try to make them happy. I invite them. I play games like paper, scissors, and stones. I play different games like that. I massage them inside the *omise*. [She laughs.] It is just like that. It is just shallow amusements they want." In contrast to the platonic style of Maki, lively conversation for most other hostesses at the club is usually of a sexual nature. I often overheard my co-workers initiate "lively conversation" with customers by pointing their customer's attention to their breasts, describing how they masturbate every day, and mentioning the sex acts they like. If not quite able to keep the customer's interests that way, my co-workers would then resort to singing and dancing. I could never quite talk about sex so openly with customers, which explains why the *mama-san* rarely ever assigned me to a table by myself. I was often just the designated "helper," an extra body whose job it was to do the dirty work of cleaning the table but whose presence was an added cost to the customer's food and drink bill.

So as not to be a complete deadweight, I did help and kept busy by cleaning ashtrays, refilling drinks, and singing while a co-worker entertained the guest with lively conversation. I also assisted in the sexual work expected of us. At the club, hostesses sexually titillate customers by intimating a relationship of sexual intimacy with them. Hostesses do this by physically holding the hands of customers, massaging them, holding their thighs, or verbally by vocalizing their physical attraction, whether real or not. I gradually grew accustomed to the suggestion of physical intimacy between customers and myself, because intimacy at a hostess club is usually nothing more than the insinuation of sex. Not long after beginning work as a hostess, I learned to share the attitude carried by most of my co-workers that "nothing will be lost from me" (*walang mawawala sa akin*) if I sometimes let customers touch my thigh and put their arm around my shoulder. As one interviewee succinctly put it, "I will not get pregnant from a hug."

When describing the types of sexual work performed by hostesses, it is difficult to make a blanket statement about the activities they do, as the extent of sexual intimacy they maintain with customers is far from uniform. As many told me, intimacy depends on the situation and differs according to the type of social tie they maintain with the customer.[9] For instance, the sexual intimacies that a hostess maintains with an "*omise* boyfriend" or a "club boyfriend" would be different from a "real boyfriend" with sex more likely to occur with the "real boyfriend" because of the feelings of affection she actually holds for him. At the same time, the degree of intimacy that hostesses maintain with *omise* boyfriends is not uniform with material provisions, good looks, and kindness increasing the likelihood of sex.

By maintaining different levels of sexual relations with customers, hostesses do a wide range of "relational work."[10] Hostesses actively determine intimate boundaries with customers, resulting in variegated levels of intimacy and multiple social relations. Most maintain platonic relations with the majority of their customers and distinguish a select few as boyfriends; this designation makes a customer a candidate for sexual intimacy. By earmarking customers according to level of intimacy, hostesses have to ensure that customers abide by the parameters they establish. This effort requires their performance of "boundary work," which refers to efforts they make to limit the extent of their sexual intimacy with customers.[11] Boundary work is necessary because hostesses cannot reject a customer directly. Instead, they can reject customers only indirectly. In other words, they can reject customers only via deflection.

At the club, customers constantly extend sexual advances to hostesses, usually expecting hostesses not to concede to these advances but to coyly deflect them. A common sight in hostess clubs, for instance, is to see hostesses ward off customers who try to rub their groin against them while dancing. The hostess cannot directly tell a customer to stop; instead she must rely on creative ways to avoid the customers' sexual overtures. This is why one often sees hostesses force customers to twirl them around the dance floor or hostesses with protruding behinds when slow dancing with customers. Discussing the skills required in physical deflection, the self-identified "comfort worker" Amanda explained:

> You entertain the customer at the *omise*, but really it is illegal for them to touch you on the breast or anywhere. You can fight the customer if they do that. That is the exception because that is a sign of disrespect. That is not part of the rules, but that just happens because Japanese men like to do that. So of course you have to learn how to protect yourself in a way that you do not hurt the feeling of the person you are resisting . . . The play there is if someone touches you, you have to know how to react. You have to flirt, for example, and say in a coy voice, "Oh, stop it. I am ticklish there. No." You do that. You have to do it in a way that you do not hurt the feelings of the customers. You need to learn how to do that. It is psychological reversal. You cannot react mad. You cannot avoid that kind of harassment because they drink alcohol. Your job is to entertain, not to have someone feel up your body. But that is up to the person. We cannot avoid them touching us because they are drunk. So what we do, we need to trick the drunken man . . . Your job is not to let them touch you. . . . You do not have to give them sex, but you have to entertain the customer.

Many hostesses describe having to deal with "men who grope you and try to kiss you" as one of the worst aspects of their job. My co-worker Teresa struggled for instance with the constant sexual harassment of customers. As she stated, "Here in Japan, you cannot say that you will not tolerate these acts of disrespect. You cannot say that you will refuse to entertain him . . . Even if your customer is sexually harassing you, you cannot do anything about it. You still have to entertain them because they are paying."

When performing boundary work, hostesses walk the fine line of deflecting the advances of customers without blatantly rejecting them. This requires the development of skills, styles, and strategies of rejection. Even first-timers soon learn creative means of doing boundary work. Cindy, for instance, would hold onto the hands of the customer to prevent him from groping her, but if she let her guard down and he managed to touch her inappropriately, she would then pretend to scold him, mockingly spanking his hands while saying in Filipino, "*Ikaw, ang likot likot mo talaga*," meaning "You, you really are quite unruly." Afterwards, Cindy would "pretend to laugh" to further hide her annoyance. When performing boundary work, hostesses hide their negative feelings, including those of disgust and irritation. Once I had to hide my annoyance when a customer caught me off guard and grabbed my breast. Out of courtesy to the proprietors of the club, I had to laugh it off so as not to lose his business.

What is the permissible extent of boundary work? To what extent can hostesses reject the advances of customers whom they designate as merely regular customers? By "regular customer," I refer to those who are not boyfriends.[12] The hostesses I interviewed often responded by saying, "*nasa kanya*," meaning "it depends on the person." Some hostesses allow more physical intimacy with their regular customers than others; some choose to participate in the direct purchase of sex, and some do not; lastly, some refuse to sit next to customers at the club. Determining these different extents of intimacy are the moral values of hostesses and the moral boundaries they maintain when it comes to the purchase of sex.

MORAL BOUNDARIES OF HOSTESSES

Although hostess work does not necessarily involve the direct purchase of sex, it is still considered sexually immoral in mainstream society because it defies the "hostile worlds view" on intimacy and economy.[13] However, in the world of migrant hostesses, the "hostile worlds view" is only one of the multiple moral constructions in the exchange of sex and money. As I mentioned earlier, there are three moral groupings of hostesses among Filipinos in Japan. *Moral conservatives* are hostesses who maintain only platonic relations with customers. They achieve this by constructing customers as "fictive kin," for instance viewing a customer as a father or an older brother whom they could turn to for emotional and material support. *Amoralists*, in contrast, are hostesses who willingly participate in the direct purchase of sex. They see nothing wrong with receiving monetary rewards for the provision of sexual favors to customers. Lastly, the largest group of women falls under the category of *moral in-betweeners*, as they are neither conservative nor amoral but fall between these two more extreme groups. Moral in-betweeners would *never* participate in the direct purchase of sex. They use their eroticism to gain intimacy with customers but would at most, if they ever did so, allow physical intimacy only with frequent customers who would pay them not directly but indirectly with gifts, including cash and in-kind presents. In other words, they have sex only with boyfriends.

These three groupings are not mutually exclusive, as the morals of hostesses are not static but instead shift along with changes in their ideology and experience. Religious beliefs, economic needs, peer pressure, and work routines all shape the views and morals of hostesses. In the process of their migration, the construction of morals for hostesses does not necessarily constitute of a teleological progression from the "hostile worlds view" espoused in a Catholic country such as the Philippines toward a greater acceptance of paid sex as encouraged by the customs at hostess clubs. Instead, some experienced hostesses could remain staunchly conservative, particularly born-again Christians. In contrast, others could become more open to the practice of commercial sex the longer they stay in Japan.

Moral Conservatives

Minorities among hostesses, moral conservatives are those most likely to agree with the "hostile worlds view" as they reject the direct purchase of sex as sinful and minimize their sexual banter with customers. Embarrassed about the stigma associated with hostesses, moral conservatives hide the nature of their work from family and friends in the Philippines, view their job as their last resort for employment, and consciously attempt to desexualize interactions with customers. They desexualize their interactions by constructing customers as "father figures," "big brothers," or friends. Not completely rejecting hostess work, moral conservatives can do their job only if it is done with minimal reference to sex.

Most of the moral conservatives whom I met were *arubaito* workers. Among contract workers, moral conservatives tend to be first-timers who had not expected their close interactions with customers to be sexually charged. I met only two such women. Because they are unlikely to pursue this line of work, it is actually rare to meet moral conservatives in hostess clubs. Moreover, if a *talent*, a moral conservative is also one of those more likely to be sent home to the Philippines prior to the end of her contract because management is not likely to tolerate those unable to adjust smoothly to the sexual undertones of club culture. For instance, stories circulate in the community about how one or two *talents* had been sent home to the Philippines because they cried hysterically every night.

Among *arubaito* workers, moral conservatives are usually born-again Christians, who do this work because of their minimal options in the labor market. Language difficulties, the lack of experience, or the hostess's undocumented status blocks her entry into the formal labor market of Japan, thus limiting her to hostess or domestic work.[14] Rie, a born-again Christian, was a typical moral conservative, as she would rather not have done hostess work but found herself without other job options. She managed to do the job because she thought what you do with the job and not the job in itself is immoral. Responding to my question on whether doing hostess work is immoral or not, she stated:

> No, it is what you do that makes it bad. Inside me, I do not think that it is bad just as long as you know how to control yourself [with customers], and you know what you need to do, and you do not let the customers take advantage of you. There are some customers who offer you indecent proposals. They want to take you to a hotel. And they promise to get you all these things. But it is in you to handle this situation in whichever way you want.

Despite the moral dilemma she faced from doing hostess work as a born-again Christian, Rie managed to "tolerate" her work conditions because she was employed at a morally conservative bar. Rie worked at a small bar where most customers were elderly men from the neighborhood who sometimes visited the bar accompanied by their wives. Not imposed with a sales quota, Rie earned the low wage of 1,000 yen (US$10) per hour for no more than six hours a night. Still, Rie would rather have worked elsewhere and done a job that she would not have felt inclined to hide from her fellow church members. At the time of our interview, Rie was looking for a job as a domestic worker in an expatriate household, as foreign diplomats and corporate executives could sponsor her temporary residency. Yet, after months of failing to secure work in a private household, she was somewhat resigned to doing hostess work. Her youth and lack of experience with child care seemed to deter potential domestic employers from hiring her.

Moral conservatives do not necessarily perform hostess work more poorly than their more morally liberated counterparts. After all, sex is not a requirement of the job and is not desired by all customers. Flirting without the provision of sex is a skill that hostesses develop with experience, including moral conservatives, and one in which the thrills of titillation could repeatedly attract customers into returning to the club. In one hostess club I visited, for instance, the highest sales earner was Rachel, a devout Catholic whom I often saw at church on Wednesday afternoons. When I asked her co-workers Amy and Reggie why they thought Rachel attracted the most customers at their club, they responded that it was because Rachel was good in Japanese, nice, deeply religious, and lastly beautiful. I learned that every afternoon Rachel would post a biblical saying on a small white board on the refrigerator that she shared with eleven of her co-workers. She also led them in a weekly prayer group before work. Rachel did not think that flirting with customers was necessarily sinful, but she told me that to engage in sex with customers, whether paid or unpaid, would be. Among moral conservatives, Rachel was one of the more sexually tolerant ones. In contrast, others thought that one unavoidably sins when doing hostess work. For this reason, moral conservatives are likely to quit if they have other labor market options in Japan.

For instance, one former hostess, Serela, quit and sought other employment after she converted to Christianity. Serela thought of hostess work as sinful because it tempts the woman to pursue extramarital affairs and encourages her to lie to customers. Likewise, Beth saw her past work as a hostess in disagreement with her core being as a Christian. When asked whether her religion disagreed with her work in an *omise*, Beth responded, "Yes, it is bad. Because it is in the Bible. It says in the Ten Commandments that you should not lie. The work at night requires you fool people." By "fooling people," Beth referred to the routine of making false professions of love to customers and lying about her marital status. Still, moral conservatives such as Beth and Serela do not completely dismiss the job of hostesses. They still see it as viable employment despite its moral challenges for conservatives. They also do not morally shun hostesses who engage in sexual relations with customers, with many saying it would be wrong for them to judge the actions of others. Personal circumstance, they told me, would result in varying moral beliefs with some able to accept the use of their sex and sexuality at work—and others not.

Amoralists

In contrast to moral conservatives are amoralists, who reject the notion of commercial sex as immoral. I met plenty of amoralists, but only a few admitted to that status during our interviews, perhaps because the stigma of prostitution deters hostesses from publicly admitting their involvement with commercial sex. Amoralists engage in commercial sex inside or outside the club. Commercial sex inside the club includes fondling or discreetly performing a hand job.[15] Commercial sex outside the club would entail the direct purchase of various services, including fellatio and sexual intercourse.

I encountered amoralists in informal settings in the community, during coffee after church services in the afternoon or after work in the early morning. Once a group of my friends surprised me when one of them began to describe her experience giving a hand job to a first-time customer at her club, vividly describing her disappointment over the size of his penis and complaining about her measly tip of 1,000 yen (US$10) for her efforts. Others soon chimed in and shared strategies for using sex to garner tips at work. In another instance, a friend who chose not to participate in my study complained to me about how a john she met at a nightclub refused to pay her after their encounter. These stories that I heard regularly suggest that some hostesses participate in commercial sex.

Yet there seems to be a moral gauge in the community in which playing around with customers inside the club is more acceptable than engaging in commercial sex outside the club. I noticed that hostesses would freely admit to "crossing the line" with customers inside the club but not outside the club. The few who admitted to engaging in commercial sex outside the club described paid sex as "easy money," valued the financial gains of sex with customers, and saw the use of their body for money as morally acceptable. Those who did were mostly long-time residents of Japan and described themselves as having become "wise" from experience with customers who broke their hearts or fooled them with empty promises of love or marriage. They also included those in dire economic circumstances.

One amoralist whom I interviewed was Aurora, a former hostess in her mid-forties who was working in a factory. More comfortable in admitting her paid sexual liaisons than her real age during our interview, Aurora offhandedly mentioned her experience with sex work when I asked her about the sexual morality in hostess work. She stated: "No, it is not bad. It is in the woman . . . It is up to her. It is in the Filipina. Someone like me, for instance, is without anything. I have had customers try to give me 50,000 yen (US$500) for a one-night stand. Of course, if you have no money at all, you will bite, won't you?" However, most hostesses whom I met in Japan were unlike Aurora as they would not "bite." Most hostesses adamantly denied that they would ever engage in the direct purchase of sex. Still, not all are moral conservatives because they would not necessarily dismiss all paid sex as personally immoral.

Moral In-Betweeners

Most Filipino hostesses in Japan are what I would call moral in-betweeners. The moral standards of in-betweeners encompass a wide range of principles concerning the intersections of money and sex. They will not hesitate to kiss frequent customers and use their sexuality to seduce customers, but they usually will not have sex with customers. As the moral in-betweener Dianne said, "I just kissed [customers]. But I did not have sex with them unless they were my boyfriend." Some do maintain ongoing relationships with customers outside the club but view their sexual relations with customers not as prostitution but instead as a form of "compensated dating" or a "compensated relationship." Unlike amoralists, they would never participate in one-night stands and "just charge for one sex act." Even if they received financial compensation from their sexual partners, they still distinguished themselves from amoralists, whom they labeled as "prostitutes" or "hookers."

Ela, a "retired" hostess who has been in Japan for more than twenty-five years, explained:

> We are formally not hookers. We are just using our head. If we are going to get together with a Japanese, we make sure that we get together with one who has money. Me, I also got a boyfriend. . . . I think people just misinterpret us to be hookers for the reason that Japanese men give us money. But I don't think we are hookers. What I mean is that our boyfriends are giving us money. Hookers are different. Hookers are those who stand around one area and get picked up by men. Isn't that what a hooker is? Someone coming up to you and asking you how much you will cost? In Japan, they are very formal. You go on a date, but you do not talk about money. That is in you if you can artfully persuade them. [In a weeping tone] "Oh, my mother died. Boo hoo hoo. I don't have money to pay for the hospital." That kind of drama

is what you could give them. They will then give you money because they feel sorry for you. That is when they will give you money. That is the style here. But asking for money for sex is not something that we do here.

Unlike moral conservatives, moral in-betweeners such as Ela accept the use of their eroticism at work, openly flirt and banter with customers, and engage in different degrees of intimacy with customers. Moral in-betweeners do not think of commercial sex as immoral. At the same time, they do not morally accept all forms of commercial sex. It depends on the circumstances, many told me. Moral in-betweeners view the direct purchase of sex as morally unsound but consider its indirect purchase morally acceptable. For instance, some hostesses whom I met had no qualms accepting a monthly allowance from a "sponsor" who in exchange would receive sexual services on a regular basis, but they would never have accepted a direct payment for the provision of any service. In other words, the relational context of paid sex defines its social meanings with exchanges that take place in the context of a durable relationship considered morally acceptable by moral in-betweeners and those that take place in the context of a fleeting encounter not.

Moral in-betweeners draw a limit to the extent of sexual intimacy they maintain with customers. They usually would allow no more than a hand on the thigh or a kiss with a closed lip on the cheek. Unlike amoralists, moral in-betweeners reject the direct exchange of sex for money. Yet, unlike moral conservatives, they are willing to maintain a financially beneficial sexual relationship with customers—but only if the exchange of sex for money occurs indirectly. For example, moral in-betweeners would engage in paid sex only with boyfriends, whether they were real or *omise* boyfriends. As Marietta, a veteran hostess with fifteen years of experience in Japan, described,

I do not do one-night stands. For example, you think, oh, this one keeps on coming back. He has been seeing me since I was a timer.[16] Oh, I should probably give in because he has been coming to see me for so long. He has been coming to the club regularly for the past six months, plus he comes with a lot of presents. So, of course, if you get a guy to do that, you feel inclined to pay him back somehow. . . . Do you think that you are just giving them your body? You have them use your body? No, because he is like your boyfriend in the *omise*. You do not think of them as a customer. You start calling them "boyfriend" in the *omise*.

Marietta admitted to having sex outside the club with some customers as a reward for their business, but she also acknowledged that she would reward only those customers whom she found attractive, even if only slightly at "5 percent." Like Marietta, many hostesses confess that their boyfriends would probably not be their choice of a boyfriend if not for the fact that they had been their frequent customers in the club.

The sexual practices of moral in-betweeners and their self-described activity of "compensated dating" with boyfriends mirror the culture of *enjo kosai* in Japan, which literally means "compensated dating" among schoolgirls—high school students—and sometimes women. In Japan, there is a cultural phenomenon of schoolgirls dating older men for the purpose of securing luxury designer goods such as a Chanel or Hermes handbag. *Enjo kosai* is sometimes understood as prostitution, but like their schoolgirl counterparts, Filipina hostesses would disagree with this view. Distinguishing *enjo kosai* from prostitution are the comments of a Japanese schoolgirl that was published in a news report. As she explained, "High school girls don't really sell their bodies for just 20,000 yen or 30,000 yen . . . People misuse the phrase *enjo kosai.* Real *enjo kosai* is when a girl plays the role of a lover to a rich man in exchange for 200,000 yen to 400,000 yen a month. We do not consider one-night relationships *enjo-kosai.*"[17] Likewise, Filipina entertainers or hostesses do not see the direct purchase of sex as a form of "compensated dating." Instead, they practice "compensated dating" with those customers whom they have distinguished as their "boyfriends."[18]

Bakla

Transgender hostesses are often stereotyped as having less conservative moral standards than female hostesses. For instance, members of the community often told me that transgender hostesses are more likely to engage in sex with customers than are female hostesses because society would not scorn them for doing so. The logic here is that, as biological males, transgender hostesses would not be subject to the same moral standards as their female counterparts. Some *bakla* would agree. Explaining the different moral standards between *bakla* and their female counterparts in the club, Rafaella nonchalantly described her ability to freely engage in sex with customers and distinguished her position as one free of the limitations brought by moral constraints on women. As she stated, "[Customers] will say, 'Later I want to taste you. I will wait for you outside of the club when it closes.' And you know how a *bakla* is always available. [She laughed.] Especially if the customer is good looking, the *bakla* will run out and go for free." Recognizing her relative sexual freedom vis-à-vis females, Rafaella continued, "The woman has a worth. And the *bakla* always want to have a story of what happened to them one night." While a *bakla* could dismiss encounters with customers as adventures, their female counterparts cannot, as they are constrained by particular moral standards that limit their sexual freedom.

Although society does not hold them to the same moral standards as females, transgender hostesses still construct and negotiate moral boundaries in the process of labor migration. "I am no whore" was a comment made by many when asked if they engaged in paid sex with customers. Not immune to mainstream "hostile worlds views" on sex and money, the question of sex work also raises a moral dilemma for transgender hostesses. Most would refuse to engage in the direct purchase of sex. Only two admitted to doing so. Some even chose to project a virginal image during our interview, responding with coyness when I asked about their sexual involvement with customers and reacting with indignation to queries about their possible engagement with sex work.

Although they sometimes choose to project an image of moral purity, transgender hostesses are quite aware that they are not held to the same moral standards as female hostesses. Unlike their female counterparts, they can admit to their sexual engagement with customers without the risk of moral condemnation. However, the extent of their amoralism usually stays inside the club, meaning that they would not engage in the direct purchase of sex outside the club but would instead allow customers to fondle them only inside the club, and then for a price. To make extra tips for the evening, transgender hostesses admit to pressuring customers to touch their bodies for a fee. Hostesses use the expressions of "hold up" or "bang bang" to describe this practice, as these idioms convey the purpose of the act which is to entrap customers into a position of having to give them money before the night's end.

The practice of "bang bang" does not exist in female hostess clubs but is one that transgender hostesses resort to if they fail to garner any tips during *show time*. Club management evidently does not condone this act and actually bans it in some workplaces. Providing us a vivid description of this practice was the retired entertainer Ana:

When [customers] enter our establishment, we tell them, "Oh, you want to touch my breasts. Then you have to pay me. OK, hold it. Squeeze it however many times you want." This is because there will be nothing lost from us. A woman cannot do that. Can you see a woman making that same offer: "OK, hold my breasts and then pay me?" I know that a woman is capable of making such an offer as well, but they have to do it in secret.

For many transgender hostesses, letting customers touch their bodies for a fee is the extent of their amoralism, which suggests that they abide by different moral rules inside and outside the club. Most transgender hostesses would not take their amoralism outside the club. Ana, for instance, would never have engaged in the direct purchase of sexual intercourse. Prior to quitting the profession, Ana had had a number of boyfriends, or "sponsors" as she also called them, who regularly provided her with an allowance. With some she had had sex; with others she had not.

In contrast to the more selective Ana, most other hostesses—whether female or transgender—had had sex without financial compensation with good-looking customers. Yet, doing so did not make them amoralists, as this practice does not necessarily translate to commercial sex. Sean, for instance, described how she would not hesitate to play with customers sexually if they fit her "type." As she put it, "If there is a young good-looking man, then we iron them. Do you know what ironing means? It means we iron them down there. [She pointed at her crotch.] You know us, the *bakla*. We just do it for fun. That is actually against the rules. But as soon as we see a good-looking Japanese man, we drop all the rules!" Notably, it is not just the *bakla* who "drop all the rules" when they see a good-looking customer. So do their female counterparts.

Perhaps because society gives *bakla* greater moral flexibility than females, they are less likely to become moral conservatives. Indeed, none of the transgender hostesses who participated in my study claimed to be one. Yet, even with their greater moral flexibility, most transgender hostesses are not likely to become amoralists. Most consider themselves moral in-betweeners, who are held back from amoralism by the social stigma associated with prostitution. They would never just have sex if the "price is right," but would selectively discriminate and gauge their degree of intimacy with clients. Sean, for instance, would have sex only with those whom she found attractive and constantly made excuses to keep her distance from unattractive men who tried to take her to a hotel. As she said, "There are those dirty old men. It is up to you what ad lib you want to use, like 'I am not ready.' 'I could not do this one, because I am shy.' You make their heads spin to get out of the situation. If you don't want to do it, they will also respect you."

SHIFTING MORAL BOUNDARIES

Can you tell me how you felt when you first came here?
I felt sorry for myself. I wanted to go back to the Philippines. I even cried. I really wanted to go back to the Philippines. I did not like the work. I knew what the work was going to be. People had told me about it.

Who?
The timers [return migrants] whom I was with in the promotion agency [in the Philippines]. Still, I was excited to come here to Japan. But, once in Japan, it was like I wanted to go home to the Philippines. [She shrieks.] I did not want to go on with my work here.

Why?
I saw a Japanese kiss one of the girls when I walked into the *omise*. I got scared. I was thinking in my head that here they let the men kiss them. I was thinking this. I felt sorry for myself.

And now?
Now, I am OK. I realize it is in the woman. It is in her style and demeanor. If you want someone to kiss you, if you want someone to touch your private part, then that is up to you.

Do you think that your morals are compromised here?
Yes. [We laugh.] You have to work hard and put all you have in the job to earn money. You do that so you can save money . . .

Do you hold hands with your customers?
Yes, I do. When they are about to leave too, I walk them to the door. Then, they want to kiss me.

Is that fine?
No.

Does that make you cry?
Not anymore. But I still get disgusted until this day, but you hide that so that when they come back, you are still the one that they *shimei*. When they leave, you just wipe your mouth with a hot towel.

Would you ever have sex for money?
Why give yourself, if you do not like the person? Isn't that right? Why force yourself to do something just for money? We are not that desperate.

I could imagine myself debating this in my head.
Sometimes I have thought about it. I have thought that if I let one of these guys use me, they would probably come to the club every night. But then my conscience kicks in, and I think, "No, it is not worth it." No matter what, I have some pride left. Isn't that right? I think it is OK to let them kiss you, but you should not give the thing that you should be guarding carefully. That should only be for the person you love. Isn't that right? [We laugh.] (Reggie, a first-timer)

Moral standards are not static but shift in the process of migration. As the excerpt of my interview with Reggie indicates, migration is a process of negotiating moral boundaries. In the case of Reggie, we see that she still held onto fairly conservative beliefs regarding the social purity of women, for instance viewing sex as something women "should be guarding carefully." This makes her quite different, at the very least more conservative, than her co-worker Amy. Contradicting the common assumption that the restrictive conditions of a hostess's migration would force her into prostitution, the fact that Reggie would earn only US$100 after six months of laboring in Japan had not tempted her to engage in any form of compensated sexual relations with customers.

In most cases, the longer a hostess stays in Japan, the greater the likelihood that her moral boundaries would expand beyond the conservative mores upheld in a Catholic country such as the Philippines. These mores would include the "hostile worlds view," the notion of women's purity, the view of female virginity as sacrosanct, monogamy, sex for reproduction, sex for love, and sex as restricted to married couples. Peer pressure and work experience largely account for the expansion of the moral boundaries of hostesses. Indeed, many consider their migration and labor experience as liberating, resulting not only in their rejection of the Catholic teaching that sex should solely be for the purpose of reproduction but also in their greater openness about the physical pleasures of sex. Conversations among hostesses frequently turn to the topic of sex from complaints over its lack to pointers on how to maximize a woman's pleasure. Indeed, magazines in the Filipino community periodically post advertisements of various sexual toys that would heighten women's sexual pleasures.

For Filipina hostesses, shifts in moral boundaries do not come easily, as most initially experience culture shock when entering the club. This is more the case for younger hostesses, as well as those from rural areas in the Philippines such as Irene, who described her initial experience of going to Japan as one of immense fear:

> I cried at the airport, and I felt alone. That is when I felt it. I felt it every day for a whole month. I had no clue about the *omise*. I had never even been to a disco. Do you know the dances in the town square? That is the only dance I had ever attended in my whole life. But a place with alcohol was never in my mind. I was so innocent. [She laughs.] I remember when the doors of the *omise* opened for the first time, it was all smoke. It was so loud. I was thinking in my head if I could take being there. I was only sixteen years old. My feeling was that I was about to enter hell.

The excitement of securing work in Japan could not quite alleviate the fears of the sixteen-year-old Irene, who came to Japan of her own volition and with parental permission. As she told me, "[My parents] allowed me to come here because life was so difficult. My father was having a hard time supporting us. He was a dispatcher at a bus terminal at Laguna." Describing the life of abject poverty she escaped, Irene explained why she decided to drop out of high school and instead seek work in Japan:

> I wanted to be able to help [my parents]. I could not take it anymore to see my parents struggle. For example, you will go to school, and your bag is old, and your shoes are old. You feel ashamed to go to school. Even if you ask your parents to buy these things for you, they cannot. It was like that for me growing up. That is why I had the determination to go to the promotion agency. I had my friend take me. They asked me to finish high school, but I was the one who was determined to go. I am hardheaded.

Following the U.S. definition of trafficking, Irene could be labeled as a "severely trafficked person" for having gone to Japan at the age of sixteen. Yet, Irene herself would have disagreed with this labeling and would have insisted that she had had the maturity and know-how needed to do hostess work in Japan. She herself told me that the situation would have been different if someone had forced her to come to Japan at such a young age or if she had not wanted to do the work. She said that neither had been the case in her situation.

Despite all of her determination to work in Japan, Irene could not help but fear the social ramifications of her close interaction with men at the club. However, experience eventually fostered her greater acceptance of commercial flirtation, resulting as well in her nonchalant attitude about close interactions with customers. Irene eventually adjusted to her work, completing more than seven labor contracts before marrying one of her customers. Likewise, Lori, whose older sisters worked as hostesses before her, eventually learned to accept her work as not immoral. As she described,

> If you are just in an *omise*, you are only entertaining. Of course you cannot really avoid the drunks who will suddenly grope you. That happens, for sure. At first, I would cry whenever someone tried to touch me. But near the end I no longer reacted like that. I got used to the work. You will get used to the work doing it everyday. Then, I also got used to drinking. If you do not drink, you really cannot work at night.

From working in Japan, Lori learned to expand her moral views on the appropriate behavior of women. For instance, she learned to accept drinking as a socially acceptable activity.

Although society imposes different moral standards on transgender and female hostesses, the greater flexibility given transgender entertainers does not mean that they are without moral dilemmas. The third-timer Nikki, for instance, was sometimes ridden with guilt over her seemingly amoral practice of having sex "with closed eyes" with a boyfriend. Describing her relationship with this boyfriend as nothing but a commercial exchange, Nikki stated,

> There is nothing I like about him except his money. And that is what makes it hard for me because I am not that kind of person, a user, doing something just for the money. I am not that kind of person, but for this job I have had to change. It's not just half of myself that I have had to change, but I have had to change myself from

head to foot. I have had to change all my principles in life. . . . All of that I have had to throw away in this job.

Nikki was one of the more remorseful hostesses I met in Tokyo. Most others considered their amoral behavior to be "wise" and "realistic."

Hostesses explained to me that it is only logical for their moral boundaries to expand once in Japan. Their work in the nightlife industry not only exposes them to greater opportunities for sexual relationships, but it also promises them greater monetary rewards. Ela explained:

The first time you come here, you are not really a hostess. You are a student in the Philippines, but then you come here because the earnings are so much bigger. But you were just pressured to come here in Japan to earn money. That is the only thing that I felt forced to do. At first, I used to cry when I had to dance with a Japanese man. It was just cheek-to-cheek dances, but because they were old, you were not into them. But near the end, you get used to it. You begin to appreciate it because you get money and tips.

Likewise, the first-timer Reggie had learned to become more overt in her use of sexuality to lure customers to the club. Described Reggie:

Before I was really quiet . . . I did not speak that much. I did not flirt with the customers all that much. But now I am thinking that you really need to have customers. You need to flirt with customers so they are pleased with you. I feel I became wise. [Laughs.] By wise, I mean I know how to joke around, and I am loud in the club. I talk a lot now.

While financial considerations may expand the moral boundaries of hostesses such as Reggie, it does not automatically make all of them—or even most of them—amoral.

The expansion of moral boundaries is not always a smooth process. Conflict could come via peer pressure, as recalled by Elizabeth, forty years old at the time of our interviews. Describing her experience as a first-timer, she remembered the moral dilemma she had faced when forced to expose her breasts during *show time*. As she explained,

[My co-workers and I] cried. We wanted to go back to the Philippines. We really did not know that we could complain. We were mostly first-timers, but there some veterans were telling us that it was no big deal. We just had to show our breasts. We first said no, and then the veterans spoke to us. They asked us if we were virgins, and if not, then it is no big deal to show our breasts. No one will be groping them. We just have to show them. We will eventually learn how to play along, the longer we stay in Japan.

The construction of morals does not always involve a predictable shift toward a greater acceptance of commercial sex. Elizabeth, for instance, never adjusted to the amoral regime of her club.

Bitterness and heartaches over failed romances also lead to ideological shifts in the views of hostesses on the intersections of sex and money and consequently their rejection of the "hostile worlds view." Experience teaches them to be less idealistic about romance and more realistic about the different meanings of sex. That sex need not always involve love is a conclusion many have made after having been duped by romantic partners in the past. Explained Ela:

What changed with me is that I realize that we become wise. It is important that women here become wise and do not let men use you. Give and take. It is not just all love. You also have to have material. Material and love together, that is the best. If you can demand anything from them, then you demand everything. OK, let's love, but let's also give materially. So buy me this, and buy me that. Isn't that right? It is because, if you don't get anything from them, you lose when they leave you suddenly, even if they impregnate you. Then nothing. You got nothing, and then on top of that he left you with a child. So it is important that you become wise.

A "hostile worlds view" would teach women such as Ela only to exchange sex for love, which would be unrealistic in a world where women suspect that plenty of the men they meet want nothing more than sex. Hence, for hostesses, to secure material compensation in romance is a strategy they utilize to protect themselves from being used by customers. Thwarted romances are made acceptable by the material gains they come away with in the relationship.

Hostesses see themselves as becoming more realistic and practical the longer they stay in Japan. Commercial flirtation becomes morally acceptable and the norm among them. Seeing nothing inherently wrong with their job, hostesses do not discourage their daughters from pursuing this line of work. For example, Ruby, a forty-one-year-old migrant who first came to Japan in 1981, encouraged one of her two daughters to work at a club. One liked to party, and one did not. To save money, she encouraged the one who liked to go out at night to be a hostess. Explained Ruby,

> My eldest, she likes to drink. She enjoys that and parties. So instead of her spending for that, she might as well work and get paid doing what she enjoys. Is that not right? My oldest is like that. She likes to go out drinking, and here it is expensive. So it is better you just work in an *omise*. You have company, as well.

MORAL REGIMES OF COMMERCIAL SEX IN HOSTESS CLUBS

Having just presented different moral grouping of hostesses, I would now like to address the question of whether hostesses can do their work without violating their moral boundaries. I address this question so as to return to the claims of their human trafficking posed by the U.S. Department of State. Many hostesses insist that they carry a semblance of control over their relations with customers. As they repeatedly told me, the extent of intimacy between a customer and a hostess depends on the hostess. As they would say, "*Nasa kanya*," meaning, "It is up to the person." However, there is a limit to the control that hostesses have over their labor. It is, for instance, limited by their need to abide by the moral regime of sex in their workplace as well as their migrant status. By moral regime, I refer to the moral standards and prevailing notions of proper and improper uses of sexual intimacy in hostess clubs.

Moral regimes of sex shape the conditions of interaction between hostesses and customers, and problems can arise if the morals of hostesses do not coincide with the moral regime at their club of employment. This moral clash has the potential to result in the hostesses' moral boundaries being violated and in the possibility of their forced sexual labor. As one hostess, Mai, reflected, "Your situation really depends on the *omise* that you enter."

The Regimes

Philippine clubs in Tokyo fall under three moral regimes that mirror the moral boundaries of hostesses. There are morally conservative, amoral, and lastly moral in-betweener establishments. Clubs tend to have a reputation that accordingly determines their patronage. In other words, customers tend to visit establishments that maintain moral regimes that coincide with or match their own moral boundaries. At morally conservative workplaces, physical contact between customers and hostesses, if it does occur, is limited to infrequent dances on the floor or hands held across the table. Usually, the customer and hostess sit across the table from one another and converse, perhaps sharing sexual jokes but barely touching one another. Morally conservative establishments are usually neighborhood snack bars frequented by older men who are sometimes accompanied by their wives. Customers either pay a per-hour table fee, reaching no more than 3,000 yen (US$30) per hour in these establishments, or instead buy a bottle of liquor that they keep in-house to consume every time they visit. Usually these neighborhood establishments employ only *arubaito* workers, in other words hourly paid workers who are either permanent or undocumented residents. Among my interviewees, only a handful of women were ever placed at a morally conservative club as contract workers. More often they had to work in an establishment with a morally in-between regime.

At clubs with a moral in-betweener regime, the sexual flirtation that takes place is generally meek. These interactions are not overtly sexual, such as the heavy petting and make-out sessions that one would encounter at an amoral club. Instead, customers and hostesses usually touch only fleetingly; for instance, a quick grope on the breast or a kiss on the lips are exchanged once or twice in one evening. Hostesses overtly use their sexuality to seduce customers into becoming regular patrons at morally in-between establishments. Seduction commonly takes place via entertainment through singing and dancing in sexually provocative but nonrevealing clothes. It also takes place via conversation when customers and hostesses tease one another with compliments and sexual jokes. Yet some of these conversations could be described as more silly than seductive. Once I overheard a co-worker initiate a conversation with a customer by exclaiming how large her breasts are, which she had then jiggled to attract his attention. Clubs with morally in-between regimes run the gamut in terms of class standing and include those that would cost no more than 3000 yen (US$30) for ninety minutes to those that would cost as much as 12,000 yen (US$12,000) for two hours.

In sharp contrast to the tame sexual exchanges we find in morally in-between establishments are the raunchy conversations one would overhear in amoral businesses. At these places, customers could expect sexual acts from hostesses if they are able to provide sufficient material compensation. A 2,000 yen (US$20) tip, for instance, can sometimes secure the customer a hand job underneath the table, or a 1,000 yen (US$10) tip can reward a customer with a grope on the hostess's breast. These establishments vary in size from large clubs that employ more than twenty hostesses who perform nightly *show times* to small neighborhood bars that employ no more than three hostesses per night. In these establishments, management have been known to, but not always, demand that hostesses expose their breasts and wear skimpy and revealing attire during *show time*. In some cases, management encourages hostesses to allow customers to touch intimate parts of their body at the club or maintain sexual relations with customers outside the club. Rates at amoral businesses that I visited or heard about from hostesses ranged from 5,000 yen (US$50) per hour to 7,000 yen (US$70) per ninety minutes. Hostesses do not necessarily earn more at an amoral business, but they are likely to garner more tips and gifts from customers in exchange for sex.[19]

The Making of Moral Regimes

Moral regimes at clubs are not only imposed by management rules from above but are also constructed by the actions that occur inside the club. The culture of hostess clubs accordingly shifts from club to club. This tells us that the moral regimes of clubs are not static. The actions of those at the club, including customers, management, and workers jointly determine, but not without conflict, the moral regimes that shape customer and hostess relations. As everyday actions constitute the moral regime of clubs, changes in action could engender a sudden shift in the culture of the hostess club. This occurred at the club where I did field work, which I quit after the arrival of three new hostesses drastically transformed the moral regime of the club from a moral in-betweener club to an amoral club.

To my discomfort and that of my six other co-workers, the actions of the three new hostesses hired at our workplace fell under the moral regime of amoralism. The three new hires had no qualms about undressing on the dance floor to entertain customers. They also encouraged customers to touch them in their private parts in the view of other workers including myself. These three new workers attracted customers who would not have patronized our club if it had maintained its moral in-betweener regime. Business had been slow prior to their arrival, and so our *mama-san* was only too happy to expand her clientele and condoned the actions of the women by not reprimanding them. Surely enough, my old co-workers quit the club one by one. They worried that the actions of the new hires would reconstitute the cultural expectations of customers who now would be likely to expect a greater level of physical intimacy from them. They also did not appreciate the floor manager's sudden encouragement for us to engage in sex outside the club. His change in attitude on the appropriate dynamic between customers and hostesses seemed to have been prompted by the increased sexual energy at our club after the arrival of our three new co-workers. It was not only my co-workers who stopped going to the club. Not all customers patronize hostess clubs to pursue sex. Some are likely to want no more than the thrill of flirtation. Customers who do are likely to only visit moral in-betweener establishments and avoid amoral venues. Not surprisingly, many customers did not appreciate the shift of culture at the club. They too began to stop patronizing the club.

"Sex trafficking" becomes an issue when hostesses find themselves working in a club where the moral regime of sex does not match their own. For instance, a moral conservative working at an amoral club is likely to confront serious moral violations at work. Aggravating this situation would be their migrant status. *Arubaito* workers could reject peer pressure and quit.[20] *Talents*, as contract workers, unfortunately have less flexibility to do so.

MORAL VIOLATIONS AND THE RISK OF "SEX TRAFFICKING"

Hostesses are aware that clubs have different moral regimes and accordingly try to find work only at clubs that would match their own moral beliefs on commercial sex. For example, the *arubaito* Marietta consciously measured the moral regime of each of the clubs that she entered for work. As she explained:

> There are some *omise* where you see the women doing things. You feel pressured to follow because everyone else is doing it. I am talking about having customers feel you up, do dirty dancing. They do not care that someone like their neighbor in the Philippines is going to see them do that.
>
> *Do you avoid those kinds of omise?*
> I try to study the system. The first day I try to see if I can handle the place.

Like others, Marietta refused to work at a club with a moral regime that goes against her own moral values. In Marietta's case, she wished to avoid clubs where customers can freely grope hostesses or clubs where hostesses are encouraged to maintain sexual relations with customers outside the club.

As an *arubaito* worker with legal residency status, Marietta can basically choose her club of employment. However, not all hostesses have the ability and flexibility to choose their workplace. In contrast, *talents*, as contract workers, are bound to their place of employment. They have little control over the type of club that they will enter. Prior to their departure from the Philippines, labor recruiters have already assigned them to a club in Japan. They are contractually bound to work in their assigned club for at least three months. They usually cannot terminate their contract without penalty. It is questionable whether this condition would stand in the legal courts of the Philippines. For this reason, middleman brokers, including labor recruiters, often demand a blank check from contract workers prior to their departure and use this as a form of collateral against hostesses who quit.

Entering Japan as a contract worker, especially for moral conservatives, is highly risky. A morally conservative *talent* could find herself contractually bound to work at a club with an amoral regime. This is because morally conservative clubs are few and far between. It is in this situation that a *talent* could fall prey to forced labor, doing a job she wishes not to do but with limited recourse to leave her job. Yet, to be trapped in a situation of moral contestation does not automatically mean that hostesses are trafficked. After all, hostesses have the agency to shift their moral boundaries and adjust them to fit the moral regime of their workplace. They also have the option to leave their workplace, a choice that I acknowledge comes with difficulty for *talents*. By recognizing hostesses' agency, I am not denying that forced labor could take place. Instead, I am calling attention to the fact that forced labor is not a universal occurrence among them.

If unable to adjust their moral boundaries, *talents* could report contract violations to the Philippine Embassy. One violation they could cite is the requirement for them to sit with customers, which everyone admittedly does but is in fact technically illegal for them to do. *Talents* could use this job condition—although they knew what they would be doing in Japan prior to their departure from the Philippines—to ask the Philippine Embassy to repatriate them. One person who almost went to the Philippine Embassy was my co-worker Dianne, who complained to me about her second job placement in Japan:

> They would make us do *show time* that was scandalous when I was a second-timer. He made us do strip dancing, but we are not strip dancers. We are variety dancers. So, I fought the employer. We were there for only three months. We were sent home.

I said that is better that you send us home than do what you wanted us to do. . . . We went home.

Aware that her job description did not include strip dancing, Dianne—as the self-designated leader of her group—threatened her club owner that she would report him to the Philippine Embassy. Doing so could lead to steep fines and penalties for the club from the Ministry of Justice in Japan, which oversees the incorporation of foreign workers. Although Dianne never did report her club to government authorities, she felt vindicated. She managed to leave the club without penalty and return to the Philippines with her full salary. Notably, not all of Dianne's co-workers opted to return to the Philippines. Some she figured had no qualms about stripping.

Yet, did these hostesses truly have a choice? Did they stay because preexisting debts awaited them in the Philippines? Or did they stay to avoid potential fines that they feared middleman brokers would impose on them? If confronting moral violations, *talents* may feel coerced not to return to the Philippines because of the debts they had accrued prior to migration or the penalties that the promotion agency would impose on them, telling us that the control of middleman brokers aggravates their vulnerability to forced labor. The former entertainer Elsa, for instance, chose to tolerate her experience of moral violations at the workplace to keep a clean record with promotion agencies in the Philippines. Reflecting on her eight contract stints in Japan, Elsa recalled her second contract to be her least favorite because she was subjected to the constant sexual harassment of customers during those six months. As she described, "I did not like how frisky the customers were. That was terrible. Even if I stabbed them with a toothpick, they still would not stop. And they will come back for you. You will just walk by them, and they will grab your ass. That is what I liked the least." Although unhappy with her job placement, Elsa chose not to quit. She opted to tolerate six months of "unbearable" work at this amoral club, so as to avoid being blacklisted by promotion agencies in the Philippines. Her situation raises the question of whether she was trafficked, meaning coerced to tolerate sexual harassment. Despite her limited options, the fact is that Elsa *chose* to remain employed in an amoral club. Significantly, not all of them would do the same as Elsa. Some, such as Dianne, would demand repatriation. Others would escape the club and pursue work as a visa overstayer elsewhere. For instance, my co-worker Teresa did just that, landing at the club

Manila after she had escaped a club where hostesses were pressured to have sex with customers during a *dohan*. These different routes that hostesses take to negotiate their experience of moral violations indicate that the universal solution of "rescue, rehabilitation, and reintegration" that is advocated by the U.S. government and followed by Japan does not address all of their needs. Some may not want rescue, which for many means job elimination, but instead job improvement and labor market flexibility.

In some cases, contract workers are undeniably in need of rescue. Some may find themselves wanting to leave but believe they cannot, whether because they fear the reprisal of middleman brokers in the Philippines or they genuinely believe that their six-month contract binds them to work there. One such woman had been Elizabeth. Describing her experience as a first-timer, she recalled,

> We were modern dancers . . . We would dance for one hour. Then it became ugly. We all started crying. We had to show our breasts. That was when I was a first-timer, when I was a *talento*. But that was not in our contract. We were supposed to report that, but at that time we did not. *We did not know that we could do anything about it*. At the end of the dance, we had to show our breasts. Before we left the stage, we had to show our breasts. I am getting upset just remembering it. [*Emphasis my own.*]

Without doubt, one could argue that Elizabeth was trafficked, as she was coerced to undress on stage. The situation of Elizabeth raises the challenge of how to make sure that entertainers, specifically *talents*, leave the Philippines with the knowledge of their rights, including their right to quit their job.

Sexual coercion is not the only way entertainers are potentially trafficked. In light of the control of middleman brokers over migrant contract workers, some may argue that *all* contract workers in the nightlife industry of Japan are trafficked persons. However, such a claim disregards the fact that many enjoy their work and do not mind being bound by debt or threat of penalty to stay employed for the entire duration of their contract. Although she faced difficulty adjusting to hostess work at the age of sixteen years old, Irene, for instance, eventually found her work enjoyable, describing the experience as one that heightens camaraderie among women. Stated Irene: "Think about it. Why do you insist on coming back here, if you do not personally enjoy the work? It is fun. You are like sisters. You joke around. When customers are drunk, you make fun of them. It is a lot of fun too. I have never had an unpleasant trip.

What I like the most is the camaraderie with the women." Not all hostesses wish to terminate their contracts. Moreover, not all feel morally violated in the workplace. More often than not, the moral boundaries of a hostess match the moral regime of her workplace.

The problem remains, however, that *talents* are vulnerable to forced labor. When the moral regime of the workplace does not match the moral boundaries of the hostess, she becomes vulnerable to forced labor. We see this in the case of Elizabeth and to some extent Elsa. Their experiences raise the question of whether the mere possibility of forced labor warrants their universal rescue. Hostesses think not. Instead of the universal call for their rescue, many feel that their advocates should work toward ensuring their greater control over their labor and migration. Doing so would recognize their agency as hostesses, respect the choices they make—whether to stay or leave their job—and acknowledge their ability to negotiate experiences of coerced sexual labor in the process of labor migration.

Migrant Filipina hostesses cultivate a diverse range of intimate relations with customers. They maintain a wide range of moral boundaries, resulting in diverse sexual practices and standards. In the exchange of gifts and intimacy with customers, hostesses form, contest, and transform moral categories so as to defy the "hostile worlds view." In so doing, they call into question claims that the commercialization of intimacy would lead to their moral degradation. Hostesses do not necessarily promote an alternative universal view on paid sex. Instead, they maintain multiple moralities; they subvert the formation of a universal moral standard when it comes to appropriate hostess-customer relations. Respecting the diversity of moral standards in their community, the longer hostesses stay in Japan, the less judgmental they become of the moral standards of others. I found moral conservatives avoid judging amoral hostesses and vice versa.

Examining intimate relations between hostesses and customers through the lens of morality not only establishes the dynamic nature of hostess work but also points to the constitution of morals as a social process.[21] Individual morals need not reflect the standards imposed by mainstream society. Morals form not only from ideologies but also from life experiences. Morals are constructed in actions and practices. Through everyday interactions, morals are constantly questioned in the workplace, determining relations with customers and the personal desires of hostesses concerning sex, love, and money. Yet relations with customers depend not only on the moral standards of the hostess but also on the moral regime of sex in the workplace, peer pressure, and the hostess's migrant status.

This chapter has shown that the alarming cry of forced prostitution is not the norm but the exception among migrant Filipina hostesses. This does not mean that they are not vulnerable to abuse. In the next few chapters, I make the case that we need to see that the problem of "trafficking" is *not* the nature of people's activity, including sex work or commercial flirtation. "Human trafficking" is instead a labor and migration issue. It is caused by restrictive policies that limit the freedom and autonomy of migrants, including the conditional residency of wives, the criminalization of undocumented workers, and the limited rights of contract workers.

CHAPTER SIX

MAKING LOVE FOR A VISA

"WHAT IS YOUR VISA?" WAS A QUESTION that seemed frequently posed to me, though I later realized that is was only those with spouse or family visas who had routinely asked me this question.[1] To ask "what is your visa?" was to evoke one's sense of greater belonging in Japan, because soon after asking me about my visa status the questiononer would find a way to let me know that she had or was in the process of obtaining permanent residency.[2] Securing permanent residency status is not easy for foreigners; unless one is of Japanese descent, one would qualify for permanent residency only as a spouse or mother of a Japanese citizen. Japan does not grant long-term residency status to its non-*nikeijin* foreign workers.[3] Perhaps for this reason, wives and mothers distinguish themselves from the workers that comprise the majority of Filipinos in Japan and construct themselves as the "real" members of Japanese society.[4] Referring to other members of the community, they would frequently comment "*talent lang yan*," meaning "she's only a *talent*" or in passing threaten to report a visa overstayer who had gotten on their nerves. For the most part, wives share a sense of camaraderie with other migrant Filipinas and are unlikely to act on the vulnerability of others in the community.[5] Still, speaking of their ability to expel others reminds everyone of the greater security of their citizenship and the greater rights that the state provides them, including welfare provisions, labor market flexibility, and eligibility for permanent residency.

Wives comprise a sizable portion of the nearly 153,000 long-term legal Filipino residents in Japan.[6] Others are mothers of Filipino-Japanese children who obtained legal residency as foreign custodians of Japanese citizens.[7] Most wives and mothers initially entered Japan as entertainers, but some had met their husbands in the Philippines and never took part in the entertainment industry.[8] Among entertainers, Filipina wives are in a select group. The anthropologist Nobue Suzuki, who has written extensively on migrant Filipina wives and entertainers in Japan, estimates that only around 10 percent of migrant entertainers eventually tie the knot with a Japanese citizen.[9]

Because long-term residency is conditional on marrying or giving birth to a Japanese citizen, we could argue that long-term residency is conditional on the provision of sex. Hence, I refer to long-term legal residents in the Filipino migrant community as *sexual citizens* not only to underscore sex as a primary condition of their belonging but also to acknowledge that their citizenship, that is, their terms of belonging in Japanese society, involves sexual relations with Japanese citizens. In other words, providing sex is tantamount to the process of immigrant adaptation to the host society for this particular group of migrants. By calling attention to the status of wives and mothers as sexual citizens, I wish to underscore that in some capacity we are *all* sexual citizens. Indeed, the responsibility of reproducing populations is a constitutive element of citizenship, which is a condition that is only magnified in the situation of Filipina entertainers who want long-term residency in Japan.[10]

To examine the conditions of citizenship for wives and mothers, I address the social meanings of sexual relations that result in a long-term residency visa among migrant hostesses as a window to their migrant settlement. I see these sexual relations, which I also refer to as the process of making love for a visa, as a mirror to the sociocultural construction of marriage and the family for migrant Filipina hostesses. By referring to the act of sex as a process of making love, I do not mean to suggest that sex for a visa is always conditional to love. Instead, I acknowledge that love does not emerge from a deep interiority. While not necessarily shaped by rational calculation, love emerges not only from political economic conditions, as established by family and marriage historians such as Stephanie Coontz, Nancy Cott, John D'Emilio, and Estelle Freedman, and but it also takes shape from the particular social location of subjects in relations of race, class, gender, and nation.[11] From the particular subject-positions of Filipina hostesses, making love as well as the making of love cannot be disaggregated from the material security of a visa.

Examining sexual relations that lead to a long-term residency visa for both heterosexual female hostesses and transgender hostesses, this chapter begins by examining the constitution of love in heterosexual partnerships. Then, it moves to a discussion of marriages for transgender hostesses. I make two central arguments in this chapter. First, I show that the conditionality of sex for acquiring a visa intrinsically questions the possible disaggregation of love and money as motivations for marriage. For hostesses, marriage cannot be based solely on a profound love that is devoid of rational calculation. As such, the constitution of love for hostesses falls outside the moral stricture of romance in dominant society. This intrinsic location results in marriages void of love coexisting with those based on the deepest love, a coexistence that ruptures ideal views of romance as being void of materialism.

Then, secondly, I address the sexual partnerships that lead to a long-term residency visa for Filipina transgender hostesses, raising the question of how they navigate through the compulsory heterosexuality of sexual citizenship in a country that does not recognize same-sex marriages. I question notions of legitimacy in "marriage" by discussing the ways transgender subjects subvert the sexual and gender order of heterosexual marriages. In my discussion, I establish how they *mimic heteronormativity*, by which I mean appropriate heterosexual characteristics and ideals, to attain long-term legal residency. When mimicking heteronormativity, they engage in legitimate marriages not void of affective ties with masculine subjects, including *tomboys* or female-to-male transgender "husbands." Paying attention to the sexual relations between male-to-female transgender hostesses and their female-to-male transgender partners, my discussion establishes the undoing of both gender and sexual norms of marriage in these partnerships and their subversion of heteronormative conditions of citizenship. In so doing, the marriages of transgender hostesses disavow heterosexual marriage as a condition of citizenship and rupture the premise of their sexual exclusion.

SEXUAL CITIZENS AND NOTIONS OF LOVE

Emotions do not exist in a vacuum; instead their meanings are discursively produced and emerge from particular sociocultural processes.[12] The affective ties that develop between hostesses and customers blossom in the context of the commercial exchange of flirtation at the club, resulting in the intertwining of love and money in the constitution of romance. Likewise, marriage, resulting in the promise of permanent residency status and greater economic opportunities, bars the separation of economic rationalism from feelings of love. Indeed, in different gradations, Filipina migrant hostesses pursue marriage with Japanese men for a combination of love and material security, with some marrying primarily for love, others for both love and money, and some purely for the material security of a visa. This should come as no surprise, as there are nearly always economic dimensions in "legitimate" relations such as marriage, and likewise there are affective ties among people in market settings, including in the exchange of sex for money.[13] Viviana Zelizer puts it best when she states, "Money cohabits regularly with intimacy, and even sustains it."[14] In the case of Filipina hostesses, differentiating the comingling of money and intimacy in both their work and personal life are their moral values.

Morals do not function in bounded spheres. Therefore, the moral values cultivated among hostesses at the club would influence their social relations in noncommercial spaces. These values would also reflect their views and decisions on marriage. For instance, moral in-betweeners would find nothing wrong with marrying a man primarily for a visa—but only if they have slight feelings of affection for him. As the moral in-betweener Rikka stated emphatically, "I wouldn't have sex if I had no feelings for the man." In contrast, amoralists would marry for a visa and engage in sex for "zero love," while moral conservatives are likely to claim that they would marry only for love. These varying moral premises of marriage lead to different experiences and meanings of sexual partnerships for foreign hostesses in Japan. Yet, as I establish in this chapter, the degree to which love and money sustain relationships fluctuates, resulting in porous boundaries across the different moral groupings of hostesses.

Despite the intrinsic relations that link love and money, we still instinctively view these two as mutually exclusive of one another. The "hostile worlds view" on love and money haunts us. Anthropologist Nicole Constable would add that this is the case particularly in the West. As she describes,

> This attempt to polarize love and pragmatics and to represent them as discontinuous represents a particularly western perspective and bias. Underlying such a dichotomy is the idea that "true love" is somehow selfless and "pure," and not only incompatible with but also diametrically opposed to pragmatic or practical concerns.[15]

Consequently, scholarly representations on international marriages tend to separate cases of "true love" from those of pragmatic motivations.[16] In her study of sex workers in the Dominican Republic, Denise Brennan examines how love figures in marriages between sex workers and their foreign clients. Brennan found that sex workers are hardly ever driven by "emotion-driven love" but instead by "strategy-driven love." The term *emotion-driven love* would refer to irrational feelings one holds outside of conscious thought, while *strategy-driven love* would be motivated by one's material wants and needs. As Brennan states, "Marriage in a tourist economy—especially in an internationally known sex-tourist destination—often has nothing to do with emotion-driven love or romance."[17] Suzuki similarly distinguishes "romantic love" from the economic motivations of women:

> The discourse revolving around the capitalist logic often fails to take into consideration the fact that, on a global scale, male–female relations almost *everywhere* have developed not just around fetishized romantic love but around most women's necessity to find economic means for survival, security, and mobility and men's continuing advantage in the global labor and political-economic arenas.[18]

Likewise, Leiba Faier found that Filipina hostesses in Japan distinguish pragmatic choices from sentiments of love when making sense of their motivations for marriage.[19] Examining why Filipina hostesses in Japan evoke "love" to describe their reason for marriage, Faier explains that they do it to combat dominant assumptions that they marry for purely instrumental reasons.[20]

Building from these previous discussions on the negotiation of "true love" and pragmatic motivations, I describe the constructions of love that emerge from the subject position of Filipina hostesses as sexual citizens. I show that for them monetary transactions are integrated into "true love" to the point that what Brennan distinguishes as "emotion-driven love" and "strategy-driven love" are deeply entangled. The motivations and outcomes of their marriages—whether for love or money—belong in a moral continuum in which emotional motivations fall at one end and rational calculation at the other. In this moral continuum, we have at one end those who would marry primarily for love, with little consideration for money; in the middle are those who cannot disentangle the motivations of love and money; and at the other end are those who would admit to marrying for "zero love." Regardless of where they are at in this moral continuum, money—that is, instrumental calculations—and love—that is, emotional sentiments—comingle in the motivations and outcomes of marriage. The prominence of one does not disavow the other. Indeed, hostesses describe the most "emotion-driven love" on the basis of monetary transfers. How much a customer spends on a hostess, how often someone visits her at the club, and the extent of the monetary gifts he gives to her and her family in the Philippines would prove how much he loves her.

The subject position of Filipina hostesses as sexual citizens engenders particular ideals of love, one distinct from the kind of consummate love or pure love that individuals pursue for self-development,[21] examples being Japanese women who pursue Western men to be freed of the deeply entrenched gender division of labor in Japan[22] and the practical approach to love one finds in the class-stratified matchmaking (*o-mei*) system in Japan. Instead, migrant hostesses tend to fall in love with the men who spend money on them, lavish them with gifts, and materially provide for them. They do not seek love for self-growth but instead for material stability. As such, masculine magnanimity is the dominant trope of romance for migrant Filipina hostesses.[23]

With rare exception, hostesses describe the emotion of love solely via monetary terms.[24] Hostesses measure the enactments of love by lovers and husbands according to the weight of their financial provisions. Even tales of experiencing "love at first sight" are expressed via monetary calculations. When asked about her "love story," Rowena,[25] for instance, immediately responded, "It was love at first sight"—after which she proceeded to enumerate the expenses he incurred to demonstrate his love. First, she proudly shared with me the story of how her husband had released her from her labor contract by paying her middleman broker 150,000 pesos (US$3,000). Then, to further emphasize the weight of his love, she let me know that he frequently visited her at the club and spent a lot of money to see her. As Rowena stated:

For one and a half months, he would go to the *omise* every day. Then he went home to the Philippines with me. He owed a lot. He put it all in his credit card. In one day, he would spend 40,000 yen. He spent a lot there every day. He even calculated it. [She laughs.] He spent 2,000,000 [yen] in one and a half months from going there . . . He went every day from the start to the end.

For Rowena, the monetary expense of her husband established the depth of his love and devotion to her. Moreover, it served as proof that he indeed experienced "love at first sight," for why else would he have visited her at the club so frequently and have spent so much money on her from the moment he first met her to the moment she had to return to the Philippines, if he did not love her?

Meeting at a club does establish the centrality of monetary exchange in romance. Devotion—demonstrated by frequent visits to the hostess at the club—cannot be disentangled from financial transactions. Money becomes the central medium for displaying affection at the club, a practice that culturally shapes how hostesses in turn view and understand love. For instance, hostesses come to expect customers to display their romantic desires by acting as male providers. Explaining the provision of money by customers, Julia, a forty-one-year-old veteran who first migrated to Japan in 1981, stated, "[Japanese men give money to us, because] they are like proposing. They want you to like them. In short, they like you. They want you to be his girlfriend or mistress. Or they want you to marry them." As money becomes the way that hostesses measure the degree of affection that customers have for them, the wide range of social relations that could result from the provision of money by customers to hostesses, which includes marriage as well as a one-night stand, blur the distinction between legitimate and illegitimate romance as well as between prostitution and marriage.

With material considerations central to constructions of love among hostesses, it is no surprise then that marriage also always involves pragmatic considerations. My friend Amanda, for instance, cannot see why she needs to marry her boyfriend Hiroshi, as she has no material motivation to do so. States Amanda:

I told [Hiroshi] that I do not need to marry him. Why do I have to marry you? I have my permanent visa now. I do not need any husband. I do not need to get married anymore because I have a visa already. Other Filipinas are forced to marry because they need a visa. They will marry someone old, someone who smells like dirt, someone ugly, because of the visa, without any love, just for the visa. But in my case, I have my permanent visa. I have government support for my kids until they are eighteen years old. Why will I get married to a Japanese? That is what I was thinking even though I love him.

For Amanda, love alone cannot be the sole reason for marriage. Amanda does indeed love Hiroshi, but in her opinion love alone is not a good enough reason for marriage. In contrast, pragmatic considerations alone could justify marriage for Amanda and most other members of the Filipino migrant community. This stance, which contradicts dominant ideological beliefs on the reasons for marriage, undoubtedly emerges from their subject position as foreign hostesses whose attainment of legal status is contingent on their provision of sex and marriage. Dominant ideology dictates that people marry purely for love, with love being an abstract concept, a sentiment of mutual obligation and commitment sustained primarily by affection and friendship but driven by an irrational interiority. Yet, pragmatism weighs heavily in the constitution of love for hostesses. This ideological shift from the norm among hostesses suggests that emotions indeed evolve from particular social processes as well as subject positions.

Therefore, we should not be surprised that many hostesses enter marriage largely for pragmatic and material purposes. While they do so, we should realize that marrying for these reasons does not discount "emotionally driven love" as a factor into their decision to marry. Indeed, the utmost generosity of a not very attractive husband—even a smelly one—could lead to emotionally charged sentiments of love. Minda, for instance, describes herself as "a practical woman," who married her husband because of her "need to provide for her children" in the Philippines. She was not shy in admitting to me that she felt comatose when having sex with her husband, physically repulsed by his old wrinkly body, during the first few years of their marriage. As she told me, "I am a practical person. I married my husband, but I had no feelings for him. I remember just lying on the bed motionless while he had sex with me. I did not feel a response." Yet, after seven years of spending every waking moment with him, she described the development of her deep feelings of love for him, one engendered by her appreciation for his monthly remittance of US$1,000 to her children in the Philippines. The case of Minda tells us that feelings of love could fluctuate toward one end of the moral spectrum of emotionally charged and rationally calculated sentiments, a fact that questions our urge to distinguish the two.

Yet not all marriages that begins with "zero love" work out for hostesses. Not all eventually develop to include emotionally charged sentiments. The thirty-year-old Eden, for example, felt compelled to run away from her sixty-seven-year-old husband after a week of sleeping with him. She told me she became gaunt and sleepless after a week of marriage because she could not bear to sleep next to him for one more night. Not unlike others, Eden was quite calculating in her decision to marry a Japanese man for a visa. Like other amoralists, she entered the marriage void of affection. What is unique about the situation of Eden is that she was already married in the Philippines and that she and her husband in the Philippines had jointly decided on her marriage to a Japanese man as a means for them to obtain legal residency in Japan. To reach their goal as a family, Eden and her husband jointly decided to put their marriage on hold for five years, or however long it would take for Eden to receive permanent residency. Afterwards, Eden would divorce her second husband and then petition for her first husband to join her in Japan. According to Eden, this option was worth the sacrifice and a much better one than staying in the Philippines, where her family would only face a downward spiral to starvation. In the Philippines, Eden and her husband had been members of the working poor. With both having completed only an elementary education, they lived in the slums of Manila and struggled to feed their children. The opportunity to visit Japan as a tourist came through the invitation of her sister, who was once an entertainer and had become a permanent resident. Not wanting to stay in Japan only temporarily as a tourist, Eden looked for a potential husband immediately after arriving in Japan and met one during her first month in the country.

The case of Eden gives us an example of what Denise Brennan describes as marriage as an "advancement strategy," but in this instance it was not merely an individual but instead a family advancement strategy.[26] As amoralists, Eden and her husband have shown us how the maintenance of the most deep-seated emotionally charged love is not void of the most calculated decisions. Both of Eden's marriages occupy what historian Gail Hershatter describes as a "chaotic zone outside the reach of the state's legal and moral strictures."[27] Eden's marriage for a visa makes her morally suspect. As we see with the treatment of mail-order brides, states usually view marriage for pragmatic motivations to be morally suspicious.[28] Likewise causing a raised eyebrow is the decision of Eden and her Filipino husband to have Eden marry a Japanese man as an advancement strategy for their family. Yet, Eden's decision to seek a second husband does not necessarily fall outside of dominant moral strictures.[29] After all, most marriages are held together by a combination of pragmatism and emotions, and Eden's actions, clearly dictated primarily by pragmatism, just fall on one end of this moral spectrum. The impulse to shun the decision of women such as Eden to engage in marriages without love or the urge to dismiss marriages that depend on the commercial sexual liaisons of women as occupying a "chaotic zone" foreign to the norms of society loses sight of the fact that *all* marriages involve the intermingling of emotions and pragmatism, with certain relations falling on one or the other extreme of this moral spectrum. Eden and her Filipino husband remind us that pragmatism and emotions coexist in relationships that are seemingly held together only by emotion-driven love.

Most relations pursued by hostesses fall in the middle of this moral spectrum; often pragmatism and emotions simultaneously shape their choices in romance. In contrast to Minda and Eden, who both married Japanese men with "zero love," most other hostesses—as they are moral in-betweeners—claim to hold—at the very least—an inkling of love for their husbands, although perhaps not a passionate irrational love such as those felt by moral conservatives. Regardless, they insist on feeling some form of love for their husbands prior to marriage. Rikka, for instance, insisted, "I wouldn't have sex if I had no feelings for the man." Vivianne, a hostess for more than twenty years in Japan, similarly remarked, "Of course I love him too. I would not get married if I did not like him." Most hostesses refuse to have sex without affective ties. This includes my former co-worker Melissa, who was desperate to attain legal residency status but not to the point that she would marry someone she did not "love" or "lust." As she stated, " I think about what I have to do to get a visa without having to compromise myself. I do not want to have to do *that* to get a visa." By "that," Melissa refers to the act of sex-for-a-visa without affective ties.

Interestingly, those who do marry for only "a little love" distinguish their feelings from the passionate emotions they once had for a boyfriend in the Philippines. Financial considerations seem to play a much smaller part in their choice of lovers in the Philippines than in Japan. When hostesses marry for practical reasons in Japan, they often give up their "first love" or the "love of their life" in the Philippines by doing so, leading many to tell me, "Our love lives in Japan are very sad." When asked to differentiate and compare their lovers in the Philippines and Japan, female hostesses often complained about the lack of emotional expressiveness among the Japanese and their poor performance in the bedroom. Amanda, for instance, complains about sex with Hiroshi as "horrible. . . . You are still wearing your panties, and [he] ejaculates before you take them off." Adding to Amanda's irritation is Hiroshi's passive attitude and belief that, at nearly sixty years old, "he is too old to learn how to have good sex." In contrast, Filipino husbands are constructed as more romantic, expressive, and "sweet." Filipina hostesses in the process of their incorporation as sexual citizens in Japan negotiate these cultural distinctions in styles of romance with Filipino men constructed as more romantic and warmer and Japanese partners considered colder but more financially stable. Filipino men are generally described to be better lovers than Japanese men. Amanda, for instance, still fantasizes about her sexual encounters with her former driver in the Philippines and compares this past lover to her partner Hiroshi. Interestingly, emotions far outweigh pragmatism in the choice of Filipino partners among entertainers, thus placing these relations in the opposite end of the moral spectrum of pragmatism and emotions from their choice of Japanese partners.

While practical considerations weigh heavily in the selection of Japanese partners, the choice of a less passionate partner is not outside the purview of emotionally charged romances. For instance, some hostesses told me they would like to marry a Japanese man so they could escape their life of poverty in the Philippines. This materially based narrative of rescue fits a Cinderella story of migration, one that is not driven by cathexis but nonetheless is a story that makes difficult the disentanglement of the economic motivations of hostesses from romantic ones.[30]

Pragmatics does not always outweigh emotions as the central motivating force in relationships. Married men make up a sizable pool of the customers who interact with Filipina hostesses, opening the door to extramarital relations. For most Filipina hostesses, their judgment and reason, particularly in the context of their strong Catholic morals of monogamy and their conviction of the sacredness of marriage, should make them avoid the pursuit of relations with married men. Yet many find themselves emotionally enraptured in torrid love affairs with their married customers. This was the case for Lori, a single mother of a Japanese-Filipino boy, who explained, "I did not think about the situation, even though I knew he was married." Pragmatic considerations did not influence Lori when she fell in love with one of her married customers. Instead, she described being unable to control her strong feelings of attraction for him "because he has a strong personality, but at the same time he is very nice." Even though she "knew that we would never end up together because from the beginning I knew he was married," she could not help that her feelings "slowly developed" the more he visited her at the club.

Extramarital affairs between hostesses and their married customers are rampant in the Filipino migrant community. Some of these affairs are more long term than others. Some result in the birth of Japanese-Filipino children, and others do not. Relationships end, and sometimes they do so in negative circumstances, as did Lori's, whose lover wanted nothing more to do with her after she decided to keep their child.[31] Sometimes relationships with married men survive the test of time and turn into storybook romances, one with the themes of destiny, missed opportunities, and rescue from poverty. Despite the prominence of emotionally charged love in these storybook romances, the entanglement of money in these relations exists in the same way that feelings of love underlie pragmatic choices made by hostesses in selecting their marriage partners. We see this in the case of Elsa, a mistress of a Japanese business owner for more than fifteen years and one whose storybook romance of joy and tragedy was sustained by monetary transactions.

Elsa

To many members of the Filipino community, Elsa was considered a winner. She did not have to work, received full financial support from her lover, and kept herself busy by attending church and taking up floral arrangement classes. Elsa's lover even purchased a house for her in an exclusive neighborhood in

Manila and put more than US$100,000 in her Philippine bank account, telling her he wanted to make sure that she was well taken care of in case something happened to him. Elsa deeply appreciated his financial support, not only to her and their child but also to her entire extended family in the Philippines. Growing up in abject poverty, having to scavenge for food in trash cans as a child, Elsa could not eliminate financial gains as a motivating factor in determining her emotional desires for and attraction to her wealthy lover. Yet, one problem lingered for Elsa, which was that she remained a visa overstayer. Trapped in a relationship with a married man, Elsa did not have the option of finding someone else, possibly someone who could help her attain legal status in Japan. Being with the "love of her life" left Elsa in legal limbo, one aggravated by his refusal to allow Elsa to marry anyone else, even if only in paper, while they remained together.

While her lover, whom she called her "husband," refused to divorce his wife, he maintained an ongoing relationship with Elsa. He visited Elsa at their home every night after work, spending at least three hours with her before he returned to his wife in another area of Tokyo. During the three hours they would spend together, Elsa prepared his bath and change of clothes, served him dinner, and then relaxed with him, usually by watching television. Afterwards, he returned to his wife, never spending the night with Elsa unless he took her on a business trip or visited her in the Philippines, as he had in the past before her return to Japan. Devoted to Elsa, he regularly visited their child in the Philippines, who until recent changes in the law had not qualified for Japanese citizenship because she had been born out of wedlock.[32]

Despite her material security and his devotion, Elsa described her life of "being in love" as "painful" and "lonely." She craved the marital status of the many other Filipinas around her, imagining a deep love that would come with marriage and monogamy. Yet, it seems that the relationship of Elsa and her lover fits ideal constructs of a pure and somehow selfless love much more so than the pragmatically driven marriages of other Filipina hostesses whom I met, as surely the pain tolerated by Elsa through her continued devotion to her "husband" suggested a love free of pragmatic concerns. Even the love story relayed by Elsa does not fit the usual reduction of love-to-monetary calculations as it did for most other hostesses. Instead, Elsa framed her relationship around the theme of fate and rescue.

Elsa described her "love story" as one that had happened against all odds, which projected a sense of inevitability to the relationship. That is, it had happened due to fate and destiny. Elsa first met the man whom she would later consider her "husband" in 1988, when she was a second-timer in Tokyo. While he had been a somewhat regular customer of hers at the club, he was nothing more than just a customer. For instance, he and Elsa did not meet regularly outside the club, as one would do with a boyfriend, and they also never exchanged phone numbers and communicated with one another outside the club. At the end of her contract, Elsa had no intention of ever seeing him again. She did not even know whether she was going to return to Japan for a third time because she had not liked her experience with frisky customers at that particular club. Tired and burnt out, Elsa stayed in the Philippines for more than a year before opting to return to Japan once again, going through another round of auditions until she was booked to work at a different club in Tokyo. It was at this club that she had a chance meeting with her "husband." According to Elsa, "Fate had brought us together." As she described:

> Then, what happened when I came back a third time, I saw him at the club where I was working. It was just a coincidence that he went there. He had been there before. His friend from out of town he brought there, but when it comes down to it, he does not like Philippine clubs. He just brings his customers there. He takes his customers who like Filipino women there. So he brought this customer there, and it just happened that I was there. When I saw him, I thought he looked so familiar. . . . I was looking at him, thinking that I know him. That became the father of my child. I kept on looking at him, and then I got moved to [his table] so that I could meet new customers. So we looked at each other, and he was looking at me as if he knew me. I told him that we knew each other from the last club. He was so excited. He hugged me. After he saw me that time, he kept on coming back there. He would go there every week or even twice a week. He told me that he liked me even before. That is the beginning of our love story.

After that chance meeting, Elsa and her "husband" began to see each other regularly. At the end of her contract, he even accompanied her back to the Philippines. They continued to pursue their relationship after she returned to Japan as a fourth-timer; the only reason she took the job was the chance to be closer to him. Elsa eventually decided to stay in Japan indefinitely as a visa overstayer and set up house with him. He rented an apartment for her in Tokyo, still maintaining that apartment for her around the time I met her fifteen years later. Except for a two-year stint in the Philippines, which is where Elsa decided to give birth to their child, Elsa and her "husband" have maintained this ongoing arrangement of his nightly visits since the early 1990s.

Despite her material security, Elsa remained deeply dissatisfied in her relationship. Yet she had no plans to leave him, not because of financial dependence but because of her selfless love for him. After all, Elsa could have returned to the Philippines and lived comfortably with all the money and property that he had already given her. Instead, complained Elsa:

> What I got out of this is—I got a lot of money. I never thought I could hold that much money. But, you know, I do not want money. I do not want it to be just money. I want it to be love too. I told him that I will not survive on money alone even if I grew up poor. I need more than money. I am not happy just to have money . . . He knows it is not just money that I want. . . . I told him what I want is for him to be by my side and to be with him always. I like talking to him. Years I have waited. Years I have suffered. I am the type of person who needs love. Ever since I was young, I did not feel love from my parents.

Elsa's cry for love stood in contradistinction to the pragmatic concerns and desires of other hostesses such as Rowena, who calculated love via her husband's monetary expenses. Despite the difference in priorities between Rowena and Elsa, we should recognize the comingling of pragmatic considerations and emotional desires not only in Rowena's but in both of their feelings. For instance, masculine magnanimity also engendered Elsa's emotional desires; her initial attraction to her "husband" had been stimulated by his generosity as a customer.

I bring up the case of Elsa and describe her current heartache to show the mingling of pragmatically driven love and emotionally driven love, telling us that these distinct motivations belong in the same moral spectrum. The impulse in the literature to disaggregate the two not only imposes Western standards and definitions of romance, as argued by Nicole Constable, but also loses sight of the meanings of romantic love engendered by the intersections of rationalism and emotions and consequently blurs our understanding of the constitution of love for migrant Filipina hostesses.[33] As importantly, the varying degrees of pragmatism and emotions in the relationships formed by hostesses call into question the boundaries that distinguish the moral groupings of hostesses. As the case of Minda shows us, deep emotional ties could sustain marriages that are initially motivated by pragmatic gains. Likewise, deep emotional ties—as Elsa has shown us—often unconsciously stem from pragmatic gains. These examples indicate that the moral groupings of migrant hostesses are distinguished by artificial boundaries, challenging us to let go of our impulse to disaggregate money and love when making sense of social relations among spouses, lovers, and friends.

CULTURAL CLASHES IN MARRIAGE

With Japanese, probably only 5 percent have a good relationship with their husband. I have not seen any happy marriages between Filipinos and Japanese. In my long time here, I have not seen any happy marriages. Most of the time, I hear them tell me they are stressed over their spouses. No one has told me, "I love my husband very much." (Amanda)

These cynical remarks shared by Amanda echo the dominant views on marriage between Japanese men and Filipino women in the Filipino migrant community. Fairy-tale endings rarely happen in the community, with marriages resulting not always in divorce but in frequent marital strife, according to the wives whom I met in Tokyo. Declarations of love for a hostess's husband are usually followed by a laundry list of the difficulties in their marriage. These include problems with Japanese in-laws, unhelpfulness of Japanese husbands with translating important documents such as school memos and government residency forms, and lack of support for extended kin in the Philippines. For Amanda, it had been the absence of her husband from the day-to-day affairs of their family life, an absence magnified by her illiteracy in Japanese, that ended her marriage.

The rate of divorce between Filipino women and Japanese men hovers slightly above the national average at around 40 percent,[34] telling us that most couples weather the storm in their not-so-perfect marriages. Racism in Japanese society represents one major hurdle in international marriages. If they have racist family members, husbands find themselves with the difficult situation of having to straddle their allegiance to their family of orientation, that is, their Filipina wife and their children, and their family of origin. Some of my interviewees had never even met their Japanese in-laws. This included Len-len, whose husband wished to shield her from the racism of his parents. This also included Sheila, whose racist in-laws wished never to meet their Filipino-Japanese grandchildren. As Sheila described, "Me, I do not get along with them [her in-laws] either. We have not been together at all. We have not spent time together. They have not met the grandchildren. They do not like foreigners. Is that unbelievable or what?" In some cases, Filipina wives wish to just stay away from their in-laws so as to avoid racist altercations. This included Rowena, who complained: "My in-laws would come to our house weekly. They were offering me divorce papers . . . They do not want a foreigner for their son." While many Japanese families hold racist views against their foreign daughters-in-law, some hostesses such as Marietta were more fortunate and managed to develop good relations with their in-laws. A single mother, Marietta received financial support from her mother-in-law for the care of her daughter.[35]

Additionally getting in the way of marital bliss are the cultural clashes that come with international marriages and the pressure for international wives to conform to the norms, values, and culture of their husbands.[36] In Korea, the state participates in the inculcation of cultural norms of the family on international brides, a process described by sociologist Minjeong Kim as the disciplining of "maternal citizenship."[37] In Japan, the process of cultural assimilation for foreign brides occurs less formally, primarily through the husband and his family but also through schools, imposing cultural norms of maternalism on foreign mothers. Making daily *obento* boxes, participating in school sports events, and attending frequent meetings with other mothers are just some of the activities inculcating a Japanese way of life for Filipina mothers in Japan. The state also impresses notions of child rearing on foreign mothers during custody battles. Since 1996, the Japan government has recognized the residency of foreign custodians of Japanese citizens.[38] Yet foreign mothers do not have the guarantee of custody after divorce, as Japanese grandparents and fathers can sue for custody of the child. Sometimes they do this to secure the deportation of the foreign wife whose residency would be conditional on her custodianship of their Japanese child if she had been without permanent residency prior to divorce. To minimize the risk of being perceived as unfit mothers by the courts, foreign wives monitor not only their sexual behavior but also their occupation after divorce. For instance, many quit hostess work, even if only temporarily, and pursue work that would not disagree with ideal notions of mothering in Japan. Marietta, for instance, sought work in a laundry shop soon after her divorce, returning to hostess work only after she had successfully secured permanent residency.

Regardless of the involvement of the state, marriage of a Filipina hostess to a Japanese is never as simple as just incorporating Japanese values and ways of life onto her own, because this process usually constitutes of a clash of cultures, one that results in acts of resistance by Filipina wives against the dominant values and cultural expectations of Japanese husbands as well as their common refusal to give up their own cultural practices. One salient example is the conflict that arises over the insistence of Filipina hostesses of maintaining financial support for extended kin in the Philippines. The continued financial support of one's natal family after marriage is said by Filipina hostesses to be foreign to the Japanese but is a common practice in the Philippines. Marriage in the Philippines constitutes a union of families in which each spouse gains membership in the family of the other spouse bilaterally.[39] The absence of government provisions and the poor state of social welfare make the care of elderly kin the family's private responsibility in the Philippines, becoming a greater responsibility for those with financial means.[40] As Filipina hostesses tend to have been among the poorest of the poor in the Philippines, they usually carry a tremendous burden to sustain their families. Illustrating this responsibility are the words that Amanda's mother shared with her: "Please take care of yourself. What will happen to us if something happens to you?"

The notion of filial piety does exist in Japan.[41] Consequently, Japanese husbands sometimes understand the sense of responsibility that their Filipina wives have to their natal family in the Philippines. Yet a continued affinity to their own kin could also make it all the more difficult for husbands to negotiate the racism of their family. However, Japan has seen a decline in filial piety since industrialization.[42] The decline of filial piety may enable husbands to minimize their ties with racist family members, but at the same time it may also encourage their disapproval of extending financial support to in-laws in the Philippines.

Elderly care, which is manifested in the financial obligations of hostesses to their family in the Philippines, is a common source of conflict between Japanese husbands and Filipina wives. Rowena, for instance, worried about the well-being of her parents in the Philippines after her husband recently decided to no longer send them financial assistance. Stated Rowena:

> He does not want me to send money to the Philippines. As far as he is concerned, we should just worry about our well-being here. We have needs here, too. He does not think that my family should be his responsibility as well. That problem started not so long ago. Before, whenever I asked for money, he would ask me what the money would be for, and I would say school, and he himself would send the money through the bank. Now he no longer wants to do it. I think it is because our expenses here are increasing . . . I think you have to pay for your breath here [laughs].

Although Rowena tried to nonchalantly laugh off her problem, during the interview I could sense her distress over it. To deal with her problem, Rowena—a stay-at-home mother for the last ten years—began to shave off a percentage of the food budget that her husband alloted every month. The small amount of money she managed to send to her family in the Philippines somehow reassured her that they would not starve back there.

In some cases, husbands have the best intention of sending money to their kin in the Philippines but simply cannot afford this added expense to their monthly household budget. It is in these cases that husbands support the return of their wives to the labor force. To balance the escalating cost of living in Japan and their continued responsibility for kin in the Philippines, plenty of Filipina wives turn to the labor market. So as not to impose the financial burden of providing for their family in the Philippines onto their husbands, many Filipina wives in Japan simply work. Yet, language difficulties limit their labor market options to the low-wage sector. Plenty of Filipina hostesses, for instance, are illiterate in the Japanese language.

Many of the married Filipino women whom I met in Japan held two jobs: They did low-wage service work, usually as a cashier or hotel chambermaid, during the daytime and worked at night as a hostess in one of the many clubs in Tokyo. Limited labor market options have made hostess work all the more attractive, as it is far more lucrative than other low-wage service jobs. Cleaning rooms as a hotel chambermaid earns Filipina hostesses in Tokyo no more than the minimum wage of 950 yen (US$9.50) per hour, but a job as a hostess could earn them anywhere between 1,000 and 2,500 yen (US$10 to 25) an hour, depending on their sales. Yet, in some cases, they turn to hostess work not for the higher wages but because they maintain a passion for singing and entertaining. Some also find hostess work more palatable than the more labor-intensive jobs available to them such as hotel housekeeping.

Yet the solution of working as a hostess to support one's family in the Philippines potentially opens the door to marital strife; it leads to the temptation of extramarital affairs, triggers jealousy among spouses, and lessens the time that couples spend together. To ease potential protests from their husbands and to legitimize their work, many Filipina wives earmark the use of their earnings from clubs solely toward helping out their families in the Philippines. Having a morally legitimate reason for doing hostess work somehow justifies their employment.[43] Julia, for instance, still worked as a hostess after being married for more than fourteen years. When asked how much she usually sent to the Philippines, she responded:

> All my income from my nighttime job. For example, I earn 200,000 [yen] at night, and I give that all to [my family in the Philippines]. Then, my earnings from the day job are what we use for our living expenses. I work in a supermarket, so I have a discount. I save a lot doing that work. So even though the salary is low, working there is very helpful. I get a 50 to 80 percent discount. Even with rice, I can get that much of a discount. That is why I struggle to stay employed in the supermarket.

By holding two jobs, Julia maintained her financial obligations to *all* of her family members, both her family of orientation in Japan and her family of origin in the Philippines. In Japan, she maintained the responsibility of providing food for her family, while her husband took care of the cost of housing and utilities. In the Philippines, she cared for her parents as well as some of her siblings and their children. Juggling these two obligations required Julia to work more than sixty hours a week.

Another motivation for wives to enter the labor market is to gain some independence from their husbands. Being a stay-at-home wife could leave them insecure and uncomfortably dependent on their husbands. This was the case for the born-again Christian Serela, a mother of three children, whose husband, a dentist, maintained complete control over her by denying her access to any money when she did not work outside the home. He would occasionally give her 10,000 or 20,000 yen (US$100 or 200) but would often refuse her requests for more. He paid for all of the expenses in the household, including their food, clothes, and other responsibilities traditionally allocated to women in the family in Japan. In protest, Serela decided to return to the labor market and work once again at a hostess club. This happened after nearly a decade of tolerating her precarious situation living under the complete control of her husband. Her youngest child was four years old at the time. She would leave after putting him to bed and would return before he woke up. Her older daughter was there to help. Serela explained her situation:

> Of course, I had material desires. I kept on asking him for money that it was stressing me out. It was because he was not giving me an allowance. I was stressed. He would buy for me what I asked. But it is different to have your own money. It is a different feeling to have your own money in your wallet. You know that feeling, right?

Serela worked at the club for three years, quitting after her husband started giving her 100,000 yen (US$1,000) per month. Her strategy of working at the club so as to gain some control over her situation eventually worked, but it was a slow process that withstood plenty of fights and turmoil in her marriage.

On marriage, a Filipina hostess, as a foreign spouse in Japan, technically becomes a dependent of her Japanese spouse. First, her legal status is conditional on her husband's continued sponsorship of her one- to three-year visa until she gains permanent residency. Foreign spouses do not qualify for permanent residency until after five years in Japan, technically making them legal dependents of their husbands and leaving them vulnerable to abuse. Aggravating their situation of dependency is the problem of their illiteracy. These two forms of dependency combined potentially debilitate Filipino women, putting them at risk, for instance, of abusive husbands who refuse to renew their visas or free them from their marriage. Further aggravating their situation of dependence is the refusal of their husbands to give them access to financial resources, as illustrated by the case of Serela. Describing the vulnerability of foreign wives to abuse, Nobue Suzuki observed, "In other cases I encountered, due to their wives' illiteracy in Japanese, other—busy, lazy, or exploitative—husbands hid their divorce records or did not help their wives process applications for visa renewal."[44] The wives' situation—as conditional residents vis-à-vis their husbands—tells us that their greater rights of long-term residency than other members of the Filipino community—specifically visa overstayers and *talents*—come at the expense of their own set of vulnerabilities. Representatives of local nongovernmental organizations as well as the Embassy of the Philippines, for instance, cite domestic violence as the most salient social problem affecting the Filipino migrant community in Tokyo. In an interview, a representative of the Philippine Embassy told me that in any given month approximately 150 Filipino women complain about their marital problems with Japanese men.[45] Complaints include problems with womanizing husbands, domestic violence, and the denial of an allowance. In contrast, only five hostesses on average come to the Philippine Embassy to complain about their work conditions, with the most common complaint being the requirement of going out on a *dohan*.

THE SEXUAL CITIZENSHIP OF TRANSGENDER HOSTESSES

"Japan is a paradise for gay men," Bambi emphatically said in our interview. This claim was one repeatedly echoed in my conversations with transgender hostesses. As the transgender hostess Ana stated, "Japan is a place that God created for the *bakla*." The positive perception of Japan among the transgender hostesses who participated in my study sharply contrasted with the more negative sentiments shared by female hostesses, who were more apt to complain about customers, club management, or their husbands. Partially accounting for the overall positive view of Japan among transgender hostesses was their attitude about hostess work. Another factor is their treatment as "real women" in Japan. While most female hostesses *tolerate* their jobs, transgender hostesses thoroughly *enjoy* them. Transgender hostesses can enjoy their work more freely because they do not have to negotiate the social stigma attached to females for doing hostess work. Transgender hostesses also enjoy their work because it makes them feel "like real women." According to Peachy, transgender hostesses feel "like real women" when customers regularly visit them at the club and when they become the object of their customer's affection. Feelings of being "like real women" are further reinforced when romantic relationships develop between customers and transgender hostesses. Yet the fact that transgender hostesses are only "*like* real women" and not *actually* "real women" poses a problem for those wishing to pursue long-term relations with their romantic partners and for those wishing to stay in Japan for more than six months. Hence, not being women not only results in poorer labor conditions for transgender hostesses, which makes their positive outlook over their labor all the more ironic, but it also results in their unequal sexual citizenship vis-à-vis heterosexual female hostesses.

Settlement in Japan mandates ascribing to nationalist ideologies of reproduction, as compulsory heterosexuality dictates the requirements for long-term residency. For foreigners, long-term legal residency in Japan is conditional on their participation in a heterosexual union with a Japanese national either through marriage or by giving birth to a child. Same-sex marriages are not recognized in Japan, potentially precluding long-term residency for transgender hostesses. Yet, of the eleven transgender hostesses who participated in my study, five attained long-term residency as a foreign spouse, with two having entered what they would refer to in the community as an "imitation marriage," meaning a "fake marriage" or "paper marriage" that one enters without the intention of consummating the relationship. The three others pursued genuine romantic relationships that led to their eventual attainment of a *kekkon* (marriage) visa. Two pursued romantic relations with females, and one married the mother of her romantic partner. To gain legal residency, transgender hostesses clearly manipulate the law. In so doing, they do not insist on their sexual citizenship, which in this case would refer to their right to determine their intimate relations, as they do not insist on the acknowledgment of their sexual preference, which is to be with a masculine male; instead they subvert the principles of sexual citizenship in Japan via their marriage to masculine females or to those they describe as "normal" women.

While belonging in the nation-state promotes heterosexual marriages, the marital unions of transgender hostesses undeniably subvert the institution of marriage as an emblem of heterosexuality. This is particularly true in their marriages to masculine females. These partnerships of "gender reversals," a term used by my informants to describe the rearrangement of the gender order in their marriages, mock the idea that there is an "original" gender, a gender order associated with sex and the body. These marriages trouble the categories of gender via their performance, reminding us of the contingency of gender identities and the possibilities of their resignification and reconstitution.[46]

Transgender hostesses become wives, while their female-to-male partners become husbands, telling us that the gendered categories of wife and husband are not of an "internal essence of gender" but instead they are "manufactured through a sustained set of acts, posited through the gendered stylization of the body."[47] In this section, I interrogate the ways transgender hostesses circumvent and challenge what Diane Richardson calls "heteronormal" conditions of citizenship when they enter marriages with biological females so as to secure long-term residency in Japan.[48] How does their undoing of gender and sexual norms in the institution of marriage subvert heteronormal conditions of citizenship? What do their acts signify about their identity as gay men or transgender subjects? Moreover, how does their marriage to biological females, as self-identified male-to-female transgender or transsexual subjects, question notions of authenticity in marriage and lead to the subversion of marital culture?

If given the choice, the transgender hostesses who participated in my study would have preferred to marry a masculine male. They all self-identified as *bakla*, ascribing to a feminine persona as they sexually desired normative male partners.[49] The transgender *bakla* in Tokyo ascribe to the same sexual desires and gender identity as the *bantut* studied by Mark Johnson in the Southern Philippines.[50] The term *bantut* traditionally refers to men who adopt feminine practices and at the same time desire masculine, that is, normative, male partners. The *bantut* self-identify as gay as did the transgender hostesses whom I met in Japan. Considering that these transgender hostesses did not insist on same-sex marriages with their ideal romantic partner, that is, a normative male, we could argue that their marriages to females, even masculine ones, did not question the heterosexual principles of marriage in Japan but in fact maintained the continued exclusion of gay marriages. Yet I wish to point out that the subversion of heteronormativity need not be a zero-sum game of sexual citizenship. After all, transgender hostesses legitimately attain long-term residency via marriage, even if not to their preferred partner of a masculine male, by subverting the gender order associated with marriage.

Marriage is a politically contentious issue in queer communities, with the right to same-sex marriage seen as a battleground for sexual citizenship.[51] Diane Richardson argues that citizenship is nothing more than "naturalized heterosexuality," as homosexuality is banished to the private sphere with the denial of public recognition of same-sex marriages.[52] Likewise, Jeffrey Weeks argues that rights to "intimate citizenship," meaning the control of one's body, emotions, identity, and relations, should include the recognition of sexual diversity in the public sphere.[53] For many, the right of same-sex marriage is tantamount to the citizenship of nonheterosexuals, an inclusion that both normalizes and transgresses the moral order of marriage.[54] While acknowledging that marriage is a battleground for political struggles over "sexual citizenship," I do not wish to engage in a debate on the pros and cons of gay marriages. Instead, I wish to focus on the process of becoming a citizen for a transgender hostess and the meanings of her subversion of both the gender and sexual order of marriage when she marries a transgender female-to-male husband, or a biological female in general, to attain citizenship in Japan. In other words, I wish to examine the process of these transgender hostesses becoming sexual citizens from the subject-position of being "like real women" in Japan.

While "real" Filipino women do not necessarily come to Japan to seek romance, most transgender hostesses do. Japan offers them opportunities for romance otherwise closed to them in the Philippines. Bambi, a veteran hostess whose drug problems had barred her from working in most transgender clubs in Tokyo, refused to go back to the Philippines despite her precarious job situation. Keeping her in Tokyo were her relationships with men, whose financial support made her feel "like a real woman." Explaining her preference for Japanese men over Filipino men, Bambi stated: "I realize when I go back to the Philippines, I do not enjoy myself in the Philippines. It is different here. Here we are women. Here we get courted. Here men do not scam you for money. Usually, it is men that give you money." Bambi complained that sexual relations between the *bakla* in the Philippines and their male partners do not fit traditional gender relations of male providers and female nurturers that *bakla* like her crave to validate their feelings of being "like real women." In the Philippines, the *bakla*, instead of receiving, provides financial support to her sexual partners, a reality that reflects the sexual dynamics between the *travesti* studied by Don Kulick in Brazil and their masculine male lovers.[55] Asked if her gay identity were an issue for potential male lovers and providers in Japan, Bambi said it was not. She instead claimed: "They do not care, as long as they are in love with you. Even if you have three breasts and two penises, they do not care. What matters for them is they love you. Even if you are crippled, if they love you, then they love you no matter what." The opportunity for love is a central reason that transgender hostesses frequently claim that "*ang Japan ay paraiso para sa mga bakla*," meaning "Japan is the paradise of gay men," or as they likewise say in English, "Japan is paradise for the gays."

Like female hostesses, transgender hostesses view love as intrinsically tied to money. Exchanges of flirtation-for-money that take place in the club unavoidably influence their constructions of love. Mirroring the narratives of love shared by female hostesses, descriptions of love by transgender hostesses often measure the commitment of masculine partners according to their generosity. Rafaella, for instance, knew that her boyfriend loved her because he gave her 100,000 yen (US$1,000) or sometimes even 200,000 yen (US$2,000) per month. Married, he had recently told her he wanted to leave his wife for her, leaving her ridden with guilt over this news. Rafaella did have the option of living with him as she had a *kekkon* (marriage) visa. She was at the time of our interview in an "imitation marriage" with a transgender female-to-male, who in exchange for giving Rafaella a long-term resident visa got to live rent-free in Rafaella's apartment. They planned to keep this arrangement for five years until Rafaella secured permanent residency status.

Hostesses not only engage in paper marriages with female-to-male transgender subjects, but they also pursue genuine romantic relations with them. May, for instance, married a female-to-male transgender who romantically pursued her. One of the three interviewees who underwent an operation for a sex change, May had no intention of "falling in love" with a person whom she described as a "woman," as she had always had a sexual preference for masculine men. One of the reasons she had her operation, for example, was to have sex with men without the pressure "to hide it." She explained that her male partners usually knew of her sexual identity but "lost interest" when they saw "it." Still, May fell in love with a "woman." Explaining the circumstances that led to her marriage to a "woman," May described how feelings of love and affection developed between them while they worked together at a club:

> We used to work together. He applied to work at our club. I was the head of the *talents*. All applicants, including the Japanese, I interviewed. Then, I accepted him. But there was no love interest there. He is a tomboy, right? Before I knew it, he started pursuing me. . . . Then he eventually became my friend. It was the first time that he worked in a place with a *show time* at night. I used to teach him the ropes in the club until he started courting me. . . . He did not formally court me. He did not follow

traditional [Filipino] ritual and visit me at home. Since we were together at the club, every time he came to work he had something for me like a hamburger or whatever he can think of for me. When we do *show time*, he will wipe my back. I will tell him that he does not have to do that. I saw him just as a friend. Little did I know that he saw me differently.

Being an object of affection instilled feelings of being "like a real woman" for May. Further enforcing these sentiments had been the demonstration of *ligaw*, meaning traditional Filipino courtship, by her co-worker. In the Philippines, the courtship ritual of a man visiting a woman at home and offering her gifts is the ultimate symbol of heteronormativity. May's participation in this heteronormative courtship ritual could only have reinforced her feelings of being "like a real woman," thus fulfilling one of the reasons why she migrated to Japan.

As one of the primary reasons for her migration had been to experience life like a woman, it is not surprising that May soon became fond of her "husband." Without doubt, his actions reinforced her feminine identity. They had recently separated, however. A distraught May claimed that they carried a "normal" relationship until he strayed and broke her heart when he had an affair with a woman. Explaining the circumstances of her heartbreak, May said,

He was the first one to flirt. He found another woman. Maybe he is more satisfied with a real woman because that is what he really wants. He is a tomboy after all. So I gave in to him. I told him it was OK. I could understand him, so I said it was fine.

Though she had accepted the affair, May admitted to being unhappy about it. What had been particularly hurtful for May about the affair was the different gender dynamic that her "husband" accorded his relationship with his female mistress. May complained that he gave money to that woman but never gave her any. He even asked May for money to give to the woman. May admitted to feeling jealous of the greater benevolence that her "husband" had extended to the woman. What was particularly hurtful about this situation for May was that it reminded her that she was not a real woman after all. The lesser financial support that her "husband" had provided her during their time together indicated to May her lesser worth than a real woman would have to her husband.

Another transgender hostess who married someone female was Bambi, who pursued marriage not so much to feel like a woman, as did May, but instead to act on her sudden urge to have a family. Bambi decided to marry a woman who romantically pursued and courted her, she explained, to see whether she could have a family with a husband, wife, and children. Yet Bambi's marriage could not last as her desires for a family contradicted her gender and sexual identity of wanting to be "like a woman." Bambi could not explain her motives for suddenly wanting to raise a family. Perhaps it was her Catholic faith, she said, or perhaps it was also societal pressure in the Philippines to abide by normative standards of sexuality. Regardless of her reasons, Bambi entered her marriage to a woman in good faith. As she explained, "At first, I really tried to make the marriage work. I wanted to have a family of my own." Like May, Bambi engaged in sexual relations with the woman, not really enjoying it as it only reinforced her sole preference for men. As she described, " I could not really enjoy it. I did not really feel it. She loves me. But me, I realize that I like her only as a family. That is what I wanted. Like she is an older sister to me." Penetrating the woman whom Bambi called her "wife" also contradicted her identity of wanting to be "like a woman," which at the end only reinforced her desire to be penetrated by men. For Bambi, the reaffirmation of her gender identity did not come down to being the object of male affection as had been the case for the transsexual May but instead, similar to *travesti* in Brazil, it was centrally determined by being penetrated in sex.[56] To be "like a real woman" for Bambi meant she did not penetrate but instead was the one penetrated.

Underlying the pleasures of participating in heteronormal courtship rituals for transgender hostesses such as Rafaella, May, and Bambi is the ultimate fantasy of becoming a bride, a status that symbolically represents the achievement of true womanhood for heterosexual women and hence one frequently cited by transgender hostesses as a fantasy they wish to fulfill by finding "true love" in Japan. Ana, an incredibly gorgeous transsexual woman, narrated such a desire for coming to Japan:

I was in elementary, imagine, and that was when I first heard about sex changes. That was when I first made it a goal to have a sex change. I said, I would be rich. I also aspired to get my dream car of a BMW. Then, third, I wanted to be a woman. Actually, my first dream was to be a woman. I wanted to become a woman, a rich one. Then my wildest dream was that I would marry a man who will accept me as I am, who will see me as a real woman, and who will love me. We would get married, and I would wear a wedding gown. That was my dream since I was in the sixth grade. I was already *baklang bakla* [very *bakla*, or a very feminine man] ever since I was young. Then think about it, look at my situation, my wildest dream was the one that became true. Now it's all done. I have reached all those dreams of mine.

Ana was in a relationship with a masculine male, a highly successful stockbroker who had recently purchased a BMW to fulfill Ana's dream of owning such a car. Deeply in love with Ana, her boyfriend looked at her as a "real woman," even going to the Philippines to ask for her hand in marriage from her parents, to which her father replied, Ana shared with a giggle, "Young man, do you know what you are getting yourself into?" Most people who saw Ana would gawk at her, not because there is a gender ambiguity in her appearance as one would expect of transgender persons but because of her flawless beauty with her China-doll face, porcelain skin with the natural strawberry hue on her cheeks, and long thick black lashes that made her eyes more prominent and alluring. To put it simply, Ana was stunningly beautiful.

While Ana looked more like a woman than most women, she unfortunately could not marry the "man of her dreams" as they were both legally male. In Japan, foreigners obtain a marriage certificate by first getting a security clearance from their respective foreign embassy, after which they must register their marriage at city hall. Then, the couple files for the foreigner's legal residency at the immigration office. Surprisingly, neither May nor Bambi faced any gender-related difficulty at either city hall or the immigration office, even though their gender appearances had not matched their sex of record. According to May, the performance of gender does not factor into one's eligibility for marriage in Japan. Regardless of gender, the state would recognize the partnership as long as the marital union involves two people with differently sexed bodies.[57] Even though May and her "tomboy" spouse's visits were usually met with amusement at city hall, May knew that her application for legal residency could not be dismissed because of the legality of her marriage. We discussed her situation:

The "tomboy" and you, when you went to Immigration, were they OK with you?
When it comes to the papers that we walk, like for instance in city hall, they call me "wife." and they treat me as the wife. I tell them no, and I tell them that I am the mister. I have not changed my name, that is why.

What do they say?
Nothing. They find it amusing.

And at Immigration?

They are also amused. They do not mind. They think it is normal. They think it is a normal marriage because it is with a male and female. Others [that is, legally male transgender women] have a sex transplant . . . and they marry a man. That is more dangerous. They do not recognize those kinds of marriages.

For May, marrying a tomboy, as it conformed to the heterosexual principles of marriage, posed no legal dilemmas. In contrast, Ana—regardless of her sex change surgery—could not marry her boyfriend. The exclusion of same-sex marriage in Japan hindered the legal recognition of Ana's partnership with her boyfriend.

To circumvent the law and enable Ana to reside in Japan, Ana's boyfriend's mother decided to marry her. In fact, his parents—who were still in a relationship—divorced for the sole purpose of allowing the mother to marry Ana. Now able to stay in Japan conditionally as a *kekkon* (marriage) visa holder and legal husband of an elderly woman, Ana was able to not only pursue a romantic relationship with her boyfriend but also to perform her ultimate fantasy of becoming a wife. According to Ana, she and her in-laws all lived in one household, as "one happy family." Incorporated into her boyfriend's extended kin, Ana filled the shoes of a traditional daughter-in-law, assisting her mother-in-law, who is technically her wife, with the running of the household and duly accepting her responsibilities for caring for her in-laws as they get older. Being with an only child gave Ana these responsibilities, which she embraced—she told me—because it reinforced her identity as a woman.

Not quite satisfied with her situation, Ana would eventually have liked to solidify her relationship with her boyfriend through marriage, which she hoped they could do if she could declare herself legally female. Shortly before I met Ana, Japan passed the Law Concerning Special Cases in Handling Gender for People with Gender Identity Disorder, otherwise known as Law 111. This law allows transgenders to petition for an amendment to their legal gender. Ana mentioned this law to me, expressing her plans to attain not only permanent residency but eventually also citizenship so she could petition for a change in gender and ultimately marry her boyfriend. Remaining a Philippine citizen would bar her ability to do so as it would be the Philippines and not Japan declaring her legal gender identity. However, Ana faced an uphill battle, as qualification for citizenship required her complete cultural immersion, which would entail years of schooling in Japanese language classes. Law 111 is seemingly inclusive; yet it restricts the reproductive rights of transsexuals. Only those who are "presently unmarried," "childless," and among other criteria "possess no gonads or persistent lack of gonadal function" qualify to petition for a change in their legal gender identity.[58] Sexuality studies scholar Susan Stryker observes,

> Reproductive freedom is denied to transgender people, and the national citizen's registry comes to function as a de facto instrument of discrimination to the extent that discordances in administrative records pertaining to a transgender person's gender result in denial of state benefits, or other harmful actions or consequences (job, family, public accommodation, health care services).[59]

Returning to the case of Ana, her desire to become legally female so as to have a family with her boyfriend was thwarted by the removal of her reproductive rights. Ana wished to eventually adopt a baby, but she would be best able to do so if she remained legally male.

For transgender hostesses such as Ana, Bambi, and others, the performance of gender, in this case of femininity, in itself does not constitute their identity of being "like women." Instead, it is the acknowledgment of these performances, their recognition, and validation with masculine gestures that would constitute their feminine identity. My insistence on situating gender in a social context forces us to expand Judith Butler's assertion that gender's performance and reiteration of such a performance would on their own constitute the notion of a stable gender identity.[60] Instead, I wish to argue that the social relations constituted in the performance of gender are what gives meaning to gender, reaffirming the assertion of R. W. Connell that meanings of gender are not constituted in a vacuum.[61] Moreover, meanings of gender always emerge relationally. As Connell asserts, "Masculinity and femininity are inherently relational concepts which have meaning in relation to each other, as a social demarcation and a cultural opposition. This holds regardless of the changing content of the demarcation in different societies and periods of history."[62] Hence, performances of femininity by transgender hostesses cannot stand on their own in the constitution of gender. Instead, as the sociologist Jane Ward has observed, reciprocal acts of masculinity must confirm gender performances of femininity and vice versa.[63] In other words, acts of masculinity must validate the performances of femininity by transgender hostesses in the constitution of their gender identity of being "like real women." If not, the making of identity through the feminine performances of transgender hostesses does not come into fruition. In Japan, transgender hostesses feel "like real women" because of the recognition of their gender performances by men and female-to-male transgender subjects, who in manifold ways respond to their acts of femininity with masculine gestures. In the world of transgender hostesses, reciprocations of gender performances of masculinity and femininity take place in their participation in traditional courtship rituals, performance of marital relations, and participation in sexual acts.[64]

Transgender hostesses' reliance on acts of gender reciprocations of masculinity and femininity in their quest to experience life "like a real woman" seems to suggest the reiteration of heteronormativity. What do we make of these seemingly heteronormative relations that they pursue with masculine subjects in Japan? Borrowing the notion of "dubbing" posed by anthropologist Tom Boellstorff in his discussion of homosexual culture in Indonesia, we could argue that Filipina transgender hostesses likewise "dub" the "mass mediated messages" of heteronormativity in their construction of a gender identity.[65] As Boellstorff explains, the subject position of gay and lesbians in Indonesia emerges from their practice of *dubbing culture*, particularly the dubbing of Western sexual subjectivities, which in the process of imitation transforms into a particular sexual subjectivity unique to its context. We could argue that transgender hostesses, in dubbing heterosexual culture, do not re-create it but instead create a fusion that questions the authenticity of heteronormativity by their very performance of it. In making this argument, we do not, however, underscore the subversion of culture, particularly of the institution of marriage, by transgender hostesses.

Instead of dubbing, I wish to pose the idea that transgender hostesses *mimic heteronormativity* in their gender performances, as the making of their identity to be "like real women" rests on their simultaneous recuperation and subversion of heterosexuality. The idea of mimicking defines their process of becoming "like a real woman" as well as the process of their becoming long-term residents of Japan. My formulation of "mimicking heteronormativity" utilizes Homi Bhabha's concept of colonial mimicry, which refers to the process by which colonized subjects appropriate characteristics and ideals of the colonizer.[66] In making sense of the actions of transgender hostesses in Tokyo, we could extend Bhabha's discussion of colonialism to apply to heteronormativity as an oppressive force of domination. As we learned earlier in this chapter, foreigners in Japan qualify for long-term residency only via marriage unless they are legally adopted, which would be unusual for an adult, or if they gain custodianship of a Japanese dependent. To become a long-term resident usually requires that a transgender hostess abides by the script of heterosexual marital unions, which she could potentially do by *practicing heterosexuality* and performing a masculine self. She could imitate normalized dimensions of heteronormativity by performing masculinity in marriage to a woman in Japan. Bambi, for instance, seemed to have done just that by marrying a person whom she described as a "normal woman" and carrying out "normal" sexual relations with her. Yet, as expected, they mostly reject this route. For example, Bambi still retained her feminine gender identity during her marriage to a "normal" woman. Instead, they subvert the heterosexual script of marriage by seeking not feminine partners to gain citizenship but instead masculine partners. They mold heteronormativity to fit into their lives as male-to-female transgender beings in Tokyo.

According to Bhabha, "Colonial mimicry is the desire for a reformed, recognizable Other, *as a subject of a difference that is almost the same, but not quite.*" The process of mimicking in this case "emerges as the representation of a difference that is itself a process of disavowal."[67] In other words, mimicking involves a process of subversion, what Bhabha refers to as "mockery," that disavows dominant cultural practices. Indeed, the practice of "mimicking heteronormativity" is "almost the same but not quite" as transgender hostesses choose not to embody a heterosexual self that abides by dominant cultural scripts of the sexes.[68] When mimicking heteronormativity, they do not practice heterosexuality. As men, they choose not to embody a masculine self and pursue a feminine partner. Instead, they maintain a feminine self and ascribe to Japan's heteronormative laws of citizenship so as to attain long-term legal residency in Japan. They marry a masculine transgender, the mother of their male partner, or completely subvert the law by pursuing a paper marriage.

What do acts of mimicking heteronormativity tell us about the constitution of gender and sexual norms in the institution of marriage? How does mimicking heteronormativity open the door to the subversion of the institution of marriage and consequently lead to the possibility of the greater tolerance for same-sex marriages? The marriages of transgender hostesses to females, whether with masculine ones or elderly grandmothers, disconnect heterosexuality from the institution of marriage with their recognition by the state, as the sanctioning of such marriages acknowledges the subversion of the gender and sexual order in heterosexual marriages. Still, we should acknowledge that perhaps the undoing of gender could occur only because marriage is deeply entrenched in heterosexuality. Regardless of how "abnormal" or "amusing" its gender arrangement, marriage remains morally acceptable as long as it involves two people with differently sexed bodies.

The designation of transgender marriages as "abnormal" does point to their transformative limits. When asked if she faced any difficulty with the acceptance of her marriage by state officials, Bambi responded, "They could not do anything about it because our marriage is legal. Even though I am abnormal, the woman still loves me. So they cannot do anything about that one." By insisting on maintaining her "abnormal" gender on her marriage to a female, Bambi insisted on the resignification of the gender categories we generally associate with marriage. At the same time, the self-definition of Bambi as "abnormal" does indicate the liminality of her position as an "abnormal" husband or wife. She inhabited what Butler would call

> . . . middle regions, hybrid regions of legitimacy and illegitimacy that have no clear names and where nomination itself falls into a crisis produced by the variable, sometimes violent boundaries by legitimating practices that come into uneasy and sometimes conflictual contact with one another.[69]

The state of "abnormality" inhabited by Bambi calls attention to her lack of recognition, even self-recognition, as normative gender and sexual categories of marriage remain entrenched in her mimicking of heteronormativity.

Despite its transformative limits, the resignification of gender in these marriages does, however, challenge the categories we attach to the institution of marriage. We see the unquestionable subversion of sexual and gender norms, for instance in the earlier described experience of May when she registered her marriage to a "tomboy" at both city hall and the immigration office. May's marriage to a masculine female clearly questioned the gender order of marriage with her avowal of her status as a "mister." By presenting herself as a feminine mister, May insisted on the mimicking and not the practice of heterosexuality.

By establishing the normalcy of her marriage, May also reminded us that the government refuses to recognize same-sex marriages, restricting the options for long-term resident eligibility of transsexuals such as herself who find their gender identity limited by their legal status as male. While May called attention to the denial of sexual citizenship to gays and lesbians, that is, the denial of state and public recognition of same-sex marriages, she also mocked the basis of their exclusion. May's circumvention of the law via her marriage to a female, that is her mimicking of heterosexuality, challenged the very premise of gay and lesbian exclusion with the subversion of the gender and sexual norms of marriage.

The recognition of masculine wives, feminine husbands, male brides, and female grooms by the state troubles not only the categories of gender but also the sexual norms of heterosexual marriage. Yet the repetition of these recognitions is ultimately necessary for the subversion of the gender and sexual order in marriage. Indeed, the marriages of May and Bambi are not considered anomalous among members of the Filipino community, who frequently hear of the queer marriages practiced by not only the *bakla* but also by heterosexual females who engage in nonsexual unions to gain long-term residency visas. For many hostesses, the process of becoming sexual citizens entails their participation in an asexual marriage. This has increasingly become the case with the crackdown on the migration of *talents* since their identification as sex-trafficked persons by the U.S. government. Asexual marriages redefine marital fidelity. They challenge us to expand what we consider are legitimate bases of marriage and to recognize nonsexual commitments, such as friendships, as genuine partnerships. Bambi and her wife, for instance, have chosen to remain married even after they had stopped engaging in sexual intercourse. They remained deeply committed to one another, even if only as friends. We should see these nonnormative marriages as one other way that migrant Filipinos in Japan redefine marital norms when they try to establish long-term residency through the circumvention of the heteronormal conditions of marriage. Without doubt, these asexual marriages, along with the marriages of transgender hostesses, both in their different ways subvert sexual norms that we associate with the institution of marriage.

This chapter has described the conditions of citizenship for long-term legal residents via the lens of marriage. It has used marriage as a springboard to examine settlement so as to underscore the subject position of long-term residents as sexual citizens. As my discussion in this chapter has showed, particular struggles of citizenship arise from this subject position, including for instance the issue of the vulnerability engendered by conditional residency for wives whose legal residency in Japan is conditional to their continued marriage to a Japanese citizen. This, coupled with their illiteracy, increases the susceptibility of these women to domestic violence. Another evident struggle concerns the exclusionary measures confronted and subverted by transgender hostesses in the process of establishing long-term residency in Japan.

While I use marriage as a springboard to examine citizenship, I do not unquestioningly uphold the sanctity of marriage in my discussion of the challenges confronted by migrant hostesses as sexual citizens but instead simultaneously question the premise on which marriage is used to distinguish certain groups of migrants as more legitimate members of Japan than others. I question the notion that marriage is a "purchase on legitimacy."[70] I call into question the basis of legitimacy for long-term legal residents in Japan by arguing that marriage belongs in the same moral continuum as sex work; it is merely one of many settings of commercial exchange in society. Hence, I question the moral distinction that wives tend to make of themselves vis-à-vis Filipinas with entertainer visas. As Lieba Faier noticed in her study of Filipina wives in rural Japan, they tend to think of hostessing as morally compromising and resulting in negative impressions of Filipino women.[71] Yet, contrary to the moral distinction Filipina wives make of themselves, acquiring legal status as sexual citizens implicitly involves the commercial exchange of receiving a visa for sex, regardless of the affective ties that one maintains in marital relationships. Additionally, I illustrate the instability of the sexual and gender categories that uphold the institution of marriage by describing the subversion of sexual and gender norms in the marriages of transgender hostesses, a process that questions the moral standards of heterosexuality in marriage. This chapter dismantles the categories that uphold marriage not solely for the sake of their mere dismantlement but to call attention to the displacements of citizenship that confront long-term legal residents, addressing the question of who gets excluded and what forms of vulnerability the dependency on marriage engenders for migrant hostesses.

CHAPTER SEVEN

THE INVISIBILITY OF HOSTESSES

IN THE PHILIPPINES, THE MOST COMMON euphemism for an irregular or undocumented migrant is T-N-T, which is an abbreviation for *tago-ng-tago*, meaning to hide and hide. Indeed, the phrase *tago ng tago* best captures the everyday life of migrant hostesses without legal residency in Japan; they remain acutely conscious of the threat of deportation and seek an inconspicuous existence from police and immigration authorities. They inhabit what Victor Talavera and his colleagues describe as a "conditional state of possible deportation."[1] To avoid getting caught by immigration authorities, undocumented workers perpetually monitor their behavior so as to remain inconspicuous. They also limit their interactions in the public sphere. Their lives are often bound between home and work, which is a constriction that leads to their isolation and defines their settlement as one of limited geographical mobility.[2] Giving us an example is the long-time undocumented worker Yvonne, who came to Japan only to attend her sister's funeral but ended up staying in Japan illegally after she decided to be the primary caregiver for her niece, whose mother, Yvonne's sister, had died in a car accident. She described the existence of many undocumented workers like herself when she talked about her daily routine of going to and from work, "Me, I have been here for a long time. I have worked in an *omise* for many years. . . . I never go out. That is bad. I just go to work and home, work and home. That is why I do not know anything. I do not know many places here." Like Yvonne, undocumented migrant hostesses in the nightlife industry of Japan rarely venture in public spaces, contain their interactions to home and work, and experience migration as a life of isolation. Most rarely leave the vicinity of their neighborhood, with some, I learned, not knowing how to walk to the nearest train station from their house, even if it is a mere four blocks from their doorstep.

For undocumented migrants across the globe, deportability is a product of the criminalization of illegal residency, which according to anthropologist Nicolas de Genova is a disciplining measure imposed by the state; the policing of public spaces serves to "discipline undocumented migrants by surveilling their 'illegality' and exacerbating their sense of ever-present vulnerability."[3] In Japan, the absence of civil rights exacerbates the vulnerability of undocumented migrants to deportation, resulting in their heightened surveillance.[4] To look foreign is reason enough to invite interrogation by state authorities; one need not commit a crime to be questioned by authorities in public spaces. In the Filipino migrant community, stories circulate about how authorities can randomly approach non-Japanese-looking individuals and demand proof of legal residency. Those without legal documents are immediately taken to the police station, where they will be booked and transferred to immigration authorities. Migrants are then placed in detention until their deportation. Identification leads to indefinite incarceration, as migrants are deported only if they can without assistance from the state raise the funds needed to cover the cost of their airfare to return to their country of origin.

Many undocumented hostesses claim not to mind being sent home to the Philippines. As many noted, "If it is time, then it is time." What they do mind is the humiliation of incarceration, which is a procedural step in the process of involuntary deportation from Japan.[5] Maki, once an undocumented worker in Japan, was one of the few hostesses whom I met who had experienced incarceration. She had been caught in a raid of a *hosto* club that she visited with a friend after work. Describing the extreme humiliation of her detention, Maki recalled:

> That was intense. I had to wear the prison garb. Then you were chained like a dog on your waist. Then you have two bodyguards. They do that when they take you for an interview. . . . While detained, we only had ten minutes to shower and we would have to do it together. You cannot take a bath. There were different people there. The people with me were of different races . . . Then, when we eat, they put our food through this small hole . . . I felt like they were feeding us like we were dogs. We had no money, so we could not eat what we wanted to eat. Then the time to wash up is only five minutes. You do not do anything the whole afternoon . . . Then you smoke only during the designated time for smoking. I think it is ten minutes. You are all together. All of you are chained together. It was very hard. I was there for three months.

Maki had finally managed to leave prison after one of her customers paid for her fare back to the Philippines. Stories, such as the one shared by Maki, on the hardship and humiliation of incarceration circulate among migrant Filipina hostesses and consequently instill fear among visa overstayers.

To underscore their precarious situation of settlement, this chapter describes not just the everyday life of undocumented migrant hostesses but also the constant fear and vulnerability of their settlement, what anthropologist Sarah Willen would describe as the embodied experience of "being-in-the-world."[6] Recognizing the perpetual fear of deportation that characterizes the being of undocumented migrants in Japan, I refer to them as invisible citizens.[7] Distinct from their counterparts with legal status in Japan, the terms of belonging for undocumented migrants require that they continuously hide during the process of settlement. Seeking invisibility is a state of being shared by migrant Filipina hostesses with undocumented migrants elsewhere. In Switzerland, Hans-Rudolf Wicker describes the liminal existence of undocumented workers as "structurally integrated but symbolically and socially excluded to such an extent that they become invisible."[8] In Israel, Sarah Willen likewise found that undocumented migrants inhabit the extreme margins of society. As she states, most occupy "structurally as well as geographically, socially, and politically peripheral" spaces.[9] Anthropologist Leo Chavez identifies two trajectories of settlement for undocumented migrants in California.[10] There are those who rarely interact with the institutions and members of the larger society, and then there are those who manage to blend in and become integrated into the host society and culture.

We often hear about the latter group, whose citizenship is described by the leading migration scholar Saskia Sassen as one that is "unauthorized yet recognized."[11] Although citizenship evades them, some undocumented workers still manage to work and raise a family in the host society. Arguing that membership in the modern nation-state need not require legal residency, Sassen notes that there are "multiple dimensions of citizenship which engender strategies for legitimizing informal or extra-statal forms of membership."[12] Agreeing with Sassen, sociologist Yasemin Soysal argues that the membership of guest workers, a group that includes undocumented workers in her formulation, supersedes the territorial dimensions of national citizenship to accord a form of postnational membership on the basis of rights and protection grounded in the principles of human rights. Soysal argues that migrants in Europe have realized their rightful membership in the host polity because of their experience of "a shared public social space; a set of abstract principles and responsibilities (such as human rights, respect for justice . . . and a 'productive life'); and the rationalized organization and routine of everyday praxis."[13] In other words, the limited national rights of guest workers are made irrelevant by the influence of universal human rights. Yet the case of migrant Filipina hostesses reminds us that some migrant workers remain outside the purview of mainstream society, and the marginal space they inhabit elides them human rights protection. Instead of finding membership as "unauthorized yet recognized" subjects, they are instead *unauthorized and unrecognized.*

Illustrating the lives of undocumented hostesses in Japan, this chapter describes their state of being "unauthorized and unrecognized," or invisible citizenship. It establishes that this state of being, one that is engendered by their conditional status of deportability, leaves them vulnerable to human rights abuses. My description of the invisible citizenship of undocumented workers follows Sarah Willen's "critical phenomenology of illegality," in which she captures the precarious status of illegal migrants by documenting the embodiment of illegality, including their sensory and perceptual experience of it as well as the emotional instability engendered by their vulnerability to deportation.[14] At the same time, I not only recognize the phenomenological insecurities generated by the conditional state of deportability but also scrutinize the ways migrants minimize it. Following Foucault's notion of "governmentality," citizenship as experience is constructed not only by how the state defines one's terms of belonging but also by how the self negotiates these terms. As I noted, undocumented migrants negotiate their vulnerability to deportation via their conscious efforts to achieve invisibility. They diffuse the threat of deportation by remaining inconspicuous. To avoid identification and its consequent result of deportation, they minimize their interactions in the public sphere and, when in the public sphere, they employ strategies of blending in with the crowd, which is a task made difficult by their distinct phenotype, darker than most Japanese.

Negotiating the threat of deportation via maintaining invisibility not only keeps undocumented migrants living in the shadows of the law but also leaves them outside the protection of the law. They are in what Susan Coutin describes as a state of being "physically present but legally absent, existing in a space outside of society, a space of 'nonexistence.'"[15] By forcing migrants to a state of invisibility, the criminalization of undocumented migrants by the state renders them vulnerable to the abuse of employers and coethnics.[16] Undocumented migrants frequently depend on their employers for housing; transportation whenever they venture outside their home, for instance to work, the supermarket, and church; and access to banks for remittances. Common sights outside churches holding Filipino masses on Sunday are white vans that transport hostesses, leaving the impression that employers imprison these workers. Yet this is more likely an agreed-upon arrangement preferred by a worker either because she is undocumented or, if a *talent*, unfamiliar with the way to church. Regardless, the unequal dependency between undocumented migrants and their employers renders the migrants extremely vulnerable to abuse. For example, employers have frequently been known to withhold the wages of undocumented workers. Coethnic abuse also arises as those with legal documents profit from the inability of undocumented workers to secure housing, open bank accounts, and remit funds to the Philippines.[17] In other words, the criminalization of illegal residency leaves migrant workers who are "unauthorized and unrecognized" susceptible to human rights violations and elides them the protection granted by the discourse of human rights. This in turn suggests that it is the criminalization of undocumented workers that renders them vulnerable to forced labor. By calling attention to the vulnerabilities engendered by the criminalization of illegal residency, this chapter provides another example of how current laws in place are actually to blame for the susceptibility of Filipina migrant hostesses to "human trafficking." Alongside the protectionist laws described in Chapter One, we see in this chapter how punitive laws against undocumented migrant workers in host societies expose them to abusive situations in the process of migration.

THE UNDOCUMENTED

Official government figures give a fairly small number of Filipino visa overstayers, totaling 28,491 in January 1, 2007, with an estimated number of 9,323 men and 19,168 women.[18] Yet the informal count shared by nongovernmental organizations reaches 40,000. In Japan, illegal migrants are referred to as visa overstayers regardless of the circumstances of their migration. Lumped in the category of overstayers are those who exceed the limit of either their tourist visa or their entertainer visa. During the time of my fieldwork, community members referred to visa overstayers as *bilog*, which in Filipino means "round." *Bilog* is a translated reference to the letter *O*, which members of the migrant community use as an abbreviated reference to the word *overstay*.[19] Of fifty-six participants in my study, twenty-six had been undocumented at some point of their stay in Japan. At the time of my interviews, only thirteen remained undocumented. The others had managed to obtain long-term legal residency through either marriage or giving birth to a child recognized by the father as a national of Japan.

Considering the precarious nature of their status, why would a hostess choose to overstay her visa and risk harassment from authorities? Visa overstayers fall under three main groups: (1) club escapees, that is, previous *talents* who escaped their club of employment; (2) younger sisters, that is, family members sponsored to enter as tourists by Filipina wives of Japanese men; and (3) smuggled hostesses, that is, those who pay migrant brokers to facilitate their illegal entry into Japan as tourists. Of those who participated in my study, most (nineteen) were club escapees, while only five were the younger sisters of an earlier migrant from the Philippines, and two had been smuggled by middleman brokers. In distinguishing among these three groups of undocumented workers, I acknowledge the different conditions of their illegality as well as their different degrees of vulnerability to abuse by employers and coethnics. We can assume that those with familial support, that is, younger sisters, are less vulnerable to abuse, while smuggled hostesses are likely to have the weakest social networks and consequently are most susceptible to coerced labor and other forms of human rights violations.

Club Escapees

Most hostesses who enter with entertainer visas opt not to overstay their visas, even though they would earn significantly more as overstayers with the wages of an *arubaito.* For instance, an *arubaito* would earn no less than what would be equivalent to $10 an hour in an *omise.* In contrast, a first-time contract worker would take home no more than $500 per month. Many do not overstay their entertainer visas for various reasons, including their desire to return to the Philippines, fear of illegality, fear of penalties imposed by middleman brokers, and lastly not wanting to break the law. Indeed, most contract workers become visa overstayers only as a last resort. There are those who escape their clubs because they fear that they would face difficulty securing another contract to work in Japan and as a result lose their only source of income, and then there are those who escape their club because they found work conditions to be intolerable.[20]

In some cases, contract workers risk becoming visa overstayers due to the larger amount of earnings they could garner as an *arubaito.* One transgender hostess, Nikki Ann, for instance, escaped her club so she could earn the money she would need for a sex change. The *talents* who escape their club to earn more usually have a set goal for the greater funds they would earn as an *arubaito.* Many claim that they plan to return to the Philippines as soon as they meet their goal, but sometimes meeting it would require years of work, as some become visa overstayers to build a house in the Philippines or to send younger family members to school. One of my co-workers, Sara, for instance, escaped because she needed to financially support the education of her nieces. As she explained, "I was thinking about my family. If I stayed a *talent*, I was going home with only 150,000 pesos (approximately US$3,000) for six months of work. That is small. And you still owe money to your manager for the costs of putting you up at their house. It is difficult, isn't it?" After running away, Sara saw a manifold increase in her earnings. She described, "I have been able to send 100,000 pesos (approximately US$2,000) a month. I send it to my family—to my mother and older sister. I send a total of 100,000 pesos a month. I am sending two to school, two of my sister's children. I also provide for their milk." While Nikki Ann hoped to leave Japan in two to three years, Sara planned to stay indefinitely.[21]

Hostesses such as Nikki Ann and Sara, those wishing to flee solely to earn a greater income, were quite rare in my study. This is perhaps because many want not to risk exposure to the vulnerabilities of illegality but also because many wish to avoid the penalties that they would incur if they fail to complete their labor contract. Hostesses who escape are usually saddled with a massive penalty, amounting as much as US$5,000, to the middleman brokers who had arranged their migration. Nikki Ann and Sara each amassed a debt of more than US$3,000 for refusing to finish their labor contracts. To pay for her debt, Sara sent a portion of her monthly earnings to her promotion agency. Nikki Ann ignored hers.

Like Sara, many other hostesses who had run away from their club prior to the end of their contract have had to pay or continue to pay for the penalties they incurred for "breaking a contract" with their promotion agency. While some did so because they feared that their promotion agency in the Philippines would harass their family, others felt that they had a moral obligation to cover the financial loss of their manager and promotion agency. They paid for their debt until they felt that those who had initially invested, and hence enabled, their migration had seen a profitable return on their investment. Still, not everyone feels compelled to cover whatever is her supposed debt. This is particularly the case for those who have escaped to avoid sexual harassment and maltreatment in their workplace. Escaping to avoid a grim situation, many reason, should absolve them of any financial penalty by the middleman brokers whose job it had been to protect them from unfair and unsafe working conditions. While a few flee their clubs soon after arriving in Japan as first-time contract workers, others complete a few contracts before they choose to escape and seek the higher wages of an *arubaito*. Having completed a few contracts, these hostesses usually refuse to pay middleman brokers any penalty because they reason that brokers had already amassed a sufficient profit from their labor in past years.

Some hostesses choose to run away after they realize that they are nearly at the end of their career as a *talent* and have a dim chance of securing another labor contract once they return to the Philippines. Hostesses also run away if unwilling to deal with the headache of meeting new visa requirements. As I described in Chapter One, certification requirements for prospective migrant entertainers change periodically, and experienced *talents* are never grandfathered into the new policy; instead they must undergo the new set of course requirements instituted for prospective migrants each time. Hostesses not willing to deal with the hassle of meeting new requirements escape their club prior to the end of their contract and avoid returning to the Philippines. Rafaella, for instance, chose not to return to the Philippines after the government changed the certification process for migrant entertainers from the "yellow card" to the Artist Record Book in 1994, as this change had required return migrants like herself to complete additional training before requalifying for work in Japan. Explaining why she became a visa overstayer, she stated, "I did it when it was getting harder to come back inside Japan. They were requiring an ARB (Artist Record Book)." During the time of our interview, Rafaella had just secured her legal residency via marriage after being a visa overstayer for more than a decade. Likewise Julia, who has since married one of her customers, saw changes in visa requirements as potentially hampering her flow of income as a circular migrant worker and for this reason ran away. She explained, "Before I would work six months and then go back home six months. I would stay there until I ran out of money, then I would come back here once again. Then, there came a time that they were getting stricter with *talents*, so we decided no longer to go home. We just escaped our *omise*."

Most club escapees plan to stay in Japan indefinitely. Some stay because they perceive hostess work as their most viable source of income. This is, for instance, the case for those who escaped because they feared disqualification from reentry. Yet, most hostesses became visa overstayers unintentionally and yet stay indefinitely because they have come to depend on their income in Japan. Most know that they would earn a pittance in the Philippines with their low level of education and lack of work experience other than hostess work in Japan.

Interestingly, most visa overstayers I met had not intended to become illegal. Most inadvertently became illegal after they ran away to avoid abusive conditions in their workplace. Some left when they learned that they would not earn an income after completing six months of contract labor; others fled to avoid their placement in a "flying booking"; some escaped because they felt unfairly overworked; and lastly some wished not to tolerate the moral violations they experienced at work.

Due to the stronghold of middleman brokers in the migration process, many hostesses accrue a significant amount of debt prior to migration. In some cases, they amass debt worth more than their cumulative earnings during their first contract stint in Japan. This situation encourages hostesses to escape their club prior to returning to the Philippines at the end of their contract, as many cannot accept going home to the Philippines empty handed after six months of working in Japan. Maki, for instance, escaped after she learned that she would not receive a salary from her promoter at the end of her contract. While unsure of the expenses that led to her accrued debt, Maki could not accept returning to the Philippines with nothing to show for her six months' work. Maki comes from the poorest of the poor in the Philippines. She went to Japan to provide for her family, as her father had been unemployed and her mother earned almost nothing selling candy on the streets of Manila. Not being able to give her parents any money after working for six months abroad was Maki's primary reason for running away. As she explained,

> I found out that we were not going to be given a salary. That is why we ran away. I was going to go home without money. I could not help but think of my poor family. My father had no work. I would go home without any money. So my poor family would have nothing. I also did not know if I was going to get another opportunity to come back to Japan. So, I did not think twice about it. I just tagged along with the woman who ran away.

As Maki noted, also encouraging hostesses to escape is the fact that they do not have the guarantee of returning to Japan to complete another contract once they are back in the Philippines. To secure another contract would require them to undergo another audition at a promotion agency. For these combined reasons, Maki overstayed her visa in order to at the very least guarantee a steady flow of income for her family in the Philippines. Except for a short stint in the Philippines after she was deported, Maki has for the most part remained undocumented since the early 1990s.[22] She had only recently secured legal residency status via marriage.

In other instances, hostesses escape to avoid moral violations. Hostesses unwilling to participate in commercial sex acts required by their club of employment are likely to run away. This was the case with my former co-worker Teresa, who as a moral in-betweener could not stomach the amoral regime of her workplace. She complained, "They told us to have sex with customers, and if we could not get ourselves to have sex, then just give them a blow job. Our co-workers there let customers finger them, but I think they did that already in the Philippines." Unwilling to participate in any form of commercial sex act, Teresa fled not long after arriving in Japan. She opted to escape rather than demand to return to the Philippines because she would otherwise have to go home empty handed. With five children to support, Teresa could not afford to quit and return home. Oftentimes, hostesses who face abusive conditions in the workplace would rather escape than demand to return to the Philippines because returning prior to the end of their six-month contract would mean that they would have to forego their earnings, which as I described in Chapter One are withheld from them by their promoter until their very last day in Japan. A *talent* returning to the Philippines prior to the end of her contract also is at risk of getting blacklisted by promotion agencies, making running away an attractive option for those facing violations at the workplace.

Hostesses need not face moral violations to face abuse at work. Some confront a hostile work environment with strict rules that encourage them to run away. For instance, my co-worker Arissa ran away after she could no longer tolerate the unreasonable demands imposed on *talents* at the last club where she worked prior to Manila. There club management expected *talents* to go out on a *dohan* every day. She complained:

> You can leave early only if you go on a *dohan*. For example, if you leave the house early, you have to be going out on a *dohan*. But if you have no *dohan*, you cannot go out. You can only go out at 5:00 PM. If you are on a *dohan*, you are allowed to go out at 2:00 PM or 1:00 PM. It was like that.

Aggravating the misery of Arissa had been her unsanitary living conditions. She recalled,

> The house had a lot of cockroaches. You would feel sorry for us because they never checked the conditions of the house. There were just too many cockroaches there. If you opened the washing machine, it would be filled with these small cockroaches. That is why sometimes we were practically putting our food in suitcases [she laughs] so the cockroaches will not get to them. If we had leftover food and covered it, the

cockroaches would start circling around the cover. It was so disgusting. As in, it was really disgusting. Even if you went outside to hang your clothes to dry, you would see the small cockroaches. You really would not be able to bear living there in the house.

In addition to her miserable living and working conditions, what also pushed Arissa to run away had been her placement in a "flying booking." As a hostess with a "flying booking," Arissa's legal status was akin to a visa overstayer. Getting caught would result in her automatic deportation and disqualification from reentry for at least five years. With the only difference between a flying booking and a visa overstayer being the much higher earnings of the latter, as she would earn wages not as a *talent* but an *arubaito*, Arissa figured that she might as well maximize her earnings and run away.

Hostesses are more likely to run away if they have co-workers willing to come along with them. I have yet to hear of a hostess running away on her own. Teresa, for instance, ran away with Sara, and both Melissa and Arissa escaped with other co-workers. Runaways, I noticed, move in packs. They tended to stick together for support, moving from one job to another together. In addition to the support of their fellow runaways, hostesses also would not escape their club if they were without an established network of support outside the club, which could be composed of customers as well as Filipino old-timers with whom contract workers had preestablished ties prior to migration. Teresa and Sara, for instance, turned to one of Sara's distant relatives for help, while Melissa turned to friends she knew from the Philippines who had since settled in Japan. Yet hostesses who run away find themselves in a relationship of unequal dependency with those who help them. Maki, for instance, had most of her wages at the new club that she entered after running away withheld from her by the Filipina old-timer who had helped her escape in the first place.[23] This coethnic withheld her wages for two months, forcing Maki to seek the help of yet another person to run away from a worse situation than what she had fled initially. While stories abound on how customers and coethnics take advantage of the vulnerability of runaways, not everyone acts on the weakness of others. Hostesses who experience abuse also often garner the sympathy of others, who more than willingly help them start afresh by providing them with free housing, job leads, and even cash.

Younger Sisters

In his study of illegality in Switzerland, Hans-Rudolf Wicker distinguishes illegality according to four categories.[24] He labels illegal migrants who legally entered Switzerland with work permits, such as contract workers in Japan, as "illegalized persons." Those who overstay their tourist visas he considers "overstayers." Then "illegals" are those who enter Switzerland clandestinely, similar for instance to Mexican migrants who cross the border. Lastly, he places "convicted foreigners" in a separate category, referring to foreigners whose legality is revoked after their conviction for a crime. In Japan, scholars have not made a similar distinction among visa overstayers.[25] Yet, making a similar distinction gleans insights into the circumstances of illegality for Filipina hostesses, and arguably other foreigners in Japan, and how these circumstances lead to varying degrees of vulnerability to abuse by coethnics and employers.

While one element that all illegals have in common is the constant threat of discovery, the circumstances of their entry into Japan determine their vulnerability to human rights violations. Those best able to shield themselves from abusive situations are the hostesses who entered Japan to follow their older sisters. Among my interviewees, five hostesses had entered Japan with the tourist visa designated to those entering to visit a family member.[26] Of these five, two remained visa overstayers. Unlike their counterparts who have run away from a club, visa overstayers who enter Japan with the assistance of a family member are likely to benefit from the social networks of the older sister who sponsored their migration. They can use her networks to secure employment or housing. They can also use their sister's identity to gain access to basic services they are denied, such as the use of a bank to remit funds to the Philippines. Still, there is a limit as to how much their sisters can protect them from abuse because their illegal status might preclude their sisters, especially if accountable to a Japanese spouse, from assisting or housing them.[27] Moreover, illegality by itself strips the migrant of rights, including access to the most basic of services such as, in addition to banking, leasing an apartment. Lastly, conflicts in the family could end the support of older siblings, which was the case for one of my interviewees. Despite these limitations, the younger sisters whom I met faced less abusive circumstances as visa overstayers than did their counterparts who had escaped clubs. For instance, none had ever had her wages withheld from her by her employer, as had been the case with most club escapees.

Younger siblings who overstayed their tourist visas did not necessarily enter Japan with the intention of doing so. Some had come to Japan to do no more than go on a holiday and spend time with their sister, but then, after being exposed to the much higher wages they would earn as hostesses than as professionals in the Philippines, opted to stay in Japan indefinitely. For instance, Rie, introduced in Chapter Four as the moral conservative who disdained hostess work, came to Japan only to be a temporary replacement in the *omise* for her sister who had to miss work for at least two weeks because of a scheduled surgery. While initially not wanting to work as a hostess due to the social stigma attached to the job in the Philippines, Rie soon changed her mind after realizing how much more she could earn working as one in Japan rather than as a bank teller in the Philippines. Recalling her disbelief over the salary she could earn as a hostess, the college-educated Rie exclaimed,

> I got my salary, and I was thinking, "Wow, I do not make this much in how many months in the Philippines." I was thinking that what I can make here in a week would take me months to earn in the bank in the Philippines. I was thinking that that was so big. When I first started, I got paid very little because I did not know Japanese yet. So, I only earned 1,200 yen per hour (approximately US$12 per hour). I think I got more than 40,000 yen (approximately US$400) for a week's work, and that would take me more than a month to earn in the Philippines. That was only a few days, not even a complete week's worth of work.

While initially excited about her wages, Rie later developed a keen dislike for hostess work. All the younger sisters whom I had interviewed had completed either a two-year or four-year tertiary degree prior to migration. In the Philippines, they had held a variety of professional jobs reserved for college graduates, such as a bank teller or hotel front desk clerk. Due to their experience of "conflicting class mobility," experiencing downward mobility in occupational status but upward mobility in financial status, younger sisters are those who struggled with accepting their work as hostesses.[28] Rie for one felt demoralized about performing a low-status occupation after having graduated from the premiere public institution of higher learning in the Philippines. Among younger sisters, those able to secure other forms of employment did so. Baby, for instance, sought work in a factory as soon as she legalized her residency. Rie continued to work as a hostess but wanted to quit and was actively seeking a job as a nanny. Lori managed to start an after-school program teaching English to Japanese children by renting a room in the public library. Mai chose to concentrate on being a housewife as soon as she got married. Only one younger sister, Jane, who happened to be Rie's housemate, did not have a problem with working as a hostess and continued to rely on this job as her primary source of income.

While most younger sisters come to Japan without the intention of overstaying their visa, some do. These include those who had wanted to pursue work as *talents* but could not secure the certification required of overseas performance artists in the Philippines. They then had to resort to entering Japan as tourists, usually with the sponsorship of their sister's Japanese spouse. Mai, whose two older sisters had worked as hostesses in Japan since she was in grade school, was one of them. She entered Japan as a tourist only after failing to receive accreditation as a professional dancer. She recalled,

> I was able to pass in the academic [portion], but in the ballet, no. Because I was not able to straighten my hands [laughs hysterically]. If you dance the ballet, then you really have to dance with your arms straight. I could not at all do it. That is where I flunked. I tried two times, and I just could not do it. I was told it's just the straightening of the arm that was preventing me from going to Japan. [We laugh.] So my sister told me that she will have me come as a tourist instead. Then, I was thinking in my head, they should have just given me that option to begin with instead of making me struggle like I had to for that ARB [Artist Record Book].

Mai began training to become an overseas performance artist at a much older age than her sisters, who actually did not support Mai's decision to join them in Japan. They had wanted her to hold a higher-status occupation as a symbol of upward mobility for their family.

Before working as a hostess in Japan, Mai, with her older sisters' financial support, had actually trained to become a midwife in the Philippines. Mai recounted her story of migration:

> This is what happened. After I graduated from high school, I told my sisters that I wanted to go to Japan. They are so pretty, right? I was wondering what kinds of opportunities were available to me in Japan. My sisters were so beautiful every time they returned from Japan. And even their clothes, they smelled so good. Then, they had so many fruits that they brought back with them. So I wanted to taste their life. I wanted to also go to Japan. At that time, my sister asked me if I wanted to be a hostess like her and our older sister, or would I rather not go to college. So, I decided to go to college. What you learn is something no one can ever take away from you.

So I studied in college . . . Then afterwards, I was able to graduate as a midwife, and I was a board passer. I worked in our country, and my salary was so low. You know, as a trainee I received an allowance of only 800 pesos a month [approximately US$16].

Soon after completing an internship in a hospital, Mai landed a job as a midwife in the United Arab Emirates, but there she earned a salary much lower than what her sisters brought back home when they had worked as *talents* a decade earlier. As a midwife, she earned no more than US$250 a month, which she subsidized by also working as a food server for a catering company. Her low salary only reaffirmed her desire to pursue hostess work in Japan.

Despite the disapproval of her sisters, Mai eventually prevailed in her insistence to join them in Japan. To appease them, she initially sought work as a front desk clerk at a hotel because such a job would better suit the "professional" status that her sisters wanted her to maintain. Yet, after a year, Mai switched to hostess work to double her salary. As she explained,

It was after a year in a hotel that I told my sister that I might as well work in an *omise*. I told her that it would be too bad if I let go of the opportunity to make money. In a hotel, my salary did not even reach 1,000 yen. I did not know how to speak Japanese. In an *omise*, I would make as much as 2,000 yen in one hour. Then, I was a stay-in, so I did not pay for housing.

Switching to hostess work paid off for Mai. Since working as a hostess in Japan, she had managed to purchase two houses in the Philippines, one in her hometown in a remote area of the Philippines and another one in Manila. Mai told me that her goal for going abroad had always been to purchase a home, which was something she could not quite do with the meager wages she had earned as a professional in the United Arab Emirates. For Mai, owning a home was keenly important because of her childhood experience of growing up in abject poverty. Because of the dilapidated state of her childhood home, she and her siblings, she recalled, had to seek shelter underneath a table in their house whenever it rained. Having a roof over her head through the purchase of not just one but two homes since coming to Japan symbolically represented for Mai her triumph over her childhood poverty.

Among my interviewees, not many hostesses had initially entered Japan as tourists. The majority came in legally with an entertainer visa. Local nongovernmental organizations note that those who enter as tourists are vulnerable to situations of coerced labor. This is clearly not the situation for those who enter Japan with the assistance of their older sisters, but, as I describe in the next section, this is indeed the case for hostesses who rely on middleman brokers to enter Japan illegally with tourist visas. Contrary to the repeated claim in the TIP Report that migrants who enter Japan with entertainer visas are susceptible to human trafficking, I found that those who are smuggled illegally into Japan, specifically with fake tourist visas, are more likely to find themselves in situations of coerced labor. In other words, they are the ones who are most likely to fall prey to "human trafficking."

Smuggled Migrants

Migrant Filipina hostesses are smuggled into Japan in two primary ways, with a fictitious passport that is stamped either with a tourist visa or with an entertainer visa. While persons smuggled into Japan are more vulnerable to exploitative work conditions than those who enter legally, smuggled hostesses' degree of vulnerability to forced labor is not uniform; individuals smuggled into Japan with tourist visas as opposed to entertainer visas are more prone to exploitative work conditions. The greater vulnerability of those smuggled with tourist visas arises from the fact that, unlike those who enter with entertainer visas, they need not report to the Embassy of the Philippines after they arrive in Japan. In other words, their entry into Japan remains in the shadows outside the law. Adding to their vulnerability is the fact that they will likely have limited social ties once in Japan. With the exception of long-term legal residents (that is, wives and mothers) and their sisters who later follow them, the contacts of migrant hostesses, even experienced ones, are usually limited to their workplace. Thus, the combined factors of being clandestine and being without social networks puts hostesses at risk of exploitation.

Supporting my assertion that individuals smuggled with entertainer visas are not as vulnerable to "human trafficking" as those smuggled with tourist visas, none of the hostesses who procured entertainer visas illegally in my study found herself in a situation of forced labor once in Japan. These hostesses resorted to the use of forged identities either because they were underage at the time of migration or unable to qualify for certification. Each had been integrated into her workplace in the same way as her counterparts who had entered Japan using their "real" identity. Differentiating their experiences as contract workers, however, was the greater debt that middleman brokers had imposed on them and their greater susceptibility to peonage. However, a larger debt does not necessarily translate to different work conditions or relations to club owners. This tells us that there is no direct correlation between human smuggling and "human trafficking."[29]

While none of my interviewees who had used another person's identity to secure an entertainer visa fell prey to human trafficking, the two interviewees who had used tourist visas with the assistance of not a friend or relative but instead a middleman broker did. The experiences of these two hostesses, Aiwa and Rika, suggest that individuals smuggled with tourist visas are more prone to forced labor than those smuggled with entertainer visas. Both of their initial experiences of migration in Japan fit the stereotypical image that the media paint of trafficked victims: entrapped with withheld wages and limited physical mobility. Notably, neither one had been forced into prostitution. However, employers held them against their will with no means of escape.

Neither Aiwa nor Rika still worked for her traffickers by the time I met them; more than a decade had passed since each had escaped from her precarious situation. Both have stayed in Japan since then, with Aiwa describing herself as a "permanent overstayer" and Rika securing permanent residency after she married a truck driver with whom she has one son. Neither wanted to return to the Philippines; instead both wished to settle in Japan permanently.

Aiwa first entered Japan in 1991. Much older than most other prospective migrant contract workers seeking employment in Japan, Aiwa at the age of twenty-seven struggled to get noticed and selected by promoters in auditions. After failing to secure a contract, Aiwa jumped at the chance given to her by a Japanese labor broker (that is, a promoter) whom she had met at a promotion agency in Manila. He had offered to help her secure a visa to enter Japan "under the table." Recalling the circumstance of her migration, Aiwa described,

> Two weeks I met the Japanese, and in two weeks I was in Japan. I was surprised. I never thought I could get here. It was not in me. The Japanese told me he would come back in two weeks, and he would get me. I did not hope. But he came back. When he came back, he had papers. He made me go to Davao. I went to Davao at 7:00 AM, and I arrived there at 9:00 AM. There, I applied for my passport. By 11:00 AM, my passport was released. At 1:00 PM, I applied for a visa. I waited for three days. Then, in three days I had a visa.

The labor broker had approached Aiwa at a promotion agency in Manila, when she had visited to inquire about upcoming auditions, but suspiciously he had asked her to process her papers in Davao, which is in the southern part of the Philippines and nearly a two-hour flight from Manila. Even more suspicious was the fact that the labor broker charged no fee for the passport and visa Aiwa used to enter Japan. Yet, Aiwa chose to overlook her feelings of doubt over the situation because she desperately wanted the opportunity to work in Japan. As she explained, "Because I heard of all the countries that Filipinos go, Japan offers the highest salary . . . I also used to hear that women were prostitutes before I came to Japan . . . The people in the Philippines were trying to scare me about life in Japan, but they were not scaring me."

Entering Japan with a passport other than her own and as a tourist put her at high risk of being trafficked. Aiwa knew this but still took the risk of migrating. Yet, Aiwa was not so fortunate. On her arrival in Japan, she found herself practically enslaved by her employer, the *mama-san*, who had paid for the cost of her travel to Japan. As Aiwa herself said, "She imprisoned me. She told me that I could not go out. She told me that if I go out, the police would catch me, and they would arrest me. Because it was my first time in Japan, I got scared. I hardly ever went out." While Aiwa was not imprisoned in the classic sense that her *mama-san* had locked her up, she did feel entrapped. She felt the constant gaze of her *mama-san*, who stayed in the apartment adjacent to hers. Aiwa continued,

> No, she did not lock me up. But I lived next to her. We lived next to each other. Only a wall separated us. We had different apartments. Then there was no shower. I would take a bath from the sink. I would boil water. That was in Osaka. I could not leave because I was scared. She would give me food only at night. She would not give me food in the daytime. I would be so hungry. She was Japanese. She told me I could not go out without her.

Denied her salary for nearly two months, Aiwa felt entrapped by her *mama-san*, who managed to take advantage of Aiwa not just because her limited language skills deterred her from seeking help from others but also because she had no access to friends who might help her escape.

An opportunity for Aiwa to seek help eventually came when her *mama-san* left her alone one day, allowing Aiwa to use the public phone downstairs to call her family in the Philippines. She recalled,

> One time she left, and I was so hungry. There was no one there, so I went downstairs. I saw a telephone. I made an international call to the Philippines. I knew she was not there when I went downstairs. I called the Philippines. I asked them to look for the telephone number of my classmate who is here in Japan. When they gave it to me, I called her. We were neighbors in the Philippines. She was surprised. She went to Osaka to pick me up. That is how I escaped.

Fortunately, Aiwa had the foresight to make a collect call not only to her family in the Philippines but also to her friend in Japan. Aiwa recalled that she had managed to arrange her escape in no more than an hour.

In a similar situation as Aiwa, Rika likewise entered Japan with the use of a passport other than her own and as a tourist. Rika had trained for months with a promotion agency to secure her certification to be an overseas performance artist but could not quite qualify to be a dancer. Her situation mirrored that of Mai, the younger sister whom I described in the previous section, but unlike Mai she did not have family to assist her with securing a tourist visa.

The circumstances of Rika's migration were quite similar to those of Aiwa. She was also not charged for her use of forged documents. The migrant broker even gave her money prior to migration. When I asked if she had to pay a hefty fee for the passport and visa just like my interviewees who had entered with "fake" entertainer visas, Rika responded, "No, it was free. I did not pay a cent. They even gave my mother 20,000 pesos [approximately US$400]. But my father was afraid because he knew that it was a *yakuza* that was handling my migration." A risk taker since she was young, Rika thought her toughness came from growing up in the most poverty-stricken area in Manila. Growing up utterly poor, Rika did not think she had much to lose going to Japan with the *yakuza*.

Once in Japan, the labor recruiter placed Rika along with her companions at a club that employed *arubaito* workers. Unlike their co-workers, Rika and her companions were not paid directly by the club owner; instead he paid their labor recruiter, who then would, according to Rika, garnish their earnings by at least 80 percent. Rika stayed in this situation for fourteen months, earning a mere US$600 per month—similar to a *talent* but, unlike them, without the option of returning to the Philippines. The recruiter technically did not imprison Rika, who actually had greater freedom of movement than Aiwa. She could come and go from her house as she pleased, having only to report to work during her shifts.

Still, Rika chose to stay bound to her recruiter for more than a year. Perhaps unfamiliarity with Japan, the absence of other job choices, and poor language skills deterred her from quitting. Yet, Rika claimed it had not been any of these factors but instead it had been her sense of moral obligation to her labor recruiter that discouraged her from fleeing her situation. As she explained, "It is *utang na loob* [debt of the soul] . . . to those who helped us." Although Rika knew that her migrant broker garnished most of her wages, she still thought of him "as a really good person . . . he did not enslave us, or imprison us." This latter fact alone, she said, is "why it was easy for [them] to escape."

The moral obligation of Rika toward her trafficker stemmed from her gratitude that he enabled her to escape her life of abject poverty in the Philippines. As far as Rika was concerned, he had to make enough of a profit from her labor to make their arrangement a win-win situation. Yet, regardless of the moral obligation binding Rika to her broker, she without doubt fits the definition of a "trafficked person" because ending their arrangement was not given to her as an option. She was bound to work for him indefinitely. After fourteen months, Rika did finally decide to escape. As she said, "I wanted to be free. My money will be my own. I knew how to speak Japanese at that point." According to Rika, it was relatively easy for her to run away. She simply solicited the help of a hostess who had married a Japanese man. Running away paid off for Rika, as she more than tripled her earnings at the next club she entered, taking home more than US$2,000 per month.

Neither Aiwa nor Rika were ever shackled in the process of migration, but at some point they had been unfree workers. They were indefinitely bound to their place of employment, without the option to quit, and they did not own their labor, as their wages were either withheld from them or severely garnished. Their situation supports the observation of representatives of the Philippine Embassy at Tokyo, who note that women they have identified as trafficked in Japan almost always entered illegally—not as contract workers but instead as tourists who were supposedly entering Japan to visit their family members. Ironically, the war against trafficking, as it has restricted the flow of migrants with entertainer visas, has only increased the number of hostesses resorting to the use of tourist visas to enter Japan, suggesting that this war has not protected migrant hostesses but instead has inadvertently placed more of them at risk of being abused.

EVERYDAY LIFE OF INVISIBILITY AS A *BILOG*

In many of our slow evenings at work, my co-worker Teresa would utter, "*Sana meroon akong bala*," meaning "I wish I had a bullet." Frustrated that she could not develop a customer base from the minimal traffic that plagued Manila, Teresa wished she worked not at the periphery of Tokyo but in the center in areas such as Kinshicho and Shinjiku, where she had once worked as a *talent* and where she had enjoyed the patronage of a steady flow of customers. Being a visa overstayer, in other words being without the "bullet" of legalized status, unfortunately limited Teresa's labor market options.

The restricted labor market options for the likes of Teresa suggest a shift in the culture of surveillance in Japan. In his autobiographical account of overstaying his visa in Japan, Ray Ventura describes how the police and migration authorities often played a charade of intentionally overlooking unauthorized migrant workers.[30] Yet the heightening of what de Genova calls the "deportation regime" in more recent years has constrained the integration of undocumented migrants. Instead of being overlooked, undocumented workers now feel as if they are being hunted.[31] This at least is the case in the nightlife industry of Japan, where undocumented hostesses often complained about the increased hesitation of clubs to hire them due to the spike in raids by the police and immigration authorities.

The fear of getting caught not only affects the behavior of club owners but also inhibits and at the same time disciplines the actions of visa overstayers. As I noted earlier, visa overstayers wish to remain inconspicuous to avoid detection by immigration authorities. They consequently employ multiple strategies to downplay their presence in the public sphere, including avoiding public spaces, consciously detracting from their race and "not acting Filipino," and keeping their actions in the public subdued, for instance by never riding a bicycle or talking loudly. Visa overstayers assume that being inconspicuous will significantly reduce their chances of getting caught by immigration authorities.

My undocumented co-workers, for instance, rarely ever went out; if they did, our *mama-san* or floor manager would usually accompany them. Sometimes they would dare to venture to one of the more popular shopping districts of Tokyo with me because they were confident that my stature as a professor and an American citizen would somehow shield them from interrogation by the police. After all, my foreign registration card indicated my affiliation as a visiting professor at one of the more prestigious universities in Japan. They assumed that the mere display of my card would deter the police from interrogating us. While we never proved this to be the case, my co-workers still felt somewhat confident about exploring Tokyo with me. Yet we did not go out all that often. Instead, they usually stayed indoors, either at home or at work, and if they did go out it was to walk to the corner store near their apartment.

Undocumented hostesses often choose to stay indoors because police and immigration authorities can approach them without reason and demand to see proof of their legal residency. They need not commit a criminal act. In Japan, looking foreign by itself invites inquisition from authorities.[32] For this reason, many undocumented Filipina hostesses fear walking around in public, even in their own neighborhoods. Explaining why she never went out before, the runaway Maki described how the police could just randomly approach her for no reason and demand to see her residency permit:

> Sometimes they will just nudge you. We have a co-worker who got caught. She went to the train station, and the police nudged her and asked her for her passport. She could not show any, so they brought her to the station until she was sent back home to the Philippines. Then now I have this gay friend who also got caught in the train station. Almost all of them are caught in the train station. That is where everyone is getting caught. Then everywhere, really; if you look Filipina, they come up to you. They ask you for your passport and alien card. If you have nothing to show, they will take you away. They will surround you. You are like a criminal. They treat you like a criminal. They are terrible here.

Fearing arrest and imprisonment, Maki restricted her interactions in the public sphere until her recent marriage to a customer.[33]

Life for undocumented hostesses is made difficult by its extreme isolation. One of my co-workers Sara, for instance, complained to me one afternoon about how she generally felt entrapped in Tokyo. Life in Tokyo, she told me, "is difficult" because she could not do anything but "hide and hide." Sara told me that she could not even go to the supermarket that was within walking distance from her house. She chose not to go because she would have to walk pass a police booth to reach it from her apartment. Unable to go to the grocery store, except if a customer accompanied her to one when they were out in a *dohan*, Sara usually bought her food in the 7-11 right below her apartment. For dinner, she and her roommate, my other co-worker Teresa, usually ate nothing but canned tuna, which they fried with onion. They picked up this can from 7-11. When I asked her if she ever got to eat vegetables, she told me "no" and explained, "We cannot. We just buy the food that costs 99 yen. That is it. Sometimes we will eat hot dogs. We just fry whatever is easy. That is what we eat." Although fed up with her limited dietary options in Tokyo, Sara was resigned to the fact that she "cannot do anything about it." Living in fear also limited her lifestyle in other ways. For instance, she shopped at home, not online but from magazines that cater to Filipina hostesses. She paid not with a credit card but instead gave cash on delivery.

Besides rarely going out, visa overstayers also consciously try to minimize their ethnic and racial distinction. Many told me that they tried not to look Filipino. When I asked how one could achieve this, a group of hostesses once told me that they try to dress differently from other Filipinos. They explained that Filipinos unconsciously conform to a uniform style of dress of "jeans, t-shirt, high heels, and dyed hair." On their description, I immediately took note of how none of the five of them had dyed hair. Additionally, none of them wore jeans. Instead, they wore blouses and dress slacks, which seemed a little too formal to wear at five o'clock in the morning. After I took note of their appearance, I could not help but acknowledge that no one would ever guess that they were in fact hostesses who had just clocked out of work. When I asked if they had worn the same outfits to work, they all laughed and snickered, clarifying what I had already assumed would not be the case.

Another way undocumented Filipina hostesses try to downplay their racial-ethnic identity is by avoiding being seen with crowds of Filipinos in public. When I went out with a fairly large group of Filipinos, I often noticed that undocumented hostesses would not take the train with us. Instead, they would split from our group and choose to travel with only one other person. Undocumented hostesses also avoided Filipino ethnic businesses. As Jane, one of the younger sisters whom I interviewed, complained, "I used to go to Filipino stores more often. But now that I do not have a visa, I avoid those places. It is perhaps because many people have been caught. It is dangerous." Further reflecting on how she negotiated her undocumented status in public, she continued, "I have changed the way I move. I do not go around as much as I did before. I just go to places that are close. I only go to places that are familiar.

If I am not familiar with a place, I get nervous. For example, I do not visit my sister as much. It is dangerous."

Undocumented hostesses hardly ever go out, and when they do they usually act in a subdued manner. For instance, they do not speak loudly, they keep to themselves, and they also avoid public transportation if they can, instead relying on employers to provide them with the service of "*hatid-sundo*," meaning "drop off-pick up," to go not just to and from work but also to church and the grocery store. In fact, most undocumented hostesses whom I met had a phobia about taking the train because police are known to approach and ask Filipina hostesses for their residency permit in train stations. So as not to draw attention to themselves, undocumented hostesses also avoid riding bicycles, instead preferring to walk. In the Filipino migrant community, it is said that to ride a bicycle is an easy way to get noticed and stopped by police. For this reason, many recommend that undocumented hostesses avoid riding a bicycle at any cost. As one Filipina old-timer said, "The *bilog* are so hard headed. You tell them that they should not ride a bike. Yet, they still ride a bike. They should know better."

Interestingly, the undocumented hostesses' restricted movement deceives plenty of outsiders into thinking employers hold them against their will. One well-intentioned Japanese feminist, for instance, on hearing of my research project could not help but make a comment about how migrant Filipina hostesses are trafficked persons. She sometimes saw them, she had told me, forcibly escorted in white vans. She told me that she never saw them out and about on their own; instead, when in public they seemed to be always guarded and transported from door to door in the vans. While it is true that plenty of migrant Filipina hostesses suffer from their forcibly controlled movements in Japan, making the description of my feminist colleague somewhat accurate, the primary cause of their constraint is the criminalization of their illegal residency and not their having fallen prey to human trafficking.

VULNERABILITIES OF SETTLEMENT

Punitive policies arising out of the "deportation regime" not only limit the job options of illegals and constrain their movement in public spaces; they also diminish the access of illegals to the most basic of services and resources, including remitting funds to the Philippines and securing housing. Moreover, they discourage illegal migrant workers from claiming their labor rights, as most fear seeking intervention from the proper government authorities would only bring them unwanted attention from immigration authorities.

Employer Abuse

While the risk of police harassment petrifies visa overstayers in the public sphere, the threat of withheld wages equally frightens them in the private sphere. When asked what is the most difficult experience they have had in an *omise*, many undocumented hostesses without hesitation told me, "when you are not given your salary." As Rafaella complained,

> One time you were not given your salary. You cannot do anything about it because you do not have a visa. That is difficult when you do not get paid . . . we were left to expect that we would eventually get paid. His phone was always off. He would tell us he will pay us on the fifteenth, and then the fifteenth will come and he says at the end of the month . . . so we eventually moved to another club.

Although they have recourse to demand their unpaid wages,[34] visa overstayers almost always just walk away and seek employment elsewhere. Indeed, most club escapees in my study experienced the workplace violation of unpaid wages. With the exception of one woman, all opted not to demand back wages.[35] Employers can easily deny visa overstayers, or for that matter legal residents, their wages because of the informal structure of the industry. Hostesses are usually paid in cash, making it difficult or nearly impossible to document wage payments.

Coethnic Abuse

Legals and illegals coexist inside and outside the workplace. They often work alongside each other in Philippine clubs, attend the same Mass in English or Filipino, and patronize the same Filipino restaurants.[36] Coethnics with legal residency status enable visa overstayers to integrate in Japanese society, whether by securing housing, using the bank, accessing private transportation in a car or a van, or doing other mundane activities most of us do not think twice about but are inaccessible to visa overstayers in Japan. For instance, I learned that they cannot pawn jewelry, as several of my co-workers asked me to go to a pawnshop on their behalf and collect whatever funds they could from the presents they had received from former customers. While migrants with various types of visas do coexist, they do not always do so harmoniously. Coethnics have been known not only to alleviate the vulnerability of the undocumented by giving them access to otherwise inaccessible businesses but also to take advantage of them.

I learned that visa overstayers cannot remit funds to the Philippines. Yet, they rarely grumbled about their lack of access to banking services, including their inability to open a bank account, because, as they often joked, they do not have much money to put in the bank anyway. If they do have money, they usually send it to family in the Philippines. Any surplus would then go to their bank account in the Philippines, one that an entrusted family member could have access to in an emergency. Yet it is not unheard of for the entrusted family member to misuse these funds. In two separate cases, I heard that a family member had depleted the savings of undocumented hostesses whom I had interviewed. In one case, a sister who had power of attorney over the property of my interviewee even sold her house behind her back to support her own gambling problem. Such a betrayal not only questions the common assumption that the family is a cohesive unit whose members have uniform interests; it also tells us that the vulnerability to coethnic abuse of visa overstayers extends transnationally to their family in the Philippines.

Perhaps because they wish to have control over their monies, in some cases visa overstayers opt not to send their earnings to their family in the Philippines but instead choose to retain a bank account in Japan. Yet they can do so only under the name of a legal resident. In other words, to maintain a bank account in Japan, visa overstayers would have to borrow the identity of another person. In so doing, they put a great deal of trust in the other person who can easily take away whatever funds are under their name. When I was about to leave Japan, for instance, my co-worker Melissa asked me for my bank account, wanting to take over the use of it. She wanted my ATM card and code as well as my bank book, all of which I gave to her, even though I kept wondering what she would do if the ATM card suddenly got demagnetized.

It is not uncommon for visa overstayers to use another person's identity to maintain a bank account. Rafaella, for instance, did so, telling me, "I have about 100,000 yen in the bank. I use the bank card of my friend who has a visa. *Bilogs* cannot have bank accounts. So the bank account is in her name." Wondering if she is at all scared that her friend would deplete her account, Rafaella told me, "No, because I trust her. She is *bakla*, too. She went home, and she left me her passbook and cash card. She is back here now. She is a *talent*." Rafaella explained to me that her friend is not likely to steal her money because she herself had once been "*bilog* for a long time," and for this reason she is likely to be more sensitive to the vulnerability faced by the likes of Rafaella.

Undocumented migrants are not just without access to a bank account, but as I noted earlier they also cannot remit funds to the Philippines via formal channels. Instead, they can send money only through informal money couriers in the community. Informal couriers charge significantly more than formal institutions such as Western Union or Philippine National Bank. While formal institutions charge a flat fee of 2,000 yen (approximately US$20) per remittance, couriers in the community charge an adjustable rate with the fee increasing according to the amount remitted by the sender. The *mama-san* of the club where I worked, for instance, charged Teresa US$100 for sending US$2000 on her behalf. Our *mama-san* told me that charging a 5 percent fee for remittances is quite low, as others charge undocumented workers 10 percent for sending money back to the Philippines.

Visa overstayers are also disadvantaged when it comes to housing. Legally unable to lease their own apartments, visa overstayers, particularly club escapees, are commonly saddled with overpriced housing. While some clubs provide visa overstayers with free housing, many overcharge them. For example, I realized that two of my co-workers paid too much for their apartment, which should have rented for no more than US$600 for its size and location in the periphery of Tokyo. Instead, our *mama-san* charged each of them US$600, allowing her to reap a profit from the rental unit. When I complained on their behalf and asked our *mama-san* why she charged so much for their housing, she explained that the utilities, including cable television, are not calculated in the base rent. Yet I knew from having my own much larger apartment in the center of Tokyo that it was highly unlikely that my co-workers' monthly utilities would add up to US$600. Not surprisingly, soon after complaining my two disgruntled co-workers quit working at Manila, later calling me to let me know that they had secured better employment, positions that not only paid more but did not require them to go on a *dohan*.

In other cases, visa overstayers must secure their own housing independent of the club. Those who do frequently rely on a coethnic with legal residency. They are almost always forced into a dormitory type of rental arrangement. Instead of renting a room or an apartment, they rent a bed along with other visa overstayers. Landlords usually amass a significant amount of profit when renting to "bed spacers." Moreover, those who share their apartments with visa overstayers usually reap a profit that exceeds the amount of their actual rent. In one apartment I visited, three visa overstayers stayed in one room as "bed spacers," and the couple renting the unit lived in the other room. The rent charged to the three "bed spacers" covered the rent of the entire unit.

In some situations, legal residents amass a significant amount of profit from overcharging visa overstayers for housing. They usually can do this to newcomers, those with the weakest social networks, and those who are recent runaways from their clubs. One of my interviewees, Lori, recalled how she overpaid for housing during her first year as a visa overstayer, renting a bed along with fourteen other Filipina visa overstayers in one apartment from a Japanese man and his Filipina wife. Lori believes that they amassed at least US$10,000 in profit per month from setting up a "bed spacer" system for visa overstayers in the community. As Lori described,

> There was a Japanese here who married a Filipina. They rented this [apartment] out like a dormitory. He would put five Filipinas per one room, and he would charge us rent. Our work was walking distance to our house. We were like *talents*, but we were all visa overstayers. . . . It was very expensive. It was 50,000 yen. Imagine, we lived in bunk beds, and we would be five per room. He charged 50,000 per person. Then he charged us water and electricity . . . when they come over in the morning, they require you to buy jewelry and clothes from them. It is like they force you to buy these things. You cannot not buy from her. The good thing about that place was it was close to the *omise* where we worked. . . . I think they made more than 1,000,000 yen. They had two apartments. They made a lot of money. There were fifteen of us on one floor and fifteen on another floor. I think that the man's family owned the building. So instead of renting out the unit, they would rent the place out by bed.[37]

Illustrating how vulnerable she had been, Lori actually did not know that she had had other rental options in Japan. She realized that she did only after one of her customers, one who became her boyfriend and the father of her son, helped her secure her own apartment. To her surprise, her rent for an entire one-bedroom apartment was not much more than the 50,000 yen she had paid to rent a "bed space." Explaining how she finally left her exploitative situation, Lori continued,

> I met a Japanese who was going to the *omise* who helped me get an apartment. Instead of me paying 50,000 yen, I could get a whole apartment just for me for 70,000 yen. There were two of us, and we split the apartment. We both left the dorm. What you just need is a sponsor.

Her former landlords did not take Lori's departure lightly, however, as her action triggered the end of their business. As she explained,

> They were mad that I left the house and I got my own apartment. After I did that, many of the women copied me. A lot of the women left. That is why she was really mad at me. Most of the overstayers are from the province. So, they did not know that they had other options. After they found out that they could get their own apartment, they of course asked their customers to sponsor them for an apartment. That is why that couple is very mad at me. I am the one who initiated this trend. The women thought that they had no chance here and that that was the only place where we could live. That is why they got mad at me. But I was having a very hard time at that house. It was very difficult. There were so many of us. I think there were fifteen of us in that apartment. It was a three-room apartment.

While Lori's housing situation was far more exploitative than those of my other interviewees, most visa overstayers at some point had experienced the misfortune of being subjected to overpriced housing, albeit in different degrees, through their employer or a coethnic.

WHY STAYING IN THE PHILIPPINES IS NOT A BETTER OPTION

Most visa overstayers would agree with Sara and her description of her life as an illegal in Japan to be not just difficult but incredibly lonely. The heightening of the deportation regime without doubt has pushed them further into the periphery of the social landscape of Japan. Yet, visa overstayers prefer to bear the social isolation of illegality in Japan due to its reward of financial stability. In sharp contrast, they claim that life in the Philippines is nothing but financially disabling. While I am sure that many migrant hostesses have successfully retired in the Philippines after their stint in Japan, as some of the sisters of the hostesses who participated in my study had done so, not all manage to convert their earnings in Japan to self-sustaining business ventures in the Philippines. In some cases, hostesses have attempted to retire in the Philippines but eventually depleted their savings. This happened to four overstayers in my study—Charmaine, Lori, Melissa, and Teresa. Every single one of them returned to the Philippines with a sizable amount of savings, yet each of them eventually had to return to Japan to replenish her bank accounts.

Teresa, whose life I described at length in Chapter Three, had to return to Japan to earn money to cover her children's tuition. Melissa, another of my co-workers, planned to settle in the Philippines after completing nine labor contracts as a highly paid *talent* but returned to Japan after she depleted her savings in three years. Without any income except for what she could earn from singing in local venues around Manila, Melissa decided to return to Japan, where at the time of our interviews she had been an undocumented worker for nearly a year.

Charmaine, in contrast, managed to stay for more than ten years in the Philippines but then came back after her partner's bad business decisions nearly depleted her savings of US$160,000,[38] which she amassed from working as a visa overstayer in one of the most exclusive hostess clubs in Tokyo. Charmaine never managed to operate a successful business, instead venturing into one losing enterprise after another, forcing her to return to Japan. Among the businesses she operated were a real estate office and a used car lot.

Return migrants such as Teresa, Melissa, and Charmaine do not fail for a lack of trying. As they told me, earning money in the Philippines is nearly impossible for someone who is without the right connections, especially if she has become used to a certain level of income that she has been exposed to abroad. Illustrating how difficult it is to succeed financially as an entrepreneur for return migrants, Lori described in detail the difficulties she faced during the two years she tried to settle in the Philippines:

I tried so many businesses. I had this high school classmate who for her work would go to Hong Kong and Bangkok. She would buy clothes there. I went along with her. I also bought clothes. She told me that those sell. That was around 1995. We bought blouses, shirts, polos. She sells those items in Greenhills.[39] So, I tried it as well. But I had a hard time because my mind was still in Japan. It seems as if whatever I tried in the Philippines, I would compare to Japan. I could see that I could earn so much more here. I would think that my earnings would come so much more quickly in Japan. In the Philippines, it is much slower. I was also having a hard time. Then, I also tried running a kiosk in a supermarket. I would go to Quiapo[40] at 5:30 in the morning. I would buy the [rice cakes] sold there, and I would bring them to the supermarket. That would be every day. But my profits were so low. I was getting tired for so little. From 10:00 AM to 8:00 PM, I would be there in the supermarket. I was in one of those little stalls you see as you walk out. The profits were really low. And you would be there the whole day. I did not make much, something like a 100 plus pesos [US$2]. If you did not experience earning money abroad, you would probably be satisfied with what you are earning there. But I would always compare my earnings here to what I could possibly earn there. It was so hard. We even did a shwarma business with my sister in Makati. We sold that business too. We had a hard time because our focus was not there.

After a couple of years, Lori eventually returned to Japan, where she put her entrepreneurial skills to use. Quitting hostess work after securing her legal status via her son's citizenship, Lori had been running an after-school program for elementary school children; she taught them English for three hours a day from Monday to Friday, earning an income comparable to what she would earn from working more than forty hours a week in a hostess club.

The plights of these four return migrants confirm what many hostesses repeatedly told me, including both *talents* and *bilogs*: One earns in Japan and spends in the Philippines. Once exposed to First World wages, many struggle to get used to the much smaller earnings that they would garner as small business owners in the Philippines. Financial difficulties force them to return to Japan, where their financial stability becomes worth the sacrifice of their social isolation.

Visa overstayers face a particular dynamic of indentured mobility: Financial stability comes at the cost of invisibility. In contrast to long-term legal residents whose citizenship entails the negotiation of intimate relations with Japanese citizens, visa overstayers must negotiate their criminalization as illegals. Residing in Japan requires them to live in the shadows of the law. As illegal residents, they live in constant fear of identification by police and immigration authorities. Consequently, invisibility becomes tantamount to their residency as visa overstayers; the threat of deportation is the most salient factor that shapes their settlement. This state of being brings its unique set of challenges to visa overstayers, one that places them at great risk of exploitation.

As invisible subjects, hostesses are *unauthorized* and at the same time *unrecognized*. In other words, they are easily exploited because they occupy a sphere outside the boundaries of the law. They are subjected to the withholding of their wages, overpriced housing, and, for those most vulnerable, such as Aiwa and Rika, enslavement. While the settlements of visa overstayers share the common element of the threat of deportation, it is important that we recognize variances in their experiences. Distinguishing their means of entry to Japan shows that visa overstayers are a diverse group with different access to resources; club escapees, younger sisters, and smuggled migrants experience different degrees of vulnerability to exploitation by their coethnics and employers. While we see stark distinctions among visa overstayers, social isolation is one challenge they share, one that they endure for the reward of greater material security but one that undeniably imposes a series of hardships and places them at risk of severe exploitation.

The next chapter takes a look at the challenges of settlement for *talents*, who historically have constituted the largest group of Filipina hostesses in Japan. In contrast to permanent legal residents, whose citizenship is conditional to their negotiation of intimate relations with Japanese partners, and visa overstayers, whose integration is conditional to the threat of deportation, *talents* must negotiate the control of middleman brokers as well as the temporal boundary of their settlement. These differences reinforce my assertion regarding the variety of experiences among hostesses, the diversity of their issues, and, in contrast to the universal solution of rescue posed by the United States in regards to trafficked persons, our need to develop empirically grounded solutions that adequately address the nuances in the varying experiences among those who are vulnerable to forced labor.

CHAPTER EIGHT

THE SEGREGATION OF HOSTESSES

Hostess clubs celebrate not the entertainer's arrival but her departure. They host a party, which members of the community refer to as a *sayonara*, an event in which entertainers wear gowns—long evening dresses—that range from Philippine couture to generic taffeta or chiffon prom dresses. At the *sayonara*, festive décor would brighten the club, such as a banner announcing the departure of one or a group of entertainers, balloons pinned on walls and ceilings, and party favors on tables.

The *sayonara* represents the finale of a temporary contract worker's six months in Japan. Temporary contract workers, otherwise known as *talents* or entertainers, view this event as perhaps their last opportunity to say goodbye to customers and also their last chance to collect presents. Rarely do they return to the same club for their next contract, as management prefers to offer customers a fresh batch of new hostesses to meet on a regular basis. There is also the strong likelihood that the departing *talent* will not get another opportunity to work in Japan. Most *talents* who wish to return to Japan must undergo another rigorous application process in the Philippines. But with the supply of prospective migrant hostesses far exceeding the demand for them at Japanese clubs and the clubs' preference for young *talents*, there is a high likelihood that prospective return migrants will not have the opportunity to come back, making the *sayonara* an even more important event and source of income for them. Still, some have the opportunity to return to Japan, and those who do are usually able to lure their customers to visit them in their new club of employment. But because the opportunity of return is not guaranteed, *talents* aspire to receive as many gifts and cash presents as possible in their *sayonara*. The presents that they receive range from cash presents to the latest electronics such as a high-definition flat-screen television or a portable DVD player. During the height of the "bubble economy" of Japan in the late 1980s, *talents* left Japan with much larger presents than they do today. Back then, they could aim for a "*bahay, lupa, kotse*," meaning "house, land, car." Reflecting the decline in the Japanese economy, *talents* by 2005 could expect cash presents that would only amount to no more than 10,000 yen (US$100) from regular customers and 50,000 to 100,000 yen (US$500 to $1000) from special customers, meaning customers who were particularly fond of them.

Although the *sayonara* takes place during their last night of work in Japan, *talents* begin to make preparations for this event soon after arriving in Japan. This is almost always the case in transgender clubs, where the *sayonara* is a more spectacular event than in female hostess clubs. In their *sayonara*, transgender hostesses must perform a solo dance performance while those in female clubs do not. In transgender clubs, each hostess wears a gown during a *sayonara*, while in female clubs only those leaving do.

The experience of one's *sayonara* in a transgender club, including its preparation, illustrates how labor migration for *talents* in Japan becomes a process of making plans to return home to the Philippines. For instance, *talents* begin to design *sayonara* gowns not long after they arrive in Japan, envisioning not just the design but also color and material. Then, two months after working in Japan, they have a designer in the Philippine sew the gown. On average, these hostesses spend US$200 on the gown, which is significantly less than the cost of a comparable dress in Japan. However, risks come with sending the design back to the Philippines, as the designer will sometimes alter or misunderstand the instructions and drawing of the hostess. Hence, *talents* much prefer to receive their gown months before the actual *sayonara* so that they have time to alter it or lose weight if it does not quite fit. They also prefer to have their gown in advance so they can envision a solo dance performance that suits the dress. A hostess rarely dances wearing her gown, but she would instead design a special attire for the dance performance that would coordinate well with the character projected by her gown.

In the *sayonara* events I attended, entertainers projected their own unique characterization of a sophisticate, an angel, a femme fatale, a beauty queen, or a superstar. They displayed this characterization not only in the gown but also in the dance performance, the speech, and lastly their final walk on stage. For instance, Nikki, a twenty-seven-year-old with a tall svelte figure, wanted to project the image of someone "naughty and nice" for her *sayonara* party. She had designed a baby blue taffeta gown that looked quite demure from the front but revealed a backless rear. Keeping up with her "naughty and nice" motif, Nikki played the character of an angel for her solo dance performance and wore a white sequined halter top with feathered wings and form-fitting white pants. With a wand sprinkling angel dust, Nikki ran around the club as if she were soaring through the sky to the song "If I Could Reach Out" by Gloria Estefan.

Nikki gave quite an emotionally uplifting performance, which I had known she dreaded for weeks. She practiced this dance during her last month in Japan. Yet the solo dance performance was only one of her worries. Nikki also dreaded having to deliver a speech, which she memorized and practiced in front of me at least three weeks before her *sayonara*. Like a beauty queen, a hostess in a transgender club delivers a "goodbye" speech and then gives her final walk on stage, before approaching each of the guests to individually thank them for attending her *sayonara*. This last goodbye is usually the final opportunity for a hostess to secure a tip from a customer. Nikki told me that the speech is very important for compelling customers to extend that tip. Accordingly, Nikki wrote, practiced, and memorized her speech, which she had to deliver in Japanese. She practiced the speech with customers to correct her grammar and also to remind them of her impending departure. In the speech, she described how she had learned and grown as a person in the last six months;

for this she felt a tremendous gratitude to Japan and its people. It must have been an effective speech, as I noticed that quite a few customers handed her a 10,000 yen ($100) bill after her final walk on stage.

It is not only transgender hostesses who begin to anticipate their return to the Philippines not long after they arrive in Japan. So do *talents* in female clubs, who worry about the material acquisitions they can take back to the Philippines from Japan soon after their arrival. Open and partially filled *balikbayan* boxes, six-cubic-foot cardboard containers, greet any visitor entering *talents*' resident apartments. When I saw these boxes the first time I entered some *talents*' apartment, I could not help but mistakenly assume that some of them must soon be returning home to the Philippines. After all, *balikbayan* literally means to return home, and return migrants usually use these boxes to store foods, including chocolates and canned goods, that they plan to bring home to the Philippines. Scattered throughout the crowded apartments of *talents* whom I visited were boxes that unavoidably became tables if not sealed and stacked in a corner. Transported via cargo ships, *balikbayan* boxes arrive in the Philippines in fifteen to twenty-one days and cost approximately 9,000 to 10,000 yen (US$90 to US$100) to send to Manila regardless of weight and a few thousand more to other areas of the Philippines.

Talents begin to acquire goods to fill these large cardboard boxes within their first two months of arrival in Japan, if not earlier. They aspire to send three boxes back to the Philippines before their labor contract ends in six months. Yet, as they usually send these boxes for their own consumption of Japanese goods once they return to the Philippines, they usually do not send the boxes until closer to their date of return. Still, in anticipation of their eventual return to the Philippines, entertainers purchase items to throw into a *balikbayan* box as part of the daily routine of life in Japan. For this habitual practice, they would visit *hyaku* (one-hundred) yen shops to buy chocolates, kitchenware, soaps and detergents, school supplies, and many other sundry items. I even participated in this practice by giving each migrant contract worker whom I interviewed a case of *ramen* and two or three bags of chocolates to put in their *balikbayan* box. Relations with customers would often revolve around *balikbayan* boxes, as courtship and friendship rituals in the club would involve the gift-giving of items *talents* desire for *balikbayan* boxes, including CDs of popular Japanese music, gourmet chocolates, cups of noodles, and stuffed toys.

The practices of planning *sayonara* parties and sending *balikbayan* boxes home to the Philippines symbolize the sojourn of migrant contract workers—*talents*—and illustrate how they migrate to improve their lives in the Philippines. Each suggests that *talents* remain conscious of their short duration of migration. This consciousness accordingly shapes their actions, behaviors, and attitudes about settlement, discouraging them from establishing roots in Japan while encouraging their continued ties to the Philippines.

Despite the decline in their numbers, *talents* continue to enter Japan. Since 2007, the flow of *talents* has decreased to around 7,000 per year, which is a marked decline from the early 2000s when their numbers hovered at around 70,000 per year.[1] Nongovernmental organizations speculate that the tightening of visa requirements for *talents* in 2005, which came in response to the U.S. recommendation for Japan to more closely monitor the flow of Filipino migrant entertainers, has led to an increase in visa overstayers and fake brides, two groups whose illicit status makes them vulnerable to forced labor.[2]

Continuing with my elaboration on the citizenship of migrant Filipina hostesses, this chapter focuses on the settlement issues of *talents*. Unlike permanent or indefinite migrants, *talents* are temporally bound in Japan. They enter Japan knowing they are to work for no more than six months, and most do not intend to overstay their visa. How does a hostess's knowledge of her short duration of stay in the host society shape her experiences of migrant settlement? Does it hamper the *talent*'s assimilation or feelings of belonging? Dominant paradigms on migrant settlement are based on the experiences of permanent or long-term settlers and often fail to account for experiences of settlement for sojourners. Studies have yet to consider how a temporally bound duration of settlement would impede the sojourners' integration. Instead, it is assumed and asserted that sojourners would inevitably become long-term settlers.[3] As Tsuda describes of Japanese-Brazilians in Japan, "Despite the initial intentions of the migrants themselves and the governments that receive them, more often than not migrant workers who are deemed 'temporary' become a permanent presence in the host society."[4] Yet not all sojourners settle in the host society. Their permanent presence, as Tsuda also recognizes, could be due to the continuous flow of temporary migrants.

Regardless, scholars have yet to examine how a temporally bound experience of migration would shape the orientation and conduct of sojourners. Indeed,

I found that *talents* remain conscious of their limited duration of settlement during the entire span of their migration. This awareness discourages their integration into Japan and consequently makes their settlement a process of returning home to the Philippines. The particular configuration of migrant settlement for *talents*—segregated and homeward bound—invites a paradigmatic shift in our formulation of migrant settlement as one of inevitable assimilation, forcing us to drop our assumption that all sojourners eventually become permanent migrants and challenging us to learn how migrants' qualitatively different orientations, with one aiming to settle permanently in the host society and the other aiming to return to the home society, would distinguish their very experience of settlement. In so doing, we would not only recognize the diversity of experiences among hostesses but also identify the vulnerabilities unique to those whose settlement is one of segregation.

THE SEGREGATION OF *TALENTS*

The homeward bound migration of temporary labor migrants distinguishes their experience of migration from those of other hostesses. As temporary labor migrants, their movement between the country of origin and country of destination is oriented toward building their life in the country of origin.[5] They are circular migrants who have little investment in building a life in the host society. This homeward bound orientation leads to the experience of migration as one of segregation, more specifically, temporal, social, and spatial segregation, all of which aggravate their greater feelings of affinity for the home society and fortifies their limited integration in the host society.

Temporal Segregation

In Japan, migrant contract workers with entertainer visas are granted a three-month duration of stay that they can renew once for a maximum stay of six months.[6] This time constraint undoubtedly shapes the experience of settlement for *talents*. Migrant contract workers often describe migration as a process of putting their life in the Philippines on hold while in Japan. They limit their integration and make minimal efforts to anchor themselves in the host society, which they for instance could do by investing in home furniture or décor, taking language classes, and exploring Japan by leaving the vicinity of their neighborhood.

Although they limit their integration, *talents* must to a certain extent still acculturate, although definitely not to the same extent as would long-term migrants. At the very least, they must acquire some language skills to interact with customers. At the end of six months, *talents* usually have acquired a rudimentary knowledge of the language, which they attain from speaking with customers nearly every night. While they may not speak grammatically correct Japanese, they do manage to carry on a conversation with customers before the end of their first labor contract. Making an effort to learn Japanese usually endears them to customers, resulting in more generous *sayonara* presents, and increases the likelihood of their return as a contract worker.

Despite their efforts to acculturate, Filipina *talents* for the most part still view migration as a process of putting their life in the Philippines on hold. This was the case with Nikki, the third-time contract worker whose *sayonara* I described earlier. She told me that she never looked forward to her return to Japan when in the Philippines. Instead, she usually tried to extend her stay in the Philippines until she had depleted the savings she had accrued during her last contract in Japan. Explaining why she preferred to stay in the Philippines, Nikki described her poor mental health when in Japan:

> I have not really fully adjusted to this place. The emotional trauma of being away is still there. For example, there are times you get so lonely. You feel so homesick. You look for the people who can be there for you in times of need, even with the small things. Before, I just make a phone call, and my friends all come right away. Here, I have no one to call. No one is here to take care of me except myself . . . But I have feelings of needing to force myself to work. This is because I need to make a living. But let me tell you, it is hard. It is very hard. There is not one day here that I do not cry. Everybody does here.

Once in the Philippines, it had taken Nikki some time to get over the "pressure" and "exhaustion" of working in Japan. She would rarely think about Japan when in the Philippines. Moreover, she rarely maintained social relations with people in Japan when in the Philippines, but in contrast communicated regularly with people in the Philippines while in Japan. For many Filipina entertainers, food and phone cards are the staple necessities of life in Japan.

Angie, a twenty-three-year-old female entertainer who was finishing her fourth contract to work in Japan, similarly described how working in Japan entailed having to put her life as a mother in the Philippines on hold. As she told me, "I want to be with my child. But my money is better here. If you work, you have money monthly. In the Philippines, if you do not have a job, then you struggle . . . you just let go of money, and money never comes in." Angie likewise saw her migration as nothing more than a means of earning money that she could spend in the Philippines. If given a chance, she would rather have run a business in the Philippines, such as an Internet shop or a small eatery. Yet Angie realistically knew that while she was fairly young her best option for earning money would be to work as a *talent* in Japan. Angie was like Nikki in that she often thought about her life in the Philippines when in Japan and rarely about her life in Japan when in the Philippines. But unlike Nikki, Angie did maintain ties with at least one or two customers while in the Philippines. She entertained their phone calls so she could later turn to them for financial assistance in case she depleted her earnings before she got another opportunity to return to Japan.

Nikki and Angie maintained a fragmented lifestyle of "earning abroad to spend money in the Philippines." Their temporal segregation in Japan promoted this fragmentation. We can imagine that temporary labor migrants elsewhere share this same lopsided sense of greater belonging in the country of origin than in the country of destination. In the case of *talents*, their temporal dislocation aggravates this sentiment as they are nighttime workers whose schedule further limits their social interactions with other members of the Filipino migrant community.

Social Segregation

Hostesses, particularly *talents* and visa overstayers, usually keep to themselves, interacting only with customers and co-workers while in Japan. They rarely, if at all, interact with other members of the Filipino community or for that matter other members of Japanese society. Two central factors account for their social segregation: the temporal location they occupy as nighttime workers and the social stigma attached to their work.

Hostesses maintain a time clock that they have termed in the community as "vampire hours." They are awake when most of Japan is asleep. They work from seven o'clock in the evening to four o'clock in the morning, or for a shorter period of time between these hours. Their different rhythmic pattern of daily life fosters their social segregation from most of Japanese society.

Even though I also worked as a hostess during the course of my research, I never quite got used to the different rhythm of life led by those around me so that I could, like them, adjust by replacing day with night. At four o'clock in the morning, I would rarely have any energy left to stay awake and would fall asleep as soon as I arrived home from work. In contrast, my co-workers, who often slept over at my apartment, would stay awake for a few more hours. After work, they would stay up—eat, talk on the phone, watch a video recording, or read a Filipino romance novel.

The different temporal location of hostesses fosters their social segregation in Japan, which undoubtedly intensifies the orientation toward the Philippines among *talents*. Being awake at night and asleep during the day segregates hostesses from most members of dominant society. Because of their work schedule, they attend to their business and leisure activities from four to nine o'clock in the morning and/or from four to six o'clock in the late afternoon. During this small window of time they would go grocery shopping, dine out, attend Mass, do laundry, cook, rent bootleg recordings of Filipino TV programs, and take care of other daily activities.

Due to their different time clock, hostesses tend to be socially isolated not only from members of the dominant society but also from other members of the Filipino migrant community, meaning the nonhostesses, including wives, domestic workers, male construction workers, factory workers, and other low-wage service workers.[7] While these other members of the community would go to church at noon, patronize a restaurant at eight o'clock in the evening, or go to the bank at one o'clock in the afternoon, the rhythm of life for hostesses, with the exception of wives who clock out of work earlier than others, prevents them from performing such activities during the same temporal locations. It is therefore rare for hostesses and Filipinos who are not working in the nightlife industry to meet, resulting in the bifurcation of the Filipino migrant community. Even if they do meet, they rarely interact socially. Various members of the Filipino migrant community usually meet only on Sunday afternoon at church, mingling after Mass in the crowd gathered around the food vendors set up outside for churchgoers.

The social bifurcation of the Filipino migrant community in Japan often leads to a misunderstanding of hostess work among other migrant Filipinos. Their minimal interactions with hostesses frequently result in the common misconception that hostess work is nothing but prostitution. In the autobiographical account of his life as an undocumented worker, for instance, Ray Ventura mistakenly asserts that "many of the girls who go out as entertainers end up as prostitutes, and many others know exactly what the deal is from the start."[8] Interestingly, he confesses to rarely engaging hostesses in conversation about their work. As he admitted, "I never spoke directly to Daisy and Margie about their work," referring to the two hostesses he encountered regularly.[9] Still, he feels comfortable enough to assert that they most likely engaged in prostitution. Interestingly, he makes his claim based solely on his observation of their choice of clothing: "high heels, tight fitting pants, revealing blouses, spray-netted hair."[10] Assumptions such as Ventura's clearly circulate not only in the Philippines but also among the hostesses' Filipino coethnics in Japan. Perhaps it is to contest the misconception of their work that many of hostesses whom I met rarely wore sexy attire when outside of the club. Instead, they would often choose to wear what could be described as demure clothing. After all, one complaint that hostesses frequently shared with me is the misconception of their job as nothing but prostitution.

The different rhythm of daily life of entertainers partially explains why I struggled to find interviewees during my first two months in Tokyo, as I visited Filipino business establishments such as restaurants during the day and not during the night. I was later advised to visit Filipino restaurants at three o'clock in the morning, which I eventually did, despite the difficulty of traveling in the middle of the train's nonoperational hours. After circling various areas in and around Tokyo, I soon took notice of the nontypical operating hours maintained by Filipino grocery stores and restaurants. In Roppongi, for instance, Nanay's Lugaw, a small restaurant near the Philippine Embassy, caters to nightlife industry workers after midnight and embassy patrons during the day, staying open twenty-four hours a day. Catering to hostesses, Flash Philippines, a small restaurant in the working-class neighborhood of Oyama on the periphery of Tokyo, is open from three o'clock in the afternoon to eight o'clock in the evening and then reopens from two o'clock to six o'clock in the morning. Bahay Kubo in Nishi-Kawaguchi, a working-class area in the neighboring prefecture of Saitama, is open from six o'clock in the evening to six o'clock in the morning. Likewise, the restaurant Jungle, located in the working-class neighborhood of Higashi-Jujo on the periphery of Tokyo, similarly operates from eight o'clock in the evening to eight o'clock in the morning. So does Boracay, in the red light district of Kinshicho. Many Filipino food stores reopen from two until six in the morning to cater to hostesses.

The different time clock of migrant hostesses tells us of their minimal interaction with members of dominant society, but this is not reason enough for the homeward bound orientation of *talents*. After all, they could adapt to life in Japan within their temporally bound ethnic community. Visa overstayers, for instance, do. Further pushing their greater orientation toward the home country is their marginalization in the migrant community, which only partially results from their different time clock. The social stigma attached to their occupation promotes entertainers' segregation from other members of the community. Other members of the community, for instance, wives—including those who used to work as entertainers—tend to shun them. Additionally, key institutions in the ethnic community, specifically banks and the Philippine Embassy, ignore their needs. Most community advocacy and support groups do not prioritize the concerns of this socially stigmatized group. Only churches have made significant efforts to adjust to the schedule of hostesses. For instance, one church in Tokyo offers prayer services to Filipino workers at four o'clock on Wednesday afternoons, which is a time slot that actually fits the schedule of hostesses. Churches also perform afternoon Mass in addition to the twelve o' clock Sunday Mass attended by most other Filipinos. In contrast, branches of Philippine banks do not acknowledge entertainers as one of their constituency, insisting on closing at three o'clock in the afternoon like other banks in Japan. Likewise, the Philippine Embassy closes at five o'clock in the afternoon. The inaccessibility of the Philippine Embassy for migrant hostesses calls into question whether this governmental institution adequately protects and advocates for them, which is troubling in light of the U.S. government's identification of *talents* as severely trafficked persons.[11]

Perhaps more troubling is the fact that *talents* were not a target group of the Overseas Workers Welfare Administration (OWWA) in Japan during the time of my research. OWWA is the designated government agency assigned to protect and promote the welfare and well-being of Filipino contract workers and their dependants. With offices located in most high destination areas of migrant Filipino workers around the world, OWWA operates in two locations in Japan—Nagoya and Tokyo. In Tokyo, OWWA is located in the Embassy of the Philippines and operates during the same hours as the embassy. The operating budget of OWWA comes not from the government but from the US$25 annual fee collected from temporary migrant workers deployed by the government, a fact that makes it all the more ironic that OWWA in Tokyo does not address the needs of its largest group of constituents but instead works mostly with non-OWWA members, specifically wives of Japanese men, as well as the smaller group of domestic workers. In Tokyo, the welfare officer has devoted much of her energy to developing a community-based theater group, which without doubt empowers the community by addressing the plight and difficulties of migrant Filipina workers in Japan. Yet, not one *talent* participates in this group, and only one hostess does so; the issues that this theater group addresses in its performances concern those confronted by wives and domestic workers.

Likewise, hometown associations have not reached out to *talents*. The reasoning of various community leaders whom I met is that *talents* are in Japan for only six months, which ignores the facts that they may still have some needs arising during this brief period of time and that their constant circulation between Japan and the Philippines guarantees that there will be some present in Japan at any given time. The community advocate groups' tendency to ignore the needs of *talents* tells us that their temporal segregation inadvertently results in their social segregation, which further encourages their homeward bound orientation and consequently their limited integration.

It would not be farfetched for us to assume that the social stigma attached to hostesses is a central reason behind their marginalization. Indeed, the welfare officer of OWWA informed me that she prioritizes not *talents*, or for that matter hostesses, but other members of the community (that is, wives and domestic workers) to "uplift the image of the Filipino community." In its quest to improve the public image of Filipinos, OWWA sees it as a priority to inform the public that not all Filipinos in Japan are hostesses, which we could speculate to mean that not all Filipinos are sexually loose women. The dismissal of hostesses as a public embarrassment for the identity of the nation not only indicates their marginal status in the community, but more importantly it tells us that OWWA, at least under the leadership of the welfare officer during the time of my field research, has not addressed the needs of its largest constituents in Tokyo. Giving community leaders the benefit of the doubt, this is perhaps because of the temporal inaccessibility of *talents*. Regardless, *talents* and other hostesses remain in the shadows of the Filipino migrant community.

Spatial Segregation

Aggravating the orientation of *talents* toward the Philippines is their experience of spatiality in Japan, or more specifically "the partition of [their] space" from others in the host society.[12] In Japan, it is not just visa overstayers but also *talents* who live geographically constrained lives. Like visa overstayers, *talents* are concentrated not only in a specific locale but in private spaces within this locale, resulting in their experience of spatial segregation on settlement. Suggesting their imprisonment, *talents*—like visa overstayers—spend most of their free time indoors in apartments and, when outdoors, are restricted within their neighborhood.

Without doubt, appearances could be deceptive, as the absence of *talents* in public spaces seems to suggest their imprisonment, hence "trafficking," by employers. Yet, for the most part, *talents* we should note stay indoors not by force but by choice, one that they make in the context of the constraints that they face as temporally segregated migrants who see their settlement in Japan as a period of putting their life in the Philippines on hold. In contrast, visa overstayers keep indoors due to the criminality of their illegal residency. Hence, they stay hidden by force. But *talents* stay within the confines of their apartment so as to minimize their expenses; as sojourners, they would rather spend their money in the Philippines and not in Japan. While they may choose to stay indoors, other factors constrain their spatial actions, including the proximity of their residence and workplace, their temporal location, and the fact that businesses are closed when they get off work at two or four o'clock in the morning, the six o'clock curfew imposed by most club management on *talents*, and lastly their illiteracy, which discourages them from traveling by bus or train outside of their neighborhood. When spending time with *talents*, one soon notices that most do not venture outside the vicinity of their neighborhoods during the three to six months they work in Japan.

The settlement of *talents* in Japan is one of spatial segregation, as we see not only in their confinement in particular neighborhoods but also in their concentration and restricted movements in their place of residence. *Talents* spend most of their free time in their apartments. It is where they shop for clothes, remit money, and communicate with their family in the Philippines. Peddlers—many being Filipina wives of Japanese men—sell *omise* clothes, usually brightly colored polyester dresses, to *talents* in their apartments. Some also sell phone cards, and most *talents* I met purchased at least one 1,000 yen ($10) phone card per week. One card would usually give them nearly an hour phone call with someone in the Philippines on their cellular phone, which they usually acquired courtesy of one of their many customers at the club. Other entrepreneurs also sell jewelry or offer door-to-door remittance. Because of the banks' inaccessibility, most have to rely on the peddlers who visit their apartments to send money to the Philippines. Some take the risk of relying on the postal service, but most opt for the greater security offered by remitters in the underground economy. While banks charge no more than 2,000 yen ($20) per remittance, door-to-door peddlers, as I discussed in the previous chapter, charge a much higher prorated fee of 5 to 10 percent.

During the course of my research, I had the opportunity to visit a few of the contract workers' apartments. I first had the chance to do so when I accompanied a nun who regularly visited them at their place of residence as part of what she called her "pastoral care" to her constituency in Tokyo. The apartment that I first visited was located amid other nightlife industry businesses such as pink salons for sexual massages, soaplands for assisted baths, and adult health clubs for sexual role-play. Greeting me when I entered this apartment was the rancid smell of used cooking oil that permeated the thick air. All the other apartments I visited in the course of my research were a lot like this first one I entered, as they are usually dark, squalid, and cramped units.

Talents claim that they get free housing as part of their contract to work in Japan, but this is questionable. Labor contracts of hostesses with entertainer visas filed at the Embassy of the Philippines stipulate a 30,000 yen ($300) monthly salary deduction for housing. Considering that anywhere between 10 to 12 *talents* occupy each residential unit, which are usually no bigger than 400 square feet and usually only a two-bedroom and one-bath apartment, clubs could make a tremendous amount of profit from the rent of *talents* and earn as much as 300,000 yen ($3,000) in monthly rent for each unit. Not located in prime neighborhoods but more likely in seedy red-light districts, the average two-bedroom apartment should rent for no more than 100,000 yen ($1,000). For example, I learned that one of the comparable units in a building with apartments that house *talents* costs the tenant only 60,000 yen per month.

Management usually bars the entry of outsiders into the apartments of *talents*, and only those peddlers preapproved by management can come and go regularly. Management supposedly does so to discourage customers from entering these spaces, but perhaps a more apt reason would be to hide their unsanitary conditions. Mold, mildew, cockroaches, and mice are common sights in these apartments, where visitors are not expected to take off their shoes on entry as they would in other residences in Japan. Cockroaches of different sizes crawled throughout the apartments I visited. Unfortunately, rodents also infested some of the units I entered, with many *talents* complaining to me that "Mickey Mouse" had eaten their food.

Aggravating the public health risks of *talents* is the lack of ventilation in these residential units. Due to their odd schedules, *talents* cover their bedroom windows with cardboard boxes to block the sun while they sleep during the day. Consequently, air rarely circulates in these apartments, leaving *talents* at risk of tuberculosis and other airborne diseases. Lessening their risk of disease, *talents* must pass a clean bill of health to be eligible to work in Japan. However, even if with less risk of contagion from tuberculosis, they are still prone to illness from overcrowding, lack of ventilation, and the unsanitary conditions of their residence.

Symbolically mirroring their experience of migrant settlement as one of spatial restriction, *talents*' apartments tend to be crowded units where they cannot move around freely. These cramped and enclosed quarters cannot offer entertainers much solace from the close monitoring of their movements in the workplace. *Talents*' residences tend not to have a common living area. Moreover, hallways are often blocked by jumbo *balikbayan* boxes, while kitchens would rarely be conducive to anything other than eating a quick meal. For example, kitchens do not always have a table, and *talents* tend to use not chairs but instead small plastic pails as seats.

Sometimes apartments are too small to accommodate all of the *talents* assigned to live there, so that some are relegated to make do with the hallway or kitchen as their bedroom. This happened to Rachel and Kay, two experienced return migrants whom management assigned to sleep in one corner of the kitchen. Complaining to me one afternoon, Rachel showed me how the wall separating her bedroom from the kitchen is actually only three layers of cardboard boxes and a tarp hanging from the ceiling. Showing a great deal of ingenuity in their part, Kay and Rachel created a bedroom by putting two bunk beds against each other and separating them with layers of cardboard. They sleep on one bunk bed and use the other, which is technically in the kitchen, as storage for their suitcases and *balikbayan* boxes. Inside their "bedroom" is one bunk bed and two plastic bins that they use as drawers. According to Rachel, her "bedroom" did not look anything like this when she first arrived in Japan; instead it looked more like a storage room piled with junk and furniture. She and Kay had to figure out how to clear the space, getting rid of the excess furniture and junk crowding their "bedroom," before they could feel they had a semblance of a home in Japan. Since clearing their room, Kay and Rachel had been able to personalize their space, which they had primarily done by tacking photos of their families on the cardboard adjacent to their bunk bed.

Bunk beds and not bedrooms are usually the sanctuary of *talents* in Japan. Each bunk bed would be enclosed with blankets that hang from the ceiling or the top bunk to give *talents* some semblance of privacy. *Talents* do everything except eat on their bed. This is where they do their make-up, read, write letters, watch DVDs, and talk on the phone with their families in the Philippines or customers from the club. Personalizing these spaces are the *talent*'s family pictures, usually those of siblings, parents, or children, pinned on the side of the bed.

Despite their limited space within the cramped quarters of their apartments, *talents* still spend most of their free time in there. Looking at the private spaces occupied by *talents*, the enclosed spaces of the bunk bed and the apartment with sealed windows metaphorically represent their segregation in Japan. Considering that *talents* spend most of their free time in the encaged space of their apartment, it is not difficult to see why they would not feel entrenched in Japanese society but instead would view migration as a process of putting their life in the Philippines on hold.

THE BIFURCATED COMMUNITY OF FILIPINO MIGRANTS IN JAPAN

While their temporal segregation and dislocation limit the spatial integration of *talents*, these temporal conditions also lead to the spatial division in the Filipino migrant community between hostesses and nonhostesses. The bifurcation of the Filipino migrant community in Tokyo reflects the spatial practices of its members, with *talents* and hostesses generally occupying different spatial and temporal locations from others in the community; the public faces of the community are arguably those of nonhostesses. For this reason, it took me a while to locate hostesses and identify the spaces they occupy outside work. The absence of hostesses in the public was quite glaring. For instance, events that represent the Filipino community in Tokyo and serve as gateways to the community rarely included hostesses. To give one example, a beauty contest I attended in Tokyo during my first month in Japan surprisingly had not one hostess among its contestants. Instead, most were domestic workers.

In the ethnic community, the spaces that hostesses and nonhostesses occupy are usually distinct. Some spaces like to be known as hostess spaces and some do not. When talking to the owner of a grocery store in the southwestern neighborhood of Meguro, I took note of the absence of "hostesses" in her response to my question on what types of jobs Filipinos hold in Japan. She responded, "A lot, but mostly maids. There are some professionals in the office, but most are maids. A lot of jobs. Some are in construction." In contrast to the store at Meguro, which is run by a woman whom I mistakenly thought had once been a hostess due to her tight-fitting attire, heavy jewelry, thick makeup, and dyed blond hair, is the store run by another woman in the northeastern neighborhood of Oyama. Like the storeowner from Meguro, this storeowner also wore her hair long and dyed and preferred tight-fitting clothes. Yet, in contrast to the store in Meguro, this storeowner did not deny the presence of hostesses in the community but actually catered to them, as she operated her business from three to six o'clock in the morning as well as from three o'clock in the afternoon to eight o'clock in the evening.

The stigma of hostess work in the Filipino community leads to a stratified relationship between the spatially and temporally marginalized hostesses and the rest of the community. To find interviewees, I had to visit the community not during the day but at night, and not in the most visible public spaces but in the subcultural spaces of Filipino restaurants and host clubs. I encountered hostesses during the day only at church. This is actually where the paths of hostesses and nonhostesses are likely to cross, but when they do meet there, they rarely have direct social interaction. The few Catholic churches that offer Filipino- or English-language Masses in Tokyo are the specific spaces where hostesses and nonhostesses are likely to encounter one another. The largest of these churches is St. Ignasius by Sophia University, which holds an English-language Mass at noon every Sunday. Outside of St.Ignasius there would be a line of vendors selling Filipino food on the sidewalk facing the church. During a brief period before and after Mass, the place turns into an open market with vendors selling various cooked meat dishes, served with rice, as well as desserts of rice and milk cakes. These food products are mostly prepacked into *obento* boxes for customers to conveniently take home.

Vendors begin to set up their stalls a little after eleven o'clock in the morning and stay only until around two o'clock, approximately one hour after the Mass ends, leaving people, including hostesses and nonhostesses, with little time to socially interact with one another. About eight vendors sell food outside of the church. Others sell nonperishable products such as underwear, bootlegged videos of Philippine TV shows, and religious images and figures of the Virgin Mary, Santo Niño, and various saints. One vendor sells a variety of Filipino food products such as dry noodles, sauces, and cooking mixes. Vendors, I notice, do not sell any drinks at the site but just cooked foods or other snacks. Customers also tend not to eat there. Most purchase food to take home. A snack of rice porridge, fried hotdog, or fried banana is the most one could eat on the premises.

The leisure spaces inhabited by hostesses generally differ from those of nonhostesses. The restaurants, grocery stores, and after-work drinking holes frequented by hostesses cater to their hours and operate between midnight and nine in the morning. This explains why I struggled to find interviewees during my first two months in Tokyo, as I visited Filipino business establishments such as restaurants during the day and not during the times that hostesses would be there. All this changed after I started venturing in the community past midnight, at three o'clock in the morning.[13]

Indicative of the stratification in the community, I rarely saw *talents* at formal institutions such as the embassy or banks, which are places where I had expected to encounter a representative sample of Filipinos in the community. Because these establishments operate during usual business hours of nine o'clock in the morning to three o'clock in the afternoon in the case of banks and until five o'clock in the evening in the case of the Philippine Embassy, I rarely if ever encountered hostesses in these public spaces. Service is usually so slow in these establishments that the short span of free time that hostesses have in the afternoon would not be sufficient to complete the simplest transaction, such as sending money to the Philippines. For example, the tedious process of remitting money can take up to an hour at Philippine National Bank, even if only a few customers are waiting in line to send money.[14] Because of the banks' inaccessibility to *talents*, most choose to send money by way of door-to-door remittances through peddlers who visit their apartments. Although more expensive and risky, *talents* still resort to door-to-door remittance options because of the inconvenience of banking in Japan. Likewise, they rarely venture to the Philippine Embassy because one would have to spend the whole day there to order a passport, file a marriage license, or do any other business that needs certification from the Philippine government.[15] One can imagine how those who become victims of forced labor would find it difficult and inconvenient to go to the Philippine Embassy, which ironically should serve as their primary source of protection as labor migrants in Japan.

Without doubt, *talents*' desire to return home is fostered by the poor conditions of their migration. However, although better housing and living conditions and greater access to community assistance would not necessarily result in their desire to settle permanently in Japan, they would result in an improved quality of life. Yet, *talents* do not receive adequate support from local organizations to improve the conditions of their settlement, which is ironic considering their identification as trafficked persons by the U.S. Department of State. Club owners have yet to be fined for the subpar housing conditions of *talents*. Moreover, those who impose inhumane curfew restrictions as punishment to *talents* unable to meet their sales quotas are never penalized. Indeed, poor living and working conditions are the norm and not the exception among *talents*. Only those facing extremely egregious working conditions are likely to turn to governmental organizations for support. The inaccessibility of assistance discourages *talents* from complaining. The hours maintained by governmental and nongovernmental organizations have yet to accommodate the different temporal location that hostesses inhabit. Considering that the membership fees of contract workers fund the operation of OWWA, it is quite ironic then that the hours maintained by OWWA bar access to *talents* who have need of OWWA's services.[16]

Instead of improving the conditions of their labor and migration, the solution to the *talents*' plight has been their rescue as advocated by the United States and pursued by Japan with the disqualification of most Filipino overseas performance artists from reentry. Rescue, however, has not necessarily protected *talents* from human rights abuses. Ineligibility for reentry has only encouraged plenty of them to go underground and remain in Japan as visa overstayers. As addressed in the previous chapter, visa overstayers face their own set of vulnerabilities, which some would argue are worse than those faced by *talents* because they are without government protection from employer and coethnic abuse.

Of the *talents* whom I met in Japan, it seems transgender *talents* are those who fared well after being barred from reentry into Japan, which makes sense considering that they generally come from a higher-class status than their female counterparts. Some utilized their English language skills and pursued jobs in call centers in the Philippines.[17] One went abroad to Australia to complete her master's degree in education. Others operate small businesses in the Philippines. Only one complained to me that she had gone back to becoming a member of the working poor since her disqualification from reentry. In contrast to transgender *talents*, most of their female counterparts returned to their life of abject poverty in the Philippines, with some still in debt to their promotion agencies and talent managers. Others managed to pursue hostess work elsewhere, for instance in Korea. Others shared with me plans to become entertainers in Cyprus, ironically identified by the U.S. Department of State as another hotbed for human trafficking.[18] A few managed to return to Japan as *talents*, while a large number took the risk of remaining as visa overstayers. For the most part, hostesses did not fare better after their "rescue," which suggests that eliminating the only viable occupation they have held as members of the poorest of the poor in the Philippines was not the best solution for the abuses and vulnerabilities they had confronted in the *omise*. Instead, solutions that would have assured them greater control over their labor and migration, solutions that would have enabled their independent migration, and solutions that would have guaranteed their continued employment are perhaps what would have empowered them as low-wage workers in the Philippine diaspora.

CONCLUSION

ENSURING THE SAFE PASSAGE OF MIGRANT HOSTESSES

MANY WILL COME AWAY FROM READING this book with the conclusion that migrant Filipina hostesses in Tokyo are trafficked persons. Anyone following the U.S. definition of a severely trafficked person would conclude that Amy, Irene, Rowena, Teresa had all fit this description because they pursued hostess work before they turned eighteen years old. According to the U.S. Department of State, severely trafficked persons would include minors induced to perform commercial sex acts regardless of their consent; persons made to perform commercial sex "by force, fraud or coercion"; and lastly persons who were held in "involuntary servitude, peonage, debt bondage or slavery" through fraudulent or coercive means.[1] Irene, who migrated to Japan at the age of sixteen, entered Japan using a fake passport for which she was saddled with a debt of 100,000 pesos (US$2,000). Quitting her job prior to the end of her six-month contract would have resulted in penalties imposed by middleman brokers. Migration made Irene a severely trafficked person in two ways: First it subjected her to peonage or indentured servitude; secondly, she was a minor involved in commercial flirtation.

Yet Irene would disagree with her identification as a trafficked person. Instead, she would insist, as did many other hostesses, "We are not human trafficking." How do we resolve the discrepancy between the perspective of Irene and the antitrafficking activists who wish to save her from enslavement and child prostitution?[2] Irene is now nearly thirty years old, and she looks back at her decision to pursue migrant hostess work at the age of sixteen without any regret. Perhaps she is one of the fortunate ones who survived her subjugation unscathed. When I talked to Irene about the question of human trafficking and whether she holds any regrets for what many would describe as her lost youth, Irene insisted that it was she who wanted to go to Japan and that she was not pressured by her parents or the brokers. In so doing, she reminds us that definitions of human trafficking dismiss the will of individuals, including minors such as she had been years ago. For Irene, the problem of the discourse of human trafficking was its failure to consider the different needs of "victims." To those who would label her a severely trafficked person forced into sexual slavery as a minor, she would respond that she did not have a childhood that needed protection from her indentured mobility in Japan. Contrary to their view, she would insist that her labor migration had been her means of salvation from abject poverty. For Irene, the problem with most antitrafficking activists is that they define the situations of migrants and pose solutions without taking into account the experiences and perspectives of supposed victims. In the process, they disregard the wants and needs of the actual victims they seek to rescue and protect. For these reasons, Irene found the passionate zeal of antitrafficking activists unpalatable.

According to Irene, her debt did not completely erase her autonomy. When she returned to the Philippines at the end of her first contract, she actually contested her debt and refused to pay her brokers the 100,000 pesos they charged her for the use of a fake passport. She dared them to sue her, telling them that they would be imprisoned for sending an underage migrant worker to Japan. To return to Japan for a second contract, Irene processed her travel documents using her real name. In this way, she managed to return to Japan free of the reins of a talent manager. Disregarding the control of the promotion agency and promoter over her migration, we could argue that Irene suddenly became an independent labor migrant the second time she worked in Japan. Irene's situation might be exceptional. Irene knew that not all hostesses, including older ones, have the guts to fight back against their middleman brokers. The twenty-year-old Kay, for instance, feared that not acknowledging her agreement with her talent manager would land her in prison.[3]

Being underage, in Irene's perspective, does not automatically render one a trafficked person or a severely trafficked person. To make her point, she shared a story about her Indonesian co-workers. Irene told me that she saw herself in the situation of her two underage co-workers from Indonesia. As a mother of two young children, she told me she could not help but feel protective toward her two teenage co-workers, whom she learned are sixteen and seventeen years old. She wishes that they had other options in life rather than having to work as hostesses in Japan at such a young age. Yet she was not in a position to tell them what to do or not to do; instead, as a fellow migrant worker, an older one, she was just there, she explained to me, to help them. As she told me,

> One day they just entered the *omise*. They were so young. That is why I asked the Indonesians why they are there. Did they know that they were entering this kind of work? They told me, yes. *Because if they said no, then you want to help them escape.* But they knew what they were getting into. *So if you know what you were getting into, then you are willing to be there.* Because some do not know what kind of work they will be entering, and they only find out after they have arrived there. I feel sorry for those people. [*Emphasis my own.*]

As a seasoned migrant worker, Irene knew that situations of coerced labor are probable among migrant hostesses. She had had plenty of co-workers who felt morally violated at work. The co-workers she felt sorry for were those who had entered hostess work not prepared to engage in the sexual activities expected of them by club owners. These moral violations could be as mundane as flirting at the table but could be as risqué as undressing during *show time.* Irene knew that these tasks became a problem for those unwilling to perform them because the control of middleman brokers made it difficult for them to quit. Yet Irene also knew that not everyone felt morally violated at work—not everyone needed "rescue" from her situation. Recognizing the will of her Indonesian co-workers and their desire to stay employed as hostesses, Irene did not think she should force their rescue but that she should instead recognize their personal desires as migrant workers.

According to U.S. definition, debt bondage, peonage or enslavement does not automatically make one a severely trafficked person. Only those placed in such a position via "force, fraud, or coercion" would be severely trafficked persons. Indeed, if servitude or peonage automatically leads to human trafficking, then plenty if not *all* migrant contract workers in the twenty-first century would arguably be a trafficked person.[4] Filipino au pairs in the Netherlands and Denmark, migrant domestic workers employed as temporary contract workers in Asia, and migrant domestic workers in the Live-In Caregivers Program in Canada are just some of the trafficked victims who would need rescue.[5] This is because across the world the condition of migration for domestic workers binds them to the sponsoring citizen, which appeases anti-immigrant sentiments by limiting their citizenship rights but leaves them vulnerable to abuse.[6] Additionally, many amass a huge debt to cover the placement fee that middleman brokers charge prospective migrant workers, which could reach US$3,500 in Taiwan, US$6,250 in Italy, and US$3,000 in Hong Kong.[7] Lastly, most are live-in workers. Yet indentured servitude or peonage would constitute trafficking only if enforced via force, fraud, or coercion. This means then that, as is the case with foreign domestic workers, most hostesses would technically not be "severely trafficked persons" or for that matter trafficked persons, if we are to follow the U.N. definition, because they knowingly agree to migrate as indentured workers and do so not via "force, fraud, or coercion." Yet this technicality should not justify the servitude of migrant Filipina hostesses or for that matter any migrant worker. The threat to their autonomy and freedom by the stronghold of middleman brokers or by exclusionary migration policies that bind migrant workers to their employers, without question, should be eradicated. This is especially the case considering that migrant entertainers, as well as many other migrant workers, are unable to terminate their employment without the threat of financial penalty.[8]

While migrant Filipina hostesses are technically not "severely trafficked persons," they undeniably are migrants who face severe structural constraints. These structural constraints include the stronghold of middleman brokers, the absence of regulation in their workplace, the lack of labor market flexibility for contract workers, and lastly the criminalization of those who become undocumented workers. An overhaul of their migration process, for instance the implementation of a system of checks and balance to prevent abusive behavior by middleman brokers; the implementation of labor standards such as regular days off, eight hour per evening work schedules, the elimination of the requirement of the *dohan*, the illegalization of the penalty system including the imposition of a curfew, and the direct payment of hostesses by club owners; and lastly the recognition of their labor contributions via legalization by the state are some of the solutions that would increase hostesses' control over their labor and migration. These are the types of solutions that are premised on the understanding that hostesses are labor migrants who face severe structural constraints and solutions that antitrafficking advocates should focus on, instead of rescuing and eliminating the hostesses' occupation, which are not pragmatic responses to their subjugation but instead are impulsive reactions motivated by passionate zeal of antiprostitution activists.[9]

This study has illustrated the severe structural constraints that migrant Filipina hostesses confront in the process of their migration to Japan. It has called attention to the stronghold of migrant brokers over their labor migration and the absence of regulation in their workplace. In so doing, it has drawn attention to their vulnerability to coerced labor. Interestingly, the middleman brokers' stronghold is actually *not* why migrant Filipina hostesses were identified as trafficked persons by the U.S. Department of State. Instead, the annual TIP Report called attention to their "debt bondage" and forced sexual exploitation by club owners. The inaccuracy of these speculations suggests that the identification of Filipina hostesses as trafficked persons was not based on their actual experiences, which calls into question the viability of the top-down solutions offered by the U.S. Department of State.

If we are to adequately free migrant workers, particularly female migrant workers, of the threat of forced labor, we need to disentangle our antitrafficking ventures from antiprostitution efforts. We would be motivated by the goal of ensuring the independent migration of women and not the "aspirational morality" of antiprostitution.[10] We would acknowledge the will of migrant hostesses, including the choice of some to engage in sex work. Without doubt, the situation of migrant hostesses entails coercion but also choice; it is one of indentured mobility. Claims of their human trafficking, however, flatten their experience of migration to be solely one of coercion. As such, universal rescue would become the only solution to their subjugation. Harm reduction and safe passage are not seen as viable solutions. Yet, if we acknowledge the desires of most hostesses to work in Japan, then our solutions to their subjugation should be geared toward ensuring their independent labor migration.

The depiction of migrant Filipina hostesses as victims in need of rescue is actually puzzling because it is a far cry from the usual descriptions of migrant women in the rich literature on gender and migration. Empirically grounded studies repeatedly find that women make gains in status, autonomy, and resources on migration. Personal autonomy, financial independence, self-reliance, and sexual freedom are just some of the gains women make in migration.[11] In other words, grounded empirical studies that are based not on speculation but instead on interviews with countless of migrant women have repeatedly found that migration is a liberating and empowering experience for them. This would be the case for domestic workers bound to their employers in relations of "legal servitude" in Taiwan and Hong Kong as well as for Mexican and Dominican migrants in the United States.[12] This is not to say that migrant women are not without difficulties in the process of migration. Oppressive work conditions haunt them globally, and patriarchal relations with men still subjugate them in the home front.[13] Regardless, leading feminist migration scholars, including Saskia Sassen and Pierrette Hondagneu-Sotelo, find that the experience of empowerment outweighs the setbacks that women face in migration.[14]

If migration is indeed liberating and empowering, then the near eradication of the migration flow of hostesses from the Philippines to Japan threatens female empowerment. Hostess work is without doubt a challenging job. No one could argue that the work conditions of migrant hostesses are also oppressive. Still, none of the hostesses whom I encountered in Japan, including in the *yakuza*-operated establishment where I worked alongside them, wanted rescue from their employment. After all, it is not the occupation itself but the conditions, from long hours to stringent penalty systems, that hostesses do not like. For the majority of them, it is these conditions that made them cry almost every night, and not their forced prostitution, as many antitrafficking activists have repeatedly asserted but without proof. Instead of rescue, most migrant hostesses desire freedom from their middleman brokers, improved labor conditions, workplace flexibility, and access to continued migration. Recognizing the desires of migrant hostesses forces us to recognize them as labor migrants, perhaps not independent labor migrants but instead migrants subjected to indentured mobility.

Not unlike other migrant women, hostesses in Japan also see their migration as liberating and empowering. Migration has made them breadwinners in the family, a position that grants them decision-making power and earns them the respect of kin. Participating in commercial flirtation also sexually liberates them, allowing them to challenge conservative norms that limit the acceptable sexual activities of women. We need to recognize that the migration of hostesses challenges the sexual subjugation of women. Hostess work morally transgresses the gendered sexual hierarchy that limits the legitimate sexual activities and relationships for women more than those of men. As such, the migration of hostesses challenges patriarchal boundaries. We should therefore not celebrate the forced return migration of hostesses to the Philippines but instead lament the setback it has posed to the empowerment of migrant women.

ACKNOWLEDGMENTS

FIRST AND FOREMOST, I AM GRATEFUL TO the Filipinas in Tokyo who have let me into their lives. I thank many of them not just for their participation in this study but also for their friendship.

The opportunity to conduct the research for this book was made possible by an invitation to be a visiting professor at the Institute for Gender Studies in Ochanomizu University from its director, Professor Kaoru Tachi. I am grateful to the staff and faculty at the institute for their generosity, hospitality, and financial support during my stay in Japan. My deepest thanks go to Professor Yayoi Sugihashi for her help as I adjusted to Tokyo and navigated its bureaucratic maze of immigration offices. Professor Ruri Ito of Hitotsubashi University spearheaded the invitation for me to visit Japan. Her tireless work as a translator during my lectures and meetings with key individuals was more than invaluable. I am deeply grateful to her not just for the opportunity to do this project but also for enabling me to visit and collaborate with feminists in Japan. The staff of the Institute for Gender Studies also provided support during my stay in Tokyo, including Natsuko Hayashi, Naomi Hanaoka, Seiko Miyazaki, and Masashi Harada.

I could not have completed this research if not for the teaching flexibility that my colleagues in the Department of Asian American Studies at the University of California, Davis, granted me in 2005 and 2006. For this, I extend my gratitude to my colleagues Isao Fujimoto, Darrell Hamamoto, Bill Hing, Wendy Ho, Richard S. Kim, Sunaina Maira, Susette S. Min, Stanley Sue, Caroline Kieu Linh Valverde, and Nolan Zane. I am also deeply appreciative of Billie Gabriel and the staff support she provided while I taught at Davis. Much of the writing of this book took place while I was a faculty member in the Department of American Studies at Brown University. Both inside and outside my department, wonderful colleagues and students at Brown stimulated my intellectual inquiries and analytic trajectories in this book. I am grateful to the collegiality extended by Robert P. Emlen, Matthew Garcia, Elliott Gorn, Beverly Haviland, Robert G. Lee, Steven Lubar, Richard Alan Meckel, Ralph Rodriguez, Susan Smulyan, and Samuel Zipp, as well as Paja Faudree, Evelyn Hu-DeHart, Marie Myung-Ok Lee, Karl Jacoby, Jessa Leinaweaver, John Logan, Naoko Shibusawa, and Kay Warren. This book also benefited from the research assistance of Maria Hwang, including her help with the index, and the staff support provided by the magnificent office manager Jean Wood. I completed this book in the monastic and intellectually stimulating space provided by the Center for Advanced Study in the Behavioral Sciences. I could not have had a more ideal setting. Other scholars at CASBS provided me with plenty of food for thought, in particular Victoria McGeer, Samuel Perry, Philip Pettit, Anupama Rao, Carrie Rentschler, Nancy Whittier, and Eric Worby. For granting me the sabbatical I needed to complete this book, I am thankful to my colleagues in the Department of Sociology at the University of Southern California.

One could say that I navigated the world as I developed, shared, and worked through the ideas in this book. This manuscript benefits from comments shared to me by audiences at the All the Women of the World Conference in Reykjavik, Iceland; Arizona State University; the Asian Research Institute at National University of Singapore; Barnard College; Colorado State University; Northwestern University; Oberlin College; Pomona College; the University of California, Berkeley; the University of California, Los Angeles; the University of Iceland; the University of Rovira and Virgili in Tarragona, Spain; the University of Sao Paolo in Brazil; the University of South Australia in Adelaide; the Woodrow Wilson Center in Washington,

DC; and Yale Law School. I extend a deep appreciation to my hosts in these various institutions.

My understanding of human trafficking owes a great deal to my participation in a working group organized by Denise Brennan, Janie Chuang, and Janet Halley. This study has been made all the better by conversations I had with them at these meetings along with Ali Miller, Ann Jordan, Anne Gallagher, Aziza Ahmed, Carol Vance, Chantal Thomas, Dina Haynes, Elizabeth Bernstein, Hila Shamir, Kamala Kempadoo, Kay Warren, Kerry Rittich, Prabha Kotiswaran, and Sealing Cheng.

Several more individuals have been most important to the specific shape and direction this work has taken. While I take full responsibility for any mistakes or misrepresentations, I acknowledge that this book benefited immensely from the comments shared by various friends and colleagues. Many individuals read earlier portions of this book and gave me valuable feedback including Nina Bandelj, Eileen Boris, John Christman, Brian Hackney, Kimberly Hoang, David Leheny, Pardis Mahdavi, Hasan Mahmud, Rheana Parreñas, Ali Rogers, Felicity Schaeffer-Grabiel, Jonathan Twaddell, and Jane Ward. Conversations with Roberto Gonzalez, Sonya Michel, Jerry Miller, and Elena Shih also enhanced the contents of this book. Three anonymous reviewers provided informed and constructive critiques. Nobue Suzuki and Keiko Yamanaka assisted with the translation of key government records. For their intellectual stimulations, scholarly advice, and, most importantly, friendship, I owe special thanks to Rick Baldoz, Eileen Boris, Juliana Chang, Nicole Fleetwood, Maria Hwang, Heather Lee, Steve McKay, Dina Okamoto, Celine Parreñas Shimizu, Rheana (Juno) Parreñas, Lok Siu, Noah Tamarkin, Hung Thai, Viviana Zelizer, and Min Zhou.

I could not have found a better home for this book than at Stanford University Press. I am grateful to my editor Kate Wahl, her assistant editor Joa Suorez, the copy editor Margaret Pinette, and the other staff for their work in shepherding this book through the production process.

Lastly, I dedicate this book to Gugma and Pangga, who would never know how much their love, loyalty, and companionship fueled me through the writing process.

R.S.P.
Stanford, CA

NOTES

NOTES TO INTRODUCTION

1. See International Organization for Migration, 1997. For example, Aurora Javate De Dios, a member of the abolitionist group Coalition against Trafficking in Women, speculates that "Filipina entertainers are immediately forced into prostitution as soon as they arrive" (De Dios, 1992: 50). She bases this speculation on what she assumes to be their financial desperation.

2. See the annual *Trafficking in Persons Report* (TIP Report) issued by the U.S. State Department. U.S. government–sponsored research in 2006 concluded that there are an estimated 800,000 individuals trafficked across international borders. See U.S. Department of State, 2007.

3. The 2004 TIP Report asserts, "On arrival at their destination, victims are stripped of their passports and travel documents and forced into situations of sexual exploitation or bonded servitude. . . . For example, it is reported that Japan issued 55,000 entertainer visas to women from the Philippines in 2003, many of whom are suspected of having become trafficked victims" (U.S. Department of State, 2004: 14).

4. See the Philippine Overseas Employment Administration website on the number of deployed overseas workers at www.poea.gov.ph/html/statistics.html, last retrieved on January 4, 2010. Also see a report issued by Human Rights Osaka, www.hurights.or.jp/news/ 0702/b01_e.html, last retrieved on January 4, 2010.

5. The United States lauded Japan for the decline in the number of Filipina entertainers. The TIP Report states: "There has also been remarkable progress in the government's efforts to tighten the issuance of 'entertainer visas' to Philippine nationals, which has resulted in a sizeable reduction in the trafficking of Philippine women to Japan" (U.S. Department of State, 2006: 149).

6. In 2007, of newly hired overseas contract workers, 146,337 were women and 160,046 were men (Kanlungan, 2008).

7. Of Filipina undocumented workers apprehended by the Ministry of Justice in Japan between 1987 and 1990, 87 percent were hostesses and 3.4 percent were strippers (Morita and Sassen, 1994: 159).

8. See Osteria, 1994; Anderson, 1999; Suzuki, 2003.

9. See Leigh, 1997. Carol Leigh, a longtime activist, coined the term *sex work* to refer to prostitutes and other workers in the sex industry to reduce the negative connotation of this type of work and to emphasize prostitution as legitimate labor. While Leigh's definition of sex work encompasses a wide variety of labor, the use of the phrase is often reduced to encompassing only prostitution. Amalia Cabezas (2009) also challenges us to reconfigure common understandings of sex work and consider "new forms of flexible contingent practices that may contain elements of partial commodification but that do not conform to rigid categories of commercial sex work" (21). Cabezas actually rejects the use of the term *sex work* when it comes to commercial sexual interactions that involve durable social ties.

10. By casting a wide definition of sex work, I place prostitution in a moral continuum with other jobs that involve the exchange of sexual excitement and money.

11. Following the definition of human trafficking in the U.N. Protocol, human trafficking involves a three-part process. First, it involves the movement of an individual; second, the movement must be by force, fraud, or coercion; and third, the movement must take place for the purpose of the individual's exploitation. The United Nations defines human trafficking as:

> "Trafficking in persons" shall mean the recruitment, transportation, transfer, harbouring or receipt of persons, by means of the threat or use of force or other forms of coercion, of abduction, of fraud, of deception, of the abuse of power or of a position of vulnerability or of the giving or receiving of payments or benefits to achieve the consent of a person having control over another person, for the purpose of exploitation. Exploitation shall include, at a minimum, the exploitation of the prostitution of others or other forms of sexual exploitation, forced labour or services, slavery or practices similar to slavery, servitude or the removal of organs.

See Article 3 of the 2000 U.N. Protocol to Prevent, Suppress, and Punish Trafficking in Persons, Especially Women and Children, Supplementing the United Nations Convention against Organized Crime (also known as the Palermo Protocol).

12. Only one of the fifty-six individuals I interviewed had not known that she would be required to entertain customers at the table. She had assumed that her work as an "entertainer" in Japan would be no different than her past work as a lounge singer in Shanghai.

13. While most clubs ban hostesses from engaging in explicit sexual interactions with customers, they all require hostesses to interact closely with them.

14. Japan bans the labor migration of unskilled workers, making it illegal for hostesses with "entertainer visas" to converse with their customers. For a thorough list of the criteria for entry to Japan, see *A Guide to Japanese Visas*, Appendix 1: Ministerial Ordinance to Provide for Criteria pursuant to Article 7, Paragraph 1(2) of the Immigration Control and Refugee Recognition Act (Ministry of Justice Ordinance No. 16 of May 24, 1990), retrieved on July 31, 2006, from www.mofa.go.jp/j_info/visit/visa/appendix1.html. Also see Tsuda (2006) for a discussion of immigration policies in Japan.

15. For most of the book, I refer to "entertainers" as hostesses, because even though contract workers with "entertainer visas" cannot legally do hostess work, that is, interact with customers at the table, management still expects most if not *all* of them to flirt illicitly.

16. DeStefano, 2007.

17. Su, 1997; Chacon, 2006.

18. See Free the Slaves website; retrieved on October 4, 2010, from www.freetheslaves.net/Page.aspx?pid=301.

19. U.S. Department of State, 2007: 10.

20. See the UNICEF website; retrieved on October 25, 2010, from www.unicef.org/protection/index_exploitation.html.

21. See International Organization for Migration website; retrieved on October 4, 2010, from www.iom.int/jahia/Jahia/counter-trafficking. Also see U.S. Department of State, 2007.

22. See the U.N. Office on Drugs and Crime website, retrieved on May 29, 2011, from www.unedc.org/unodc/en/human-trafficking/faqs.html.

23. See annual U.S. Department of State TIP Reports since 2000.

24. By forced labor, the International Labor Organization refers to "work or service exacted from a person under threat or penalty, which includes penal sanctions and the loss of rights and privileges, where the person has not offered him/herself voluntarily" (Ruwanpura and Rai, 2004: 3).

25. Underlying the construction of trafficked persons as "victims" in need of rescue is the moralistic view that women must stay close to hearth and home so as to protect their femininity. See Cheng, 2010; Doezema, 2001. Laura Agustin argues that the conflation of migrant sex work and trafficking romanticizes female domesticity. Constructing migrant sex workers as trafficked victims in need of protection suggests that women migrate (that is, leave the comforts of home), only when "pushed, obligated, coerced, or forced" (2007: 111).

26. See Scarpa, 2008; Destefano, 2007.

27. Scholars, government agencies, nongovernmental organizations, and the media alike blindly reproduce stories of human trafficking. The eminent migration scholar Saskia Sassen, for instance, describes the situation of migrant Filipina entertainers in Japan as one of forced prostitution:

> The rapid increase in the number of women migrating as entertainers can be traced to the more than five hundred "entertainment brokers" that now operate in the Philippines outside the state umbrella. These brokers provide women for the Japanese sex industry, which is basically controlled by organized gangs rather than through the government-sponsored program for the entry of entertainers. Recruited for singing and entertaining, these women are frequently forced into prostitution as well. (Sassen, 2003: 271–272)

28. Pettit, 2004: 55–57.

29. For a discussion of the moral regulation of Indonesian migrant women, see the works of Rachel Silvey (2000, 2005, 2007). Nana Oishi (2005) provides us with a splendid overview of migration policies in countries of emigration in Asia, illustrating how nations enact "value laden policies" to make sure that the movement of women does not disagree with gendered social norms. Lastly, Martha Gardner and Eithne Luibheid both describe the moral regulation underlying U.S. migration policies. See Luibheid, 2002; Oishi, 2005; Gardner, 2005; and Silvey, 2000.

30. Luibheid, 2002.

31. Gardner, 2005.

32. Ibid.

33. Cheng (2010) also observes that morally laden views on women's sexual integrity act as a controlling factor of migration for migrant entertainers. Also see Miller, 2004.

34. Mary Douglas and her theorization of pollution also help us make sense of the moralistic foundation of antiprostitution. According to Douglas, the body is a metaphor for society and, as such, "Certain cultural themes are expressed by rites of bodily manipulation" (2002 [1966]: 158). For the sake of maintaining order in society, we are imposed with sexual scripts that dismiss certain acts—adultery and incest, for example—as being acts of "sexual pollution" (2002 [1966]: 174). Paid sex is likely to be also an act of sexual pollution.

35. Zelizer, 2000, 2005.

36. Zelizer, 2000: 823.

37. As Nussbaum explains, "People committed to gender hierarchy, and determined to ensure that the dangerous sexuality of women is controlled by men, frequently have viewed the prostitute, a sexually active woman, as a threat to male control of women" (1999: 286).

38. Ibid.: 287.

39. Rubin, 1984.

40. Feminists who do not think there is anything inherently wrong with engaging in sex work disagree with radical feminists such as Kathleen Barry. See Barry, 1995. Philosopher Martha Nussbaum questions the stigmatization of prostitution and the notion that "taking money or entering into contracts in connection with the use of one's sexual or reproductive capacities is genuinely bad" (1998: 695). As many feminist ethnographers have documented, sex workers do not necessarily alienate their sexuality on the grounds that they receive payment for sexual services (Bernstein, 2001; Brennan, 2004; Chapkis, 1997; Kempadoo, 1998; Truong, 1990).

Moreover, paid intimacy does not necessarily taint but can coexist with noncommercial intimacy. Various forms of intimacy have always coexisted with one another. For instance, looking at child care, payments rendered to nannies for the care of children do not make them worse caregivers than unpaid mothers. These two forms of caregiving can coexist. The different social relations of the child to the paid caregiver and unpaid mother mark the boundaries that define the social meanings of payment. Child care is a socially accepted form of commodified intimacy, which by its existence questions the stigma attached to the commodified intimacy of sex work.

41. See Zigon, 2007. Following Zigon's formulation, a study on migrant Filipina hostesses allows for an anthropology of moralities. According to Zigon, an anthropology of moralities can be pursued only through an analysis of "moral breakdowns." As he notes, "It should be limited to those social and personal moments when persons or groups of persons are forced to step-away from their unreflective everydayness and think-through, figure out, work on themselves and respond to certain ethical dilemmas, troubles or problems" (2007: 140).

42. Pushing for want he calls an "anthropology of morality," Zigon advocates for the documentation of "how people we study conceive of, negotiate, and practice morality in their everyday lives" (2008: 3). He views the process of moral negotiation as a more fluid process than I do. As he notes, morality should not be conceived as "a code or set of principles and rules to be followed, or transgressed, rather morality is variously conceived . . . as a form of embodied dispositions, cultural scripts, or moral choices intimately tied with emotions and feelings" (2008: 8). While I agree that morals are constructed via experience, I think society espouses dominant moral views as a means of maintaining social order, and members of society accordingly negotiate these moral views—either accepting them, contesting them, or reconstructing them. I show in this book that this social order is gendered. Durkheim (1953) notably sees that society regulates behavior via morality. See his essay on "The Determination of Moral Facts."

43. Nussbaum, 1998; Rubin, 1984.

44. The framework I develop in this book builds on the pioneering work of feminist geographer Rachel Silvey, who introduces the concept of "moral geographies" to illustrate how women negotiate their sexual morality in migration. See Silvey, 2000. According to Silvey, particular moral codes, or gendered normative ideologies, shape women's actions and options in migration. In contrast to Silvey, who focuses on how gendered moral geographies delimit the options of women, I examine how women contest the moral codes that shape their experiences.

45. See Foucault, 1985. According to Foucault, individuals are guided by a "prescriptive system that is explicitly or implicitly operative in their culture, and of which they are more or less aware" (26). Individuals undergo a "mode of subjection . . . the way in which the individual establishes his relation to the rule and recognizes himself as obliged to put it into practice" (27). The "moral prescriptions" that guide our behavior, argues Foucault, determine our sense of self and guide our actions in the making of a "moral subject" (1997: 263). For Foucault, one becomes an ethical subject according to the extent to which one abides by the moral codes of society. In my reading of the moral subjection of migrant entertainers, I illustrate that they do not just abide by the morals norms and codes that shape their being, but they could also contest them and construct alternative moral standards. The

process of negotiating moral norms results in the formation of multiple moralities. In this process, hostesses construct alternative moral standards that guide their sense of becoming an ethical subject.

46. See Butler, 2005. In *Giving an Account of Oneself*, Butler explicates on Foucault's theorizations of morality. She explains, "Even if morality supplies a set of norms that produce a subject in his or her intelligibility, it also remains a set of norms and rules that a subject must negotiate in a living and reflective way" (2005: 10).

47. As Emile Durkheim has noted, "There is not just one morality but several and as many as there are social types." Durkheim, 1984: 335.

48. Foucault, 1985.

49. Kim Price-Glynn (2010) likewise found different attitudes among strippers about their labor. Some embraced it, while others found it embarrassing. We can speculate that the various reactions among strippers to the "stigma" of their occupation are partially attributable to the diversity of their sexual morals.

50. Durkheim observes the existence of moral plurality. Morals that are dictated by society vary by social grouping whether that grouping is a family, a nation, or humanity. While Durkheim acknowledges moral distinctions according to social groupings, I insist that members of the same social grouping could have different moral standards. Differences in experiences and subject positions lead to different moral groupings within the same social grouping.

51. By "indentured servitude," I refer to "contractual but unfree labor" (Steinfeld, 1991: 3).

52. For example, Kevin Bales, a leading pundit on the abolishment of slavery and human trafficking, asserts, "The greatest obstacles we face in ending slavery are not poverty and violence; they are the toxicity of some cultures and the perversion of organized crime" (Bales, 2007: 231). Likewise, the U.S. Department of State TIP Report repeatedly blames the pervasiveness of trafficking on transnational organized crime syndicates. Lastly, the office responsible for the Palermo Protocol is the U.N. Office on Drugs and Crime.

53. My understanding of citizenship builds from critical citizenship scholarship (Bosniak, 1999–2000; Turner, 1994). In this perspective, I see citizenship, borrowing the words of the legal scholar Brenda Cossman (2007), "as invoking the ways that different subjects are constituted as members of a polity, the ways they are, or are not, granted rights, responsibilities, and representations within that polity, as well as acknowledgement and inclusion through a multiplicity of legal, political, cultural and social discourses" (5). It is the way subjects are constituted as citizens and the way citizenship itself is constituted.

54. Haney-Lopez, 2006; Lowe, 1996; Ong, 2003; Park, 2004; Siu, 2005; Yuval-Davis, 1997.

55. Rosaldo, 1998.

56. As Lowe forcefully articulates,

> While the nation proposes immigrant "naturalization" as a narrative of "political emancipation" that is meant to resolve in American liberal democracy as a terrain to which all citizens have equal access and in which all are equally represented, it is a narrative that denies the establishment of citizenship out of unequal relationships between dominant white citizens and subordinated racialized noncitizens and women (1996: 27).

57. Ong, 2003: 6.

58. Citizenship, according to Ong, is a sociocultural process of simultaneously negotiating and being subjected to technologies of government, meaning "the policies, programs, codes, and practices [unbounded by the concept of culture] that attempt to instill in citizen-subjects particular values [self reliance, freedom, individualism, calculation, or flexibility] in a variety of domains" (Ibid., 6).

59. See Foucault, 1990.

60. Kim, 2008.

61. With the exception of one adopted daughter of a Japanese citizen, the rest of the twenty-seven long-term *legal* residents who participated in my study attained their visa status via marriage or by giving birth to a Japanese national.

62. Near the club were five other Philippine clubs, meaning clubs that solely employ Filipinas, as well as one or two Japanese, Korean, Russian, and Chinese clubs. The club was located amid *pachinko* parlors (gambling establishments), soap lands (where customers receive a bath), fashion health clubs (where customers purchase sexual intercourse with women in uniforms), pink salons (where customers purchase a hand job or blow job), and numerous other hostess clubs.

63. I worked in a hostess club noncontinuously across three months. I first worked for nearly a month, and then I would return regularly to fill in whenever the club was short on women. Many of our customers were members of the *yakuza*, but we more often had to serve working-class men (for example, carpenters and painters) and low-level salaried men. In the club, the women, including myself, spoke a combination of Japanese, Tagalog, and English with customers. Many of the customers had not yet visited the Philippines but had gained a rudimentary knowledge of Filipino because they frequented Philippine hostess establishments, some as often as twice a week.

64. As the U.S. Department of State TIP Report claims, "Japanese organized crime groups (*yakuza*) that operate internationally are involved in trafficking" (2005: 113).

65. The first seven hostesses who agreed to an interview with me cancelled our appointments.

66. Douglass, 2003.

67. Religious clergy, including nuns and priests, have gained the trust of members of the hostess industry. They visit the clubs and the homes of hostesses as part of their "pastoral care." Club owners also turn to them for advice and assistance when working with hostesses facing difficulty adjusting to the culture of hostess clubs.

68. I was an inept hostess, as acting feminine did not come naturally to me. I was also considered one of the less attractive hostesses, being much bigger and older than my co-workers, who were usually around 100 pounds in weight and, with the exception of one, no older than twenty-seven. Not seeing me as competition, my co-workers often showed me the ropes, teaching me how to act around customers and helping translate my conversations with them. I had only rudimentary knowledge of Japanese. At the club, some customers spoke English and Filipino.

69. I conducted open-ended interviews that were tape recorded, which I later fully transcribed. The interviews ranged from one to three hours in length. They were conducted in Filipino. Interviews were conducted in places where hostesses felt comfortable in speaking openly about their experiences. They included their apartments as well as restaurants and cafés not frequented by other Filipinos. They felt comfortable giving interviews in public spaces because our language choice of Filipino gave them a semblance of privacy.

70. Hostesses told me that bags of chocolate and packs of ramen would be appreciated by contract workers.

71. I scheduled most interviews, but some I did right on the spot. I used the snowball method for only a handful of interviewees. Usually, I identified potential interviewees by direct contact.

72. Notably, religious clergy were the ones who helped me gain access to the more secluded group of temporary contract workers.

73. I conducted supplementary interviews with the following individuals in Japan: one promoter; four club owners; two social workers; three representatives at the Embassy of the Philippines; and three representatives at the Ministry of Justice. While based primarily in Japan, my study also considers the labor migration process from the angle of the sending country. I spent two weeks in Manila and interviewed representatives and owners of two management agencies and two promotion agencies. I also visited two nongovernmental organizations that work on behalf of migrant Filipina hostesses as well as representatives at the Overseas Workers Welfare Administration and the Philip-

pine Overseas Workers' Administration. During my brief stay in the Philippines, I managed to watch one audition and one practice session for prospective migrant entertainers.

74. In my study, only thirteen individuals (twelve female and one transgender) initially entered Japan as other than contract workers. Three entered with family visas, two entered in 1980 with what they referred to as "business" visas, and eight entered with tourist visas that they successfully attained by securing the sponsorship of a Japanese citizen, often the husband of their mother, sister, or other female kin. Those who entered as tourists had a higher level of education. For instance, six of them had completed bachelor's degrees prior to migration. This is not surprising because securing a tourist visa, even with the sponsorship of a Japanese citizen, usually requires proof of income and/or savings.

75. Many of the hostesses in my study came from very impoverished backgrounds. As an example, the family background of Lenlen was like that of many of the female hostesses whom I met in Japan. Recalling the life of poverty she left behind in the Philippines, she described:

> We were also very poor. You would not believe how poor we were. We could eat only once a day. That is the kind of life I had growing up . . . we picked through garbage. I remember being so hungry, and I saw food in the garbage, and I ate it. And we used to sell vegetables. We had plenty of vegetables outside. Early in the morning, we would pick those vegetables to sell so we could have money to bring to school. Sometimes we would use it to buy rice. I also experienced having to sell plastic in the wet market. Sometimes I would sell things at the bus terminal. I would sell whatever you can sell. I would sell *pinyato* [pop rice], *hopia* [bean cake], peanuts, and all those things that could be wrapped in plastic. There are a lot of food vendors. So you get it from there, and you sell it for them. You do not have capital. You just take products from them.

76. Philippine Overseas Employment Administration, 2006.

77. In contrast, migrant domestic work requires an initial recruitment fee that is unaffordable to most of those who become hostesses in Japan (Lan, 2006; Oishi, 2005).

78. One struggled to find employment in her chosen field of study of elementary education and had to settle for assembly-line work in a factory in the Philippines before securing a contract as a dancer in Japan. The other finished her course work in dentistry but, soon after getting pregnant, followed her two older sisters to Japan. The pressure to earn greater income as a single mother led her to migrate.

79. Among my female interviewees who entered Japan initially with entertainer visas, nineteen had not completed college, four had graduated from high school, and ten had failed to complete high school.

80. Existing data do not tell us the precise number of transgender entertainers. We can assume, however, that they make up a sizeable number of the male performance artists (that is, singers, dancers, choreographers, composers, and musicians) who are annually deployed to Japan from the Philippines. These male performing artists also include those who work at *host* bars, that is, the male version of hostess clubs. In 2003, 2,559 male performers were deployed to Japan from the Philippines. In 2004, we saw a slight increase of 2,998 male performers entering Japan from the Philippines. In 2005, their numbers declined to 1,376 male performers. See Philippine Overseas Employment Administration's Deployment Per Country Per Skill (New Hires), retrieved on December 14, 2010, from www.poea.gov.ph/.

81. When working in a female club, the transgender entertainer is usually made the leader, otherwise known as the *chi-mama*, whose work is to discipline and keep the younger female workers in line. For example, the *chi-mama* ensures that entertainers are well prepared for their variety shows in the club.

82. While most would not pursue a sex change, many turn to plastic surgery to look more feminine. The more feminine they are, the more employable they are in Japan. However, unlike the

travesti of Brazil, the *bakla* do not inject themselves at home with industrial silicon (Kulick, 1998). They invest in cosmetic surgery with a certified medical professional in the Philippines, Thailand, or Korea. They seek breast enlargements, eyelid surgery to make their eyes more slanted like the Japanese, and rhinoplasty surgery to create a bridge on their nose. They also spend a great deal of money on skin-lightening creams as well as whitened foundation to make their brown hue look much lighter in the dimly lit clubs. As they told me, looking Japanese makes them more marketable.

83. Patrick Califia, writing about transgenderism, claims that

> while third-gender identities may serve as roles that can be adopted by people we might label as transsexuals, hermaphrodites, and effeminate homosexuals, I believe that if hormones and surgery were made available to third-gender people in traditional societies, the great majority of them would opt for sex changes. (2003 [1997]: 179)

This was not the case for the majority of Filipino transgender hostesses I met in Japan, most of whom believed that while one can play with gender, one cannot do so with sex.

84. It is difficult to label this group of interviewees. Some described themselves as a "woman born a man." Most considered themselves "gay men." As men, they acknowledged the greater flexibility they had than their female counterparts to engage openly in sexual liaisons.

85. Yet, labeling them as transgender does have its pitfalls (Valentine, 2007). For instance, not all of those whom I placed in the category of "transgender" identified with this category. Three of them were transsexuals who identified as a "*babae*," meaning woman. Others described themselves not as a woman but a "woman trapped inside a man's body," categories that they insisted are different. Indeed, most did not see themselves as "women." Among the *bakla* I met in Japan, many refused to go through with a sex change, describing the process as a violation of the natural body parts that God had given to them. The core of their self-perception as *bakla* was their attraction to masculine subjects, particularly men but also butch lesbians. Notably, some insisted on still being seen as "men" but distinguished themselves from most other men as being "abnormal" or members of the "third sex." They also considered themselves to be different from their female counterparts in hostess clubs, and as "men," or for having a man's body, they believed they had more flexibility to engage in sexual intercourse with customers. For having a man's body, they were aware that they were not held to the same moral standards concerning sexual practices as were women, whose promiscuity would violate notions of female social purity in the Philippines and risk stigma (Sobritchea, 1990; Encanto, 2004). What they did share with women was a sexual predilection for masculine subjects. The lure of close intimate interactions with male subjects in the hostess club served as a huge motivating factor for seeking work in Japan.

86. All five were married to Japanese women.

87. This had not been the case for their counterparts in Brazil (Kulick, 1998).

88. Some complained that cross-dressing *bakla* are ghettoized in stereotypical labor market sectors such as cosmetology and fashion design.

89. Lunsing, 2005.

90. The U.S. Trafficking in Persons Report claims that migrant Filipina entertainers are held in debt bondage (U.S. Department of State, 2004). I found this to be inaccurate. Instead the subjugation of migrant Filipina entertainers is one of peonage, meaning a system in which debtors are bound in servitude until their debts are paid. It could also be more accurately referred to as indentured servitude, which is a condition that contractually bounds the worker only for a set period of time. In contrast, debt bondage applies to persons who are bonded in perpetuity. The United Nations defines "debt bondage" as "the status or condition arising from a pledge by a debtor of his personal services or of those of a person under his control as security for a debt, if the value of those services as reasonably assessed is not applied towards the liquidation of the debt or the length and nature of those services are not respectively limited and defined" (Section 1, Article 1[a]).

See the 1957 U.N. Supplementary Convention on the Abolition of Slavery, the Slave Trade, and Institutions and Practices Similar to Slavery. In the case of migrant Filipina entertainers, their relationship of bondage to middleman brokers is not necessarily *indefinite*. Their situation is thus better described as servitude, indentured servitude, or peonage.

91. My recommendation echoes those made by the authors in the anthology *Trafficking and Prostitution Reconsidered* (Kempadoo, 2005).

92. Soderlund, 2005.

93. See Chacon (2006) for a thorough discussion on how the U.S. global antitrafficking campaign puts greater focus on prosecution over protection and prevention.

NOTES TO CHAPTER ONE

Portions of this chapter have been adapted from Rhacel Parreñas's "The U.S. War on Trafficking and the Moral Disciplining of Migrant Women," *The Force of Domesticity: Filipina Migrants and Globalization*, New York University Press (2008), and "Trafficked? Filipino Hostesses in Tokyo's Nightlife Industry," 18 *Yale Journal of Law and Feminism* 145 (2006).

1. Trafficking Victims Protection Act (TVPA) defines "severe forms of trafficking" as:

> (A) sex trafficking in which a commercial sex act is induced by force, fraud, or coercion, or in which the person induced to perform such act has not attained 18 years of age; or (B) the recruitment, harboring, transportation provision, or obtaining of a person for labor or services, through the use of force, fraud, or coercion for the purpose of subjection to involuntary servitude, peonage, debt bondage, or slavery.

United States Congress. 2000. Victims of Violence Protection Act of 2000. Washington, DC: GPO. H.R. 3244; 106th Congress, Section 109(8).

2. In the Philippines, a strong sense of filial piety dictates intergenerational relations and leaves children with the moral duty to support parents financially. See Medina, 2000.

3. "Jeepney" refers to a popular mode of transportation, a multipurpose vehicle reflecting a hybrid of a jitney and jeep, made from U.S. military jeeps left over from World War II.

4. See Lan (2006) for a discussion of foreign domestic worker migration to Taiwan and Constable (1997) for the situation of foreign domestic workers in Hong Kong. Prospective migrant domestic workers also do not have to pay a placement fee if placed to work in noncoveted destinations such as Jordan, where migrant employment pays little and workers are known to be susceptible to abuse.

5. Article 24(2), Chapter 2 of the Labor Standards Act (Act No. 49 of April 4, 1947) states that "wages shall be paid at least once a month at a definite date."

6. The amount I provide in U.S. dollars is an estimate based on the approximate rate of exchange during the time I conducted fieldwork.

7. The first wave of entertainers from the Philippines entered Japan as cultural performers. See Faier (2009).

8. Tsuda (2006) provides a thorough description of Japan's immigration policies and cites the reinforcement of the long-standing ban on unskilled migrant laborers by the Immigration Control and Refugee Recognition Act of 1990.

9. See Tsuda 2006: 13–16.

10. Meeting with representatives of the Ministry of Justice, Tokyo, Japan (November 11, 2005).

11. See U.S. Department of State, 2004: 14, 96.

12. See TVPA, Sec. 103(9).

13. See U.S. Department of State, 2004.

14. According to Nana Oishi (2005), "value laden policies" constrain the migration options of women in various sending countries in Asia. Such policies impose minimum age requirements for migrant women or restrict the types of jobs they can pursue abroad. For instance, Bangladeshi

women are barred from entering domestic work in foreign countries, India sets forth a minimum age requirement for its nurses, and the Philippine government has likewise repeatedly changed its minimum age requirement for entertainers in Japan. In contrast, no country delimits the types of jobs that men can seek outside of its territories.

15. *Oxford English Dictionary,* Web Edition. Draft revision June 2005. Retrieved on July 29, 2006, from www.oed.com/.

16. See A Guide to Japanese Visas, Appendix 1: Ministerial Ordinance to Provide for Criteria pursuant to Article 7, Paragraph 1(2) of the Immigration Control and Refugee Recognition Act (Ministry of Justice Ordinance No. 16 of May 24, 1990). Retrieved on July 31, 2006, from www.mofa.go.jp/j_info/visit/visa/appendix1.html.

17. Meeting on November 11, 2005, with representatives of the Ministry of Justice, Tokyo, Japan.

18. Ibid.

19. Collective Position Paper by 11 Filipino NGOs on Japan's New Immigration Policy. "Anti-trafficking and Human Rights, Anti-trafficking Initiatives in Asia." Retrieved on January 26, 2005, from www.vitalvoices.org.

20. See Maria Angela Villalba, n.d. *Philippines: Good Practices for the Protection of Filipino Women Migrant Workers in Vulnerable Jobs.* GENPROM Working Paper No. 8. Geneva, Switzerland: International Labour Office, Gender Promotion Programme, 24. For migrant entertainers, "academics" interestingly refer not to their aptitude but instead moral values. A report released by the International Labour Office in Geneva, Switzerland, found that

> academic training is designed primarily to help dancers in their early twenties, who perform on stage in a club or hotel from evening till dawn, to manage their unique and hazardous work environment. Contents of the academic training include positive and appropriate values, behavior and attitudes development, communication and language skills, good grooming and social graces, spirituality and human relations. In other words, women are taught to "entertain" the male audience without sexual services. (24–25)

21. Under the system of the ARB, the certificate of training, including the academic training, is not a precondition to assessment and certification, but only if "they are certified by their respective artists' guilds or associations duly recognized by TESDA" (Republic of the Philippines Department of Labor and Employment, 2001).

22. Philippine Overseas Employment Administration. 2004. *Memorandum Circular No. 12. Subject: Guidelines on the Certification of Overseas Performing Artists.* Manila: Philippine Overseas Employment Administration.

23. Meeting with Ministry of Immigration Officials, Tokyo, Japan (November 11, 2005).

24. Discussion with Professor Ruri Ito, Tokyo, Japan (November 11, 2005).

25. These standard contracts are available at the Philippine Embassy in Tokyo.

26. See Villalba, n.d.

27. The estimated calculation I provide is based on the exchange rate during the time of my field research.

28. Memorandum Circular No. 10. Series of 1997. "Guidelines on the Accreditation of Japanese Principals Hiring Filipino Performing Artists (OPAs)" (May 5, 1997).

29. Xiang, 2007.

30. Not all clubs are eligible to hire foreign entertainers. For instance, eligibility is restricted to clubs meeting certain criteria, including a stage, five full-time employees, and an operator with three years of experience working with foreigner entertainers. See www.mofa.go.jp/j_info/visit/visa/appendix1.html.

31. Philippine Overseas Employment Administration, 1997.

32. In the late 1980s, first-time *talents* took home around US$450 per month. In the mid-2000s, the average salary of a first time contract worker was US$500. Food allowances of *talents* have also remained stagnant in the last twenty years. As they did in the late 1980s, *talents* received the same supplementary food allowance of 500 yen a day in 2005, which was not very much. To put this amount in perspective, 500 yen in Tokyo would not cover even one combination meal in a low-end fast food restaurant such as Mo Burgers, let alone three meals.

33. Steinfeld, 1991: 3. As indentured workers, migrant entertainers do not have labor market flexibility to choose their workplace.

34. The withholding of wages by promoters (who notably had been paid in advance by club owners) not only deters entertainers from quitting prior to the end of their six-month contract but also puts them at risk of never getting paid or being unable to contest any questionable wage deductions imposed on them.

35. As John Stuart Mill argues, "He abdicates his liberty; he foregoes any future use of it beyond that single act. He therefore defeats, in his own case, the very purpose which is the justification of allowing him to dispose of himself . . . The principle of freedom cannot require that he should be free not to be free. It is not freedom, to be allowed to alienate his freedom" (In Pateman, 1988: 74–75). Following the argument of Mill, the abdication of freedom when agreeing to indentured servitude translates to enslavement.

36. Pettit, 2011.

37. While many of us would be uncomfortable with the illiberal choice of the hostess to become an indentured worker, we cannot deny that she had the attributes of autonomy when making that decision—"normal cognitive function, basic perceptual and inferential abilities, and those reasoning capacities considered basic to elementary thinking and reflection" (Christman, 2001: 201). As an autonomous person, a migrant Filipina entertainer is one who chooses in the context of their constrained options to become an indentured servant to middleman brokers.

38. Christman, 2001.

39. Christman, 1991: 344.

40. Helping us make sense of the argument that migrant Filipina entertainers are not without their freedom when choosing indentured servitude, political theorist John Christman provides the example of a "happy slave" who chooses enslavement after the removal of external obstacles. As he describes,

> Imagine that the "happy slave" is a Tibetan monk who has spent the last several years in the same room meditating and sitting quietly (being fed by acolytes) and from which he will never desire to move. If chains are then put on the door to the room, a room he does not want to leave, then his freedom of action is simply unaffected by these chains.

(See Christman, 1991: 354.) The situation of most migrant Filipina entertainers mirrors those of the Tibetan monk. We cannot deny that problems potentially arise when they do wish to leave the room but face the constraints of the chains put on the door. The point however is that most of them—like the Tibetan monk—wish not to leave the room. Many even wish to reenter the room after they leave it. Most Filipina hostesses wish to maximize their labor market opportunities and desire reentry to Japan on the termination of their six-month contracts.

41. Interview with representatives of two promotion agencies, in Manila, Philippines (August 9, 2005).

42. Meeting with representatives of the Ministry of Justice, Tokyo, Japan (November 11, 2005).

43. Following the logic of the *balato*, talent managers would sometimes still charge former clients a marriage fee, even after the end of their "contract." One former entertainer who had to pay her former manager such a fee is Marietta, who explained, "I was done with [my contract] for a year. But I was supposed to pay them 50,000 pesos [US$1,000] if I got married, even if my contract was over . . . The way they [promotion agencies and managers] think about it is that you would never

have met that person if they did not send you to Japan. They think like that because they are the ones who did your booking. . . . They think of it as *utang na loob* [debt of gratitude]. So, if you get married, they think it is their right to know. That is their mentality."

44. Sometimes knowledge of the law gives entertainers the strength to contest the penalties brokers have saddled them with. Those likely to contest their penalty are hostesses who had been mistreated at their club of employment, those who feel brokers had made enough of a profit from their labor, and lastly those who feel they have received inadequate compensation for their past labor.

45. As a last resort, some may even turn to spirit possession as a strategy to quit their job without penalty. Similar to the factory workers observed by Aihwa Ong in Malaysia during the 1980s, those possessed become overcome by evil spirits inside the club in front of customers or in their residence with other hostesses to the point that they disrupt business or the well-being of their co-workers (Ong, 1987). Spirit possession is a regular enough occurrence among migrant entertainers that Filipino nuns and priests have sometimes performed more than a few exorcisms per year. If their efforts to exorcize evil spirits are unsuccessful, the club then sends the entertainer home to the Philippines without penalty. To be sent home by a club is the best option for entertainers wishing to return to the Philippines because they are not saddled with a penalty. Unfortunately middleman brokers saddle those who merely quit with penalties.

46. During the time of my research, the exchange rate was $1 to 50 pesos.

47. I interviewed six entertainers who migrated to Japan below the minimum age of eighteen years old, with the youngest being fifteen years old. All had freely decided to pursue work in Japan with the consent of their parents, none of whom had originated the idea of sending their daughter to Japan. All said they came to Japan "to escape poverty." All had been acquainted with previous migrants—neighbors or distant relatives—and had some inkling of the type of work they would do in Japan.

48. According to my interviewees, deportees are banned from returning to Japan for five years.

49. For example, in one family, I interviewed one sister who had used the identity of another sister who later on decided to go to Japan and then had to use the identity of yet another sister. In this family, all three sisters worked in Japan using someone else's identity.

50. In some unusual cases, entertainers have the acumen to know not to pay the fee for the use of a fake passport. This had been true for Irene, an experienced contract worker, who complained: "I had a fight with my promotion agency because I did not pay for the fake name. They were forcing me to pay for a penalty of 100,000 pesos. I told them that if I had that much money, I would invest it in a business. Why would I give that much money? . . . They were trying to scare me. They try to scare women, especially if they are only twenty years old or eighteen years old. And young people do not understand the law. They do not understand the law. The promotion agencies have plenty of scams."

51. The law in Japan makes clubs ineligible from hiring foreign entertainers if they employ workers who have been convicted of violent crimes or those found guilty of soliciting or procuring prostitution. See A Guide to Japanese Visas, Appendix 1 Ministerial Ordinance to Provide for Criteria pursuant to Article 7, Paragraph 1(2) of the Immigration Control and Refugee Recognition Act (Ministry of Justice Ordinance No. 16 of May 24, 1990); retrieved on July 31, 2006, from www.mofa.go.jp/j_info/visit/visa/appendix1.html.

52. I use the word *supposedly* because the sources of such estimates are unclear. See page 10 of U.S. Department of State (2007) for estimated number of trafficked persons worldwide.

53. Pettit, 2004.

54. Chacon, 2006: 3029–3030.

55. See Commission on Security and Cooperation in Europe News Release, "Commission Charman: 'It's Time to Declare War on Sex Traffickers': Calls for Passage of H.R. 1356, a Bill 'To End International Sexual Trafficking'" (June 28, 1999); retrieved on July 6, 2010, from www.house/gov/csce/.

56. See Gardner, 2005; Luibheid, 2002, Rand, 2005.

57. See Gardner, 2005; Luibheid, 2002.

58. Gardner, 2005; Odum, 1995.

59. U.S. Department of State, 2005: 5.

60. U.S. Department of State, 2004.

61. Ibid.: 14.

62. U.S. Department of State, 2006: 151.

63. Ibid.

64. U.S. Department of State, 2005: 14.

65. Government of Japan, 2005: 4.

66. U.S. Department of State, 2005: 132.

67. Ronalyn Olea, "Undocumented workers most vulnerable among migrants," bulatlat.com/GMANews.TV, November 11, 2008. Retrieved on January 3, 2010, from www.gmanews.tv/story/131847/undocumented-workers-most-vulnerable-among-migrants.

68. Sealing Cheng (2010) makes a similar observation, noting that one of her informants purchased fake marriage papers for $5,000 to return to Japan.

69. Interview in Tokyo with Lilibeth Pono of the Philippine Embassy (May 26, 2005).

70. Ventura, 1992.

71. Tripp, 2005: 51.

NOTES TO CHAPTER TWO

1. From my field notes, July 16, 2005.

2. In contrast, Filipino men find employment in construction as day laborers. See Ventura, 1992.

3. Because of the similarity in the labor required across various types of *o-mise* in the community, my discussion in this chapter does not distinguish among pubs, bars, and clubs; instead I generally refer to their workplace as a hostess club.

4. See Development Action for Women Network (DAWN) 2003; 2004. Organizations such as DAWN should be commended for their work in addressing the social problems of Filipina migrants to Japan, especially their advocacy for the rights of Filipino children of Japanese men. Many of these children are in the Philippines without financial support from their fathers and before June 4, 2008, had been without the benefits of Japanese citizenship. For a discussion on the welfare of the children of Japanese-Filipino children, see Nobue Suzuki's dissertation (2003). However, DAWN's radical feminist stance and abolitionist view do cloud their objectivity when it comes to the welfare of hostesses. We see this in the inconsistency of the claims in their report *Pains and Gains*, which is based on a survey of 120 hostesses. For example, they report the finding that "women were usually informed by [Overseas Performance Artist] timers about the work that they would be doing there" (21) but a few pages later contradict this finding with the claim that there is a "lack of awareness about the work of OPAs in Japan" (35) among prospective migrants.

5. Fujimoto, 2007: 3.

6. While some Filipinas wish to solely do hostess work, most relish the opportunity to perform on stage. They value their skills as dancers or singers. However, most wish to perform only on "special occasions" because doing so on a daily basis would increase their workload, requiring them to regularly practice new dance routines and songs.

7. Allison, 1994; Leheny, 2006.

8. Chung, 2004.

9. Oishi, 2005.

10. *Arubaito* is derived from the German word *arbeit*, meaning work.

11. Stringent government requirements limit the ability of club owners to hire *talents*, forcing some to settle for *arubaito* workers. I address these requirements extensively in Chapter One.

12. Medina, 2000.

13. Douglass, 2003.

14. Golden, 2001.

15. Allison, 1994: 9.

16. Downer, 2001.

17. Golden, 2001.

18. Allison, 1994: 131.

19. Sobritchea, 1990.

20. In the Class B clubs that I visited, food usually cost double the price of that in a regular restaurant, as a fruit plate or a plate of fried chicken would cost me at least 3,000 yen (US$30) each, while each song programmed in the karaoke machine would cost either 100 or 200 yen (US$1 to US$2).

21. Beer is marked as unfeminine and likely to cause weight gain. In contrast, there seemed to have had no negative association with beer drinking in the hostess establishment where Allison (1994) conducted her fieldwork.

22. In these cases, clubs would not pay the minimum monthly salary of 200,000 yen to middleman brokers.

23. Higher-end Class B clubs would feature a few Class A workers, while lower-ranked clubs would have lower-paid Class C workers. Class B venues cater not to higher-end professionals but instead to middle- and working-class men, with the difference between higher- and lower-ranked Class B venues being the degree of professionalism in the delivery of the variety show performance and the attractiveness of hostesses.

24. *Manila* is a pseudonym.

25. The Akebono's real name is Chad Rowan. Because Akebono hails from Guam, the customer might also have been making a remark about my ethnicity.

26. Leheny, 2006.

27. Ibid.: 68.

28. The term *salary man* refers to an office worker.

29. I later learned these photos were remnants of the previous business, a restaurant, that had inhabited the space.

30. Suzuki, 2005: 137.

31. Allison, 1994.

32. Hartmann, 1981.

33. Married hostesses frequently mentioned that they had to lie about their marital status. The undocumented worker Marie explained,

> I do not tell (customers) that I am married. That would scare them away. There are some customers who could tell you have a husband and children. Some would accept that. There are customers who would not accept that. You would lose your customer if you told them that. If you are a hostess, you have to be single . . . I tell them that I am single, but I tell them that I have children.

34. In the Philippines, *lapad* means wide. Members of the community refer to a 10,000 yen bill as a *lapad* in reference to its wider size than bills of a smaller amount in the Japanese currency.

35. I could only laugh in response and take his comment as a joke, but I was frustrated that I could not quite generate a quick comeback either in Japanese or English.

36. Braverman, 1974.

37. Pun, 2005; McKay, 2006.

38. Leidner, 1993.

39. Snack bars, as they usually employ only five women, are too small to enforce the table rotation system.

40. Bars are less apt to feature *show time.*

41. Hostesses acquire phones either by using their commission from the club or with the financial assistance of customers.

42. Foucault, 1990.

43. Transgender hostesses told me that this is the case because management does not see them as being in need of protection as they do women. When I asked them about attitudes toward gays and lesbians, they claim that they are "safe" and not at risk of harassment when walking the streets of Tokyo. In contrast, they say that they are constantly harassed and taunted when in public spaces in the Philippines.

44. Hondagneu-Sotelo, 2001.

45. Menjivar, 2006.

46. A kilo is approximately 2.2 pounds.

47. Likewise, sex workers in the Dominican Republic preferred to establish continuous relationships with customers. See Cabezas 1999: 99 and chapter 5 in Padilla, 2007.

48. As I mentioned earlier, a *shimei* will remove the hostess and customer from the table rotation system and guarantee the customer approximately one hour with the hostess.

49. While hostesses compete for the loyalty of a customer, they also help one another develop a customer base. Newcomers usually get more help than others. For instance, hostesses try to be gracious to newcomers and give them the first chance to secure a new customer before they seek his business. Those who violate this unwritten rule are seen negatively.

50. In the Philippines, a *bakla* generally refers to a male homosexual, but the term comes with broad connotations and conflates homosexuality, transvestism, and effeminacy. See Benedicto (2008).

51. Kelly, 2008: 69.

52. Turner, 1967: 96.

53. Ibid.

54. Mackie, 2008.

55. Ibid.: 414.

56. Cannell, 1995; Johnson, 1997.

57. Palumbo-Liu, 1999.

NOTES TO CHAPTER THREE

1. Her co-workers, who earned more than the US$700 monthly salary that she received as a tenth-timer in Japan, had to generate upward of 1,000,000 yen (US$10,000) in sales per month.

2. Fortunately for Janet, the knot on her back eventually disappeared but only after she had met a customer willing to help her out with her sales quota. This customer claims to have fallen in "love at first sight" with Janet; for this reason he said he did not mind spending money on her to help her meet her sales quota. Once he even brought his parents and daughter along to the club to meet Janet and watch her perform during *show time.* Her transgender identity made no difference to him. To survive her six months in Japan without the risk of being sent home prior to the end of her contract or with minimal reproach from management, Janet solely relied on this one customer to meet her sales quota. Yet, relying on only one customer is unrealistic for most, whether they are female or transgender, as most customers of Philippine clubs tend to be poor and of the working class and cannot afford to singlehandedly support a hostess. Fortunately for Janet, her customer had enough expendable income to lavish on her. He earned enough from managing his father's auto dealership.

3. See Allison (1994) for a thorough description of male rituals in hostess clubs.

4. For a discussion of gender's relational construction, see Connell, 1995.

5. For a definition of aesthetic labor, see Warhurst et al. (2000) and Warhurst and Nickson (2009). Wacquant (1995) describes bodily labor. See Hochschild (1983) for an extensive discussion of emotional labor.

6. Hardt defines "immaterial labor" as "labor that produces an immaterial good, such as service, knowledge, or communication" (1999: 94).

7. Pierre Bourdieu defines *capital* broadly to refer to "accumulated labor (in its materialized form or its 'incorporated,' embodied form) which, when appropriated on a private, i.e., exclusive, basis by agents or groups of agents, enables them to appropriate social energy in the form of reified or living labor" (1986: 241).

8. My discussion of capital uses the theories of Bourdieu but diverges from his assertion that capital comes naturally or as a logical outcome of one's habitus, meaning the set of dispositions that generate perception and classification (Bourdieu, 1990). Capital, according to Bourdieu (1986, 1990), emerges from an unconscious inculcation. As he states, "Cultural capital can be acquired, to a varying extent, depending on the period, the society, and the social class, in the absence of any deliberate inculcation, and therefore quite unconsciously" (Bourdieu, 1986). Instead, I assert that hostesses consciously acquire capital, whether it is bodily, emotional, or cultural, as part of their workplace strategies of reaping material gain. One could imagine that in other settings capital comes not from habitus but from conscious acquisition. This would be the case, for instance, for a working-class child who is transported to a private college as a scholarship student or for a new immigrant learning to speak the native language.

9. Hardt, 1999: 93–98; Hardt and Negri, 2001.

10. Hardt, 1999: 89.

11. We need to acknowledge that economic relations between customers and hostesses are not completely subsumed by the relations between customers and club owners or middleman brokers. If they were, then we could argue that the cultivation of capital only aggravates the exploitative extraction of surplus value by the club owner from the labor of hostesses.

12. The material gains of the hostess suggests that the immaterial labor of producing masculinity does potentially subvert the capitalist project, as speculated by Hardt, providing hostesses with "autonomous circuits of valorization" from their employers (Hardt, 1999: 100).

13. Hostesses returning from a *dohan* need not participate in the table rotation system. The *dohan* is interrupted only if another customer requests her company.

14. DAWN, 2004.

15. U.S. Department of State, 2004.

16. Because of the *appointment dohan*, hostesses can entertain more than one *dohan* in a night. Some interviewees have had a "double *dohan*" evening, meaning a night in which they have the extension of two *dohan* invitations. However, they can go out on only one "regular *dohan*" per evening.

17. Hostesses can go on a date with customers after a club closes. This outing would be independent of the club and would not require a *dohan*.

18. Sales quotas instill competition among hostesses, encouraging them to fight over customers. Conflicts arise when customers curtail their patronage of a particular hostess and begin to visit another hostess regularly at the club. Explained my co-worker Arissa,

> "The customers will come, and then they will request you. Then another group comes [from the Philippines], and then the other woman will be requested. Then a fight will break out. 'Why was she requested? That one used to be my customer.' That kind of fight will always happen. I witnessed that kind of fight. The women were pulling each other's hair. They were cussing each other out, 'I will kill you.'

Because of the sense of ownership that hostesses develop for customers, customers usually learn of the protocol that they are expected to extend a *shimei* or *dohan* to only one hostess per club.

The search for customers results in a high level of distrust among hostesses, sometimes turning into actual fistfights and hair pulling, as described by Arissa, but more often resulting in the badmouthing of coworkers. Elsa, a long-time visa overstayer, recalled the intense competition she experienced as a contract worker:

> There is so much jealousy going around in the club. Especially if you have a good customer, they will badmouth you. They will tell the customer that you have a boyfriend or a child in the Philippines, or even a husband. You feel sorry for those Filipinas who get ruined by their co-workers. Especially if they know that a woman has a very rich customer, they will talk badly about you. They will tell him that you already have a Japanese boyfriend or a husband in the Philippines.

When a customer drops a hostess, she usually displaces her anger onto the new main of the customer, because the unequal power relationship between hostesses and customers prevents her from expressing her disgruntlement to the customer. As such, hostesses frequently hold grudges against their co-workers whom they suspect of stealing their customer. While intense competition exists among hostesses in the club, they do try to build feelings of camaraderie with one another and ease the jealousy, backbiting, and competition that equally define their relationships at the workplace. They would frequently assist one another with reaching their sales quota, by asking their customer to extend a *shimei* to their friend. Usually those who reach their quota with the help of others reward them, or share their material gains with them, which in Filipino is a practice referred to as giving *balato,* in other words sharing of one's winnings.

19. This amount is calculated according to the food and drink consumption of the customer, sometimes with the inclusion of the cost of the *dohan* and *shimei* minus the commission of the hostess.

20. Hostesses claim they can get by on a food budget of 500 yen a day. One explained to me that one could purchase bread and hot dog for less than 500 yen. Another told me she could eat rice, which is provided by the club, with a chicken yakitori available at 7-11 for 80 yen a stick. Their 500 yen a day food allowance made me feel guilty for consuming at least one latte per day as a latte cost 400 yen per cup. The 500 yen food allowance is also not enough to cover one meal at McDonald's. To make do, hostesses usually combine their allowances and contribute to a grocery budget for the household. My field notes describe one such pool maintained by hostesses:

> In this household, there are nine women who contribute 1,500 yen per ten days to the groceries. They use this money to go food shopping. A few among them would prepare food, which would be available when they got back from work and when they were about to leave for work. They said it is so much cheaper than eating at McDonald's, which their 500 yen daily allowance cannot cover. Interestingly, there were four dishes when I came in their house. One was cooked by Angie, another by Jeanne, one came from a Filipino restaurant, and the other was made by someone else. During the interview, Jeanne had cooked rice. She said they always have rice ready for the women, so they always feel as if food is available to them. For example, Jeanne told me, if there is rice and no main dish (*ulam*), one could just fry an egg and eat it with rice. She said sometimes it is difficult to accommodate the needs of all because some are allergic to seafood, for instance. But for the most part they do not always eat there. They also eat out with their customers during a *dohan*. This then leaves more food for others. Some days they run out of food, and sometimes they barely touch the food cooked for them. (July 10, 2005)

21. At the time we met, Lenlen no longer worked as a hostess but stayed at home as a wife in Japan.

22. Building on the theorizations of capital by Pierre Bourdieu, we should remember that capital is a "social relation," specifically a "social relation, i.e., an energy which only exists and only produces its effects in the field in which it is produced and reproduced, each of the properties attached to class is given its value and efficacy by the specific laws of each field" (Bourdieu, 1984: 113). This means

that particular forms of capital with specific meanings uniquely arise in every social field, including in the social field of a hostess club.

23. See Wacquant (1995) for a more extensive discussion of bodily labor, and Warhurst et al. (2000) and Warhurst and Nickson (2009) for aesthetic labor.

24. During our interviews, older hostesses did not spend as much time looking at the mirror as did their younger counterparts, but stored in their cellular phones would be older photographs that many of them would proudly show me after our interview. They wanted to show me how good they had looked when they had passed their first rigorous audition as a *talent* many years ago.

25. Schaeffer-Grabiel, 2006.

26. Kang, 2003: 826.

27. Glenn, 2008.

28. According to her, it would likely cost her 40,000 pesos for a nose job (US$800) and 300,000 pesos for her silicone implants (US$6,000).

29. To help hostesses achieve a sensual aesthetic, the same magazine also features sexy underwear, usually thongs and g-strings, which I found out from ordering a few are made of the hardest and most abrasive material one could imagine.

30. *Emotional labor* refers to the emotional regulation of a worker who as part of her or his job displays particular emotions. See Hochschild, 1983.

31. Past studies on emotional labor have not focused on the productive aspects of this labor. Instead, studies have repeatedly described such work as oppressive to women. See Pierce, 1995; Patel, 2010. Emotional labor is often depicted negatively in the literature; it is said to maintain gender inequality through the performance of feminine subservience and to lead to the extraction of unrecognized labor from the mostly female low-wage workers who perform it. In other words, emotional labor is said to be invisible work that requires the performance of feminine subjugation or the reinscription of gender stereotypes. In offshore call centers, for instance, men are more frequently assigned to become bill collectors, while women are assigned to work for the airline industry (see Patel, 2010: 32). In law firms, we find "Rambo litigators" and "mothering paralegals" (see Pierce, 1995). Yet, in the case of hostess work, the performance of emotional labor could lead to positive gains for the worker.

32. Distinguishing the process of building emotional capital from emotional labor, the former relies not only on the manipulation of emotions (emotional labor) but also storytelling. Second, unlike past discussions on emotional labor, the emotional manipulations of hostesses entail the use of acting as a consciously acquired skill.

33. Hochschild, 1983: 7. Emotional labor has a use value, which benefits the club owner. In Hochschild's formulation, the surplus value of emotional labor does not necessarily benefit the hostess but instead the capitalist (for example, the club owner).

34. I describe the work of hostesses as the accumulation of capital and not "affective labor" because I see the former as a labor process. In contrast, "affective labor" is not described by Hardt (1999) and later Hardt and Negri (2001) as a labor process. Instead, it is presented as a commodity, one of the goods produced in postindustrial economies. As such, the performance of this type of labor, that is, the process of the production of emotions, is not one that they explicate.

35. Hardt, 1999: 89. See Bourdieu (1984) for his discussion of capital as a "social relation."

36. Seeing "affect" as a "good" and not so much as a form of capital, Hardt and Negri do not elucidate on the values of the "affects" produced by the worker.

37. Zelizer, 2005.

38. Padilla, 2007: 157.

39. Shimizu, 2007.

40. Bernard, 1981.

41. See Tsuda (2006) for a discussion on labor migration policies in Japan and the restriction against the migration of unskilled workers.

NOTES TO CHAPTER FOUR

1. Romantic affairs are admittedly a two-way exchange, but as I had not interviewed customers for this study and had interacted with them only while I worked as a hostess, the romantic affairs that I illustrate in this chapter draw primarily from the perspectives of hostesses. Still, the experiences of customers are not absent in my discussion, as the actions of hostesses occur not in a vacuum but in response to their relations with customers, the reactions of customers to their suggestions of intimacy, and the ways customers, as hostesses described to me, attempt to manipulate hostesses with their own professions of love and the lure of permanent residency in Japan via a marriage visa. In short, salient in my interviews with hostesses are descriptions of the actions of their customers.

2. Takeyama, 2005.

3. By morals, I refer to the rules or habits of conduct, particularly sexual conduct, that comply with standards of right and wrong. Morals guide as they attach social and ethical meanings to the actions and behavior of individuals.

4. Zheng (2009) makes a similar observation of hostesses in China.

5. Suzuki, 2003.

6. *Casa* is a euphemism for brothel in Filipino. It means "house" in Spanish.

7. Bernstein, 2007b.

8. Ibid.

9. Kelly, 2008.

10. Bernstein, 2007b.

11. This is not the case for the sex workers studied by Bernstein. See Bernstein, 2007b.

12. This coincides with the fact that interactions between hostesses and customers occur within a commercial sphere of "free-floating eroticism" (Bauman, 1998).

13. Hochschild, 1983.

14. Unlike the Filipina women that Lieba Faier (2007) observed in the rural area of Nagano, the hostesses in my study managed to remain emotionally distant from their labor. However, this did not close off the possibility for love to develop between them and customers because of the permeability between "surface acting" and "deep acting."

15. My fieldnotes provide an example of the one-month courtship mentioned by Charmaine. As we see from the experience of another interviewee Kay, the customer during this one-month period would usually lavish the hostess with presents in hopes that she would be seduced to engage in sex. As I describe in my fieldnotes,

> As I was sitting there waiting for Reggie to finish taking a shower, I looked around the room and suddenly noticed eight blue boxes from Tiffany's. I asked Kay about the boxes. She told me that they are from a customer, a fifty-three-year-old bald man who wants to have sex with her. He told her that he would visit the *o-mise* every day; after thirty days, if she still has not had sex with him, then he will stop going to the club. Indeed, he had stopped going. However, during those thirty days that he did visit, he had given her a lot of jewelry. Interestingly, Kay did not know about the store Tiffany's, so I had to explain to her that the jewelry sold at that store is very expensive. I promised to bring her back a catalog. (July 18, 2005)

16. See Hershatter (1999) for a similar discussion of relational dynamics between courtesans and customers in early twentieth-century Shanghai.

17. Sinclair, 2006: 32.

18. Hochschild, 1983: 90.

19. Korczynski, 2002.

20. Payne, 2009.

21. According to Hochschild, we resolve the emotive dissonance in surface acting by "changing what we feel or by changing what we feign. When display is required by the job, it is usually feeling that has to change; and when conditions estrange us from our face, they sometimes estrange us from feeling as well" (Hochschild, 1983: 90).

22. Chapkis, 1997.

23. Sallie Yea (2005) likewise observes the forging of emotional ties and long-term relationships by Filipina entertainers in Korea as a strategy of fortifying their relations with customers.

24. Zelizer, 2005.

25. Viviana Zelizer defines "relational work" as "the establishment of differentiated social ties, their maintenance, their reshaping, their distinction from other relations, and sometimes their termination" (Zelizer, 2005: 35).

26. The possibility of multiple relational ties between hostesses and customers emerges from the porous boundaries that set apart our relations in society. As Zelizer perceptively notes, "In any particular social setting . . . multiple ties of different kinds coexist and often extend across the setting's boundary into other settings" (2005: 33). Actions do not necessarily change across relational ties, but their meanings do. For instance, displays of affection by hostesses would not necessarily differ from one customer to the next, but the meanings of these displays would. Yet, despite the sameness in their behavior with customers across a vast relational terrain, hostesses are not quick to transform relations with customers. Courtships without doubt could lead to love and romance (Faier, 2007). However, hostesses resist this transition and remain emotionally guarded.

27. Likewise, Patty Kelly (2008) observed that sex workers morally classify sex acts. Only "normal" sex acts, such as straightforward vaginal intercourse, are morally acceptable for them to perform. Morally questionable acts include fellatio, cunnilingus, and anal sex. According to Kelly, sex workers maintain their dignity by limiting their services to "normal" acts.

28. See http://rss.xinhuanet.com/newsc/english/2007-09/09/content_6690258.htm for the online article "150,000 Abandoned Filipino-Japanese Kids in the Philippines," *China View* (September 9, 2007); retrieved on June 18, 2011.

29. The threat of physical assault outside the club also deters hostesses from acquiring a "boyfriend." Afraid of the strange sexual proclivities that they have observed among their customers—some of whom have requested to purchase not only their panties but also their panty hose—hostesses fear the potential danger of entering hotel rooms with customers because even long-time visitors to the club are in some ways still strangers. As many noted, for all they know their customer could have a sexual proclivity for violence. Indeed, the threat of violence also looms over those who end up with possessive "boyfriends." It is not unknown for some "boyfriends" to have physically threatened hostesses.

30. As Patty Kelly likewise observed, sex workers in Mexico do not engage in sexual relations without the guarantee of material gain. However, they would not reduce all of their compensated sexual acts to acts of prostitution. They make a distinction between clients who pay directly and romantic partners who pay indirectly (Kelly, 2008: 184). They further distinguish their sexual relationships between boyfriends and customers by reserving particular sexual intimacies such as the fondling of breasts and kissing to their boyfriends.

31. Zelizer, 2005.

32. Similarly, Elizabeth Bernstein (2007b) notes the shifting dynamic in prostitution; customers want the exchange of sex to go beyond the physical act but to also include a degree of emotional and personal connection, one that is denied to customers by the fast pace of life and extension of work hours in late capitalism. Customers want sex workers to act like they really care for them. Also see Albert, 2002; Cabezas, 2002; Wonders and Michalowski, 2001.

NOTES TO CHAPTER FIVE

Portions of this chapter have been adapted from Rhacel Parreñas's "The Morals of Money and Sex," in Nina Bandelj, ed., *Economic Sociology of Work, Research in the Sociology of Work*, Volume 17, 207-232, 2009, and "Cultures of Flirtation: Sex and the Moral Boundaries of Filipina Migrant Hostesses in Tokyo," in Eileen Boris and Rhacel Salazar Parreñas, eds., *Intimate Labors: Cultures, Technologies, and the Politics of Care*, Stanford University Press, 2010.

1. Retrieved on December 9, 2009, from www.merriam-webster.com/dictionary/prostitution.

2. Kelly (2008) observed the same distinction among sex workers in Mexico.

3. For a thorough description of the labor of prostitution, see Agustin, 2007; Bernstein, 2007b; Chapkis, 1997; White, 1990. These works establish a blurry line between sex-for-money and flirtation-for-money, thus questioning the distinction that hostesses make of their labor from prostitution. White (1990), for instance, documents that prostitutes not only provided sex in early twentieth-century Nairobi; they also provided "the comforts of home" to transient male laborers whom they also fed, bathed, and provided with conversation. White's observations suggest striking similarities between prostitution and hostess work.

4. See Tony McNichol, "The Show's Over," *Japan Times* (April 26, 2005); Lisa Katayama, "Sex Trafficking: Zero Tolerance," *Mother Jones* (May 5, 2005); Jeremaiah Opiniano, "Teacher Culls Bar-Girl Work to Flay US Anti-Trafficking," *Philippine Today* (November 20, 2006). For the Opiniano article, see www.philippinestoday.net/index.php?module=article&view=101; retrieved on January 20, 2007.

5. The term *comfort women* generally refers to the Filipina and Korean women who were held as sex slaves by Japanese soldiers during World War II. Seemingly unaware of the politically charged use of this term, Amanda used it—in English—to describe her work as a hostess.

6. Leidner, 1993.

7. Connell, 1995.

8. To my surprise, many of our regular customers spoke a little bit of Tagalog. This is because many had frequented Philippine pubs for more than a decade, and some had married Filipino women.

9. Zelizer, 2005.

10. Ibid.: 28.

11. My definition of *boundary work* differs from that of sociologist Thomas Gieyrn (1983), who coined the term to describe the process by which boundaries are constructed to distinguish fields of knowledge. In this process, selected characteristics, such as practices, organizations, and knowledges, are attributed to particular institutions for the purpose of constructing a social boundary. Since then, other sociologists have applied the concept of boundary work to apply to social groups, including Michelle Lamont (1992) and Pei-Chia Lan (2006). I look at "boundary work" merely as the practice of instituting corporal boundaries in hostesss clubs.

12. Hostesses feel genuine emotional attachments to "real boyfriends," which could be romantic love but also sexual lust.

13. Zelizer, 2000: 823.

14. Domestic workers are a minority in the Filipino community. They rarely work for Japanese households but instead cater to the expatriate community.

15. Such acts would be cause for dismissal in most hostess clubs.

16. "Timer" is a euphemism for a *talent* or contract worker.

17. In Leheny, 2006: 71.

18. The standing of "boyfriend" distinguishes a customer as not just a frequent but also a preferred customer. What is key here is that such a man is first and foremost a customer. As Alice described, "He is your boyfriend. But there is a limit. If you are not with each other, then he is no longer your boyfriend. It's not like a real boyfriend that he will still be your boyfriend if you are not with each other."

19. By sex, I refer to a wide range of acts that need not involve intercourse. Some of these acts include genital touching, fondling, and masturbation. Notably, clubs would not receive a portion of the earnings of hostesses in paid sexual transactions.

20. While *arubaito* workers have greater labor market flexibility than *talents*, I acknowledge that among *arubaito* workers those who are visa overstayers have far lesser control of their labor market options than those who have legal residency status.

21. As Foucault writes,

> Of course, all moral action involves a relationship with the reality in which it is carried out, and a relationship with the self. The latter is not simply "self awareness" but self-formation as an "ethical subject," a process in which the individual delimits the part of himself that will form the object of his moral practice, defines his position relative to the precept he will follow, and decides on a certain mode of being that will serve as his moral goals (1985: 28).

NOTES TO CHAPTER SIX

1. Visas are otherwise referred to as "condition of residency" in Japan. Those with marriage as their condition of residency are married to a Japanese national or a long-term resident such as a Zainichi Korean who does not have citizenship but has special status of residency.

2. After learning of my visa status as a "*kyoju*" or "professor," they would always give me a puzzled look. They did not know what to make of my unusual status. Usually, they would ask, "What is that?" Immediately afterwards they would proceed to let me know they were "permanent" or "*kekkon*," meaning "marriage."

3. *Nikei-jin* refers to a person of Japanese descent. Foreigners could obtain fourteen kinds of working visas. They include professor, artist, religious activities, journalist, investor/business manager, legal/accounting services, medical services, researcher, instructor, engineer, specialist in humanities/international services, intracompany, entertainer, and skilled labor visas. Filipinos mostly enter to work as an "entertainer." A smaller number enter with a "general visa," as a student, trainee (meaning a professional entering not as a worker but intern), or a dependent. See the official government site for an enumerated list of short-term and long-term visas in Japan; retrieved on September 12, 2008, from www.mofa.go.jp/j_info/visit/visa/03.html.

4. Husbands of Japanese women comprise a small proportion of the Filipino migrant community.

5. Gonzalez, 2009.

6. See Government of Japan website on number of foreigners, www.e-stat.go.jp/SG1/estat/List.do?lid=000001031723. Verified by Professor Nobue Suzuki on October 8, 2008.

7. Since 1996, the Japanese government has recognized the residency of foreign custodians of Japanese children. Historically, the state had not granted Japanese nationality to children born out of wedlock to Japanese fathers and non-Japanese mothers, even if the Japanese fathers acknowledged the children as their own. Japanese nationality was given to children of non-Japanese mothers and Japanese fathers only if recognized in utero by the Japanese father as his child. In June 4, 2008, the Supreme Court in Japan ruled that the marital status of the parents had no bearing on the nationality of the child, thereby increasing the number of Japanese-Filipino children who are eligible for citizenship. This ruling opens the door to legal residency for Filipino women, who are now able to seek residency as foreign custodians of their Japanese children.

8. Potential husbands visiting the Philippines include both tourists and businessmen (Suzuki, 2003).

9. Personal conversation, Tokyo, Japan; July 2005.

10. Berlant, 1997; Weeks, 1985.

11. Cott, 2002; D'Emilio and Freedman,1998; Coontz, 2005.

12. Abu-Lughod, 1986; Illouz, 2007; Lutz and White, 1986.

13. Bernstein, 2007b; Brennan, 2004; Cabezas, 2004.

14. Zelizer, 2005: 28.

15. Constable, 2003: 128.

16. Suzuki, 2003.

17. Brennan, 2004: 96. Seemingly devoid of emotions, sex workers, according to Brennan, "are hard at work selling romance" (98) and engage in the performance of being in love. They pursue marriage and act in love as an "advancement strategy" (Brennan, 2004: 155–182). Notably, some hostesses admitted to me that their pursuit of marriage was an "advancement strategy," but they interestingly seemed to extend Brennan's formulation, marrying not as an individual-based strategy but instead a family-based one. Some hostesses admitted to being married in the Philippines and having the consent of their Filipino husband to marry a Japanese as a way of securing legal residency in Japan. The strategy of the family would require the husband and wife to temporarily separate, but still remain married, as divorce is illegal in the Philippines, and then have the wife marry a Japanese man with the intent of divorcing him after she obtains permanent residency, which would take at least five years. Afterwards, she would then petition her husband in the Philippines to join her in Japan. This long-term strategy of securing residency is not unheard of in the community.

18. Suzuki, 2003: 18.

19. Faier, 2007.

20. As Faier describes of one of her informants, "Girlie delineated two types of people: those who were cold and calculating and those who were loving and decent. She suggested that loving one's husband was a measure of both morality and humanity—of an emotional interiority evidenced by love" (Faier, 2007: 155).

21. Giddens, 1993.

22. Kelsky, 2001.

23. We could also say they are similar to the Japanese women who marry American men to obtain a U.S. green card regardless of whether they hold passionate sentiments of love for their husbands (Kelsky, 2001). Yet, the situation of the women in Kelsky's study cannot be reduced solely to this rationalist construction of love as they also fit the notion of "pure love" that Giddens (1993) describes in the posttraditional world in which individuals seek partnerships based on personal growth. In this case, Japanese women rid themselves of rigid Japanese traditions when seeking partnerships with Western men.

24. Likewise, anthropologist Sealing Cheng observed that "money is proof of love" for Filipina entertainers in Korea (2010: 145).

25. At the time of our interviews, Rowena was a housewife and mother of two children in Tokyo, having married the customer who had helped release her from her labor contract after only one term as a contract worker. Rowena was only fifteen years old when she began working in Japan. Despite her youth, her father gave her permission to marry the customer, a man nine years senior, telling her "whatever happened to me would be my responsibility."

26. Brennan, 2004.

27. Hershatter, 1999: 381.

28. Constable, 2003.

29. Mirroring the morals of Eden and her husband, husbands in New York and Shanghai have been known to manage the commercial sexual activities of their wives with other men (Clement, 2006; Hershatter, 1999). Some may even find these liaisons lucrative.

30. Amanda, for instance, stays with Hiroshi not for the sexual pleasures of romance but instead for the stability their relationship provides her children. Explains Amanda:

> I am not an ordinary mommy. I sacrificed my whole life for [my children]. I tell them that I have an affair with a man not for my own pleasure, but for them. I told them that. I told them that Hiroshi is my boyfriend, and I have sex with him because of them. He is the

one who helps them with their assignments. Mommy cannot do that. I am not Japanese. I do not understand *kanji*. So, in return, I respect the man's feelings. Because Hiroshi respects us, I respect him.

Despite the "bad sex" between them, one cannot disentangle the instrumental calculations that Amanda makes in her relationship with Hiroshi from her "love" for him because, according to Amanda, she would not even consider such calculations if she did not love him. Likewise, Amanda astutely points out that Hiroshi's feelings for her are not devoid of instrumental calculations, thus further questioning our impulse to distinguish emotions from pragmatism or emotionally based decisions from rationally based ones. Part of the attraction of Hiroshi for Amanda is her children and the opportunity he has to help raise them. In fact, Hiroshi thinks that "destiny brought [them] together." Explains Amanda:

> He thinks destiny brought us together. His wife left him and took his daughter, so he never experienced being a father. With my children, he gets to experience what he lost when his wife took their daughter at two years old. My children and Hiroshi have a good relationship. He told me that it is destiny that brought us together because he wants children, and I need a father for them.

The otherwise lonely Hiroshi, who Amanda tells me has no contact with his only child, finds joy in helping out her children with their homework and as a bonus gets sex from her. Evaluating her situation, Amanda explains, "I know he will not completely love my children if I were not here for him. I am here; that is why he loves my children. In a way, we are using each other." The case of Amanda and Hiroshi, "using each other," suggests we should not construct "strategy-driven love" and "emotion-driven love" as mutually exclusive emotions but instead see how they possibly sustain one another, as indicated by the deep gratitude Amanda feels toward Hiroshi and the joy that Hiroshi feels for helping raise a family.

31. He has since refused to legally recognize their child as his own.

32. On June 4, 2008, the Supreme Court of Japan ruled to grant Japanese citizenship to children born out of wedlock to a non-Japanese mother and a Japanese father. Prior to this ruling, only children recognized in utero by a Japanese father would receive Japanese citizenship.

33. Constable, 2003.

34. The average divorce rate was around 33 percent in the early 2000s (Suzuki, 2003).

35. Marietta's mother-in-law also went against her son in court and supported Marietta when she filed for sole custody of her daughter after their divorce. Marietta's situation was unusual, but perhaps Marietta and her mother-in-law bonded over their shared troubles over the criminal activities of Marietta's husband, who was a member of the *yakuza* before his death.

36. Kim, 2008; Yuh, 2002.

37. Kim, 2008.

38. Suzuki, 2003.

39. Medina, 2000.

40. Ibid.

41. Asai and Kameoka, 2005.

42. As Asai and Kameoka describe, "Adult children are now less apt to take in and care for their aged parents. Among young people, the concept of filial piety is even less meaningful. They perceive their parents as people who care for and pamper them, but not family members to whom they are obligated to provide care" (2005: 112–113).

43. The negotiation of morals among sex workers is not exclusive to hostesses. Denise Brennan likewise found that Dominican sex workers justify the moral transgressions of their work by claiming that they do it for morally good reasons, claiming for instance to be motivated by "family obligation

and sacrifice" (2004: 174). Likewise, Lieba Faier (2009) notes how Filipina hostesses in the Central Kiso area justify their work by claiming to do it for their family.

44. Suzuki, 2003: 180–181.

45. Interview with Lilibeth Pono, Embassy of the Philippines, Tokyo, May 26, 2005.

46. Butler, 1990.

47. Ibid.: xv.

48. Richardson, 2000.

49. We should note that they are a particular kind of *bakla*, as this identity also includes masculine males who sexually desire men.

50. Johnson, 1997.

51. Butler, 2004.

52. Richardson, 2000: 78.

53. Weeks, 1998.

54. Bell and Binnie, 2000; Weeks, 1998.

55. Kulick, 1998.

56. Ibid.

57. In Japan, Article 24 of the Constitution declares marriage is "based only on the mutual consent of both sexes" (Norton, 2006: 6).

58. Ibid.: 5.

59. Stryker, 2009.

60. Butler, 1990.

61. Connell, 1987; 1995.

62. Connell, 1995: 44.

63. Ward (2009) specifically documents the gender labors that transgender female-to-males require of their femme partners to validate their masculinity.

64. My findings disagree with those of Raine Dozier (2005) who found that female-to-male gender identities did not have to be bolstered by the contrasting gender of their sexual partners.

65. Boellstorff, 2005: 81.

66. Bhabha, 1994: 121–131.

67. Ibid: 122.

68. Ibid.: 127.

69. Butler, 2004: 108.

70. Ibid.: 106.

71. Faier, 2009: 215.

NOTES TO CHAPTER SEVEN

1. Talavera et al., 2010: 167.

2. Talavera and his colleagues found that the isolation similarly experienced by undocumented individuals in the U.S.-Mexico borderlands lead them to various emotional anxieties, including angst, despair, loneliness, and depression. For the most part, these emotional states of being did not reflect the experiences of my interviewees.

3. De Genova, 2002: 438. Also see De Genova and Peutz, 2010; Mahler, 1995.

4. Although Article 14 of the Constitution of Japan declares that "all of the people are equal under the law and there shall be no discrimination in political, economic or social relations because of race, creed, sex, social status or family origin," Japan does not have civil rights legislation that penalizes discriminatory activities committed by citizens or businesses. The Constitution of Japan, Prime Minister of Japan and His Cabinet; retrieved on January 5, 2010, from http://74.125.155.132/search?q=cache:R8c9h

_KUt8kJ:www.kantei.go.jp/foreign/constitution_and_government_of_japan/constitution_e.html +%22Constitution+of+Japan%22&hl=en&client=firefox-a&gl=us&strip=1.

5. Immigrants who surrender, that is, voluntary deportees, can avoid incarceration if they show proof of intention to leave the country.

6. Willen, 2007b: 10.

7. Filipinos comprise a substantial number of all undocumented migrants in Japan. In recent years, it has been estimated that there are 240,000 undocumented migrants in Japan (Shipper, 2008).

8. Wicker, 2010: 238-239.

9. Willen, 2007a: 2.

10. Chavez, 1992.

11. Sassen, 2006: 85.

12. Ibid.

13. Soysal, 1994: 166.

14. Willen, 2007a, b.

15. Coutin, 2007: 9.

16. In my study, the undocumented workers' vulnerability to abuse did not result in their forced prostitution by physical threat or intimidation, but this vulnerability could have forced some to resort to commercial sex. As one of the older hostesses I had interviewed, Baby, explained, "No, no one is forced to *do* it. But some women are forced *into* it. . . . Sometimes some women, when they see money, they will do anything. They do that because life is very hard. But to say you are forced to *do* it, no."

17. In Japan, only those with legal residency status can use banks to wire transfer money.

18. Japan monitors the entrance and exit of foreigners. We can safely assume that the government subtracts the number of exits from entrances to calculate and provide an estimated number of visa overstayers. I gratefully acknowledge the assistance of Nobue Suzuki and Keiko Yamanaka in gathering these numbers. Please see www.estat.go.jp/SG1/estat/List.do?lid=000001031723; last verified by Keiko Yamanaka on October 9, 2008.

19. *Walang bala*, meaning to be without a bullet, is another common reference to visa overstayers that I heard in the community.

20. One interviewee escaped so she could spend more time with her lover, who was a married man. Her situation was an exception among hostesses.

21. Not long after running away, Nikki Ann managed to secure legal residency via her marriage to a self-identified lesbian.

22. Not long after she was deported back to the Philippines, Maki managed to return to Japan as a contract worker. She escaped the club where she was assigned not long after arriving in Japan.

23. She complained, "I let it go after two months because I had *utang na loob* [debt of the soul]. They were the ones who helped me run away. So after they were able to get my salary for two months, I was given in Philippine money only 50,000 pesos, but they were making 500,000 pesos off me. I worked for that money . . . I gave them two months of my salary, and then I ran away again."

24. Wicker, 2010: 230-232.

25. Douglass and Roberts, 2003; Ventura, 1992.

26. Entering Japan as a tourist is difficult for most Filipinos, but those who could secure a letter of invitation from a resident of Japan increase their likelihood of obtaining a visa. One of my interviewees, Baby, remarked, "You just need an invitation letter. A guarantee. That is what is important. Because the guarantor promises to cover all of your expenses while you are here. That is what that meant."

27. As I discussed in Chapter Six, Filipina wives of Japanese men frequently complained about how the familial responsibilities of their spouses rarely extended to include extended kin. The Japanese spouses of Filipina wives also feared the ramifications of harboring an illegal and rarely allowed visa overstayers, even if kin, to live with them.

28. Parreñas, 2001a.

29. One could argue that the stronghold of the debt could make a hostess susceptible to "human trafficking" because it would hamper her ability to negotiate any moral violations that she might face at work. Yet, among my interviewees, none of those who faced some form of moral violation acquiesced because of a debt. The moral in-betweener Teresa even acquired debt just to escape a moral rationalist club because she wished not to capitulate and perform the sexual acts encouraged by club management. Debts do not seem to debilitate hostesses. Providing another example, Irene refused to recognize the debt she had been saddled with for the use of a "fake" passport. Refusing to be bullied, she threatened to report the middleman brokers to the appropriate authorities if they refused to forgive her debt. To sever her ties with the middleman brokers who charged her for the use of a "fake" passport, Irene opted to work with another promotion agency and insisted on using her "real" name the second time around.

30. Ventura, 1992.

31. De Genova and Peutz, 2010.

32. In Arizona, the passage of SB 1070 and its signing into law by Governor Jan Brewer in January 2010 also allows authorities to apprehend foreign-looking individuals without good reason.

33. In 2004, Maki was caught in a police raid at a host club. She was arrested, incarcerated, and later deported. Soon after, she returned to Japan as a *talent*. In her mid-thirties, she managed to compete successfully in auditions against much younger overseas performance artists because she is quite attractive, is petite and hence "cute," and is adept in Japanese.

34. "Illegal" immigrant workers are entitled to rights and protection under Japan's Labor Standards Act (Government of Japan, 1947). From the outset, Japanese labor law prohibits discrimination of workers on the basis of their "nationality, creed or social status" (Article 3 Labor Standards Act). The law does not distinguish between "illegal" and "legal" workers. Simply, the law describes a worker who is entitled to rights and protections as "one who is employed at an enterprise or place of business (hereinafter referred to as an enterprise) and receives wages there from, without regard to the kind of occupation" (Article 9 Labor Standards Act). Thus, as workers, undocumented migrants in Japan are entitled to the protections of Article 23, which states that

> Upon a worker's death or retirement, in the event of a request by one having the right thereto, the employer shall pay the wages and return the reserves, security deposits, savings, and any other funds and valuables to which the worker is rightfully entitled, regardless of the name by which such funds and valuables may be called, within seven days.

This section merely mentions "death and retirement," but the Tokyo Employment Service Center for Foreigners, managed by Japan's Ministry of Health, Labor, and Welfare, cites this article as the basis for worker's entitlement to receive wages seven days after their resignation. See www.tfemploy.go.jp/en/spec/spec_1c.html. I acknowledge the research assistance of Maria Hwang, who helped me identify how the law protects the labor of visa overstayers.

35. Quite persistent, Marie was the only undocumented hostess I interviewed who demanded her salary from her employer. As she told me,

> My third job in Shinjiku was once again with a *yakuza*. He did not pay my salary . . . He was addicted to gambling. I worked there, and then I lived upstairs in the bar . . . At first I got paid, then at the end . . . he started paying me in installments. That is OK because he was still paying me. But then near the end, one month, two months had gone by, and he told me to wait a little bit more. I had this bad feeling he was not going to pay me. So I searched for his house. I did not know where he lived but I found it . . . I told him, if you don't pay for my salary, I will report you to the police even if I am *bilog*. So he met me in a coffee shop . . . I got my salary. I was able to get 160,000 yen.

36. As Nicholas De Genova observes, "Concretely there are no hermetically sealed communities of undocumented migrants. In everyday life, undocumented migrants are invariably engaged in social relations with 'legal' migrants as well as citizens, and they live in quite intimate proximity to various categories of 'documented' persons" (2002: 422).

37. If we calculate on the high end that such an apartment would cost 200,000 yen per month, then we can estimate that the couple reaped a significant profit as they collected at least 750,000 yen per month for rent.

38. Charmaine managed to smuggle that much money back into the Philippines by stuffing cash in her carry-on and giving some of the money to the Japanese man who accompanied her home as well as two close friends whose plane tickets she covered. As she described, "I separated the money and hid it in my suitcase. And I put some money with the Japanese who went home with me. Then I had close friends who went home with me. I had them go home with me. I paid for their tickets. They were also undocumented before like me. They were going home as well."

39. Greenhills is a shopping center in Manila.

40. Quiapo is an area in Manila with open markets that sell cheap goods.

NOTES TO CHAPTER EIGHT

Portions of this chapter have been adapted from Rhacel Parreñas, "Homeward Bound: The Circular Migration of Entertainers between Japan and the Philippines," *Global Networks*, Volume 10, Issue 3, pages 301–323, July 2010.

1. Philippine Overseas Employment Administration, 2009.

2. Representatives of nongovernmental organizations give a larger count of undocumented migrants than government figures and estimate that there are more than 40,000 undocumented Filipina migrants in Japan, exceeding the current annual flow of contract workers but still a small percentage of the cumulative count of *talents* who have entered Japan in the last ten years. We have also seen a jump in the number of marriages between Filipina brides and Japanese grooms, for instance spiking to 10,427 in 2005 from fewer than 7,000 in the previous year (Tutor, 2007).

3. Castles and Miller (1998) formulate a stage model of migration in which migrants initially arrive as temporary workers but prolong their stay, then sponsor the migration of their family, and eventually become permanent settlers. Also see Castles, 1984; Massey, Durand, and Malone, 2002; and Tsuda 1999.

4. Tsuda, 1999: 689.

5. Slany and Malek 2005.

6. The visa restricts the employment of the entertainer to the sponsoring club.

7. Ventura, 1992.

8. Ibid.: 30.

9. Ibid.: 30.

10. Ibid.: 30.

11. For example, see U.S. Department of State 2004; U.S. Department of State 2005. During the time of my research, the embassy began to operate on Sundays but still closed its doors at five o'clock in the afternoon.

12. De Certeau 1984: 123. Also see Lefebvre, 1992.

13. Besides restaurants, the leisure space of choice among hostesses is host bars, meaning bars that are the male equivalent of hostess bars. During the course of my research, friends, co-workers, and interviewees repeatedly invited me to visit Philippine host bars. Like hostess bars, host bars vary by ethnicity. There are Korean host bars, Philippine host bars, and Japanese host bars. Philippine host bars cost less than hostess bars, as the cover charge in Philippine host bars is no more than 1,000 yen for the entire evening. The bar makes most of its profits from food and drinks. These bars operate

from midnight to nine in the morning and are located in areas known to have hostess bars. Customers often accompany hostesses to these clubs after hostess bars close at four o'clock in the morning, which would just be in time for the variety show performance of the male hosts. Philippine host bars are quite popular among hostesses, including those from Korea, Romania, and the Philippines. Perhaps they go there for the nightly *show time* performance that is unique to Philippine host bars, as Korean and Japanese host bars do not provide this form of entertainment. In host bars, I could not help but frequently notice large groups of Filipino women accompanied usually by only one Japanese man, whom we can safely assume to be a customer. Often a hostess would accommodate the request of a customer to get something to eat after her club closes; but unless she is out with her boyfriend, she will likely go out with the customer only if she is chaperoned by a co-worker or two.

14. My field notes indicate how wearisome the process of sending money could be through the official channel of a banking institution:

> It was slow at the bank. It also took a long time to get remittances processed as a few and not one individual processes the remittance. It begins when one signs up with the receptionist, who then guides the remitter to fill out a form and inserts this form along with one's remittance identity card in a clear folder. The remitter is then instructed to wait until someone calls out his or her number. This folder is then taken and processed by another person. In my case, this process took more than an hour despite the fact that there were only around eight of us waiting to send money to the Philippines. To send money, one can do (1) an immediate deposit to a Philippine National Bank branch; (2) a deposit that will take two to three business days to another bank; or (3) "advice and pay" for those without a bank account, meaning they are advised by phone that they have money waiting for them at a specific branch. The receiver goes to the section "Remittances," which is a special line in the bank to which individuals who receive remittances go to collect their money. This type of remittance is also called "over the counter."

15. To cater to the large number of service workers in the community, the embassy now operates on Sundays, but still most entertainers find the embassy's hours of operation inconvenient to their work schedule.

16. In Japan, much of OWWA's attention went to Filipinos who were technically not part of its constituency: wives and domestic workers. This latter group is technically not part of OWWA's constituency because they are not migrant contract workers whose overseas labor is facilitated by POEA. Only those whose migration is facilitated by POEA become members of OWWA, as part of their processing fee is designated to the funding of OWWA.

17. Severe discrimination against transgenders in the Philippines closes the options of most other professional occupations for them, making call centers a rare and welcome opportunity for transgenders who wish to hold a professional job in the country.

18. See U.S. Department of State, 2006.

NOTES TO CONCLUSION

1. See the Trafficking and Violence Protection Act definition of "severe forms of trafficking" (U.S. Department of State, 2007: 9).

2. Bales, 2007.

3. Kay agreed to complete at least five labor contracts in Japan and share 50 percent of her earnings with her manager.

4. In a recent presentation by Amy O'Neill Richards, senior advisor to the director in the U.S. State Department's Office to Monitor and Combat Trafficking in Persons, she suggested that all live-in contract workers are trafficked persons. According to Richards, live-in workers are inherently without freedom and autonomy. This would make them trafficked persons, in other words people in

need of rescue. Considering that most migrant women workers are domestic workers, this statement inadvertently discourages the migration of women. Richards's presentation was made at the "Driving Change, Shaping Lives: Gender in the Developing World" Conference at the Radcliffe Institute for Advanced Study, Cambridge, MA (March 3, 2011).

5. For a discussion of the oppressive work conditions of au pairs in socialist democratic nations in Europe such as Denmark and the Netherlands, see Marchetti, 2005; Stenum, 2008, 2009. The migration of au pairs is considered by labor advocates to be a backdoor to unregulated domestic work in Denmark and the Netherlands. The terms of migration for au pairs bind them to their employer and limit their ability to negotiate for fair working conditions. To learn more about the legalized indenture of migrant domestic workers in Canada, see Bakan and Stasiulis, 1997; Pratt, 2004. In Canada, migrant domestic workers' eligibility for permanent residency is contingent on two years of live-in service. Critics have argued that this requirement practically enslaves migrant domestic workers. Lastly, both Pei-Chia Lan and Nicole Constable have documented migrant domestic workers' limited rights in Taiwan and Hong Kong, respectively. These limited rights hamper their ability to negotiate for fair working conditions. Pei-Chia Lan additionally has documented that most migrant domestic workers in Taiwan are not in a position to quit their jobs because they enter heavily into debt, with many expecting all of their first year's wages to go into paying that debt. Migration fees charged by middleman brokers account for the primary expense that places them in debt. See Constable, 2007; Lan, 2007.

6. Parreñas, 2008, 2010.

7. Lan, 2006: 52; Lindio-McGovern, 2003: 520.

8. In addition to the penalties imposed by middleman brokers, lenders impose exorbitantly high interest rates on migrant workers. In Italy, for instance, lenders imposed a monthly interest rate of 10 percent (Parreñas, 2001a).

9. The fact that the current solutions advocated by the U.S. State Department are not based on practical reason suggests that it is the moral regulation of women, the desire to protect feminine respectability in the process of migration, and the moralistic assumption that hostesses can't possibly want to do their job of flirting with customers that have spurred the identification of migrant Filipina hostesses in Japan as trafficked persons.

10. Pettit, 2004.

11. Hondagneu-Sotelo, 1994; Gonzalez-Lopez, 2005.

12. Lan (2007): 53. Also see Hondagneu-Sotelo, 1994; Singer and Gilbertson, 2003; Lan, 2006; Constable, 2007.

13. Espiritu, 2003; Menjivar, 2000.

14. Hondagneu-Sotelo, 2003; Sassen, 2006.

BIBLIOGRAPHY

Abend, Gabriel. 2008. "Two Main Problems in the Sociology of Morality." *Theory and Society* 37: 87–125.

Abu-Lughod, Lila. 1986. *Veiled Sentiments: Honor and Poetry in a Bedouin Society.* Berkeley and Los Angeles: The University of California Press.

Agustin, Laura. 2007. *Sex at the Margins: Migration, Labour Markets and the Rescue Industry.* London: Zed Books.

Albert, Alexa. 2002. *Brothel: Mustang Ranch and Its Women.* New York: Ballentine Books.

Allison, Anne. 1994. *Nightwork: Sexuality, Pleasure, and Corporate Masculinity in a Tokyo Hostess Club.* Chicago: University of Chicago Press.

Anderson, Bridget. 2000. *Doing the Dirty Work.* London: Zed Books.

Anderson, James N. 1999. "Filipina Migrants to Japan: Entertainers, House Helpers, and Homemakers," *The Annual Report of the Institute of International Studies*, Vol. 2. Tokyo: Meiji Gakuin University.

Asai, Masayuki O., and Velma Kameoka. 2005. "The Influence of *Sekentai* on Family Caregiving and Underutilization of Social Services among Japanese Caregivers." *Social Work* 50 (2): 111–118.

Bakan, Abigail, and Daiva Stasiulis, eds. 1997. *Not One of the Family: Foreign Domestic Workers in Canada.* Toronto: University of Toronto Press.

Bales, Kevin. 2007. *Ending Slavery: How We Free Today's Slaves.* Berkeley: University of California Press.

Ballescas, Maria Rosario. 1993. *Filipino Entertainers in Japan: An Introduction,* Quezon City, Philippines: Foundation for Nationalist Studies.

Barry, Kathleen. 1995. *The Prostitution of Sexuality.* New York: New York University Press.

Barton, Bernadette. 2008. *Stripped: Inside the Lives of Exotic Dancers.* New York: New York University Press.

Bauman, Zygmunt. 1998. "On Postmodern Uses of Sex." *Theory, Culture and Society* 15: 19–33.

Bell, David, and Jon Binnie. 2000. *The Sexual Citizen: Queer Politics and Beyond.* London: Polity Press.

Benedicto, Bobby. 2008. "The Haunting of Gay Manila: Global Space-Time and the Specter of Kabaklaan." *GLQ: A Journal of Lesbian and Gay Studies* 14(2–3): 317–338.

Berlant, Lauren. 1997. *The Queen of America Goes to Washington D.C.: Essays on Sex and Citizenship*. Durham, NC: Duke University Press.

Bernard, Jessie. 1981. "The Good Provider Role: Its Rise and Fall." *American Psychologist* 36(1): 1–12.

Bernstein, Elizabeth. 2001. "The Meaning of the Purchase: Desire, Demand, and the Commerce of Sex." Ethnography 2(3): 389–420.

———. 2007a. "The Sexual Politics of the 'New Abolitionism': Imagery and Activism in Contemporary Anti-Trafficking Campaigns." *Differences: Journal of Feminist Cultural Studies* 18:3, 128–151.

———. 2007b. *Temporarily Yours*. Chicago: University of Chicago Press.

Bhabha, Homi. 1994. *The Location of Culture*. New York: Routledge Press.

Boellstorff, Tom. 2005. *The Gay Archipelago: Sexuality and Nation in Indonesia*. Princeton, NJ: Princeton University Press.

Bosniak, Linda. 1999–2000. "Citizenship Denationalized." *Indiana Journal of Global Legal Studies* 7: 447–509.

Bourdieu, Pierre. 1984. *Distinction: A Social Critique of the Judgment of Taste*. Cambridge, MA: Harvard University Press.

———. 1986. "The Forms of Capital." In J. Richardson, ed., *Handbook of Theory and Research for the Sociology of Education*, pp. 241–258. New York: Greenwood.

———. 1990. *The Logic of Practice*. Stanford, CA: Stanford University Press.

Braverman, Harry. 1998 [1974]. *Labor and Monopoly Capital: The Degradation of Work in the Twentieth Century*. New York: Monthly Review Press.

Brennan, Denise. 2004. *What's Love Got to Do with It?* Durham, NC: Duke University Press.

Brown, Wendy. 1993. "Wounded Attachments," *Political Theory* 21(3): 390–410.

Butler, Judith. 1990. *Gender Trouble*. New York: Routledge.

———. 2004. *Undoing Gender*. New York: Routledge.

———. 2005. *Giving an Account of Oneself*. New York: Fordham Press.

Cabezas, Amalia. 1999. "Women's Work Is Never Done: Sex Tourism in Sosúa, the Dominican Republic." In Kamala Kempadoo, ed., *Sun, Sex, and Gold: Tourism and Sex Work in the Caribbean*, pp. 93–125. Lanham, MD: Rowman & Littlefield Publishers.

———. 2002. "Tourism, Sex Work, and Women's Rights in the Dominican Republic." In Alison Brysk, ed., *Globalization and Human Rights*, pp. 44–60. Berkeley and Los Angeles: University of California Press.

———. 2004. "Between Love and Money: Sex, Tourism, and Citizenship in Cuba and the Dominican Republic." *Signs* 29(4): 987–1015.

———. 2009. *Economies of Desire: Sex and Tourism in Cuba and the Dominican Republic*, Philadelphia: Temple University Press.

Califia, Patrick. 2003 [1997]. *Sex Changes: The Politics of Transgenderism*. San Francisco, CA: Cleis Press.

Cannell, Fenella. 1995. "The Power of Appearances: Beauty, Mimicry, and Transformation in Bicol." In Vicente Rafael, ed., *Discrepant Histories: Translocal Essays in Philippine Cultures*, pp. 223–258. Philadelphia: Temple University Press.

Cargill, Thomas, Michael Hutchison, and Takatoshi Ito. 1997. *The Political Economy of Japanese Monetary Policy*. Cambridge, MA: MIT Press.

Cantu, Lionel. 2009. *The Sexuality of Migration: Border Crossings and Mexican Immigrant Men*. New York: New York University Press.

Castles, Stephen. 1984. *Here for Good: Western Europe's New Ethnic Minorities*. London: Pluto Press.

———. 2006. "Guestworkers in Europe: A Resurrection?" *International Migration Review* 40 (4): 741–66.

Castles, Stephen, and Alastair Davidson. 2000. *Citizenship and Migration: Globalization and the Politics of Belonging*. New York: Routledge Press.

Castles, Stephen, and Mark Miller. 1998. *The Age of Migration: International Population Movements in the Modern World*. London: Macmillan.

Chacon, Jennifer. 2006. "Misery and Myopia: Understanding the Failures of U.S. Efforts to Stop Human Trafficking," *Fordham Law Review* 74: 2977–3040.

Chapkis, Wendy. 1997. *Live Sex Acts: Women Performing Erotic Labor*. New York: Routledge.

———. 2005. "Soft Glove, Punishing Fist: The Trafficking Victims Protection Act of 2000." In Elizabeth Bernstein and Laurie Schaffner, eds. *Regulating Sex: The Politics of Intimacy and Identity*, pp. 51–67. New York: Routledge.

Chavez, Leo. 1992. *Shadowed Lives: Undocumented Immigrants in American Society*. Orlando, FL: Harcourt Brace Jovanovich.

Cheng, Sealing. 2010. *On the Move for Love: Migrant Entertainers and the U.S. Military in South Korea*. Philadelphia: University of Pennsylvania Press.

Christman, John. 1991. "Liberalism and Individual Positive Freedom," *Ethics* 101:2 (January): 343–359.

———. 2001. "Liberalism, Autonomy and Self-Transformation," *Social Theory and Practice* 27:2 (April): 185–206.

Chuang, Janie. 1998. "Redirecting the Debate over Trafficking in Women: Definitions, Paradigms, and Contexts," *Harvard Human Rights Journal* 11: 65–107.

Chung, Haeng-ja. 2004. "Performing Sex, Selling Heart: Korean Night Club Hostesses in Japan." PhD Dissertation. Department of Anthropology, University of California, Los Angeles.

Clement, Elizabeth. 2006. *Love for Sale: Courting, Treating, and Prostitution in New York City, 1900–1945*. Chapel Hill: University of North Carolina Press.

Connell, R. W. 1987. *Gender and Power: Society, the Person, and Sexual Politics*. Stanford, CA: Stanford University Press.

———. 1995. *Masculinities*. Berkeley and Los Angeles: University of California Press.

Constable, Nicole. 2003. *Romance on a Global Stage*. Berkeley and Los Angeles: University of California Press.

———. 2007. *Maid to Order in Hong Kong*. Ithaca, NY: Cornell University Press.

Coontz, Stephanie. 2005. *Marriage, a History: From Obedience to Intimacy, or How Love Conquered Marriage*. New York: Viking.

Cossman, Brenda. 2007. *Sexual Citizens*. Stanford, CA: Stanford University Press.

Cott, Nancy. 2002. *Public Vows: A History of Marriage and the Nation*. Cambridge, MA: Harvard University Press.

Coutin, Susan. 2007. *Nation of Emigrants: Shifting Boundaries of Citizenship in El Salvador and the United States*. Ithaca, NY: Cornell University Press.

D'Emilio, John, and Estelle Freedman. 1998. *Intimate Matters: A History of Sexuality in America*. Chicago: University of Chicago Press.

De Certeau, M. 1984. *The Practice of Everyday Life*. Berkeley: University of California Press.

De Dios, Aurora Javate. 1992. "*Japayuki-san*: Filipinas at Risk." In Mary Ruby Palma-Beltran and Aurora Javata de Dios, eds., *Filipino Women Overseas Contract Workers: At What Cost?* pp. 39–58. Manila: Goodwill Training.

De Genova, Nicholas. 2002. "Migrant 'Illegality' and Deportability in Everyday Life." *Annual Review of Anthropology* 31: 419–447.

De Genova, Nicholas, and Nathalie Peutz, eds. 2010. *The Deportation Regime: Sovereignty, Space and the Freedom of Movement*. Durham, NC: Duke University Press.

Destefano, Anthony. 2007. *The War on Human Trafficking*. New Brunswick, NJ: Rutgers University Press.

Development Action for Women Network (DAWN). 2003. *Pains and Gains: A Study of Overseas Performing Artists from Pre-Departure to Reintegration*. Manila, Philippines: DAWN.

———. 2004. *Moving on: Stories of DAWN Women Survivors*. Manila, Philippines: DAWN.

Doezema, Jo. 2001. "Ouch! Western Feminists' 'Wounded Attachment' to the 'Third World Prostitute,'" *Feminist Review* 67 (Spring): 16–38.

Douglas, Mary. 2002 [1966]. *Purity and Danger.* New York: Routledge.

Douglass, Mike. 2003. "The Singularities of International Migration of Women to Japan: Past, Present, and Future." In Mike Douglass and Glenda S. Roberts, eds., *Japan and Global Migration: Foreign Workers and the Advent of a Multicultural Society*, pp. 91–119. Honolulu: University of Hawai'i Press.

Douglass, Mike, and Glenda S. Roberts, eds. 2003. *Japan and Global Migration: Foreign Workers and the Advent of a Multicultural Society.* Honolulu: University of Hawai'i Press.

Downer, Lesley. 2001. *Women of the Pleasure Quarters: The Secret History of the Geisha.* New York: Broadway Books.

Dozier, Raine. 2005. "Beards, Breasts, and Bodies: Doing Sex in a Gendered World." *Gender & Society* 19(3): 297–316.

Durkheim, Emile. 1953. *Sociology and Philosophy.* Glencoe, IL: The Free Press.

———. 1984. *The Division of Labor in Society.* New York: Free Press.

Encanto, Georgina Reyes. 2004. *Constructing the Filipina: A History of Women's Magazines (1891–2002).* Diliman, Quezon City: University of the Philippines Press.

Espiritu, Yen Le. 2003. *Home Bound: Filipino American Lives across Cultures, Communities and Countries.* Berkeley, CA: University of California Press.

Faier, Lieba. 2007. "Runaway Stories: The Underground Micromovements of Filipina *Oyomesan* in Rural Japan," *Cultural Anthropology* 23(4): 630–659.

———. 2008. "Filipina Migrants in Rural Japan and Their Professions of Love," *American Ethnologist* 34(1): 148–162.

———. 2009. *Intimate Encounters*, Berkeley and Los Angeles: University of California Press.

Farley, Melissa. 2006. "Prostitution, Trafficking, and Cultural Amnesia: What We Must Not Know in Order to Keep the Business of Sexual Exploitation Running Smoothly." *Yale Journal of Law and Feminism* 18:109–144.

Foucault, Michel. 1977. *Discipline and Punish.* New York: Vintage Press.

———. 1985. *The History of Sexuality, Vol. 2: The Use of Pleasure.* New York: Random House.

———. 1990. *The History of Sexuality, Vol. 1.* New York: Vintage Books.

———. 1997. "On the Genealogy of Ethics: An Overview of Work in Progress." In Paul Rabinow, ed., *Ethics: Subjectivity and Truth*, pp. 253–280. New York: New Press.

Frank, Katherine. 2002. *G-Strings and Sympathy: Strip Club Regulars and Male Desire.* Durham, NC: Duke University Press.

Freeman, Amy. 2005. "Moral Geographies and Women's Freedom: Rethinking Freedom Discourse in the Moroccan Text." In Walid Falah and Caroline Nagel, eds., *Geographies of Muslim Women: Gender, Religion, and Space*, pp. 147–177. New York and London: Guilford Press.

Fujieda, Eri. 2001. "Filipino Women's Migration to Japan's Sex Industry: A Case of Transnational Gender Subjection." Ph.D. Dissertation. Department of Sociology. University of Illinois, Urbana-Champaign.

Fujimoto, Nobuki. 2007. "Three Years after the Action Plan of Measures to Combat Trafficking in Persons: Issues Facing the Japanese Government and NGOs." Press Release of Asia-Pacific Human Rights Information Center, Osaka, Japan (October 23).

Gardner, Andrew. 2010. "Engulfed: Indian Guest Workers, Bahraini Citizens, and the Structural Violence of the *Kafala* System." In N. De Genova and N. Peutz, eds., *The Deportation Regime*, pp. 196–223. Durham, NC: Duke University Press.

Gardner, Martha. 2005. *Qualities of a Citizen.* Princeton, NJ: Princeton University Press.

Giddens, Anthony. 1993. *The Transformation of Intimacy.* Stanford, CA: Stanford University Press.

———. 1997. *Sociology.* London: Polity Press.

Gieryn, Thomas. 1983. "Boundary-Work and the Demarcation of Science from Non-Science: Strains and Interests in Professional Ideologies of Scientists." *American Sociological Review* 48(6): 781–795.

Glenn, Evelyn Nakano. 2008. "Yearning for Lightness: Transnational Circuits in the Marketing and Consumption of Skin Lighteners." *Gender and Society* 22(3): 281–302.

Golden, Arthur. 2001. *Memoirs of a Geisha*. New York: Vintage Books.

Gonzalez, Joaquin. 2009. *Filipino American Faith in Action: Immigration, Religion, and Civic Engagement*. New York: New York University Press.

Gonzalez-Lopez, Gloria. 2005. *Erotic Journeys: Mexican Immigrants and their Sex Lives*. Berkeley and Los Angeles: University of California Press.

Government of Japan. 1947. *Labor Standards Act (Act No. 49 of April 7, 1947)*. Tokyo, Japan: Government of Japan.

———. 1951. *Immigration Control and Refugee Recognition Act (Cabinet Order No. 319 of 1951)*. Tokyo, Japan: Government of Japan.

———. 2005. Japan's Action Plan of Measures to Combat Trafficking in Persons. 13th Economic Forum, Prague, Czech Republic (May 23–27).

Haney-Lopez, Ian F. 1996. *White by Law: The Legal Construction of Race*. New York: New York University Press, 1996.

Hardt, Michael. 1999. "Affective Labor." *Boundary 2* 26(2): 89–100.

Hardt, Michael, and Antonio Negri. 2001. *Empire*. Cambridge, MA: Harvard University Press.

Hartmann, Heidi. 1981. "The Unhappy Marriage of Marxism and Feminism: Towards a More Progressive Union." In Lydia Sargent, ed., *Women and Revolution: The Unhappy Marriage of Marxism and Feminism: A Debate on Class and Patriarchy*, pp. 1–41. London: Pluto Press.

Hershatter, Gail. 1999. *Dangerous Pleasures: Prostitution and Modernity in Twentieth-Century Shanghai*. Berkeley and Los Angeles: University of California Press.

Hochschild, Arlie. 1983. *The Managed Heart*. Berkeley and Los Angeles: University of California Press.

Hondagneu-Sotelo, Pierrette. 1994. *Gendered Transitions*. Berkeley and Los Angeles: University of California Press.

———. 1999. "Introduction: Gender and Contemporary U.S. Immigration." *American Behavioral Scientist* 42(4): 565–576.

———. 2000. "Feminism and Migration." *Annals of the American Academy of Political and Social Science*, 571: 107–120.

———. 2001. *Domestica*. Berkeley and Los Angeles: University of California Press.

———. 2003. "Gender and Immigration: A Retrospective and Introduction." In Pierrette Hondagneu-Sotelo, ed., *Gender and U.S. Immigration: Contemporary Trends*, pp. 3–19. Berkeley and Los Angeles: University of California Press.

Iglicka, Krystyna. 2001. "Shuttling from the Former Soviet Union to Poland: From 'Primitive Mobility' to Migration." *Journal of Ethnic and Migration Studies* 27 (3): 508–18.

———. 2005. "National Paradigms of Migration Research in Poland." In Krystyna Slany, ed., *International Migration: a Multidimensional Analysis*, pp. 49–63. Cracow, Poland: AGH University of Science and Technology Press.

Illouz, Eva. 2007. *Cold Intimacies: The Making of Emotional Capitalism*. London: Polity Press.

International Organization for Migration (IOM). 1997. *Trafficking in Women to Japan for Sexual Exploitation: A Survey of the Case of Filipino Women*. Geneva, Switzerland: IOM.

Japan Times. "Costly Crackdown." *Japan Times*, December 7, 2004.

Japan Times. "Human-Trafficking at Record 79 Cases but Number More Likely in Thousands" *Japan Times*, April 15, 2005.

Johnson, Mark. 1997. *Beauty and Power: Transgendering and Cultural Transformations in the Southern Philippines*. Oxford, UK: Berg Publishers.

Kang, Miliann. 2003. "The Managed Hand: The Commercialization of Bodies and Emotions in Korean Immigrant-Owned Nail Salons." *Gender and Society* 17(6): 820–839.

Kanlungan Foundation Centre. 2008. *Fast Facts on Filipino Labor Migration 2007*. Quezon City, Philippines: Kanlungan Foundation.

Kara, Siddhartha. 2009. *Sex Trafficking: Inside the Business of Modern Day Slavery*. New York: Columbia University Press.

Katayama, Lisa. 2005. "Sex Trafficking: Zero Tolerance." *Mother Jones* (May 5).

Kelly, Patty. 2008. *Lydia's Open Door: Inside Mexico's Most Modern Brothel*. Berkeley and Los Angeles: University of California Press.

Kelsky, Karen. 2001. *Women on the Verge: Japanese Women, Western Desires*. Durham, NC: Duke University Press.

Kempadoo, Kamala. 1998. Introduction: Globalizing Sex Workers' Rights. In Kamala Kempadoo and Jo Doezema, eds., *Global Sex Workers: Rights, Resistance, and Redefinition*, pp. 1–28. New York: Routledge.

———. 2004. *Sexing the Caribbean: Race, Gender and Sexual Labor*. New York: Routledge.

Kempadoo, Kamala, and Jo Doezema, eds. 1998. *Global Sex Workers: Rights, Resistance, and Redefinition*. New York: Routledge.

Kempadoo, Kamala (with Jyoti Sanghera and Bandana Pattanaik) (eds.). 2005. *Trafficking and Prostitution Reconsidered: New Perspectives on Migration, Sex Work and Human Rights*, Boulder, CO, and London: Paradigm Publishers.

Kim, Minjeong. 2008. "Gendering Marriage Migration and Fragmented Citizenship Formation: 'Korean' Wives, Daughters-in-Law, and Mothers from the Philippines." PhD Dissertation. Department of Sociology, SUNY Albany.

Korczynski, Marek. 2002. *Human Resource Management in Service Work*. London: Palgrave.

Krzystek, Krystyna. 2008. "Integration of Female Immigrants into Labour Market and Society: Biographical Policy Evaluation. The Polish Case." In Krystyna Slaney, ed. *Migracje Kobiet: Perspektywa Wielowymiarowa*, pp. 123–139. Cracow, Poland: Wydawnictwo NOMOS.

Kulick, Don. 1998. *Travesti: Sex, Gender, and Culture among Brazilian Transgendered Prostitutes*. Chicago: University of Chicago Press.

Lamont, Michele. 1992. *Money, Morals, and Manners: The Culture of the French and the American Upper-Middle Class*. Chicago: University of Chicago Press.

Lan, Pei-Chia. 2006. *Global Cinderellas: Migrant Domestics and Newly Rich Employers in Taiwan*. Durham, NC: Duke University Press.

———. 2007. "Legal Servitude and Free Illegality: Migrant 'Guest' Workers in Taiwan." In Rhacel Parreñas and Lok Siu, eds., *Asian Diasporas: New Formations, New Conceptions*, pp. 253–277. Stanford, CA: Stanford University Press.

Lefebvre, H. 1992. *The Production of Space*. Malden, MA: Blackwell Publishers.

Leheny, David. 2006. *Think Global, Fear Local: Sex, Violence, and Anxiety in Contemporary Japan*. Ithaca, NY: Cornell University Press.

Leidner, Robin. 1993. *Fast Food, Fast Talk: Service Work and the Routinization of American Life*. Berkeley and Los Angeles: University of California Press.

Leigh, Carol. 1997. "Inventing Sex Work." In Jill Nagle, ed., *Whores and Other Feminists*, pp. 226–231. New York: Routledge Press.

Lindio-McGovern, Ligaya. 2003. "Labor Export in the Context of Globalization: The Experience of Filipino Domestic Workers in Rome." *International Sociology* 18(3): 513–534.

Lister, Ruth. 2002. "Sexual Citizenship." In Engin Isin and Bryan Turner, eds., *Handbook of Citizenship Studies*, pp. 191–207. London: Sage.

Lowe, Lisa. 1996. *Immigrant Acts: On Asian American Cultural Politics*. Durham, NC: Duke University Press.

Luibheid, Eithne. 2002. *Entry Denied*. Minneapolis: University of Minnesota Press.

Lunsing, Wim. 2005. "The Politics of *Okama* and *Onabe*: Uses and Abuses of Terminology Regarding Homosexuality and Transgender." In Mark McLelland and Romit Dasgupta, eds., *Genders, Transgenders, and Sexualities in Japan*, pp. 81–95. London and New York: Routledge.

Lutz, Catherine A., and Geoffrey M. White. 1986. "The Anthropology of Emotions." *Annual Review of Anthropology* 15: 405–436.

Mackie, Vera. 2008. "How to Be a Girl: Mainstream Media Portrayals of Transgendered Lives in Japan," *Asian Studies Review* 32 (September): 411–423.

Mahler, Sarah. 1995. *American Dreaming: Immigrant Life on the Margins*. Princeton, NJ: Princeton University Press.

Mahler, Sarah, and Patricia Pessar. 2001. "Gendered Geographies of Power: Analyzing Gender Across Transnational Spaces." *Identities: Global Studies in Culture and Power* 7(4): 441–460.

Mahhmood, Saba. 2005. *Politics of Piety: The Islamic Revival and the Feminist Subject*. Princeton, NJ: Princeton University Press.

Marchetti, Sabrina. 2005. "We Had Different Fortunes: Relationships between Filipina Domestic Workers and Their Employers in Rome and Amsterdam." Master's Thesis. Gender Studies, Utrecht University.

Martin, Philip, M. Abella, and C. Kuptsch. 2006. *Managing Labor Migration in the Twenty-First Century*. New Haven, CT: Yale University Press.

Massey, Douglas, J. Durand, and N. Malone. 2002. *Beyond Smoke and Mirrors: Mexican Migration in an Era of Economic Integration*. New York: Russell Sage Foundation.

McKay, Steve. 2006. *Satanic Mills or Silicon Islands? The Politics of High-Tech Production in the Philippines*. Ithaca, NY: Cornell University Press.

McNichol, Tony. 2005. "The Show's Over." *Japan Times* (April 26).

Medina, Belinda. 2000. *The Filipino Family*. Diliman, Quezon City: University of the Philippines Press.

Menjivar, Cecilia. 2000. *Fragmented Ties: Salvadoran Immigrant Networks in America*. Berkeley: University of California Press.

———. 2006. "Liminal Legality: Salvadoran and Guatemalan Immigrants' Lives in the United States." *American Journal of Sociology* 111(4): 999–1037.

Miller, Alice. 2004. "Sexuality, Violence against Women, and Human Rights: Women Make Demands and Ladies Get Protection," *Health and Human Rights* 7(2): 17–47.

Morita, Kiriro, and Saskia Sassen. 1994. "The New Illegal Immigration in Japan, 1980–1992." *International Migration Review* 28(1): 153–163.

Nagel, Joane. 2000. "States of Arousal/Fantasy Islands: Race, Sex, and Romance in the Global Economy of Desire." *American Studies* 41(2/3): 159–181.

———. 2001. "Racial, Ethnic, and National Boundaries: Sexual Intersections and Symbolic Interactions." *Symbolic Interactions* 24(2): 123–139.

Norton, Laura. 2006. "Note. Neutering the Transgendered: Human Rights and Japan's Law No. 111." 7 *Georgetown Journal of Gender and the Law* 187.

Nussbaum, Martha. 1998. "'Whether from Reason or Prejudice': Taking Money for Bodily Services." *Journal of Legal Studies* 27: 693–724.

———. 1999. *Sex and Social Justice*. New York: Oxford University Press.

Odum, Mary. 1995. *Delinquent Daughters: Protecting and Policing Adolescent Female Sexuality in the United States, 1885–1920*. Chapel Hill: University of North Carolina Press.

Oishi, Nana. 2005. *Women in Motion*. Stanford, CA: Stanford University Press.

Ong, Aihwa. 1987. *Spirits of Resistance.* Albany: State University of New York Press.

———. 2003. *Buddha Is Hiding: Refugees, Citizenship, the New America.* Berkeley and Los Angeles: University of California Press.

Onishi, Norimutsu. 2005. "Japan, Easygoing Till Now, Plans Sex Traffic Crackdown." *The New York Times* (February 16: A3).

Opiniano, Jeremaiah. 2006. "Teacher Culls Bar-Girl Work to Flay US Anti-Trafficking." *Philippine Today* (November 20). Available at www.philippinestoday.net/index.php?module=article&view=101.

Osteria, Trinidad. 1994. *Filipino Female Labor Migration to Japan: Economic Causes and Consequences.* Manila: De La Salle University Press.

Padilla, Mark. 2007. *Caribbean Pleasure Industry: Tourism, Sexuality and AIDS in the Dominican Republic.* Chicago: University of Chicago Press.

Palumbo-Liu, David. 1999. *Asian/America: Historical Crossings of a Racial Frontier.* Stanford, CA: Stanford University Press.

Park, John. 2004. *Elusive Citizenship: Immigration, Asian Americans, and the Paradox of Civil Rights.* New York: New York University Press.

Parreñas, Rhacel Salazar. 2001a. *Servants of Globalization: Women, Migration, and Domestic Work.* Stanford, CA: Stanford University Press.

———. 2001b. "Transgressing the Nation-State: The Partial Citizenship and 'Imagined (Global) Community' of Migrant Filipina Domestic Workers." *Signs: Journal of Women in Culture and Society* 26(4): 1129–1154.

———. 2006. "Trafficked? Filipina Migrant Hostesses in Tokyo's Nightlife Industry." *Yale Journal of Law and* Feminism 18(1): 145–180.

———. 2008. *The Force of Domesticity: Filipina Migrants and Globalization*, New York: New York University Press.

———. 2010. "'Partial Citizenship' and the Ideology of Women's Domesticity in State Policies on Foreign Domestic Workers." In Ursula Apitzsch and Marianne Schmidbaur, eds., *Care und Migration: Die Ent-Sorgung menschlicher Reproduktionsarbeit entlang von Geschlechter- und Armutsgrenzen*, pp. 127–140. Opladen & Farmington Hills, MI: Budrich.

Pateman, Carole. 1988. *The Sexual Contract.* Stanford, CA: Stanford University Press.

Payne, Jonathan. 2009. "Emotional Labour and Skill: A Reappraisal." *Gender, Work and Organization* 16(3): 348–367.

Patel, Reena. 2010. *Working the Night Shift: Women in India's Call Center Industry.* Stanford, CA: Stanford University Press.

Peiss, Kathy. 1987. *Cheap Amusements.* Philadelphia: Temple University Press.

Pettit, Philip. 2004. "Depoliticizing Democracy," *Ratio Juris* 17(1): 52–65.

———. Forthcoming in 2011. "Liberty." In Hugh LaFollette, ed., *International Encyclopedia of Ethics.* Oxford, UK: Wiley.

Philippine Overseas Employment Administration. 1997. Memorandum Circular No 10. Guidelines on the Accreditation of Japanese Principals Hiring Filipino Performing Artists. Manila: Philippine Overseas Employment Administration.

———. 2003. Memorandum Circular No 21. Subject: Guidelines on the Recruitment and Deployment of Overseas Performance Artists to Japan. Manila: Philippine Overseas Employment Administration.

———. 2006. Manpower Development Division Employment Branch. Profile of Overseas Performing Artists Deployed to Japan and Impact of the New Japan Immigration Law on the Issuance of Visa to Filipino Entertainers. Manila: Philippine Overseas Employment Administration.

———. 2009. *Statistics* 2009. Manila: Philippine Overseas Employment Administration.

Pierce, Jennifer. 1995. *Gender Trials: Emotional Lives in Contemporary Law Firms.* Berkeley: University of California Press.

Polaris Project. n.d. *Polaris Project Hotline Manual for Volunteers.* Tokyo, Japan: Polaris Project.

Pratt, Geraldine. 2004. *Working Feminism.* Philadelphia: Temple University Press.

Price-Glynn, Kim. 2010. *Strip Club: Gender, Power and Sex Work.* New York: New York University Press.

Pun, Ngai. 2005. *Made in China.* Durham, NC: Duke University Press.

Rand, Erika. 2005. *The Ellis Island Snow Globe.* Durham, NC: Duke University Press.

Republic of the Philippines Department of Labor and Employment. 2001. Subject: Revised Guidelines on the Training, Testing, Certification, and Deployment of Overseas Performance Artists. Department Order No. 10 (Series of 2001). Manila: Republic of the Philippines.

Reyes, Raquel A. G. 2008. *Love, Passion and Patriotism: Sexuality and the Philippine Propaganda Movement, 188–1892.* Singapore: National University of Singapore Press.

Richardson, Diane. 2000. *Rethinking Sexuality.* London: Sage.

Rosaldo, Renato. 1998. "Cultural Citizenship, Inequality, and Multiculturalism." In William Flores and Rina Benmayor, eds., *Latino Cultural Citizenship: Claiming Identity and Rights*, pp. 27–38. Boston: Beacon Press.

Rubin, Gayle. 1984. "Thinking Sex: Notes for a Radical Theory of the Politics of Sexuality." In Carole Vance, ed., *Pleasure and Danger*, pp. 267–319. New York: Routledge.

Ruwanpura, Kanchana and Pallavi Rai. 2004. "Forced Labour: Definitions, Indicators, and Measurement." Working Paper 18 (March). Geneva, Switzerland: International Labour Office.

Sassen, Saskia. 1998a. *Globalization and its Discontents.* New York: New Press.

———. 1998b. "The Repositioning of Citizenship and Alienage: Emergent Subjects and Spaces for Politics." *Globalizations* 2:1 (May): 79–94.

———. 2000. "Women's Burden: Counter-Geographies of Globalization and the Feminization of Survival." *Journal of International Affairs* 53:2 (Spring): 503–524.

———. 2003. "Global Cities and Survival Circuits." In Barbara Ehrenreich and Arlie Hochschild, eds., *Global Woman*, pp. 254–273. New York: Metropolitan Books.

———. 2006. *Territory, Authority, Rights: From Medieval to Global Assemblages.* Princeton, NJ: Princeton University Press.

Scarpa, Silvia. 2008. *Trafficking in Human Beings: Modern Slavery.* New York and Oxford, UK: Oxford University Press.

Schaeffer-Grabiel, Felicity. 2005. "Planet-Love.Com: Cyberbrides in the Americas and the Transnational Routes of U.S. Masculinity." *Signs* 31(2): 331–356.

———. 2006. "Flexible Technologies of Subjectivity and Mobility across the Americas." *American Quarterly* 58(3): 891–914.

Shimizu, Celine Parreñas. 2007. *The Hypersexuality of Race: Performing Asian/American Women on Screen and Scene.* Durham, NC: Duke University Press.

Shipper, Apichai. 2008. *Fighting for Foreigners: Immigration and Its Impact on Japanese Democracy.* Ithaca, NY: Cornell University Press.

Silvey, Rachel. 2000. "Stigmatized Spaces: Gender and Mobility under Crisis in South Sulawesi, Indonesia." *Gender, Place, and Culture* 7(2): 143–161.

———. 2005. "Transnational Islam: Indonesian Migrant Domestic Workers in Saudi Arabia." In Ghazi-Walid Falah and Caroline Nagel, eds., *Geographies of Muslim Women: Gender, Religion and Space*, pp. 127–146. New York and London: Guilford Press.

———. 2007. "Mobilizing Piety: Gendered Morality and Indonesian-Saudi Transnational Migration." *Mobilities* 2(2): 219–229.

Sinclair, Joan. 2006. *Pink Box: Inside Japan's Sex Clubs.* New York: Abrams.

Singer, Audrey, and Greta Gilbertson. 2003. "'The Blue Passport': Gender and the Social Process of Naturalization among Dominican Immigrants." In Pierrette Hondagneu-Sotelo, ed., *Gender and U.S. Immigration: Contemporary Trends*, pp. 359–378. Berkeley and Los Angeles: University of California Press.

Siu, Lok. 2005. *Memories of a Future Home: Diasporic Citizenship of Chinese in Panama*. Stanford, CA: Stanford University Press.

Slany, Krystyna, and Agnieszka Malek. 2005. "Female Emigration from Poland during the Period of the Systematic Transformation (on the Basis of the Emigration from Poland to the USA and Italy)." In Krystyna Slany, ed., *International Migration: A Multidimensional Analysis*, pp. 115–154. Cracow, Poland: AGH University of Science and Technology Press.

Smith, Robert Courtney. 2006. *Mexican New York: Transnational Lives of New Immigrants*. Berkeley and Los Angeles: University of California Press.

Sobritchea, Carolyn. 1990. "The Ideology of Female Domesticity: Its Impact on the Status of Filipino Women." *Review of Women's Studies* II (2): 26–4.

Soderlund, Gretchen. 2005. "Running from the Rescuers: New U.S. Crusades against Sex Trafficking and the Rhetoric of Abolition." *NWSA Journal* 17(3): 64–87.

Southern Poverty Law Center. 2007. *Close to Slavery: Guest Worker Programs in the United States*, Montgomery, AL: Southern Poverty Law Center.

Soysal, Yasemin. 1994. *Limits of Citizenship: Migrants and Postnational Membership in Europe*. Chicago and London: University of Chicago Press.

Steinfeld, Robert. 1991. *The Invention of Free Labor: The Employment Relation in English and American Law and Culture, 1350–1870*. Chapel Hill and London: The University of North Carolina Press.

Stenum, Helle. 2008. *Au Pair in Denmark: Cheap Labour or Cultural Exchange*. Copenhagen: FOA Printing Shop.

———. 2009. "'Workers Not Slaves': The Management of Temporary Filipino Au Pair Migration in Denmark." Paper to the 3rd Gendering Asian Network Conference: "Gender, Mobility and Citizenship." Helsinki, Finland, May 28–30.

Stryker, Susan. 2009. "Transsexual Genital Surgeries and the Question of Eugenics." Paper presented at (Re)producing Justice Symposium, Berkeley School of Law, November 13.

Su, Julie. 1997. "El Monte Thai Garment Workers: Slave Sweatshops." In Andrew Ross, ed., *No Sweat: Fashion, Free Trade, and the Rights of Garment Workers*, pp. 143–150. New York: Verso.

Suzuki, Nobue. 2000. "Between Two Shores: Transnational Projects and Filipina Wives In/From Japan," *Women's Studies International Forum* 23(4): 431–444.

———. 2003. Battlefields of Affection: Gender, Global Desires and the Politics of Intimacy in Filipina–Japanese Transnational Marriages. PhD Dissertation, Department of Anthropology, University of Hawaii, Manoa.

———. 2005. "Tripartite Desires: Filipina-Japanese Marriages and Fantasies of Transnational Traversal." In Nicole Constable, ed., *Cross-Border Marriages: Gender and Mobility in Transnational Asia*, pp. 124–144. Philadelphia: University of Pennsylvania Press.

Takeyama, Akiko. 2005. "Commodified Romance in a Tokyo Host Club." In Mark McLelland and Romit Dasgupta, eds.. *Genders, Transgenders, and Sexualities in Japan*, pp. 200–215. London and New York: Routledge.

Talavera, Victor, Guillermina Gina Nuñez-Mchiri, and Joshia Heyman. 2010. "Deportation in the U.S.–Mexico Borderlands: Anticipation, Experience, and Memory." In Nicholas De Genova and Nathalie Peutz, eds., *The Deportation Regime*, pp. 166–195. Durham, NC: Duke University Press.

Tripp, Aili Mari. 2005. "The Evolution of Transnational Feminisms: Consensus, Conflict, and New Dynamics." In Myra Marx Feree and Aili Mari Tripp, eds., *Global Feminism: Transnational Women's Activism, Organizing, and Human Rights*, pp. 51–75. New York: New York University Press.

Truong, Thanh-Dam. 1990. *Sex, Money, and Morality: Prostitution and Tourism in South-East Asia*. London and New York: Zed Books.

Tsuda, Takeyuki. 1999. "The Permanence of 'Temporary' Migration: The 'Structural Embeddedness' of Japanese-Brazilian Immigrant Workers in Japan." *The Journal of Asian Studies* 58(3): 687–722.

———. 2006. "Localities and the Struggle for Immigrant Rights: The Significance of Local Citizenship in Recent Countries of Immigration." In Takeyuki Tsuda, ed., *Local Citizenship in Recent Countries of Immigration*, pp. 3–36. Lanham, MD: Lexington Books.

Tsuda, Takeyuki, and Wayne Cornelius. 2004. "Japan: Government Policy, Immigrant Reality." In Wayne A. Cornelius, Takeyuki Tsuda, Philip Martin, and James Hollifield, eds., *Controlling Immigration: A Global Perspective*, 2nd ed., pp. 439–476. Stanford, CA: Stanford University Press.

Turner, Bryan. 1994. "Postmodern Culture/Modern Citizen." In Bart van Steenbergen, ed., *The Condition of Citizenship*, pp. 153–168. London: Sage.

Turner, Victor. 1967. *The Forest of Symbols: Aspects of Ndembu Ritual.* Ithaca, NY: Cornell University Press.

Tutor, B. D. 2007. "Filipinas Are Popular as Brides to Japanese," *Philippine Today* (February 8, 2007). See www.philippinestoday.net/index.php?module=article&view=211.

Tyner, James. 1996. "Constructions of Filipina Migrant Entertainers." *Gender, Place, and Culture* 3(1): 77–93.

U.S. Citizenship and Immigration Services. 2007. Available at www.uscis.gov/portal/site/uscis.

U.S. Commission on Security and Cooperation in Europe. 1986. Immigration Marriage Fraud, Hearing before the Subcommittee on Immigration and Refugee Policy of the Committee on the Judiciary, United States Senate, 99th Congress, First Session. (26 July 1985). Washington DC: U.S. Government Printing Office.

———. 1999a. Press Release, Commission Chairman: "It's Time to Declare War on Sex Traffickers." Washington D.C.: U.S. Government Printing Office. Available at www.csce.gov/.

———. 1999b. The Sex Trade: Trafficking of Women and Children in Europe and the United States. Hearing before the Commission on Security and Cooperation in Europe. 106th Congress, First Session. Washington, DC: U.S. Government Printing Office.

———. 2004. Issue Forum: Enforcing U.S. Policies against Trafficking in Persons: How Is the Military Doing? (September 21). Washington, DC: U.S. Government Printing Office.

U.S. Congressional Record. 2000. "Conference Report on H.R. 3244, Victims of Trafficking and Violence Protection Act of 2000." Honorable Christopher H. Smith of New Jersey. Proceedings and Debates of the 106th Congress, Second Session 146: 123 (October 5). Washington DC: U.S. Government Printing Office.

———. 2003. "H.R. 2620: Trafficking Victims Protection Reauthorization Act." Honorable Christopher H. Smith of New Jersey. 149: 96 (June 27). Washington, DC: U.S. Government Printing Office.

U.S. Congressional Report. 2001. Fighting *the Scourge of Trafficking in Women and Children.* 147: 163 (November 29). Washington, DC: U.S. Government Printing Office.

U.S. Department of State. 2001. *Trafficking in Persons Report.* Washington, DC: U.S. Government Printing Office.

———. 2002. *Trafficking in Persons Report.* Washington, DC: U.S. Government Printing Office.

———-. 2003a. *Pathbreaking Strategies in the Global Fight Against Sex Trafficking: Prevention, Protection, Prosecution.* Conference Proceedings (February 23-26). Washington, DC: U.S. Government Printing Office.

———. 2003b. *Trafficking in Persons Report.* Washington, DC: U.S. Government Printing Office.

———. 2004. *Trafficking in Persons Report.* Washington, DC: U.S. Government Printing Office.

——— . 2005. *Trafficking in Persons Report.* Washington, DC: U.S. Government Printing Office.

———. 2006. *Trafficking in Persons Report.* Washington, DC: U.S. Government Printing Office.

———. 2007. *Trafficking in Persons Report.* Washington, DC: U.S. Government Printing Office.

United Nations. 2000. *United Nations Protocol to Prevent, Suppress, and Punish Trafficking in Persons, Supplementing the United Conventions against Transnational Organised Crime.* New York: United Nations.

Valentine, David. 2007. *Imagining Transgender: An Ethnography of a Category*. Durham, NC: Duke University Press.

Ventura, Ray. 1992. *Underground in Japan*. London: Jonathan Cape.

Wacquant. Loic. 1995. "Pugs at Work: Bodily Capital and Bodily Labour among Professional Boxers." *Body and Society* 1(1): 65–93.

Walkowitz, Judith. 1980. *Prostitution and Victorian Society: Women, Class and the State*. Cambridge, UK: Cambridge University Press.

Ward, Jane. 2009. "Gender Labor: Transmen, Femmes, and the Collective Work of Transgression," *Sexualities* 13(2): 236–254.

Warhurst, C., Nickson, D., Witz, A., and Cullen, A. 2000. "Aesthetic Labour in Interactive Service Work: Some Case Study Evidence from the 'New' Glasgow,'" *Service Industries Journal*, 20(3): 1–18.

Warhurst, Chris, and Dennis Nickson. 2009. "'Who's Got the Look?' Emotional, Aesthetic, and Sexualized Labor in Interactive Services." *Gender, Work and Organization* 16(3): 385–404.

Weeks, Jeffrey. 1985. *Sexuality and Its Discontents*. New York: Routledge.

———. 1998. "The Sexual Citizen." *Theory, Culture & Society* 15(3–4): 35–52.

Weeks, Kathi. 2007. "Life within and against Work: Affective Labor, Feminist Critique, and Post-Fordist Politics," *Ephemera: Theory and Politics in Organization* 7(1): 233–249.

White, Luise. 1990. *The Comforts of Home: Prostitution in Colonial Nairobi*. Chicago: University of Chicago Press.

Wicker, Hans-Rudolf. 2010. "Deportation as the Limits of 'Tolerance': The Juridical, Institutional and Social Construction of 'Illegality' in Switzerland." In Nicholas De Genova and Nicholas Peutz, eds., *The Deportation Regime*, pp. 224–244. Durham, NC: Duke University Press.

Willen, Sarah. 2007a. "Exploring 'Illegal' and 'Irregular' Migrants' Lived Experiences of Law and State Power," *International Migration* 45(3): 2–7.

———. 2007b. "Toward a Critical Phenomenology of 'Illegality': State Power, Criminalization, and Abjectivity among Undocumented Migrant Workers in Tel Aviv, Israel," *International Migration* 45(3): 8–38.

Wonders, Nancy, and Raymond Michalowski. 2001. "Bodies, Borders, and Sex Tourism in a Globalized World: A Tale of Two Cities—Amsterdam and Havana." *Social Problems* 48(4): 545–571.

Xiang, Biao. 2006. *Global "Body Shopping": An Indian Labor System in the Information Technology Industry*. Princeton, NJ: Princeton University Press.

Yamanaka, Keiko. 2000. "'I Will Go Home, but When?': Labor Migration and Circular Diaspora Formation by Japanese Brazilians in Japan." In Mike Douglass and Glenda Roberts, eds., *Japan and Global Migration: Foreign Workers and the Advent of a Multicultural Society*, pp. 123–152. Honolulu: University of Hawaii Press.

Yea, Sallie. 2005. "Labor of Love: Filipina Entertainer's Narratives of Romance and Relationships with the GIs in US Military Camp Towns in Korea," *Women's Studies International Forum* 28(6): 456–472.

Yuh, Ji-Yeon. 2002. *Beyond the Shadow of Camptown: Korean Military Brides in America*. New York: New York University Press.

Yuval-Davis, Nira. 1997. *Gender and Nation*. London: Sage Publications.

Zelizer, Viviana. 2000. "The Purchase of Intimacy." *Law and Social Inquiry* 25(3): 817–848.

———. 2005. *The Purchase of Intimacy*. Princeton, NJ: Princeton University Press.

Zheng, Tiantian. 2009. *Red Lights: The Lives of Sex Workers in Postsocialist China*. Minneapolis: University of Minnesota Press.

Zigon, Jarrett. 2007. "Moral Breakdown and the Ethical Demand: A Theoretical Framework for an Anthropology of Moralities," *Anthropological Theory* 7(2): 131–150.

———. 2008. *Morality: An Anthropological Perspective*. Oxford, UK, and New York: Berg.

INDEX

Printed and bound by CPI Group (UK) Ltd, Croydon, CR0 4YY

23/04/2025

14660938-0004